Lecture Notes in Artificial Intelligence     3265

Edited by J. G. Carbonell and J. Siekmann

Subseries of Lecture Notes in Computer Science

Robert E. Frederking   Kathryn B. Taylor (Eds.)

# Machine Translation: From Real Users to Research

6th Conference of the Association for Machine Translation
in the Americas, AMTA 2004
Washington, DC, USA, September 28 – October 2, 2004
Proceedings

 Springer

Series Editors

Jaime G. Carbonell, Carnegie Mellon University, Pittsburgh, PA, USA
Jörg Siekmann, University of Saarland, Saarbrücken, Germany

Volume Editors

Robert E. Frederking
Carnegie Mellon University
Language Technologies Institute
5000 Forbes Avenue, Pittsburgh, PA 15213, USA
E-mail: ref@cs.cmu.edu

Kathryn B. Taylor
Intelligence Technology Innovation Center
Washington, D.C. 20505, USA
E-mail: kathrynbtaylor@comcast.net

Library of Congress Control Number: 2004112847

CR Subject Classification (1998): I.2.7, I.2, F.4.2-3, I.7.1-3

ISSN 0302-9743
ISBN 3-540-23300-8 Springer Berlin Heidelberg New York

Springer is a part of Springer Science+Business Media

springeronline.com

© Springer-Verlag Berlin Heidelberg 2004
Printed in Germany

Typesetting: Camera-ready by author, data conversion by PTP-Berlin, Protago-TeX-Production GmbH
Printed on acid-free paper     SPIN: 11323761     06/3142     5 4 3 2 1 0

# Preface

The previous conference in this series (AMTA 2002) took up the theme "From Research to Real Users", and sought to explore why recent research on data-driven machine translation didn't seem to be moving to the marketplace. As it turned out, the first commercial products of the data-driven research movement were just over the horizon, and in the intervening two years they have begun to appear in the marketplace. At the same time, rule-based machine translation systems are introducing data-driven techniques into the mix in their products.

Machine translation as a software application has a 50-year history. There are an increasing number of exciting deployments of MT, many of which will be exhibited and discussed at the conference. But the scale of commercial use has never approached the estimates of the latent demand. In light of this, we reversed the question from AMTA 2002, to look at the next step in the path to commercial success for MT. We took user needs as our theme, and explored how or whether market requirements are feeding into research programs. The transition of research discoveries to practical use involves technical questions that are not as sexy as those that have driven the research community and research funding. Important product issues such as system customizability, computing resource requirements, and usability and fitness for particular tasks need to engage the creative energies of all parts of our community, especially research, as we move machine translation from a niche application to a more pervasive language conversion process. These topics were addressed at the conference through the papers contained in these proceedings, and even more specifically through several invited presentations and panels. The commercial translation community weighed in through the invited presentations of Ken Rother, CIO of Bowne Global Solutions, and Jaap van der Meer, a founding partner at Cross Language. Bowne Global Solutions is the largest of the world's "Big 3" translation services companies. Cross Language is one of a handful of new consulting and services companies formed to help customers select, customize and deploy machine translation. The US Government was represented by Kathy Debolt, Chief of the Army's Language Technology Office. Panel discussions included a forward-looking dialog between current students of translation and computational linguistics. Human translators as well as current users of machine translation also discussed working with machine translation.

2004 marked 10 years since the first AMTA conference, held in Columbia, Maryland in October 1994. With our sixth biennial conference, we returned to the Washington area. The timing and location of AMTA 2004 were very special to the history of machine translation. The conference was held at Georgetown University, the site of seminal operational experiments in machine translation, beginning in 1954. To mark the 50th anniversary of the realization of automated translation, we included a panel of five of the pioneers from Georgetown (Tony Brown, Christine Montgomery, Peter Toma, Muriel Vasconcellos, and Michael Zarechnak), as well as an overview of the beginnings of MT by John Hutchins.

How are people using MT today? Lots of innovative applications are emerging. A new event at this conference was a half-day Research and Deployment Showcase. The showcase gave attendees an opportunity to see operational systems that incorporate machine translation together with other hardware and software tools to accomplish real-world tasks. The research portion of the showcase offered a preview of the next generation of machine translation in operational prototype systems developed by research groups.

One of the founding goals of AMTA was to bring together users, researchers and developers in an ongoing dialog that gives members of each of these communities a chance to hear and respond to each others' concerns and interests. AMTA 2004 made a special effort to bring users and researchers together with the goal of inspiring and motivating each.

Acknowledgements may seem like obligatory filler to readers removed by space and time from the original event, but no organizer can reflect on the process without a deep sense of gratitude to the team that did most of the real work. AMTA 2004 was informed and realized by the inspirations and volunteer efforts of:

| Jeff Allen | Publicity Chair | |
|---|---|---|
| Jennifer DeCamp | Research and Deployment Showcase Coordinator | MITRE |
| Mike Dillinger | Tutorials and Workshops Chair | Translation Technology Consultant |
| Jennifer Doyon | Local Arrangements Chair | MITRE |
| Bob Frederking | Program Co-chair: Research Focus | CMU/LTI |
| Erika Grams | Conference Webmaster | |
| Walter Hartmann | Exhibits Coordinator | MT Consulting |
| Flo Reeder | Proceedings and Publications | MITRE |
| Kathi Taylor | Program Co-chair: User Focus | ITIC |
| John White | Sponsorships Chair, Proceedings and Publications | Northrop Grumman |

Additional information about the AMTA, its mission, activities and publications, can be obtained from the association website: www.amtaweb.org, and from AMTA Focalpoint Priscilla Rasmussen, 3 Landmark Center, East Stroudsburg, PA 18301, USA; phone: +1-570-476-8006; fax: +1-570-476-0860; focalpoint@amtaweb.org

July 2004                                                    Laurie Gerber
                                                        Conference Chair
                                                              AMTA 2004

# Table of Contents

# Case Study: Implementing MT for the Translation of Pre-sales Marketing and Post-sales Software Deployment Documentation at Mycom International

Jeffrey Allen

Mycom France
91, avenue de la République
75011 Paris FRANCE
jeffrey.allen@mycom-int.com

## 1 Background

Several major telecommunications companies have made significant investment in either controlled language and/or machine translation over the past 10 years.

- Alcatel: Alcatel developed the COGRAM Controlled Language checker (linked to the EC-funded SECC checker project) and a set of writing rules in the 1980s and presented the results at the CLAW96 conference. The SECC checker was available for testing online in 1996. No further news about the Alcatel implementation has been made available since 1996. Alcatel has however shown renewed interest in Controlled Language and Machine Translation rules and technologies by organizing a workshop on the topic in Paris on 2 April 2004, sponsored by the Society for Technical Communicators.
- Lucent / Avaya: Lucent Technologies (now Avaya) became interested in Controlled Language and Machine Translation in 1997. Five years later in 2003, they had produced on their own a set of Controlled Language rules (O'Brien, 2003). These rules seemed from this analysis to be underspecified for the task with respect to 7 other sets of Controlled Language rules that had been implemented in corporate environments.
- Sony-Ericsson: Ericsson also showed interest in Controlled Language and Machine Translation in 1997. There remains to be interest in MT, yet if seems to focus more on the translation/localization of content in small screen displays (Spalink, AMTA2000).
- Nortel Networks: Nortel Networks started up approximately in 1996 a multilingual project including Controlled Language rules and checker combined with Machine Translation and Translation Memory technologies. This implemented included the integration of the MaXit Controlled English along with an internally developed/customized translation tools. They announced at CLAW1998 the implementation of the project and attended the kickoff meeting of the NCCAT consortium in September 1998. In 1999-2000, Nortel Networks sold off its language technology group (speech research and technologies, Multilingual technologies) to various entities.

R.E. Frederking and K.B. Taylor (Eds.): AMTA 2004, LNAI 3265, pp. 1–6, 2004.
© Springer-Verlag Berlin Heidelberg 2004

- The result of this project is a limited set of 15 Nortel Standard English (NSE) rules.
- Mycom International: Mycom considered these previous implementations in the telecom field and decided to take a completely different approach to implementing MT technologies in production needs for translating various documents. This has been more and example-based, osmosis learning approach. The Mycom Technical Documentation department was set up in June 2001. The department manager trained the small team of technical writers to write in a clear, concise format that would benefit both the monolingual workflow as well as a potential multilingual workflow. No mention of CLs was made but rather a simple and basic approach to good technical writing, which included CL principles. All product documentation (user, installation, responses for information, pre-sales brochures, technical overview, etc) was produced through this department, so a standardized approach was used for creating the product-related documentation. Significant text-leverage and recycling processes have been used for the creation of all documentation.

This paper describes the use of MT technologies for translating both pre-sales marketing and post-sales software deployment documentation in the software product division of Mycom International.

## 2   Software and Methodology Used

The software used for this implementation was Reverso Expert (v5), which is based on the PROMT v5 MT kernel. The implementer on the team at Mycom has significant experience in using this MT product. In order to be most productive, the team decided to use an existing method of MT implementation (created by Jeff Allen) as described elsewhere (Allen, 2001; Allen, 2003; Guerra, 2003).

## 3   Context

This implementation of MT products has been conducted on pre-sales marketing and post-sales acceptance documents, both customer-facing documents, for key customer accounts. No pilot study was conducted; rather an experienced MT user, being a subject matter expert in the field, led the implementation. One document was a Response for Information (RFI) pre-sales document (approximately 2000 words), referred to hereafter as the RFI document, which was translated from English into French using MT software and then post-edited. The second document was a Customer Acceptance Test Validation Plan, which the customer is using to test the Mycom software and determine conditional or full acceptance of the product that is deployed at the customer site.

# 4  Quality

Some translation agencies have disputed in the past that the quality of MT post-editing output is questionable when it is not conducted by translation professionals. To clarify the issue of quality in this context, the person involved in this implementation has several years of experience as a (human) translator and trainer of professional translators. The person is fully bilingual in both the source and target languages and provides training courses for industry in both languages on a range of topics. This person has been with the Mycom International product division since prototype days and has been involved with all phases of product management with key customers over the past few years. This experience has included designing, authoring, and editing an entire range of the company's user guides and manuals, marketing brochures, R&D specifications, a range of test documents, and all other types of customer facing documents. As a subject matter expert in this company's area of activity, this person is fully competent to appropriately evaluate and determine, in both languages, the level of textual quality that is necessary for complete end-to-end care of Mycom customers.

# 5  Human Translation Speed

A study led this past year on human translation speed (Allen, 2004) shows from answers received from dozens of sources of many types and sizes (translation agencies, government translation bureaus, translation dept of international orgs, etc, freelance translators, etc) that the average translator can translate approximately 2400 words per day. These published statistics are used as a comparison baseline for the present project.

# 6  Results

## 6.1  Document 1

### 6.1.1  Document Details
The first product scenario took place with a Response for Information (RFI) pre-sales document. It was an urgent request (4 March 2004) to produce a French version of an existing English language source document. English language document to be translated into French. The source language document contains 1494 words.

### 6.1.2  Measurements
The MT implementer logged the following statistics to complete the entire translation job:
- 15 min: spend time with another subject matter expect to identify the potential ambiguous terms and decide on the desired translated form for each of them.

- 45 min: dictionary entry coding and testing on the entire document to produce very high quality draft document with no post-editing.
- 2 hours: the sales representative (the translation requester) spent this much additional time post-editing the target language version of the document.

### 6.1.3 Sub-conclusion
3 hours to complete 1500 words.


## 6.2 Document Two

### 6.2.1 Document Details
The document is validation test plan for software acceptance at a customer site. The original French language document needs to be translated into English. The first half of validation test plan contains a total of 3764 words in the original text, thus approx 4000 words. The second half of the test plan contains 4600 Words to translate. The total time allowed to complete the translation was one week. Total number of words to translate: 8364 (nearly 8400)

### 6.2.2 Measurements
Every detail of the implementation was carefully timed, logged and documented.

*6.2.2.1 Section One*
Monday 29 March 2004
- 0.5 hour: file preparation/separation time
- 1.5 hours:  Text analysis and dictionary building: 76 entries made

Tues 30 March 2004
- 0.5 hour: identify poorly translated terms (on paper) of document version 1 for dictionary improvement
- 1.5 hours: create approx 50 entries
- 0.5 hour: doc analysis/dict entry work/testing
- 0.5 hour: doc analysis/dict entry work/testing

Wed 31 Mar 2004
- 2 hours: identify amig terms, dictionary coding, testing new dictionary entries
- 0.50 hour: review the output of document version 2
- 0.50 hour: read over draft 3 and identify more corrections
- 1 hour: file formatting: full copy over and reformat of final doc
- 0.50 hour: post-editing

*6.2.2.2  Section Two*
19 April 2004

- 0.50 hour: strip out all text in original document (the actual test case scenarios) that was already in English, in order to only keep the descriptive text in French.
- 1 hour 45 min: disambiguation and finishing coding dictionary for this section of test plan

### 6.2.3  Sub-conclusion

*6.2.3.1  MT interaction time*
- 7.5 hours of custom dictionary building and final translation corrections for nearly first 4000 words of the document.
- 1 hour 45 min for custom dictionary building and translation corrections of second half of document.

*6.2.3.2  Pre- and post-processing time*
There have been a total of 2 hours of document pre- and post-processing tasks, including formatting the Word doc and RTF files to work with translation system, as well stripping out English text in the original French language source document.

*6.2.3.3  Dictionary*
Over 400 dictionary entries were created during the production of the translated document.


## 7  Conclusion

An average human translator would normally produce 2400 words per day and thus take 3-4 days to translate this translation product job from scratch. This implementation shows that a fully bilingual subject matter expert, with professional translation experience, combined with excellent mastery of a commercial MT system, can complete the entire translation workflow of the translation job in slightly more than 1 day of work. This clearly shows, for this specific language direction, and on a given MT commercial tool, that the results obtained on production documents by such an individual can attain production rates that are 25%-30% of the time necessary and expected via traditional translation methods. The results of the translations have been clearly recorded in e-mail messages of congratulations on the success of both translated documents. These e-mails clearly indicate that these types of translation implementation efforts could enhance the ability for the company to write pre-sales marketing and post-sales technical documents in one language, and later translate, adapt, localize them into another language for other customers.

Both translation jobs were conducted by creating a specific custom dictionary for the technical terminology of the documentation of this company. These dictionaries are usable in the Reverso (v5) family of MT software products. The dictionaries can also be exported in hard print and softcopy formats.

## References

1. Allen, Jeffrey. March 2004. Translation speed versus content management. In special supplement of Multilingual Computing and Technology magazine, Number 62, March 2004. http://www.multilingual.com/machineTranslation62.htm
2. Allen, Jeffrey. 2001. Postediting: an integrated part of a translation software program. In Language International magazine, April 2001, Vol. 13, No. 2, pp. 26-29. http://www.geocities.com/mtpostediting/Allen-LI-article-Reverso.pdf
3. Allen, Jeffrey. 2003. Post-editing. In Computers and Translation: A Translators Guide. Edited by Harold Somers. Benjamins Translation Library, 35. Amsterdam: John Benjamins. (ISBN 90 272 1640 1). http://www.benjamins.com/cgi-bin/t_bookview.cgi?bookid=BTL_35
4. Guerra, Lorena. 2003. Human Translation versus Machine Translation and Full Post-Editing of Raw Machine Translation Output. Master's Thesis. Dublin City University. http://www.promt.ru/news-e/news.phtml?id=293
5. O'Brien, Sharon. An Analysis of Several Controlled English Rule Sets. Presented at EAMT/CLAW2003, Dublin, Ireland, 15-17 May 2003 http://www.ctts.dcu.ie/presentations.html

# A Speech-to-Speech Translation System for Catalan, Spanish, and English

Victoria Arranz[1], Elisabet Comelles[1], David Farwell[2,1], Climent Nadeu[1],
Jaume Padrell[1], Albert Febrer[3], Dorcas Alexander[4], and Kay Peterson[4]

[1] TALP Research Centre, Universitat Politècnica de Catalunya, Barcelona, Spain
{varranz,comelles,farwell,climent,jaume}@talp.upc.es
[2] Institució Catalana de Recerca i Estudis Avançats, Barcelona, Spain
[3] Applied Technologies on Language and Speech, Barcelona, Spain
{afebrer}@verbio.com
[4] Language Technologies Institute/Interactive Systems Lab,
Carnegie Mellon University, Pittsburgh, USA
{dorcas,kay}@cs.cmu.edu

**Abstract.** In this paper we describe the FAME interlingual speech-to-speech translation system for Spanish, Catalan and English which is intended to assist users in the reservation of a hotel room when calling or visiting abroad. The system has been developed as an extension of the existing NESPOLE! translation system[4] which translates between English, German, Italian and French. After a brief introduction we describe the Spanish and Catalan system components including speech recognition, transcription to IF mapping, IF to text generation and speech synthesis. We also present a task-oriented evaluation method used to inform about system development and some preliminary results.

## 1 Introduction

In this paper we describe an interlingual speech-to-speech translation system for Spanish, Catalan and English which is under development as part of the European Union-funded FAME project[5]. The system is an extension of the existing NESPOLE! translation system (cf. [4],[5]) to Spanish and Catalan in the domain of hotel reservations. At its core is a robust, scalable, interlingual speech-to-speech translation system having cross-domain portability which allows for effective translingual communication in a multimodal setting. Initially, the system architecture was based on the NESPOLE! platform. Now the general architecture integrating all modules is based on an Open Agent Architecture (OAA)[6] [2]. This type of multi-agent framework offers a number of technical features that are highly advantageous for the system developer and user.

Our system consists of an analyzer that maps spoken language transcriptions into interlingua representation and a generator that maps from interlingua into

---

[5] FAME stands for *Facilitating Agent for Multicultural Exchange* and focuses on the development of multimodal technologies to support multilingual interactions. http://isl.ira.uka.de/fame/

[6] http://www.ai.sri.com/~oaa

R.E. Frederking and K.B. Taylor (Eds.): AMTA 2004, LNAI 3265, pp. 7–16, 2004.
© Springer-Verlag Berlin Heidelberg 2004

natural language text. The central advantage of this interlingua-based architecture is that in adding additional languages to the system, it is only necessary to develop analysis and generation components for the new languages.

For both Catalan and Spanish speech recognition, we used the JANUS Recognition toolkit (JRTk) developed at UKA and CMU.

For the text-to-text component, the analysis side utilizes the top-down, chart-based SOUP parser[1] with full domain action level rules to parse input utterances. Natural language generation is done with GenKit, a pseudo-unification based generation tool[6].

The Interchange Format[3], the interlingua currently used in the C-STAR Consortium[7], is being adapted for this effort. Its central advantage for representing dialogue interactions such as those typical of speech-to-speech translation systems is that it focuses on identifying the speech acts and the various types of requests and responses typical of a given domain. Thus, rather than capturing the detailed semantic and stylistic distinctions, it characterizes the intended conversational goal of the interlocutor. Even so, in mapping to IF it is necessary to take into account a wide range of structural and lexical properties related to Spanish and Catalan.

For the initial development of the Spanish analysis grammar the already existing English and German analysis grammars were used as a reference point. Despite using these grammars, great efforts have been made to overcome important differences between English/German and the Romance languages dealt with. The Catalan analysis grammar, in turn, is being adapted from the Spanish analysis grammar and, in this case, the process is more straightforward.

The generation grammar for Spanish was mostly developed from scratch, although some of the underlying structure was adapted from that of the English grammar. Language-dependent properties such as word order, gender and number agreement, etc. have been dealt with representationally. But the generation lexica play a very important role and these have been developed from scratch. The Catalan generation grammar, in turn, is being adapted from the Spanish generation grammar and in this case the process is far more straightforward.

For both Spanish and Catalan, we use a TTS system fully developed at the UPC, which is a unit-selection based, concatenative speech synthesis system.

For the purpose of improving the system, we have developed an evaluation methodology which focuses on a subjective judgement of the fidelity and naturalness of the translations given the task at hand, reserving a hotel room. This evaluation method will be described and results of a preliminary evaluation of the system will be presented.

In Section 2 we describe automatic speech recognition and in Section 3 the language analysis side and transcription to IF. Section 4 describes the generation side of the translation process, and Section 5 the speech synthesis part of the system. Then, in Section 6 we will present an internal evaluation procedure and discuss results of a preliminary evaluation. Finally, in Section 7 we will conclude with a discussion of future directions.

---

[7] http://www.c-star.org

## 2   Automatic Speech Recognition of Catalan and Spanish

Good ASR is the first step to achieve quality in a speech-to-speech translation system. Short prepositions are particularly problematic. They are quite difficult to detect by the recognizer but are extremely valuable for the translation system.

For both Spanish and Catalan speech recognition, we used the JANUS Recognition toolkit (JRTk) developed by UKA and CMU [7].

The Spanish speech DB for training the acoustic models consists of about 30 hours of read speech from 300 Spanish speakers. Experiments were carried out with both close-talk and distant microphones. Although the latter provides a worse signal quality, the use of distant microphones should be considered for the user's comfort. Catalan models were trained on an available DB of about 30 hours, having only one close-talk microphone, but similar acoustic conditions. All Spanish and Catalan acoustic models are task and speaker independent.

Both Spanish and Catalan language models (LM) are trigram models. They were trained on text of the same topic used to build the text-to-text translation system from the C-STAR and LC-STAR[8] corpora. A subset of the LC-STAR corpus was selected related to tourist-employee conversations, with 5,162 sentences, a total of 58,646 words, and a vocabulary size of 4,201 words.

The recognizer was tested for Spanish on a subset (5 dialogues) of the TALP-MT.db database, also used for translation (cf. section 6). The acoustic models trained with close-talk microphone were used to do these experiments. These dialogues are spontaneous, but fake conversations. The agent side test subset consists of 103 sentences, for a total of 719 words, with a vocabulary of 75 words. The client side consists of 79 sentences, for a total of 536 words, with a vocabulary of 68 words. A WER of 35.95% was obtained for the agent test and of 29.43% for the client. Notice the low values of these results compared to those obtained with DB1. The main difference between both experiments is the spontaneity present in DB2 which is full of disfluencies.

## 3   Language Parsing

Parsing spontaneous speech poses unique challenges, including disfluencies, speech fragments, and ungrammatical sentences, which are not present in the parsing of written text. Users of the FAME system should feel free to speak naturally, without restricting these characteristics of spontaneous speech. Thus, the parsing module must be able to produce a reasonable analysis of all types of spoken input within the given domain.

The SOUP parser[1] was developed specifically to handle the unique characteristics of spontaneous speech. Typically one would not expect a single parse tree to cover an entire utterance of spontaneous speech, because such utterances frequently contain multiple segments of meaning. In an interlingua system, these segments are called Semantic Dialogue Units (SDUs) and correspond to a single domain action (DA). Thus, one of the SOUP features most relevant to the

---

[8] http://www.lc-star.com

FAME system is the capability to produce a sequence of parse trees for each utterance, effectively segmenting the input into SDUs (corresponding to domain actions) at parse time.

SOUP is a stochastic, chart-based, top-down parser which efficiently uses very large, context-free semantic grammars. At run-time the grammars are encoded as recursive transition networks (RTNs) and a lexicon is produced as a hash table of grammar terminals. A bottom-up filtering technique and a beam search both enhance parsing speed during the population of the chart. The beam incorporates a scoring function that seeks to maximize the number of words parsed while minimizing parse lattice complexity (approximated by the number of nodes in the potential parse tree). After the chart is populated, a second beam search seeks to minimize the number of parse trees per utterance. Only non-overlapping parse lattices are considered.

In addition, SOUP allows partial parses, i.e., some of the input remains un-parsed and the entire utterance does not fail. The Interchange Format (IF) gives a special representation to these fragments of meaning, with the goal that enough information may be preserved to complete the conversation task, and minimize frustration for the user. This special domain action signals to the generation module that only a fragment has been analyzed, and the generation output can be adjusted accordingly.

An analysis mapper completes the analysis chain by performing formatting functions on the parser output, to produce standard Interchange Format according to the IF specification. These functions include the conversion of numbers for quantities and prices as well of lists of numerals like those found in credit card numbers.

### 3.1 Language Parsing of Catalan and Spanish

The Spanish and Catalan grammars have taken as starting point the existing English/German grammars. However, the efforts invested in development have been rather different. While the Spanish one has been largely written from scratch, the Catalan grammar has made a more extensive use of the Spanish one.

The grammars have been developed using a corpus of dialogues obtained from the C-Star-II database[9]. These dialogues were recorded in English and manually translated and paraphrased into Spanish and Catalan.

Among the main differences between English and the two Romance languages considered, there is the high inflection in both Catalan and Spanish. For instance, Spanish verbs contain in their inflected ending information about tense, person, number and aspect while in English this information appears in the auxiliaries and pronouns preceeding the main verb. See the following example:

ENG: I will call tomorrow
SPA: Yo llamaré mañana
CAT: Jo trucaré demà
IF rep.: give-information+action (who=i, action=e-call-2, e-time=following,... )

---

[9] http://www.is.cs.cmu.edu/nespole/db/current/cstar-examples.db

In the IF representation the *action=e-call-2* stands for the action *call* and *e-time=following* represents the future time conveyed in English by the auxiliary *will* and in Catalan and Spanish by the inflected ending *-aré*. The large amount of morphological information has to be overcome by the use of an *@ rule*. These rules are used when there is one bottom-level token that represents more than just one IF value. However in this case, this is not the only problem to solve as *e-call-2* and *e-time=following* are not sister nodes, they appear in different levels. As a consequence, besides an *@ rule* we will also use a *nested_xxx* rule to move the *e-time=* argument up one level. The rule to be used is: *[e-call-2@nested_e-time=following]* for *llamaré*.

Another difference is that English modifiers preceed the noun whereas Spanish and Catalan modifiers usually follow it. As said before, the grammars were developed using a corpus of real dialogue data that were useful to decide which modifiers must be postponed (e.g.: specifiers, colors, sizes). For example, the adjective referring to the size of the room *big* preceeds the English noun *room* while in the Spanish and Catalan sentences the *size* follows the noun it modifies.

Word-order is also an item of distinction between English and Romance languages. English word-order is much more fixed while Spanish and Catalan are free-word order languages. For instance, English adjuncts have a fixed position either at the beginning or at the end of the sentence whereas Spanish and Catalan adjuncts are much more flexible and can appear everywhere. Example:

SPA: Tenemos el Hotel Arts en la Barceloneta.
SPA: En la Barceloneta tenemos el Hotel Arts.
SPA: Tenemos en la Barceloneta el Hotel Arts.
ENG: We've Hotel Arts in la Barceloneta.
IF rep.: give-information+availability+accommodation (experiencer=we, accommodation-spec=name-hotel_arts, location=name-la_barceloneta)

As the adjunct *en la Barceloneta* appears in different positions this should be reflected in DA-rules so that Spanish and Catalan can cover all possibilities. This optionality is expressed by means of asterisks before the argument in DA rules.

This item is also linked to the efforts made to improve the flexibility and robustness of the system to make it more user-friendly. Due to Spanish and Catalan free-word order and specially due to the flexibility of spoken language, great efforts have been performed to cover most of the possibilities by expanding top-level rules. In this way the user feels much more free because the system is able to analyze a wide range of possible structures. Apart from this, the lexicon has been widely expanded to cover as much vocabulary as possible. Although the system is aimed to a restricted domain (Hotel Reservation) and in consequence the vocabulary used is restricted to this domain, verbal forms differ quite a lot and we have tried to cover all of them in the lexicon of our grammars. To cope with this problem the paraphrased Spanish and Catalan sentences used to develop de system were really useful to have a high diversity of forms.

# 4   Language Generation

The generation module of the translation part of our interlingua-based MT system includes a generation mapper and the GenKit generator.

The generation mapper was originally developed for the NESPOLE! system. It converts a given interchange format representation into a feature structure. This feature structure then serves as input to the GenKit generator, which was originally developed at Carnegie Mellon's Center for Machine Translation[6] and has been updated and re-implemented since.

GenKit is a pseudo-unification-based generation system. It operates on a grammar formalism based on Lexical Functional Grammar and consists of context-free phrase structure description rules augmented with clusters of pseudo-unification equations for feature structures. A top-down control strategy is used to create a generation tree from an input feature structure. The leaves of the generation tree are then read off as a pre-surface-form generation. Subsequently, this pre-surface form is passed through a post-processing component, which generates the actual word strings of the generated output in the correct format.

The generator uses hybrid syntactic/semantic grammars for generating a sentence from an interchange-format feature structure. Generation knowledge employed in generation with GenKit consists of grammatical, lexical, and morphological knowledge. The higher-level grammar rules reflect the phrase structure requirements of the particular language. A lexical look-up program uses lexical entries for associating (in this case, Catalan or Spanish) words with semantic interchange format concepts and values. These lexical entries contain not only the root forms of these words, but are also enriched with, for example, lexical information pertinent to morphology generation (such as gender information in the case of nouns) and, in the case of verbs, subcategorization requirements.

Generation of the correct morphological form is performed via inflectional grammar rules that draw on additional information stored in the lexical entries (see above). In the more complex case of verb morphology, the correct form is then retrieved from an additional morphological form look-up table. Such a table turned out not to be necessary for the other grammatical categories in the case of Catalan and Spanish. The actual morphological forms are then produced in the post-processing stage.

## 4.1   Language Generation into Catalan and Spanish

The generation grammars for Spanish and Catalan were developed based on a variety of sources. Some of the underlying framework of the grammars was adapted as a seed structure for Spanish and Catalan from pre-existing English and German GenKit grammars. This skeleton was then developed and further expanded based on interchange-format-tagged development data stemming from the multilingual CStar-II database.

The grammars are semantic in nature but make syntactic generalizations if possible. They were written with two goals in mind. A GenKit grammar can be written such that the semantic rules are generalized to work with many speech act and concept combinations, or more specifically geared towards a given domain action. A smaller number of very general rules were written to cover a broad spectrum of possible domain actions, sacrificing style in some cases. One such example is the following rule for *give-* or *request- information+action*:

```
(<gri+action> ==> (<svp> % <np>) .....)
```

In other words, the desired breadth of coverage this approach achieves sometimes reduces the fluency and naturalness of the generated output to a degree. On the other hand, more specific rules were written for frequently occurring interchange format tags to ensure that generation of these is highly fluent and natural-sounding, and thus stylistically easy to read or listen to. This is the case of the following full domain-action rule for *offer+confirmation*:

```
(<cro-da> ==> (%)
  (((x0 full-domain-action) = *defined*)
   ((x0 arguments) = *undefined*)
   (*eor* (((x0 full-domain-action) = offer+confirmation)
          ((x1 value) = de1jeme_confirmarlo)) (((......))))))
```

The combination of these two directions aims at striking an optimal balance between high coverage (and efficiency of grammar writing and maintenance) on the one hand, and stylistic generation quality on the other. Ultimately, both of these aspects are crucial in determining how the generation module affects the user-friendliness of the system.

For Spanish and Catalan, several specific linguistic phenomena had to be dealt with that had not been implemented in GenKit grammars before. These include language-specific phenomena such as *que+subjunctive* constructions, pronominal verbs, clitics, pronouns, in ditransitive constructions, etc. Some of these phenomena are reflected in the lexica, which have been developed from scratch and are enriched with a considerable amount of information vital for generation. For instance, the following lexicon entry for WordNet variant *e-attend-2* indicates that in Spanish this verb is reflexive, transitive and its object must follow preposition *de*:

```
(e-attend-2 ((cat v) (root ocupar) (refl +) (trans trans) (xprep de)))
```

## 5   Text-to-Speech Synthesis

The Text-to-Speech (TTS) block in our system converts translated text into speech. For both Spanish and Catalan, we use the TTS system fully developed at the UPC. This system is a unit-selection based concatenative speech synthesis system, an approach that gives high levels of intelligibility and naturalness.

The TTS process can be divided into two blocks: (1) a linguistic block, and (2) a synthesis block. In the second block there is a concatenation of adjacent units and some modification (pitch synchronous signal processing on the time domain) if target prosody and unit attributes do not match (the UPC system defines a threshold of accepted deviation in pitch, duration and intensity and parameters are modified to fit into this accepted range).

Quality of such concatenative systems is highly dependant on the size and characteristics of the unit corpus. The system used in Spanish and Catalan uses corpora of about 2 hours per speaker. Although these corpus-based TTS systems can use task-dependent corpora to improve the quality in a certain context of sentences, no specific corpus of units has been designed for this application.

## 6   Evaluation of the Translation Component

For the time being, a preliminary evaluation of the translation component has been carried out on text input (and from Spanish into English), that is, separately from ASR. However, evaluation on the output of ASR is planned shortly. This initial evaluation has been carried out on SDU-fragmented data (cf. section 3) although the system is developed to work on full utterances. As mentioned in section 1, an evaluation methodology has been developed for that purpose, which focuses on a subjective judgement of the fidelity and naturalness of the translations given the hotel reservation task.

The evaluation data set used to test the system has been obtained from the unseen data in TALP-MT.db, a database containing nine new dialogues recorded at TALP for evaluation purposes. These dialogues were recorded in Spanish and then a) translated and paraphrased into Catalan and English, and b) IF-tagged with semantic information. Four of them were selected for this first evaluation experiment (2 from each recording session so as to try and work on as different data as possible). Each of the dialogues is approximately 25 utterances long. All dialogues are recorded in a monolingual fashion, i.e. both the agent and the client side speak in the same language for the data collection. One subject plays the role of a Spanish agent, the other plays the role of a Spanish client. The performers were given target milestones as a guideline. The target milestones are the goals which should be met by an agent-client dialogue and have the following structure:

1. Opening
2. CLIENT asks Viajes FAME AGENT for hotel reservation in Barcelona
3. AGENT finds out the following info from CLIENT: a) dates/duration of stay, b) number of people staying, and c) hotel class desired/client's budget
4. AGENT names a hotel, its approximate location and price
5. CLIENT asks to make reservation right away
6. AGENT finds out payment information from CLIENT: a) client's (first and last) name, and b) client's credit card name, number, expiration date
7. AGENT confirms/sums up reservation made
8. Closing

### 6.1   Evaluation Results and Discussion

Prior to the revision of the translation output, a set of evaluation criteria was defined. These standards considered 3 main categories (*Perfect*, *Ok* and *Un-*

*acceptable*), where the second one was further divided into *Ok+*, *Ok* and *Ok-*. Evaluation was separately performed on the grounds of *form* and *content*. In order to evaluate *form*, only the generated output was given to the three different evaluators[10]. The evaluation of *content* took into account both the Spanish input and the English output. Accordingly, the meaning of the evaluation metrics varies if they are being used to judge either *form* or *content*:

- **Perfect**: well-formed output (*form*) or full communication of speakers' information (*content*).
- **Ok+/Ok/Ok-**: acceptable output, grading from only some minor *form* error (e.g., missing determiner) or some minor non-communicated information (*Ok+*) to some more serious *form* or *content* problems (*Ok-*).
- **Unacceptable**: unacceptable output, either essentially unintelligible or simply totally unrelated to the input.

On the basis of the four test dialogues used, the results presented in table 1 were obtained. Regarding *form* 65,95% of the translations were judged to be well-formed, 22,87% were acceptable (most of them with minor mistakes) while only 11,17% were essentially unintelligible. In regard to *content*, 70,21% of the translation communicated all the speakers' information, 9,57% communicated part of the information the speaker intended to communicate (always allowing the communication to continue, even if some information was missing) and 20,21% failed to communicate any of the information the speaker intended to communicate (providing either unrelated information or no information at all. The latter seems to be due to the wider coverage of the test data, both in regards to syntax and semantics).

**Table 1.** Evaluation Results for the Translation Component

| Scores | Form | Content |
|---|---|---|
| Perfect | 65,95 | 70,21 |
| Ok+ | 12,23 | 4,25 |
| Ok | 7,44 | 1,59 |
| Ok- | 3,19 | 3,72 |
| Unacceptable | 11,17 | 20,21 |

# 7    Conclusions and Future Work

With the initial stage of system development nearing successful completion, our efforts will turn to system evaluation, to confronting the more serious technical problems which have arisen thus far and to extending the systems both within the reservations domain and to further travel-related domains. In addition to evaluating the quality of throughput of MT component using BLEU and NIST

---

[10] Two of these evaluators were familiar with the Interchange Format, but the third one was not.

measures, we have developed a user-based evaluation method of translation system as part of a hotel reservation task. We expect to carry out both types of evaluation in the coming months. In regard to difficulties, perhaps the most serious problem we confront at this point is the need to enhance the capacity of the systems to deal with the often degraded transcriptions provided by the speech recognition components. We are looking into two strategies for dealing with this issue which we hope to implement in the coming year. First, we will attempt to compile additional data both to improve the LM of the recognition system itself and to train a transcription error detection and correction procedure. Second, we will incorporate into the dialogue model strategies for requesting repetitions and reformulations of utterances by the interlocutors themselves. In this way, the users of the system can deal with many system failures through normal conversational means. Finally, we will continue to develop the Spanish and Catalan analysis and generation components within the reservations domain as well as to extend them to additional travel related domains.

**Acknowledgments** This research is partly supported by the Information Society Technologies program of the European Union under grant number IST-2001-28323 (FAME project) and by the Spanish Ministry of Science and Technology under grant number TIC2002-04447-C02 (ALIADO project).

# References

1. Gavaldà, M.: SOUP: A Parser for Real-world Spontaneous Speech. In Proceedings of the 6th International Workshop on Parsing Technologies (IWPT-2000), Trento, Italy (2000)
2. Holzapfel, H., Rogina, I., Wölfel, M., Kluge, T.: FAME Deliverable D3.1: Testbed Software, Middleware and Communication Architecture (2003)
3. Levin, L., Gates, D., Wallace, D., Peterson, K., Lavie, A., Pianesi, F., Pianta, E., Cattoni, R., Mana, N.: Balancing Expressiveness and Simplicity in an Interlingua for Task based Dialogue. In Proceedings of ACL-2002 workshop on Speech-to-speech Translation: Algorithms and Systems, Philadelphia, PA, U.S.(2002)
4. Metze, F., McDonough, J., Soltau, J., Langley, C., Lavie, A., Levin, L., Schultz, T., Waibel, A., Cattoni, L., Lazzari, G., Mana, N., Pianesi, F., Pianta, E.: The NESPOLE! Speech-to-Speech Translation System. In Proceedings of HLT-2002, San Diego, California, U.S., (2002)
5. Taddei, L., Besacier, L., Cattoni, R., Costantini, E., Lavie, A., Mana, N., Pianta, E.: NESPOLE! Deliverable D17: Second Showcase Documentation (2003) In NE-SPOLE! Project web site: http://nespole.itc.it.
6. Tomita, M., Nyberg, E.H.: Generation Kit and Transformation Kit, Version 3.2, User's Manual. Technical Report CMU-CMT-88-MEMO. Pittsburgh, PA: Carnegie Mellon, Center for Machine Translation (1988)
7. Woszczyna, M., Coccaro, N., Eisele, A., Lavie, A., McNair, A., Polzin, T., Rogina, I., Rose, C., Sloboda, T., Tomita, M., Tsutsumi, J., Aoki-Waibel, N., Waibel, A., Ward, W.: Recent Advances in JANUS : A Speech Translation System. In Proceedings of Eurospeech-93 (1993) 1295–1298

# Multi-Align: Combining Linguistic and Statistical Techniques to Improve Alignments for Adaptable MT

Necip Fazil Ayan[1], Bonnie J. Dorr[1], and Nizar Habash[2]

[1] Institute for Advanced Computer Studies
University of Maryland
College Park, MD 20742
{nfa,bonnie,habash}@umiacs.umd.edu
[2] Department of Computer Science
Columbia University
New York, NY 10027
habash@cs.columbia.edu

**Abstract.** An adaptable statistical or hybrid MT system relies heavily on the quality of word-level alignments of real-world data. Statistical alignment approaches provide a reasonable initial estimate for word alignment. However, they cannot handle certain types of linguistic phenomena such as long-distance dependencies and structural differences between languages. We address this issue in Multi-Align, a new framework for incremental testing of different alignment algorithms and their combinations. Our design allows users to tune their systems to the properties of a particular genre/domain while still benefiting from general linguistic knowledge associated with a language pair. We demonstrate that a combination of statistical and linguistically-informed alignments can resolve translation divergences during the alignment process.

## 1 Introduction

The continuously growing MT market faces the challenge of translating new languages, diverse genres, and different domains using a variety of available linguistic resources. As such, MT system adaptability has become a sought-after necessity. An adaptable statistical or hybrid MT system relies heavily on the quality of word-level alignments of real-world data.

This paper introduces Multi-Align, a new framework for incremental testing of different alignment algorithms and their combinations. The success of statistical alignment has been demonstrated to a certain extent, but such approaches rely on large amounts of training data to achieve high-quality word alignments. Moreover, statistical systems are often incapable of capturing structural differences between languages (*translation divergences*), non-consecutive phrasal information, and long-range dependencies. Researchers have addressed these deficiencies by incorporating lexical features into maximum entropy alignment models [17]; however, the range of these lexical features has been limited to simple linguistic phenomena and no results have been reported.

R.E. Frederking and K.B. Taylor (Eds.): AMTA 2004, LNAI 3265, pp. 17–26, 2004.
© Springer-Verlag Berlin Heidelberg 2004

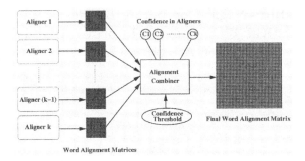

**Fig. 1.** Multi-Align Framework for Combining Different Alignment Algorithms

Multi-Align allows users to tune their MT systems to the properties of a particular genre/domain while still benefiting from knowledge of general linguistic phenomena associated with the language pair. Our goal is to induce word-level alignments for MT that are more accurate than those produced by existing statistical systems using a combination of outputs from different alignment systems. This approach allows us to eliminate the need for rebuilding existing alignment systems when incorporating new linguistic information.

Word-level alignment of bilingual texts is a critical capability for a wide range of NLP applications, such as statistical MT [1], bilingual lexicon construction [15], word sense disambiguation [4], and projection of resources (such as morphological analyzers, part-of-speech taggers, and parsers) [10,22]. The quality of word-level alignments plays a crucial role in the success of these applications, e.g., the output quality of statistical MT systems [18].

The next section presents Multi-Align, a framework for producing improved alignments through the combination of different word-alignment models. Section 3 describes a feasibility experiment using two approaches: GIZA++ [16] and DUSTer [5]. Section 4 demonstrates the effect of combining statistical and linguistically-informed knowledge on resolving translation divergences during word alignment. Finally, Section 5 describes future work on extension of Multi-Align to various linguistic resources.

## 2   Multi-Align

*Multi-Align* is a general alignment framework where the outputs of different aligners are combined to obtain an improvement over the performance of any single aligner. This framework provides a mechanism for combining linguistically-informed alignment approaches with statistical aligners.

Figure 1 illustrates the Multi-Align design. In this framework, $k$ different alignments systems generate word alignments between a given English sentence and a foreign language (FL) sentence. Then, an *Alignment Combiner* uses this information to generate a single word-alignment output. The contribution of each aligner to a particular alignment link is proportional to its confidence score on the aligned words. The decision to include a particular pair of words in the final alignment is based on a human-specified or machine-learned threshold value.

The basic data structure in Multi-Align is the *word alignment matrix*, $Z$, similar to that of current statistical-alignment approaches [19]. $Z$ is a $(m+1) \times (n+1)$ matrix, where $m$ is the number of words in the English sentence $E$, $n$ is the number of words in the foreign language sentence $F$.[1] Let $e_s$ be the word in $E$ in position $s$ and $f_t$ be the word in $F$ in position $t$. Each entry of the matrix, $Z_{st}$, corresponds to the alignment between $e_s$ and $f_t$. Rather than using binary values for $Z_{st}$, we use an alignment probability for each $Z_{st}$ of the matrix.

Formally, we assume that $k$ different aligners are used to generate the word alignments between two sentences. Let $A^i$ be the $i^{th}$ alignment system and $W^i$ be the word alignment matrix generated by this system. Each entry of $W^i$, say $W^i_{st}$, is given a probability of $p^i_{st}$, showing the probability that the corresponding words ($e_s$ and $f_t$) are aligned together. We also assume that each word alignment system is associated with a confidence value for every pair of aligned words. Let $\lambda(s,t)$ be a feature function between $e_s$ and $f_t$, and $C^i_{\lambda(s,t)}$ be the confidence of $i^{th}$ aligner on the alignment link between $e_s$ and $f_t$. This confidence value is conditioned on a feature function $\lambda$. For example, alignment links can be categorized into different groups according to the POS or semantic classes of the words involved (i.e., links involving nouns or Light-verbs, etc.), and $\lambda$ may be the link class. The contribution of the aligner $A^i$ to a specific entry $[s,t]$ of the final word alignment matrix is $C^i_{\lambda(s,t)} \times p^i_{st}$. Thus,

$$Z_{st} = \frac{\sum_{i=1}^{k} C^i_{\lambda(s,t)} \times p^i_{st}}{\sum_{i=1}^{k} \sum_{j=0}^{n} C^i_{\lambda(s,j)} \times p^i_{sj}}$$

For a given confidence threshold $\phi$, $e_s$ and $f_t$ are aligned together if $Z_{st} > \phi$.

The model includes the parameters, $W^i$, $p^i_{st}$, $C^i_{\lambda(s,t)}$ and $\phi$, to decide whether two words are aligned to each other or not in this framework. Here are some guidelines for setting these parameters:[2]

- $\boldsymbol{W^i, p^i_{st}}$: If the aligner produces a set of probabilities for every pair of words between the sentences, it is sufficient to set $W^i_{st} = p^i_{st}$ for all pairs of $[s,t]$. If there are no associated probabilities, $W^i_{st} = 1$ if $(s,t)$ is an alignment link and $W^i_{st} = 0$ otherwise.
- $\boldsymbol{C^i_{\lambda(s,t)}}$: If one of the aligners is taken to be superior to the others on certain word pairs (based on the feature function $\lambda(s,t)$), the confidence value $C^i_{\lambda(s,t)}$ for the $i^{th}$ aligner on that particular link (between $s$ and $t$) reflects a higher contribution to the final alignment matrix than the other aligners.

---

[1] The additional column ($Z_{s0}$ for $0 \leq s \leq m$) and the row ($Z_{0t}$ for $0 \leq t \leq n$) in the matrix is for unaligned English and unaligned foreign language words, respectively.

[2] Confidence values and thresholds may be human specified or set automatically using machine learning techniques.

- $\phi$: If the alignments are forced to be one-to-one, then only the entry with the highest probability in each row and column is deemed *correct*. If all aligners are treated equally, setting $\phi = 0$ is sufficient.

Multi-Align has three advantages with respect to MT systems: ease of adaptability, robustness, and user control.

- **Ease of Adaptability:** Multi-Align eliminates the need for complex modifications of pre-existing systems to incorporate new linguistic resources. A variety of different statistical and symbolic word alignment systems may be used together, such as statistical alignments [16], bilingual dictionaries acquired automatically using lexical correspondences [11,15], lists of closed-class words and cognates, syntactic and dependency trees on either side [2, 21], phrase-based alignments [12] and linguistically-motivated alignments [5].
- **Robustness:** Individual alignment systems have inherent deficiencies that result in partial alignments in their output. Multi-Align relies on the strengths of certain systems to compensate for the weaknesses of other systems.
- **User Control:** The effect of different linguistic information is difficult to observe and control when linguistic knowledge is injected into statistical maximum entropy models [17]. Multi-Align avoids this problem by helping users to understand which linguistic resources are useful for word alignment. Additionally, the contribution of each aligner may be weighted according to its impact on the target application.

## 3   Feasibility of Multi-Align: Combining Statistical and Linguistically Informed Alignments

This section describes feasibility experiments to test the impact of combining statistically-induced and linguistically-motivated alignments. Previous work demonstrated that mapping words into word classes [18] is useful for statistical alignment. We take this one step further by using semantic-based word classes and a set of general, linguistically-motivated rules from *DUSTer (Divergence Unraveling for Statistical Translation)* [5] to induce alignment improvements over GIZA++ (a state-of-the-art alignment system). The application of universal rules is similar to learning non-isomorphic tree mappings [6]; however, we require dependency trees on only one side in contrast to this method.

A central claim of this endeavor is that linguistic information is critical to the overall advancement of non-linguistic approaches to alignment. Our own error analysis of statistically-induced alignments—the output of GIZA++ on 99 English-Spanish sentences—reveals that 80% of statistical alignment errors correspond to missing alignment links. A deeper analysis also shows that 61% of these missed alignments are related to verbs, functional nouns and obliques, which form the main categories of words that are handled by linguistically-motivated components such as the universal rules of DUSTer.

We first describe the components and algorithm behind DUSTer, a linguistically-informed approach to creating partial alignments. We then describe

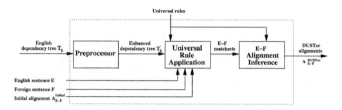

**Fig. 2.** Generating Partial Alignments Using DUSTer

the combination of DUSTer knowledge (i.e., parameterized universal rules) with statistically-induced alignments to produce a complete set of final alignment links. As shown in Figure 2, the input to DUSTer is an English sentence $E$, a foreign language sentence $F$, a dependency tree $T_E$ corresponding to $E$, and a set of initial word alignments from $E$ to $F$, $A_{E-F}^{Initial}$. The initial alignments may be produced by any existing automatic alignment system and the dependency tree may be produced by a standard parser.[3] The key idea is to relate one or more linguistically-motivated categories associated with the (English) input words to those of another language (FL); the resulting *match sets* are used to infer additional alignments from an initial set of statistically-induced alignments.

The remainder of this section presents the linguistic knowledge associated with DUSTer, after which an example of rule application is given. Finally, we describe the combination of DUSTer and GIZA++ in Multi-Align.

### 3.1   Parameters

DUSTer's universal rules require certain types of words to be grouped together into *parameter classes* based on semantic-class knowledge, e.g., classes of verbs including *Aspectual, Change of State, Directional*, etc. [13]. The parameter classes play an important role in identifying and handling translation divergences. The current classification includes 16 classes of parameters. Because the parameters are based on semantic knowledge, the English values can be projected to their corresponding values in a new language, simply by translating the words into the other language. For example, the English light verbs *be, do, give, have, make, put, take* are translated to Spanish light verbs *estar, ser, hacer, dar, tomar, poner, tener*, respectively.

### 3.2   Universal Rule Set

Universal rules relate one or more linguistically-motivated categories in English—specifically, part-of-speech (POS) labels and semantic word classes—to those of a foreign language. Each rule relates the English dependency tree

---

[3] Currently, the initial alignments are produced by GIZA++ based on IBM Model 4, and the dependency trees are generated using Collins' parser [3] trained on Penn treebank [14].

```
0.AVar.X [English{2 1} Chinese{1} Spanish{1} Hindi{1} ]
[Verb<1,i> [TenseV<2,Mod,Verb,C:i>]] <--> [Verb<1,i>]

1.B.X [ English{2 1 3} Spanish{2 1 3 4 5} ]
[PsychV<1,i,CatVar:V_N,Verb> [Noun<2,j,Subj>] [Noun<3,k,Obj>]] <-->
[LightVB<1,Verb,C:i> [Noun<2,j,Subj>] [Noun<3,i,Obj>]
[Oblique<4,Pred,Prep,C:i> [Noun<5,k,PObj>]]]
```

**Fig. 3.** Examples of DUSTer's Universal Rules

structure on the left-hand side (LHS) to the foreign-language tree structure on the right-hand side (RHS). [4] For example, the rules in Figure 3 can be used to handle two forms of conflation (Tense-Verb and Light-Verb). These rules correspond to the mappings *'will eat'* → *'eats'* and *'j fears k'* → *'j has fear of k'*, respectively. The first line shows the rule name, the languages to which the rule may be applied, and the order of the nodes in the surface form for each language involved.

Each node in the rule specification contains a *node type*—a part-of-speech category or a parameter type—followed by a list of features. The feature list includes a unique *node identifier* (e.g., *1*), an *alignment index* that relates potentially aligned LHS and RHS nodes (e.g., *j*), a *dependency relation* to the head node (e.g., *Subj*), and categorial-variation information (e.g., *CatVar:AJ_N*).[5] Because nodes with the same alignment index are viewed as translational equivalents, they are assumed to be potentially aligned in the initial alignments. Note that, in addition to the simple indices, $i$, $j$, etc., we make use of *conflated indices* (*C:i*, *C:j*, etc.) to refer to semantically light words that co-occur with high-content words but are generally unaligned in the initial alignments. Nodes marked *C:i* are taken to be related structurally to a high-content node marked $i$.

### 3.3 Application of Universal Rules for Alignment Inference

This section describes how the universal rules and parameters presented above are used to infer alignments from a sentence pair, English dependency tree, and an initial alignment, as in the example of Figure 4.

The dependency tree $T_E$ is augmented during the preprocessing step (the first module in Figure 2) with semantic parameters and CatVar information; the result is the augmented tree $T'_E$ as shown in Figure 4. The enhanced dependency $T'_E$ is next passed to the Universal-Rule Application component, along with the original $E$ and $F$ sentences and initial alignments $A^{Initial}_{E-F}$. The initial alignments $A^{Initial}_{E-F}$ are used as a strict filter on the application of the universal rules. Specifically, we require that all LHS/RHS nodes related by a simple

---

[4] The current set of universal rules supports 4 foreign languages: Spanish, Hindi, Chinese, and Arabic. There is a total of 116 overlapping rules: 21 rules for Hindi, 28 rules for Spanish, 44 rules for Arabic and 65 rules for Chinese.

[5] Categorial variations are relations between words like *jealous* (an adjective) and *jealousy* (a noun). These are extracted from a large database called CatVar [9].

| English Sentence (E): *She will fear her enemies .* | | | | |
|---|---|---|---|---|
| Spanish Sentence (F): *Ella tendrá miedo de sus enemigos .* | | | | |

**Enhanced English Dependency Tree $T'_E$**

| Node# | Word | POS | Parent | Rel | Features |
|---|---|---|---|---|---|
| 1 | She | Noun | 3 | Subj | [FunctionalN] |
| 2 | will | Verb | 3 | Mod | [TenseV CatVar:V_N CatVar:V_AJ] |
| 3 | fear | Verb | *root* | * | [PsychV CatVar:V_N CatVar:V_AJ CatVar:V_AV] |
| 4 | her | Noun | 5 | Mod | [FunctionalN] |
| 5 | enemies | Noun | 3 | Obj | [CatVar:N_AJ] |

**Initial Alignment $A^{initial}_{E-F}$:** (She, Ella), (fear, miedo), (her,sus), (enemies, enemigos)

**Fig. 4.** Example Sentences, Dependency Tree and Initial Alignment

index (i.e., $i$, $j$) have a corresponding alignment link in the initial alignments. Moreover, unindexed nodes must **not** have a corresponding alignment link in the initial alignment. Rules violating this requirement are eliminated. The remaining (potentially-applicable) rules are checked for a match against the POS and parameter labels associated with the words in the two input sentences.

In addition to checking for a match, the rule-matching process identifies specific sentence positions of matching tokens. For a given modified E-F sentence pair and a specific rule, the rule-application module returns the *match sets* corresponding to positions of words that match the RHS and LHS nodes of the rule. In the example given in Figure 4, the match sets resulting from the application of rules 0.AVar.X and 1.B.X are (([2,3],[2])) and (([1,3,5],[1,2,3,4,6])), respectively.

The final step is alignment inference, a straightforward extraction of corrected alignment pairs $A^{DUSTer}_{E-F}$ using the match sets. Formally, for each match-set element ([. . .,$e_i$,. . .] [. . .,$f_j$,. . .]), where $e_i$ and $f_j$ carry the same co-index $k$ (or the same conflated co-index), we add the pair ($e_i$,$f_j$) to the partial alignments.

### 3.4 Combining GIZA++ and DUSTer in Multi-Align

Our feasibility experiment combines GIZA++ [16] and DUSTer. For generating GIZA++ alignments, we use the default GIZA++ parameters, i.e., the alignments are bootstrapped from Model 1 (five iterations), HMM model (five iterations), Model 3 (two iterations) and Model 4 (four iterations).

GIZA++ and DUSTer are given as input alignment systems in the Multi-Align framework. Since DUSTer provides only partial alignments that are related to the translation divergences, we are interested in a union of these two systems' outputs to produce the final set of alignments. Therefore, the confidence values for each aligner are set to 1 and the confidence threshold is set to 0.[6] Figure 5 shows the set of alignments generated by GIZA++ and DUSTer and their combination in Multi-Align for the sentence pair in our example.

---

[6] As a simplifying assumption, we take the feature function $\lambda(s, t)$ to be a constant value for every $s$ and $t$. In future work, we will weight each alignment link independently using different feature functions.

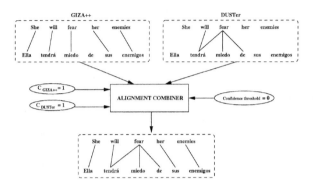

**Fig. 5.** Set of Alignments Generated by Using GIZA++ and DUSTer in Multi-Align

**Table 1.** Spanish/English Alignment Evaluation: GIZA++ vs. Multi-Align

| SYSTEM | PRECISION | RECALL | F-MEASURE |
|--------|-----------|--------|-----------|
| GIZA++ | 72.32 | 72.68 | 72.43 |
| Multi-Align | 73.01 | 73.36 | 73.12 |

## 4   Results

In order to evaluate our combined approach, we conducted an experiment to compare the alignments produced in the Multi-Align framework to those produced by GIZA++ (the industry standard) alone.[7] We measure the closeness of Multi-Align and GIZA++ output to human alignments for a test set of 100 Spanish/English sentence pairs using precision, recall and f-measure metrics.

The unit of comparison is the alignment pair, i.e., the English word and its corresponding (aligned) FL word. Let $A$ be the alignments generated by either the combined approach or GIZA++ and let $G$ be the gold standard alignments. Each element of $A$ and $G$ is a pair $(e_i, f_j)$ where $e_i$ is an English word and $f_j$ is a FL word. Formally, precision, recall and f-measure metrics are defined as follows:

$$Recall(R) = \frac{|A \cap G|}{|G|} \qquad Precision(P) = \frac{|A \cap G|}{|A|} \qquad F-measure = \frac{2 \times P \times R}{P+R}$$

Table 1 summarizes the evaluation results for both sets. The difference between the Multi-Align and GIZA++ scores are statistically significant at a 95% confidence level using a two-tailed t-test for all 3 measures.

---

[7] GIZA++ was trained on an English-Spanish training corpus of 45K sentence pairs.

## 5   Conclusion and Future Work

We have introduced a general framework, Multi-Align, to combine outputs of different word alignment systems for an improved word alignment. To illustrate the effectiveness of the framework, we conducted a feasibility experiment that combines linguistically-motivated and statistically-induced alignments to resolve structural differences between languages to add missing alignment links.

While our result appears to be a modest improvement, we have used the strictest possible application of the universal rules to obtain these results. In future, we will investigate using a bilingual dictionary and/or a POS tagger for foreign language in order to obtain better match sets on the FL side.

The most critical task in the framework is the setting of the Multi-Align parameters of the framework appropriately to decrease/increase the effects of a particular alignment system. In practice, the user may not foresee the quality of word alignments produced by a particular alignment system, therefore it may not be practical to set these parameters manually. We will investigate estimation of these parameters automatically using machine learning techniques.

The improved alignments are most useful when seen in the context of the larger goals behind our alignment work: to train foreign language parsers using the projected dependency trees and to improve the performance of both statistical and hybrid MT systems. Our next step is to conduct an external evaluation of our divergence-unraveling approach based on a quality assessment of the projected dependency trees used for parser training and the output of the trained parser. We will compare the resulting FL dependency trees with human-produced FL treebanks [7]. The goal of improving the performance of hybrid MT systems is addressed by embedding the output of our trained parser in a Generation-Heavy MT (GHMT) framework [8]. We will investigate this path and conduct evaluations using the standard MT metrics, e.g., BLEU [20].

Finally, we plan to investigate the interaction between the size of training data and the amount of injected linguistic knowledge in terms of MT output quality.

**Acknowledgments.** This work has been supported, in part, by ONR MURI Contract FCPO.810548265, Cooperative Agreement DAAD190320020, NSF ITR Grant IIS-0326553, and NSF Infrastructure Award EIA0130422. We are indebted to Andrew Fister, Ayelet Goldin, Rebecca Hwa, Nitin Madnani, Christof Monz and Eric Nichols, who assisted in developing DUSTer.

## References

1. Peter F. Brown, Stephan A. Della-Pietra, and Robert L. Mercer. The Mathematics of Statistical Machine Translation: Parameter Estimation. *Computational Linguistics*, 19(2):263–311, 1993.
2. Colin Cherry and Dekang Lin. A Probability Model to Improve Word Alignment. In *Proceedings of ACL 2003*, pages 88–95, 2003.

3. Michael Collins. Three Generative Lexicalized Models for Statistical Parsing. In *Proceedings of ACL 1997*, Madrid, Spain, 1997.
4. Mona Diab and Philip Resnik. An Unsupervised Method for Word Sense Tagging Using Parallel Corpora. In *Proceedings of ACL 2002*, Philadelphia, PA, 2002.
5. Bonnie J. Dorr, Lisa Pearl, Rebecca Hwa, and Nizar Habash. DUSTer: A Method for Unraveling Cross-Language Divergences for Statistical Word–Level Alignment. In *Proceedings of AMTA 2002*, Tiburon, CA, 2002.
6. Jason Eisner. Learning Non-isomorphic Tree Mappings for Machine Translation. In *Proceedings of ACL 2003*, Supporo, Japan, July 2003.
7. Joshua Goodman. Parsing Algorithm and Metrics. In *Proceedings of ACL 1996*, Santa Cruz, CA, 1996.
8. Nizar Habash. Generation Heavy Hybrid Machine Translation. In *Proceedings of INLG 2002*, New York, NY, 2002.
9. Nizar Habash and Bonnie J. Dorr. A Categorial Variation Database for English. In *Proceedings of NAACL/HLT 2003*, pages 96–102, Edmonton, Canada, 2003.
10. Rebecca Hwa, Philip Resnik, Amy Weinberg, and Okan Kolak. Evaluating Translational Correspondence Using Annotation Projection. In *Proceedings of ACL 2002*, pages 392–399, Philadelphia, PA, 2002.
11. Sue J. Ker and Jason S. Chang. A Class-based Approach to Word Alignment. *Computational Linguistics*, 23(2):313–343, 1997.
12. Philip Koehn, Franz Josef Och, and Daniel Marcu. Statistical Phrase-Based Translation. In *Proceedings of NAACL/HLT 2003*, Edmonton, Canada, 2003.
13. Beth Levin. *English Verb Classes and Alternations: A Preliminary Investigation*. University of Chicago Press, Chicago, IL, 1993.
14. Mitchell Marcus, Beatrice Santorini, and Mary Ann Marcinkiewicz. Building a Large Annotated Corpus of English: the Penn Treebank. *Computational Linguistics*, 19(2):313–330, 1993.
15. I. Dan Melamed. Models of Translational Equivalence Among Words. *Computational Linguistics*, 26(2):221–249, 2000.
16. Franz Joseph Och. Giza++: Training of Statistical Translation Models. Technical report, RWTH Aachen, University of Technology, 2000.
17. Franz Joseph Och and Hermann Ney. Discriminative Training and Maximum Entropy Models for Statistical Machine Translation. In *Proceedings of ACL 2002*, pages 295–302, Philadelphia, PA, 2002.
18. Franz Joseph Och and Hermann Ney. A Systematic Comparison of Various Statistical Alignment Models. *Computational Linguistics*, 29(1):9–51, 2003.
19. Franz Joseph Och and Hans Weber. Improving Statistical Natural Language Translation with Categories and Rules. In *Proceedings of ACL/COLING 1998*, pages 985–989, Montreal, Canada, 1998.
20. Kishore Papineni, Salim Roukos, Todd Ward, and Wei-Jing Zhu. BLEU: a Method for Automatic Evaluation of Machine Translation. In *Proceedings of ACL 2002*, pages 311–318, Philadelphia, PA, 2002.
21. Kenji Yamada and Kevin Knight. A Syntax-Based Statistical Translation Model. In *Proceedings of ACL 2001*, Toulouse, France, 2001.
22. David Yarowsky, Grace Ngai, and Richard Wicentowski. Inducing Multilingual Text Analysis Tools via Robust Projection Across Aligned Corpora. In *Proceedings of HLT 2001*, pages 109–116, San Diego, CA, 2001.

# A Modified Burrows-Wheeler Transform for Highly Scalable Example-Based Translation

Ralf D. Brown

Carnegie Mellon University Language Technologies Institute
5000 Forbes Avenue
Pittsburgh, PA 15213-3890 USA
ralf@cs.cmu.edu

**Abstract.** The Burrows-Wheeler Transform (BWT) was originally developed for data compression, but can also be applied to indexing text. In this paper, an adaptation of the BWT to word-based indexing of the training corpus for an example-based machine translation (EBMT) system is presented. The adapted BWT embeds the necessary information to retrieve matched training instances without requiring any additional space and can be instantiated in a compressed form which reduces disk space and memory requirements by about 40% while still remaining searchable without decompression.

Both the speed advantage from $O(log\ N)$ lookups compared to the $O(N)$ lookups in the inverted-file index which had previously been used and the structure of the index itself act as enablers for additional capabilities and run-time speed. Because the BWT groups all instances of any $n$-gram together, it can be used to quickly enumerate the most-frequent $n$-grams, for which translations can be precomputed and stored, resulting in an order-of-magnitude speedup at run time.

## 1 Introduction

A key component of any example-based or case-based machine translation system is a good index of the training instances. For shallow EBMT systems such as Gaijin [1], Brown's Generalized EBMT [2], EDGAR [3], or Cicekli and Güvenir's Generalized EBMT [4], this index is formed from either the original training text's source-language half, or some lightly-transformed version thereof. This paper addresses such a textual index and discusses how it impacts not only the speed of the system, but can act as an enabler for additional capabilities which may improve the quality of translations.

Until recently, our EBMT system used an index based on an inverted file – a listing, for each distinct word (type) of all its occurences (tokens) in the corpus. While such an index has several nice properties, including fast incremental updates that permit on-line training with additional examples, it scales poorly. Lookups not only take time linear in the amount of training text, they also require $O(N)$ additional working memory, as maximal matches are built by finding adjacent instances of a pair of words and then extended one word at a

R.E. Frederking and K.B. Taylor (Eds.): AMTA 2004, LNAI 3265, pp. 27–36, 2004.

time. Although the code had been heavily optimized (including a five-instruction hand-coded inner scanning loop), the system's overall performance was not adequate for interactive applications with corpora exceeding about five million words.

The new index format which was selected as a replacement for the existing code is based on the Burrows-Wheeler Transform, a transformation of textual data first described in the context of data compression a decade ago [5], and now the underlying algorithm in many of the best-performing compression programs such as bzip2 [6]. The following sections give a brief overview of the BWT, how it was adapted for use in Carnegie Mellon University's EBMT system, the performance improvements that resulted from replacing the index, and new capabilities enabled by the BWT-based index.

## 2 The Burrows-Wheeler Transform

The Burrows-Wheeler Transform is a block-sorting transformation which groups elements of its input lexically.

The BWT operates as follows:

1. Take the input text $T$ (of length $N$) and make it row 0 of an $N$-by-$N$ matrix $M$.
2. For $i = 1$ to $N - 1$, form row $i$ of $M$ by rotating $T$ left by $i$ places as in Figure 1.
3. Sort the rows of $M$ lexically, remembering where each row of the sorted result originated, to form $M'$ (Figure 2).
4. Due to the manner in which $M$ was constructed, columns 1 through $N - 1$ of $M'$ can be reconstructed from column 0 by providing a pointer from each row to the row which had been immediately below it prior to sorting. This vector of successor pointers is conventionally called $V$.
5. Since the first column of $M'$ now consists entirely of runs of equal elements in lexicographic order (at most one run per member of the alphabet $\Sigma$), one can discard column 0 and represent it by an array $C$ of size $|\Sigma|$ which contains the first row in $M'$ containing each member of the alphabet.

In practice, neither $M$ nor $M'$ are ever explicitly constructed. Instead, an auxiliary array of pointers into $T$ is sorted, with $M_{i,j}$ determined by retrieving $T_{(i+j) \bmod N}$. $T$ is usually a sequence of bytes, but for EBMT, a sequence of 32-bit word IDs was used.

Together, $C$ and $V$ are the output of the Burrows-Wheeler Transform. These two arrays lend themselves to highly-effective data compression because the elements of $C$ are monotonically increasing, as are the elements of $V$ within each range $C_i$ to $C_{i+1} - 1$ (see Figure 3. The transform is also reversible by starting at the position of $V$ to which row 0 of $M$ was sorted and following the successor links until all elements of $V$ have been visited; this is the final step in the decompression phase of BWT-based compression algorithms. For this example,

| m | i | s | s | i | s | s | i | p | p | i | $ |
|---|---|---|---|---|---|---|---|---|---|---|---|
| i | s | s | i | s | s | i | p | p | i | $ | m |
| s | s | i | s | s | i | p | p | i | $ | m | i |
| s | i | s | s | i | p | p | i | $ | m | i | s |
| i | s | s | i | p | p | i | $ | m | i | s | s |
| s | s | i | p | p | i | $ | m | i | s | s | i |
| s | i | p | p | i | $ | m | i | s | s | i | s |
| i | p | p | i | $ | m | i | s | s | i | s | s |
| p | p | i | $ | m | i | s | s | i | s | s | i |
| p | i | $ | m | i | s | s | i | s | s | i | p |
| i | $ | m | i | s | s | i | s | s | i | p | p |
| $ | m | i | s | s | i | s | s | i | p | p | i |

**Fig. 1.** Constructing the rotated matrix

| i | p | p | i | $ | m | i | s | s | i | s | s |
|---|---|---|---|---|---|---|---|---|---|---|---|
| i | s | s | i | p | p | i | $ | m | i | s | s |
| i | s | s | i | s | s | i | p | p | i | $ | m |
| i | $ | m | i | s | s | i | s | s | i | p | p |
| m | i | s | s | i | s | s | i | p | p | i | $ |
| p | i | $ | m | i | s | s | i | s | s | i | p |
| p | p | i | $ | m | i | s | s | i | s | s | i |
| s | i | p | p | i | $ | m | i | s | s | i | s |
| s | i | s | s | i | p | p | i | $ | m | i | s |
| s | s | i | p | p | i | $ | m | i | s | s | i |
| s | s | i | s | s | i | p | p | i | $ | m | i |
| $ | m | i | s | s | i | s | s | i | p | p | i |

**Fig. 2.** The sorted matrix $M'$

starting at $V_4$, following the pointers to $V_2$, $V_{10}$, $V_8$, etc. will reconstruct the original text.

The output of the BWT also lends itself to language modeling, as all occurrences of any given $n$-gram are adjacent in the $V$ array – thus one can count the number of occurrences simply by subtracting the position of the first occurrence from the position of the last. Further, all $n + 1$-grams beginning with the given $n$-gram have their occurrences as a sub-range of the range for the $n$-gram. For example, in Figure 2, the instances of unigram 's' occupy rows 7 through 10, while bigrams 'si' occupy rows 7 and 8 and trigram 'sis' occupies row 8. The ends of the subrange for an $n + 1$-gram can be located using two binary searches within the larger range. This leads to $O(k \ log \ N)$ lookups for the number of occurrences of any particular $k$-gram.

To deal with ambiguous lookups, the search is split as necessary. One common operation in our EBMT system is generalization via equivalence classes (e.g. days of the week, colors, or various types of proper names). When a member of an

| $M_{i,0}$ | i | i | i | i | m | p | p | s | s | s | s | $ |
|-----------|---|---|----|----|---|---|---|---|---|---|---|---|
| $V_i$ | 6 | 9 | 10 | 11 | 2 | 3 | 5 | 0 | 1 | 7 | 8 | 4 |

**Fig. 3.** The array of successors

equivalence class is encountered in the source-language text while indexing the training corpus, it is replaced by the class marker if a known translation listed in the equivalence class occurs in the target-language half of the training instance, and left unchanged otherwise. When translating, the system should match the training example in either case, so both the original word and the corresponding class marker(s)[1] form an ambiguous lookup at that position in the input.

At every word position in the input, an extension of each currently-active partial match by each alternative term is attempted; those extensions that result in a non-zero number of occurrences become active matches for the next word position. Further, a new match is started for each alternative term at that position which actually occurs in the training data, and the unextended active matches are added to the set of all phrasal matches to be processed further in the retrieval and alignment phases of translation. While this splitting of BWT matches on ambiguity could theoretically result in an exponential increase in memory and run time, in practice most alternatives peter out very quickly – usually, the bulk of the corpus matches that are found are two or three words in length. Slowdowns from ambiguous lookups have not been an issue.

## 3   Modifications for Use in Indexing

Burrows-Wheeler-transformed data is very good at showing relative positions, but in order to determine an absolute position in the original text without completely reconstructing it, some auxiliary information is required. Neither the $C$ nor the $V$ array provide any information about the *location* of an $n$-gram in the original input, only its surrounding context.

A considerable number of approaches to anchoring a BWT-based index to the text it indexes have been proposed [7], but these typically involve additional time and/or space proportional to the alphabet size. While this is acceptable when the text is considered to be a stream of bytes ($|\Sigma| = 256$), the alphabet size for our word-based index quickly reaches into the hundreds of thousands. We thus decided to take advantage of the line-oriented nature of the example base.

Because the EBMT system has no interest in finding phrases which span the boundaries between training examples, an end-of-line or end-of-record (EOR) marker can be inserted after each example. By reserving an entire range of values as EOR markers, the record number can be encoded within the marker

---

[1] A source-language word can belong to multiple equivalence classes provided the translations are disjoint.

itself. Given that the 32-bit IDs we used to represent both words and successor pointers in the $V$ array provide more than 4,200 million possibilities, 1/4 of the possible values were reserved as EOR markers. This sets the limits on the training corpus size at some 3,200 million words in over 1,000 million examples.

Further (precisely because the EBMT system does not operate on text spanning a sentence boundary, though it allows for overlapping partial translations to be merged in generating the final translation [8]), there is no need in this application to determine what text from the next training example follows an EOR marker, and it is thus possible omit the portion of $V$ corresponding to EOR. As a result, the index is no larger than it would have been had the entire training corpus been treated as a single example. There is also no processing overhead on finding matching $n$-grams resulting from the EOR markers.

In addition to inserting the EOR markers, the order of words in each training instance is reversed before adding them to the index. This allows matches to be extended from left to right even though lookups in the index can only be efficiently extended from right to left. (While the input sentence could be processed from right to left for EBMT, we also wished to use the same code to compute conditional probabilities for language modeling.)

To retrieve the training examples containing $n$-grams matching the input to be translated, iterate over the range of $V$ corresponding to the $n$-gram. For each instance of the $n$-gram, follow the pointers in $V$ until reaching an EOR, then extract the record number from the EOR and retrieve the appropriate training example from the corpus. The offset of the matched phrase within the example is determined by simply counting the number of pointers which were followed before reaching an EOR. The original source-language text is not included in the stored example since it can be reconstructed from the index if required. We opted not to store a pointer to the start position of the line in the $V$ array, since the only use our system has for the unmatched portion of the source text is for display to the user in error messages, and we can forego display of the entire source sentence in such cases. For applications which must be able to reconstruct the entire source sentence or access adjacent sentences, separately-stored start pointers *will* be required. Even without a line-start pointer, we are still able to reconstruct the word sequence from the beginning of a training example to the end of the matched portion when we need to display an error message; this is typically the most useful part of the sentence for the user, anyway.

One drawback of the BWT-based index compared to the old inverted file is that quick incremental updates are not possible, since the entire index needs to be re-written, rather than chaining new records onto the existing occurrence lists. Because on-line incremental updates in practice are performed only a small number of times before there is an opportunity for an off-line update, we have addressed the issue by using two indices – the large main index which was built off-line when the system was trained, and a much smaller index containing only the incremental updates. Although the entire auxiliary index must be re-written on each incremental update, this can be done quickly due to its small size.

## 4  Compressing the Index

For applications where space is more critical than time, the index may be stored in a compressed form which is around 40% smaller than the uncompressed form (38–46% for the corpora on which this feature was tested). Because the index comprises nearly half the total disk space consumed by the processed corpus, this results in a reduction of disk usage by nearly 20% at a cost of 20% greater CPU time. This capability has already been used to good effect on a training corpus which was slightly too large to fit completely in the machine's RAM – the reduced index size eliminated disk thrashing and thereby actually resulted in faster translations.

As mentioned above, the $V$ array consists of runs of monotonically increasing values, typically with fairly small differences between adjacent values. Thus, we opted to represent the compressed $V$ array as an array of bytes encoding either the difference from the previous element or an index into an auxiliary table of full 32-bit values.

Out of the 256 possible 8-bit values, values 1 through 191 are used to encode the actual difference from the previous entry and values 192 through 255 to encode an index within a bucket of full addresses. Value 0 was reserved to encode EOR in applications such as language modeling which do not need to encode record numbers. The $V$ array is split into buckets of 64 entries and a 32-bit pointer into a pool of full addresses is allocated for each bucket. Thus the value 192 represents the address pointed at by the current bucket's pool pointer, the value 193 represents the address following that one, etc. The best-case compression with this scheme would store 64 entries of $V$ using just 68 bytes, while the worst case is 324 bytes for those same 64 entries (8.5 and 40.5 bits per entry, respectively). On average, this method achieves a size of 18–19 bits per entry and an overall size for $C$ plus $V$ of 20–21 bits per word indexed.

The representation just described allows random access to any element of the index without decompressing any portion of the index. One simply retrieves the $i$th byte of the $V$ array and examines it. If the value corresponds to a pointer to the auxiliary array of absolute addresses, that value is retrieved; if not, scan left and accumulate the difference values until an absolute address is reached, then return the sum of that address and the accumulated difference. The number of bytes which need to be processed is typically quite small, and is bounded by deliberately forcing at least one element of each 64-entry bucket to be an absolute address (increasing the best-case compressed size to 9 bits per entry, but having negligible effect on real-world average compression). Without such deliberate breaks in the runs of difference values, common trigrams in the corpus would cause runs of difference 1 equal in length to the frequency of the trigram.

## 5  Pre-computing Phrasal Translations

One of the interesting new capabilities enabled by the BWT index is the straightforward enumeration – directly from the index – of all distinct $n$-grams of a given length $k$ together with their frequencies in time $O(kN)$ (more sophisticated approaches can no doubt reduce this time bound) using $O(k)$ space. Thus, we decided to precompute the most common phrasal translations in order to speed up the overall translation process. Doing so required very little code – 65 lines of C++ to enumerate all the $n$-grams and 150 lines more to determine the translations of the most frequent $n$-grams and add them back to the indexed corpus.

Precomputing the candidate translations for a common phrase improves translation speed because it becomes unnecessary to retrieve and align a large number of matches to determine translation probabilities. Instead, only a single instance of each of the best-scoring translations is retrieved and the stored frequency count is extracted from that instance.

## 6    Performance and Scalability

Performance was evaluated on three different corpora. The first corpus is a 100,000-sentence pair subset of the IBM Hansard corpus [9] for French-English, coupled with a 77,000-translation pair part-of-speech-tagged dictionary and some 500 context-free rewrite rules for generalization (about 2.2 million words of English). The second corpus consists of the Hindi-English parallel text collected during the June 2003 DARPA TIDES Surprise Language Exercise, less some held out sentences for testing (about 2.1 million words of Hindi). The third corpus, for Arabic-English, consists of UN proceedings and text from the Ummah newspaper (about 81 million words of Arabic).

Indexing speed when generalization is disabled is approximately equal for the old and new index formats. When generalization is enabled, lookup and retrieval of exact matches among the generalization rules account for the majority of the runtime in the old system. Thus, for the French-English test case, indexing time is cut from 58 minutes to less than 10 due to the faster lookup during generalization.

Table 1 clearly shows the $O(N)$ performance of the old index and the much better scaling of the new BWT-based index for the Hindi and Arabic test sets. The times listed are the amount of time required to locate all matching $n$-grams in the input sentences, without retrieving any of the matches from the corpus. The French test set also illustrates that the nature of the text influences the lookup time, since the French training text is much closer to the test sentences than is the case for the other languages, and as a result there are many more matches – and, in particular, long matches – against the corpus.

Pre-computing the translations of all $n$-grams occurring at least 30 times in the Hindi training corpus of 2.1 million words doubles the indexing time from 2.5 to 5 minutes, increases the total size of the indexed corpus by about 10 percent and produces a considerable speed-up in translations (see Table 2). Similarly for the Arabic corpus, training time increases from 84 minutes to about 4 hours and disk usage increases by about 18 percent when precomputing all 2- through 12-grams occurring at least 30 times each. Without the precomputation, the EBMT engine attempts to perform a word-level alignment on up to 4000 instances

**Table 1.** Index Lookup Performance

| Corpus | Train (words) | Test (words) | Time (Invert File) | Time (BWT Index) |
|--------|------|------|------|------|
| Hindi  | 2.1M | 4460 | 1.8s  | 0.5s |
| Arabic | 81M  | 5003 | 36.0s | 0.7s |
| French | 2.2M | 4628 | 7.2s  | 0.7s |

**Table 2.** Effect of Precomputation on Translation Time

| Corpus | Train (words) | Test (words) | Precomputed None | Precomputed ≥ 30 |
|--------|------|------|------|------|
| Hindi  | 2.1M | 4460 | 14s  | 1.8s |
| Arabic | 81M  | 5003 | 145s | 6.8s |
| French | 2.2M | 4628 | 158s | 8.7s |

of each distinct matching phrase, stopping after 1500 successful alignments, in order to accumulate reliable translation probabilities. Naturally, only a small percentage of $n$-grams actually have more than a small fraction of the maximum instances to be checked, but as can be seen from the run times, these account for the bulk of the processing.

The combination of new $O(log\ N)$ index and precomputation yields overall EBMT run times less than that required merely for lookups in the old index format.

## 7   Speed as an Enabler

In addition to the newly-added capability of precomputing translations already mentioned, pure speed can itself be an enabler for additional capabilities and applications.

The Carnegie-Mellon EBMT engine has in the past been used as part of a speech-to-speech translation system [10,11]. In such an interactive application, it is important for translations to be completed quickly, preferably in less than half a second. Similarly, for bulk translations of large corpora such as the Chinese portion of the TDT-3 corpus [12], a system taking tens of seconds per sentence (or, worse, several minutes per sentence) would simply not be practical.

Conversely, in applications where the previous system was fast enough, the time saved by better indexing and precomputed translation hypotheses can be applied to additional, more sophisticated processing. Or one can use a larger training corpus with the same processing as before to gain additional coverage without unacceptably slowing the translation process.

## 8   Future Work

We plan to use the pre-computed phrasal translations to help guide word-level alignment in cases where there may be too much ambiguity to perform the alignment based purely on a bilingual dicationary and the information in that particular sentence pair. Whenever a portion of the bitext mapping between the source and target language halves of a training instance is too sparse or too ambiguous to provide a unique alignment, referring to the pre-aligned phrases to restrict the possible alignments may allow the overall alignment to succeed.

**Acknowledgements.** This work was largely supported by the TIDES program under Navy research contract N66001-00-C-8007.

The author would like to thank the reviewers for their feedback, which resulted in numerous improvements to this paper.

## References

1. Veale, T., Way, A.: Gaijin: A Template-Driven Bootstrapping Approach to Example-Based Machine Translation. In: Proceedings of t he NeMNLP'97, New Methods in Natural Language Processessing, Sofia, Bulgaria (1997)
   http://www.compapp.dcu.ie/~tonyv/papers/gaijin.html.
2. Brown, R.D.: Adding Linguistic Knowledge to a Lexical Example-Based Translation System. In: Proceedings of the Eighth International Conference on Theoretical and Methodological Issues in Machine Translation (TMI-99), Chester, England (1999) 22–32 http://www.cs.cmu.edu/~ralf/papers.html.
3. Carl, M.: Inducing Translation Templates for Example-Based Machine Translation. In: Proceedings of the Seventh Machine Translation Summit (MT-Summit VII).
4. Cicekli, I., Guvenir, H.A.: Learning Translation Templates from Bilingual Translation Examples. Applied Intelligence 15 (2001) 57–76
   http://www.cs.bilkent.edu.tr/~ilyas/pubs.html.
5. Burrows, M., Wheeler, D.: A Block-Sorting Lossless Data Compression Algorithm. Technical Report 124, Digital Equipment Corporation (1994)
6. Seward, J.: The bzip2 and libbzip2 Home Page (1997) http://www.bzip2.com.
7. Ferragina, P., Manzini, G.: An Experimental Study of an Opportunistic Index. In: ACM-SIAM Symposium on Discrete Algorithms. (2001) 269-278
   http://citeseer.ist.psu.edu/ferragina01experimental.html.
8. Brown, R.D., Hutchinson, R., Bennett, P.N., Carbonell, J.G., Jansen, P.: Reducing Boundary Friction Using Translation-Fragment Overlap. In: Proceedings of the Ninth Machine Translation Summit. (2003) 24–31
   http://www.cs.cmu.edu/~ralf/papers.html.
9. Linguistic Data Consortium: Hansard Corpus of Parallel English and French. Linguistic Data Consortium (1997) http://www.ldc.upenn.edu/. (1999) 250-258
10. Frederking, R., Rudnicky, A., Hogan, C.: Interactive Speech Translation in the DIPLOMAT Project. In Krauwer, S., et al., eds.: Spoken Language Translation: Proceedings of a Workshop, Madrid, Spain, Association of Computational Linguistics and Eurpoean Network in Language and Speech (1997) 61–66

11. Black, A.W., Brown, R.D., Frederking, R., Singh, R., Moody, J., Steinbrecher, E.:
    TONGUES: Rapid Development of a Speech-to-Speech Translation System. In:
    Proceedings of HLT-2002: Second International Conference on Human Language
    Technology Research. (2002) 183-189
    http://www.cs.cmu.edu/~ralf/Papers.html.
12. Graff, D., Cieri, C., Strassel, S., Martey, N.: The TDT-3 Text and Speech Corpus
    (1999) http://www.ldc.upenn.edu/Papers/TDTi999/tdt3corpus.ps.
13. Bentley, J., Sedgewick, R.: Fast algorithms for sorting and searching strings. In:
    SODA: ACM-SIAM Symposium on Discrete Algorithms (A Conference on Theo-
    retical and Experimental Analysis of Discrete Algorithms). (1997)
    http://www.cs.princeton.edu/~rs/strings/.

# Designing a Controlled Language for the Machine Translation of Medical Protocols: The Case of English to Chinese

Sylviane Cardey, Peter Greenfield, and Xiaohong Wu

Centre L. Tesnière, Besançon (FRANCE)

**Abstract.** Because of its clarity and its simplified way of writing, controlled language (CL) is being paid increasing attention by NLP (natural language processing) researchers, such as in machine translation. The users of controlled languages are of two types, firstly the authors of documents written in the controlled language and secondly the end-user readers of the documents. As a subset of natural language, controlled language restricts vocabulary, grammar, and style for the purpose of reducing or eliminating both ambiguity and complexity. The use of controlled language can help decrease the complexity of natural language to a certain degree and thus improve the translation quality, especially for the partial or total automatic translation of non-general purpose texts, such as technical documents, manuals, instructions and medical reports. Our focus is on the machine translation of medical protocols applied in the field of zoonosis. In this article we will briefly introduce why controlled language is preferred in our research work, what kind of benefits it will bring to our work and how we could make use of this existing technique to facilitate our translation tool.

## 1 Introduction

The idea of controlled language (CL) is not a new one. It can be traced back to as early as the 1930s. It was first proposed for the purpose of encouraging a precise and clarified way of writing for the better readability of technical documents by humans (see for example [16]), both by native and non-native speakers, and especially of English [15]. Thus the users of controlled languages are of two types, firstly the authors of documents written in the controlled language and secondly the end-user readers of the documents. During its development, different names have been used for the English variants, such as "Simplified English", "Plain English", "Basic English" and "Global English". Though there are some differences among each of these, in this article we prefer to put them into one category – controlled language, an artificially defined subset of natural language (here English) as they are all more or less controlled and share more similarities. In practice, controlled languages are divided into two major categories: 1) better readability by humans and 2) ease of natural language processing (NLP) [8]. Our present work focuses on the second category, that is, natural language processing, and in particular, machine translation. We intend to design and develop a CL to control the generation of feasible and faithful texts of

R.E. Frederking and K.B. Taylor (Eds.): AMTA 2004, LNAI 3265, pp. 37–47, 2004.
© Springer-Verlag Berlin Heidelberg 2004

medical protocols which have been written by professionals, one of the two types of users of the CL, this by the means of machine translation for the end-users, the other type of CL user, being the professional or non-professional medical workers working in the field of zoonosis. There are a good many CL systems existing around the globe. Among these, those frequently cited include AECMA Simplified English, Caterpillar's CTE, CMU's KANT system, General Motors' CASL and LantMark, etc. All these different systems have made great progress in advancing the research and practice in controlled languages, and this makes us possible to benefit from them.

## 2   Why Is Controlled Language Preferred?

Controlled language is preferred for at least three reasons.  Firstly, as is known, natural language often permits an enormous amount of expression variation and allows sentences that are structurally complicated. This property of natural language often makes things much more complex, especially when one language is translated into another one either by human translators or by machine. In addition different writers tend to use specialized vocabulary (jargons), special styles and grammatical structures according to their language level or the given geographical environments while writing the documents [10]. This again increases the difficulty in understanding these documents. Furthermore, current NLP technology is still immature and cannot recognize and solve these problems. Thus phenomena such as ambiguity and the very complexity of natural language inevitably become the very problems that hinder the development of NLP, and are the most difficult predicament faced by NLP researchers. Since the 1960s, controlled language has been applied in NLP research. Numerous experiments have shown that the characteristics of controlled language can reduce the complexity of natural language if the controlled language is well designed and correctly employed. Controlled language can improve and enhance the quality of machine translation if the application domain is well defined, the lexical choices and syntactic structures are strictly restricted and personal styles are properly constrained. All this can explain why more and more attention has turned to the design and development of CLs.

Secondly, the characteristic of medical protocols, our domain for machine translation, makes it possible to use controlled language to enhance the quality of machine translation. The medical protocols we work with are those applied in the field of zoonosis – animal diseases which can be transferred to humans; in other words, zoonosis refers to diseases that are shared both by humans and animals. The medical protocols that we are concerned with are more or less similar to those in manuals or user's instructions. Such medical protocols are kinds of instructions that are used to direct certain kinds of step-by-step medical practices. For example: PAIR (Puncture, Aspiration, Injection and Re-aspiration) procedures, a kind of diagnosis or treatment method for human hydatid diseases. By their very nature, medical protocols are typically domain-specific and employ specific vocabulary and limited grammatical structures. Furthermore, they do not show as many language ambiguities and complex structures as those of general-purpose documents. Both vocabulary and grammar are thus easier to control. The biggest differences that we have observed between the medical protocols usually concern the choices of words or styles employed by different authors. This is also where jargon and dialect-like sentences are encountered. These differences produce problems both at the vocabulary level and the grammatical level. However, most of these problems can be controlled or at least can be made much less complex than those appearing in other (uncontrolled) documents. In addition, no matter how different the writing style might be, the general writing method is similar. The usual writing style is to present the step-by-step procedures as a list, one by one. Even if the procedures are not well listed or their sentence structures are confused or complex, we can always easily control them.

Finally, controlled language is particularly suitable for multilingual translation if all the languages concerned can be controlled more or less in the same way; for other work in this area see for example [11], [13]. While the work described in this paper is concerned with machine translation of English to Chinese, the same domain (medical protocols applied in the field of zoonosis) is being studied in respect of machine translation from French to Arabic. Using controlled language can greatly facilitate the eventual generation and combination of these four controlled languages. These are the very reasons why we finally chose to apply CL techniques in our research.

## 3   Some Basic Differences Between English and Chinese

In this section, we will briefly introduce a few of the major differences between English and Chinese concerned specifically with our work. English and Chinese belong to different language families. The differences between these two languages can be found at almost all levels, lexical, syntactic and semantic.

Firstly, unlike most Indo-European languages, Chinese characters do not exhibit morphological changes to show different grammatical functions. In terms of writing, there are no separators between the words. This makes Chinese word segmentation extremely difficult. For the words formed by a Chinese character or characters, it is hard to tell their grammatical categories only from their morphological forms. Traditionally, in Chinese dictionaries the grammatical category of a word is not indicated, and this is for many reasons, one of which is the lack of agreement concerning the categorization of Chinese word classes. The grammatical category of a Chinese word can only be distinguished from its place or order in a sentence. Though word order is also important in English, we can still tell the grammatical category of most English words from their morphological form out of the sentence context without much difficulty (though the presence of grammatical category ambiguity, its recognition and disambiguation is still problematic in NLP). This is usually not the case for Chinese words. For example, a Chinese word can have the function of a noun, a verb or even an adjective without any morphological change. Verbs and adjectives can appear directly as subject or object (usually no matter what constituent a word is, its morphological form will always stay the same). The person and number of the subject do not affect the verb at all. Besides, Chinese words do not have inflexions to mark the number of nouns, as English nouns, or inflexions to show different tenses and other grammatical functions as that of English verbs and so on. Thus word order becomes more important in Chinese. In order to convey the meanings of some of these different grammatical functions, Chinese uses many auxiliary words, such as *structural*, *interrogative*, and *aspectual* words (also called particles). For example, it is difficult to say exactly the grammatical category, or even what the Chinese word "翻译" refers to without any context, as is shown in the following sentences [17]:

1. **I translated** his novel.
   我翻译了他的小说。(verb)
2. The **translation** of poetry is a kind of creative activity.
   诗歌翻译是一种创作活动。(noun)
3. The **translator** is proficient in several foreign languages.
   这位翻译通晓几种语言。(noun, person who translate)

In Chinese, all these three 翻译 are morphologically identical. However in example 3 the meaning changes. Here 翻译 refers to "translator" instead of the action of translating. This is not the case in English. In English, "translated", "translation" and "translator" are not only morphologically different but are also different in terms of grammatical categories and furthermore they differ in meaning as in the $3^{rd}$ case. Here is another example:

4. 游泳是一种很好的锻炼。**Swimming** is a good exercise.

Unlike English, in Chinese, the verb "游泳" functions as subject but does not need to change its form, while the English verb swim has to adding in order to get a legal grammatical form.

Secondly, there are syntactic differences between the two languages, both at the phrasal level and sentence level. In English the attributives can be put both in front of and behind the noun, but in Chinese they are usually in front of the noun, including some of the relative clauses if these are not translated into several sentences. In our current study, a large proportion of sentences belong to these two kinds. For example,

5. experimental evidence 实验证明
6. the use of antibacterial agents 抗菌药物的使用
7. patients **who refuse surgery**. 拒绝手术的病人。
8. patients **who relapse after surgery**. 手术后复发的病人。

Example 5 shares the same word order in both languages though not necessarily the same grammatical categories. In example 5 the first word "experimental" is an adjective in English, but is a noun in Chinese. These kinds of phrases are the easiest to deal with. Another important point is that when English short relative clauses are translated into Chinese, they are usually translated into phrases instead of subordinate clauses as in example 7 and 8. But for some long and complex relative clauses the common way is to translate them into two or more sentences.

Thirdly, for simple declarative sentences, while English sentences are more dominated by SVO structure, in Chinese there are often at least three possibilities: SVO, SOV, OSV (the passive voice is excluded).

9. The doctor **examined** *the patient*.
           S          V        O

a) 医生检查了这个病人。("了 aspectual word marking past tense)
      S   V         O

b) 医生把这个病人检查了。

    S       O       V

(with the particle "把", generally referred to as "把" construction)

c) 这个病人医生检查了。

    O       S     V

This kind of different arrangements in Chinese is largely dependent upon the meaning rather than upon grammatical functions. The different arrangements lay stress on the different information intended to be transferred. As a result of the different arrangements of the sentence constituents, the semantic contents are greatly influenced. This brings extra difficulty to the analysis of Chinese sentences without referring to semantics and even pragmatics. In our work, only the first sentence structure (SVO as in example 9a)) will be recommended. These examples show in fact only a very small part of the different linguistic competence in both languages. In practice, the differences are much greater and more complex than these but we will not explain them in detail here.

The differences that we have discussed do influence the linguistic methodology or methodologies to be employed in terms of linguistic analysis. As we have remarked, the differences between the two languages can be found at almost all levels, lexical, syntactic and semantic. The methodology underlying the work described in this paper is systemic linguistics [6], [5]. In systemic linguistics, the usual decomposition in terms of "levels" (lexical, syntactic and semantic etc.) is not really what is needed to solve problems in language processing but on the contrary what is needed is to include data from these levels only as and when needed [4]. Furthermore systemic linguistic analyses are inherently traceable, and thus are suitable for applications demanding high quality as is the case of the machine translation of medical protocols. It is our experience that for the machine translation of different language family couples systemic approaches to language analysis bear fruit; we cite: Korean to French [7], Chinese to French [12], [1]and French to Arabic [1], [2]

## 4 Aspects and Principles Considered for the Design and Development of a Controlled Language

Like most other CL systems, while designing and developing our controlled language, we concentrate on two aspects: vocabulary and grammar (as style does not greatly vary, it is not within our major focus). Thus both the source (English) and target (Chinese) languages will be controlled in these two aspects. Furthermore, in order to ease the translation from source language to target language, the most similar structures in both languages are to be preferred; that is, to try to avoid structures which are difficult to translate or can produce some language-specific ambiguities in the two languages. As we demonstrated in the previous section, although Chinese allows SVO, SOV and OSV structures, the accepted structure will be SVO, conforming to that of the source language, English. The phrases and sentences that are structurally different from source language (SL) to target language (TL) have to be specified.

There are three major principles we follow: consistency, clarity and simplicity. Briefly speaking, consistency means that all the terminology and writing rules should be consistently used. There should not be any conflicts between the terms and between the rules. Clarity means that texts to be written should conform to the formulated rules. If any part of a text does not fit the rules, it should be checked and clarified. Simplicity means that while there are alternative ways of saying the same thing, the simplest one and that which is most accountable by our rules should be selected [9]. The simplest writing style is preferred. All these principles should be followed in both the source language and in the target language.

### 4.1 Vocabulary

To control the vocabulary, we concentrate on the following aspects while constructing our lexicon:

Firstly, each entry is limited to one meaning and one part of speech in most of the cases. When it is absolutely necessary that certain terms carry more than one meaning (usually no more than two meanings exist), these terms will be listed as different entries and relative semantic features will be offered to avoid possible ambiguity. Alternatively such terms can be distinguished by the syntax. Jargon will not be allowed, that is the use of different words to refer to the same thing especially words unknown by other groups of end-users. The lexicon will list all the allowed words together with allowed syntactic structures both at the phrasal level and at the sentential level, for example, by using the sub-categorization of verbs and/or nouns and other ambiguity avoiding methods.

Secondly, like most other CL systems, in our lexicon words can have several properties [14], such as:

- morphological properties describing the grammatical categories, inflexions and other grammatical features of words;
- semantic properties including the domain or field or other relative information of the word,
- and translation information offering information concerning basic forms of the corresponding word or sentence structures in the target language.

Of course this does not mean that all words will necessarily have all these properties. In fact, most of the terms in our corpus are highly domain-specific and have no more than one meaning, e.g. serology ( 血清学), alveolar echinococcosis (AE) ( 细粒棘球蚴病), bilirubin (胆红素) etc. Only a few of the terms have more than one meaning, such as "control (n.)", "solution (n.)", and "operation (n.)". Each of these terms has two meanings in our corpus. For example, "control" as a noun either means "the power to influence people's behavior or the course of events", e.g. "the prevention and control of this disease", or means "a standard of comparison for checking the results of an experiment", e.g. "control group". In this case, the semantic features of each word will be defined. As for "solution", in our lexicon its meaning is restricted to mean only "a liquid with which something is dissolved", as in "ethanol solution". "Operation" as a noun can have many meanings according to the context; in medical literature, it is mostly used to refer briefly to either "a planned activity or movement", or to "an act of surgery performed on a patient". However, in our lexicon, "surgery" will be used for the second meaning, that is, "an act of surgery performed on a patient". This means that in our lexicon, the common meaning of a word will sometimes be excluded.

Thirdly, in our corpus, many acronyms are frequently used. In order to avoid possible ambiguity, the period within and at the end of abbreviations will not be allowed. That is, acronyms will be written as other ordinary words no matter whether they are capitalized or not. For example, CT is recommended instead of C.T.; ELISA, instead of E.L.I.S.A.; also in "10-15 cc" and in "ABP 90-50 mm Hg", no period will be used. Acronyms will be treated as single entries. In addition, their meanings will be constrained in a domain-specific manner.

For example, in our lexicon US refers to ultrasound and not the United States. Acronyms can be transferred directly without translating into Chinese (which is common practice) or transferred directly together with the Chinese equivalence in parentheses.

Fourthly, we have to standardize the orthography of some of the terms. We have observed in our corpus that many terms have more than one spelling form. The most frequently occurring are those words ending by either –cal or –ic. For example, we find serological or serologic (血清学的), and immunological or immunologic (免疫学的). Other variant orthographic forms are for example onchocercosis and onchocerciasis (盘尾丝虫病) (which of the English words is preferable is still a matter of debate between specialists in English speaking countries and specialists in non-English speaking countries); lymphopaenia and lymphopenia (淋巴细胞减少), leukopaenia and leukopenia (白血球减少症) (British English and American English respectively). This kind of phenomenon is mainly caused by different habits or by geographical distinctions. In our lexicon only one form will be allowed, for example, in the case of –cal and –ic, -cal will be recommended. The others will follow the most commonly used one found in authorized dictionaries. The standardization of terminology is necessary, but this work has to be done with the involvement of field specialists. We have thus worked with them for the standardization of terminology, including examining the use of jargons. Furthermore, in the longer term for the eventual machine translation of such controlled protocols, entry of such protocols involving the choice of the correct spelling should be supported either by on-line vocabulary checking or by an integrated vocabulary checker.

Finally, in our corpus, figures are frequently used to indicate for example the quantity of drugs. We thus have to pay special attention to the use of figures.

## 4.2  Grammar

At the level of grammar, we have two things to do: to control at the phrasal level and to control at the sentential level. We have carefully examined our corpus, and we have observed that no matter what kind of style the author employs, the grammatical structures do not vary greatly. In fact, by themselves they are very limited. Moreover, the present tense is that which is the most commonly used. The passive voice is not very frequently used.

### 4.2.1  Phrasal Level

In our corpus, we have observed that many of the procedures are written just at the phrasal level. They are not at all complete sentences as shown by the following examples.

1) Serological control 血清对照
2) Prophylaxis with albendazole if possible 如果可能, 用阿苯达唑预防
3) Puncture and parasitological examination (if possible) or fast test for antigen detection in cyst fluid
(如果可能) 进行穿刺及寄生虫病检查或进行囊液抗检快速检查
4) Aspiration of cyst fluid (10-15 cc) 抽出囊液 (10-15 cc)
5) Test for bilirubin in cyst fluid 检查囊液中的胆红素

Each of these noun groups carries sufficient information for its particular purposes. Besides, these phrases are very short, and their structure is not too complex (though there are some exceptions, they can be controlled). We prefer to restrict their structure to some limited kinds for the ease of generation from English to Chinese. For example, the length of a controlled phrase will be no longer than NP + PP + PP. Most of the phrases can be controlled at the level of 1) NP (det + noun, (this is very rare in our corpus); or adj + n); 2) NP + PP; 3) NP + PP + PP; and 4) NP + p.p. + PP. Here the p.p. has two possibilities, one being the present participle, and the other the past participle.

### 4.2.2  Sentential Level

From our observations of the corpus, we find that we can constrain the sentential structures of the protocols by means of no more than 6 kinds. We set these as, 1) nouns and/or noun groups (this is mentioned at the phrasal level); 2) imperative sentences; 3) simple sentences; 4) If… then…clauses; 5) a few limited subordinate clauses, including relative clauses; and a special structure; 6) elliptical structures, such as "if possible", "if necessary", etc. Sentences which do not comply with these criteria will be considered as illegal sentences. For each simple sentence only one subject or one instruction is preferred. Besides, in human translation, for one source sentence there might be two or more corresponding target sentences. This is a common phenomenon while translating long complex English sentences into Chinese. However this phenomenon does not exist in our system. The target sentence to be generated is always one to one with its source sentence. That is, each input sentence will have only one output sentence. We give here modified examples of the five grammatical structures:

1) Inject 95% ethanol solution 注射95%的酒精溶液。
2) Cysts communcate with biliary tree. 包囊同胆树相通。
3) If bilirubin is absent, aspirate all cystic fluid
如果没有胆红素, 抽出所有囊液。
4) If protoscolices are present, continue PAIR procedure.
果有原头蚴, 继续PAIR 操作。
5) Patients who refuse surgery. 拒绝手术的病人。
6) Patients who relapse after surgery. 手术后复发的病人。
7) New parasitological control if possible 如果可能, 重新进行寄生虫对照。

Sentences like:

1.  "If no bilirubin present" will be written to "if bilirubin is absent".
2.  "if treated by β-blocking agent: stop the treatment at least one week before the procedure; replace it by another drug, depending on the nature of the treated disease, if necessary."

Sentence 2 above has firstly to be made more precise, and then rearranged. For example, "if treated by β-blocking agent" is very ambiguous, so it should be written out in full to "if the patient was treated by β-blocking agent".

The use of anaphora is not common in our corpus, and it will be avoided by limiting the use of pronouns or relative clauses. Repetition is preferred. For example in the above sentence, "replace it by another drug," the "it" can be replaced by "β-blocking agent", and the whole sentence becomes: "replace the β-blocking agent by another drug if necessary". And "depending on the nature of the treated disease" can be broadened to a complete sentence: "the choice of the new drug will depend on the nature of the treated disease".

As to the target language, namely Chinese, we also constrain the uses of vocabulary and of grammar, but in a far less rigid manner. For example, "present" in the above example will only be translated to the Chinese verb "有", and "absent" will be translated to "没有" (literally they are equivalent to "have" and "not have" respectively in English), though in this case there are several alternatives, e.g. " 出", "发现", "存在" etc. As for the syntactic structures, the standard and most commonly used structures will be suggested. Finally, the generated target texts will be stylistically similar to the controlled source language. From the above examples we can see that though different authors will write their protocols in different ways, we can still control the grammatical structures limited to the 6 kinds mentioned above and thus improve the capacity for automatic processing.

## 5   Future Work

In order not to frustrate authors, one of the two types of users of the CL, with controlled rules and facilitate their production of texts, we need to develop relative language checkers [3] to enhance the usefulness of our CL in practice. For example, a vocabulary checker can be used to check terms, forms and/or acronyms, of which the latter is particularly important. A grammar checker can be used to check the sentence or phrase lengths as well as some lexical and grammatical misuses or unacceptable sentences. A benefit will be that authors can learn the writing rules while they are using our tool without being trained specifically in the controlled language. That is, while authors are writing their texts, whenever they enter a word or phrase, the following potential structure will be suggested directly. The system will automatically direct the authors and furthermore will check for grammatical errors when any input is found which does not comply with our controlled rules. Additionally an electronic dictionary will support the checking and correction of the orthography and also will aid in finding synonyms.

## 6  Conclusion

This article has discussed the characteristics of both the natural languages concerned in our study, English and Chinese, the typical features of medical protocols and the reasons why we prefer to use controlled language as a basic technique for the machine translation of medical protocols. We have stated that the benefits of controlled languages and in particular that are easier to deal with for translation purposes. It is true that our study can only cover a very small part of the linguistic phenomena involved and will not be able to deal with the many kinds of linguistic problems outside the focus of our work. However, what we will have done during this first step will surely help broaden the future coverage of linguistic phenomena and promote further research. The grammatical structures we have defined can be applied to multilingual environments. As they are simple, they consist of the basic language structures found in all languages. Furthermore, such grammatical structures are thus easier to be analyzed and transferred from language to language. So, having designed a CL we can then finally turn our attention to a multilingual environment for machine translation applied to four different and widely used languages, namely Arabic, Chinese, English and French and the particular translation couples we are involved with (English – Chinese, French – Chinese, French – Arabic).

## References

[1]     Alsharaf, H., Cardey, S., Greenfield, P., Shen, Y., "Problems and Solutions in Machine Translation Involving Arabic, Chinese and French", Actes de l'International Conference on Information Technology, ITCC 2004, April 5-7, 2004, Las Vegas, Nevada, USA, IEEE Computer Society, Vol 2, pp.293-297.

[2]     Alsharaf, H., Cardey, S., Greenfield, P., "French to Arabic Machine Translation: the Specificity of Language Couples", Actes de The European Association for Machine Translation (EAMT) Ninth Workshop, Malta, 26-27 April 2004, Foundation for International Studies, University of Malta, pp.11-17.

[3]     Altwarg, R., "Controlled languages : An Introduction"
        http://www.shlrc.mq.edu.au/masters/students/raltwarg/

[4]     Cardey, S., Greenfield, P. "Peut-on séparer lexique, syntaxe, sémantique en traitement automatique des langues ?". In Cahiers de lexicologie 71 1997, ISSN 007-9871, 37-51.

[5]     Cardey, S., Greenfield, P., "Systemic Language Analysis and Processing", To appear in the Proceedings of the International Conference on Language, Brain and Computation, 3-5 October 2002, Venice, Italy, Benjamins (2004).

[6]     Cardey S. "Traitement algorithmique de la grammaire normative du français pour une utilisation automatique et didactique", Thèse de Doctorat d'Etat, Université de Franche-Comté, France, June 1987.

[7]     Cardey, S., Greenfield, P., Hong, M-S., "The TACT machine translation system: problems and solutions for the pair Korean – French", Translation Quarterly, No. 27, The Hong Kong Translation Society, Hong Kong, 2003, pp. 22-44.

[8]     Namahn, "Controlled Languages, a research note by Namahn"
        http://www.namahn.com/resources/documents/note-CL.pdf

[9]     Olu Tomori S. H., "The Morphology and Syntax of Present-day English: An Introduction", London, HEINEMANN Educational Books Ltd, 1997.

[10]  Ronald A. Cole *et al*, Survey of the State of the Art in Human Language Technology – Section 7.6 (1996), http://cslu.cse.ogi.edu/HLTsurvey/ch7node8.html

[11]  Sågvall-Hein, A., "Language Control and Machine Translation", Proceedings of the 7th International Conference on Theoretical and Methodological Issues in Machine Translation (MI- 97), Santa Fe, 1997.

[12]  Shen, Y., Cardey, S., "Vers un traitement du groupe nominal dans la traduction automatique chinois-français", *Ve Congrès International de Traduction,* Barcelona, 29-31 October 2001.

[13]  Teruko Mitamura "Controlled Language for multilingual Machine Translation" In Proceedings of Machine Translation Summit VII, Singapore, September 13-17, 1999 http://www.lti.cs.cmu.edu/Research/Kant/PDF/MTSummit99.pdf

[14]  Tenni, J. *et al.* "Machine Learning of Language Translation Rules" 'http://www.vtt.fi/tte/language/publications/smc99.pdf

[15]  Simplified English, userlab Inc. 1-800-295-6354 (in North America) http://www.userlab.com/SE.html

[16]  Van der Eijk, P., "Controlled Languages and Technical Documentation", Report of Cap Gemini ATS, Utrecht, 1998.

[17]  张斌《汉语语法学》Century Publishing Group of Shanghai 2003

# Normalizing German and English Inflectional Morphology to Improve Statistical Word Alignment

Simon Corston-Oliver and Michael Gamon

Microsoft Research, One Microsoft Way, Redmond, WA 98052, USA
{simonco, mgamon}@microsoft.com

**Abstract.** German has a richer system of inflectional morphology than English, which causes problems for current approaches to statistical word alignment. Using Giza++ as a reference implementation of the IBM Model 1, an HMM-based alignment and IBM Model 4, we measure the impact of normalizing inflectional morphology on German-English statistical word alignment. We demonstrate that normalizing inflectional morphology improves the perplexity of models and reduces alignment errors.

## 1 Introduction

The task of statistical word alignment is to identify the word correspondences that obtain between a sentence in a source language and the translation of that sentence into a target language. Of course, fluent translation performed by expert human translators involves reformulation that obscures word alignment. However, in many domains, automatically identified word alignments serve as an important source of knowledge for machine translation.

We describe a series of experiments in which we apply morphological normalizations to both the source and target language before computing statistical word alignments. We consider the case of aligning English and German, two closely related languages that differ typologically in ways that are problematic for current statistical approaches to word alignment.

We perform a series of experiments using the Giza++ toolkit (Och and Ney, 2001). The toolkit provides an implementation of IBM Model 1 and Model 4 (Brown et al., 1993) as well as an HMM-based alignment model (Vogel, Ney and Tillman, 1996), together with useful metrics of model perplexity. We perform five iterations of IBM Model 1, which attempts to find simple word translations without consideration of the position of the words within the sentence. The word-alignment hypotheses yielded by this first stage serve as input for five iterations of HMM alignments, which in turn serve as input for five iterations of IBM Model 4. Model 4, which models phenomena such as the relative order of a head and a modifier, is the most sophisticated model considered here. Clustering of words was performed using JCLUSTER (Goodman, 2001).

These word alignment models take a naïve view of linguistic encoding. Sentences are conceived of as little more than a sequence of words, mapped one-to-one or one-to-N from the source language to the target language. Recent research has attempted

R.E. Frederking and K.B. Taylor (Eds.): AMTA 2004, LNAI 3265, pp. 48–57, 2004.
© Springer-Verlag Berlin Heidelberg 2004

to improve machine translation by considering the linguistic structure that exists between the level of the word and the level of the sentence (see, for example, Alshawi, Bangalore and Douglas, 2000; Marcu and Wong, 2002; Koehn et al., 2003). Relatively little research has been directed towards considerations of the role of word-internal structure.

Brown et al. (1993), considering the case of English-French machine translation, perform some orthographic regularizations such as restoring the elided *e* at the end of the relative pronoun *qu'*, or separating the portmanteau *des* "of.the.PLURAL" into its components *de les*. They also speculate that additional morphological analysis to identify the relations among inflected forms of verbs might improve the quality of their models. Not until very recently have results been reported on evaluating the improvements obtainable through morphological processing, the most recent being the work by Nießen and Ney (2004) and Dejean et al. (2003).

Before presenting the experimental results, we briefly outline the salient morphological differences between English and German.

## 2   Morphological Facts

English and German are historically related; both languages are in the Western branch of the Germanic family of Indo-European. Despite this close historical relation, the modern-day languages differ typologically in ways that are problematic for statistical approaches to word alignment.

German has pervasive productive noun-compounding. English displays its Germanic roots in the analogous phenomenon of the noun group—sequences of nouns with no indication of syntactic or semantic connection. As a general rule, English noun groups translate in German as noun compounds. The converse does not always obtain; German compounds occasionally translate as simple English nouns, other times as nouns with prepositional, adjectival, or participial modifiers. When using models such as those of Brown et al. (1993), which allow one-to-one or one-to-N alignments, we would expect this asymmetry to result in poor alignment when English is the source language and German is the target language.

The order of constituents within the clause is considerably more variable in German and long distance dependencies such as relative clause extraposition are more common than in English (Gamon et al., 2002). In German, so-called separable verb prefixes may occur bound to a verb or may detach and occur in long distance relationships to the verb. Adding to the confusion, many of these separable prefixes are homographic with prepositions.

The languages differ greatly in the richness of their inflectional morphologies. Both languages make a three way distinction in degree of adjectives and adverbs. In nominal inflections, however, English makes only a two way distinction in number (singular vs. plural) whereas German makes a two way distinction in number (singular and plural), a four way distinction in grammatical case (nominative, accusative, genitive and dative) and a three way distinction in lexical gender (masculine, feminine, neuter). Nominal case is realized in the German noun phrase on the noun, the determiner and/or pre-nominal modifiers such as adjectives. Vestiges of this case marking remain in the English pronominal system, e.g. *I/me/my*.

The languages have similar systems of tense, mood and aspect. Verbal inflection distinguishes past versus non-past, with weak vestiges of an erstwhile distinction between subjunctive and indicative mood. Many complexes of tense, aspect and mood are formed periphrastically. The most notable difference between the two languages occurs in the morphological marking of person and number of the verb. Aside from the irregular verb *be*, English distinguishes only third-person singular versus non-third-person singular. German on the other hand distinguishes first, second and third person by means of inflectional suffixes on the verb. In the data considered here, drawn from technical manuals, first and second person inflections are extremely uncommon.

## 3   The Problem of Morphology

Let us now consider how these linguistic facts pose a problem for statistical word alignment. As previously noted, the correspondence between an English noun group and a German noun compound gives rise to an N-to-one mapping, which the IBM models do not allow. Differences in constituent order, however, are really only a problem when decoding, i.e. when applying a statistical machine translation system: it is difficult to model the movement of whole constituents by means of distortions of words.

The homography of separable prefixes and prepositions adds interference when attempting word alignment.

The most glaring deficiency of the IBM models in the face of the linguistic facts presented above concerns related word forms. The models do not recognize that some words are alternate forms of other words, as opposed to distinct lexical items. To put this another way, the models conflate two problems: the selection of the appropriate lexical item and the selection of the appropriate form, given the lexical item.

Since the models do not recognize related word forms, the effect of inflectional morphology is to fragment the data, resulting in probability mass being inadvertently smeared across related forms. Furthermore, as Och and Ney (2003) observe, in languages with rich morphology, a corpus is likely to contain many inflected forms that occur only once. We might expect that these problems could be resolved by using more training data. Even if this were true in principle, in practice aligned sentences are difficult to obtain, particularly for specific domains or for certain language pairs. We seek a method for extracting more information from limited data using modest amounts of linguistic processing.

With this brief formulation of the problem, we can now contrast the morphological operations of this paper with Nießen and Ney (2000), who also consider the case of German-English word alignment. Nießen and Ney perform a series of morphological operations on the German text. They reattach separated verbal prefixes to the verb, split compounds into their constituents, annotate a handful of high-frequency function words for part of speech, treat multiword phrases as units, and regularize words not seen in training. The cumulative effect of these linguistic operations is to reduce the subjective sentence error rate by approximately 11-12% in two domains.

Nießen and Ney (2004) describe results from experiments where sentence-level restructuring transformations such as the ones in Nießen and Ney (2000) are combined with hierarchical lexicon models based on equivalence classes of words.

These equivalence classes of (morphologically related) words have the same translation. The classes are obtained by applying morphological analysis and discounting morphological tags that do not change the translation into the target language. The statistical translation lexicon which results from clustering words in equivalence classes is considerably smaller (65.5% on the Verbmobil corpus).

The morphological operations that we perform are the complement of those performed by Nießen and Ney (2000). We do not reattach separated verbal prefixes, split compounds, annotate function words for part of speech, merge multiword phrases or regularize unseen words. Rather, we normalize inflectional morphology, reducing words to their citation form. Since it is not clear what the citation form for German determiners ought to be, we normalize all forms of the definite article to the nonce word *DefDet*, all forms of the indefinite article to *IndefDet*, and all demonstratives to *ProxlDet* ("proximal determiner") and *DistlDet* ("distal determiner"). We perform one additional operation on all German text, i.e. even in the scenarios characterized below as involving no inflectional normalization, we separate contractions into their constituents, in a similar fashion to what Brown et al. (1993) do for French. For example, the portmanteau *zum* "to.the.DATIVE" is replaced with the two words *zu dem*. When morphological regularization is applied this is then rendered as *zu DefDet*.

The following examples illustrate the effects of morphological processing. Words that are stemmed are shown in italics.

**English**

**Before.** If your computer is connected to a network, network policy settings may also prevent you from completing this procedure.

**After.** if your computer *be connect* to *Indefdet* network, network policy *setting* may also prevent you from *complete Proxldet* procedure.

**German**

**Before.** Anwendungen installieren, die von Mitgliedern der Gruppe Benutzer erfolgreich ausgeführt werden können.

**After.** *Anwendung* installieren, die von *Mitglied DefDet* Gruppe Benutzer erfolgreich *ausführen* werden können.

**Aligned English sentence.** Install applications that Users can run successfully.

## 4  Data

We measured the effect of normalizing inflectional morphology on a collection of 98,971 aligned German-English sentence pairs from a corpus of technical manuals and help files for computer software. The content of these files is prosaic and the translations are, for the most part, fairly close.

As Table 1 shows, while the number of words is nearly identical in the German and English data sets, the vocabulary size in German is nearly twice that of the English, and the number of singletons in German is more than twice that of English.

**Table 1.** Corpus profile

|            | German    | English   |
|------------|-----------|-----------|
| Words      | 1,541,002 | 1,527,134 |
| Vocabulary | 53,951    | 27,959    |
| Singletons | 26,690    | 12,417    |

## 5  Results

We perform stemming on the English and German text using the NLPWin analysis system (Heidorn, 2000). In the discussion below we consider the perplexity of the models, and word error rates measured against a gold standard set of one hundred manually aligned sentences that were sampled uniformly from the data.

The stemmers for English and German are knowledge-engineered components. To evaluate the accuracy of the stemming components, we examined the output of the stemmer for each language when applied to the gold standard set of one hundred sentences. We classified the stems produced as good or bad in the context of the sentence, focusing only on those stems that actually changed form or that ought to have changed form. Cases where the resulting stem was the same as the input, e.g. English prepositions or singular nouns or German nouns occurring in the nominative singular, were ignored. Cases that ought to have been stemmed but which were not in fact stemmed were counted as errors.

The English file contained 1,489 tokens; the German analogue contained 1,561 tokens.[1] As Table 2 shows, the effects of the morphological processing were overwhelmingly positive. In the English test set there were 262 morphological normalizations, i.e. 17.6% of the tokens were normalized. In German, there were 576 normalizations, i.e. 36.9% of the tokens were normalized. Table 3 presents a breakdown of the errors encountered. The miscellaneous category indicates places where unusual tokens such as non-breaking spaces were replaced with actual words, an artifact of tokenization in the NLPWin system. Compared to Table 1 morphological normalization reduces the number of singletons in German by 17.2% and in English by 7.8%.

**Table 2.** Accuracy of morphological processing

|         | English | German |
|---------|---------|--------|
| Good    | 248     | 545    |
| Bad     | 14      | 31     |
| Error % | 4.5%    | 5.4%   |

---

[1] Punctuation other than white space is counted as a token. Throughout this paper, the term "word alignment" should be interpreted to also include alignments of punctuation symbols.

**Table 3.** Analysis of morphological errors

|  | English | German |
|---|---|---|
| Failed to stem | 1 | 20 |
| Should not have stemmed | 0 | 5 |
| Wrong stem | 7 | 5 |
| Miscellaneous | 6 | 1 |

As noted in the introduction, we used Giza++ to compute statistical word alignments for our data. We performed five iterations of IBM Model 1, followed by five iterations of HMM, and then five iterations of IBM Model 4. To evaluate the effect of stemming, we measured the perplexity of the final Model 4.

Raw perplexity numbers of the final Model 4 are not comparable across the different morphological processing scenarios we want to investigate, however. Perplexity is tied to vocabulary size, and if the vocabulary size changes (as it does as a result of morphological stemming), perplexity numbers change. In order to overcome vocabulary size dependence of the results, we use the differential perplexity between the Model 4 and a uniform model operating on the same vocabulary. Below we illustrate how this amounts to simply scaling the perplexity number by the target vocabulary size.

Perplexity $PPL_{M4}$ regarding the model 4 probability $P_i^{M4}$ for a target word $w_i$ is:

$$PPL_{M4} = \exp\left[-\frac{1}{N}\sum_{i=1}^{N}\log P_i^{M4}\right] \tag{1}$$

where $N$ is the size of the sample.

A uniform probability distribution for translation would always assign the probability $P_u = P(w_i) = 1/V$ to a target word, where $V$ is the size of the target vocabulary. Perplexity based on the uniform model is defined as follows.

$$PPL_u = \exp\left[-\frac{1}{N}\sum_{i=1}^{N}\log P_u\right] = \exp\left[-\frac{1}{N}\sum_{i=1}^{N}\log\left(\frac{1}{V}\right)\right] \tag{2}$$

$$= \exp\left[-\frac{1}{N}N\log\left(\frac{1}{V}\right)\right] = V$$

We define the differential perplexity $DIFFPPL$ as the ratio of the perplexities $PPL_{M4}$ and $PPL_u$ which is equivalent to dividing the original perplexity $PPL_{M4}$ by $V$:

$$DIFFPPL = PPL_{M4} / PPL_u = \frac{PPL_{M4}}{V} \tag{3}$$

In the remainder of this paper we will, for the sake of convenience, refer to this differential perplexity simply as "perplexity".

We compute word alignments from English to German and from German to English, comparing four scenarios: None, Full, NP and Verb. The "None" scenario establishes the baseline if stemming is not performed. The "Verb" scenario performs stemming only on verbs and auxiliaries. The "NP" scenario performs stemming only on elements of the noun phrase such as nouns, pronouns, adjectives and determiners. The "Full" scenario reduces all words to their citation forms, applying to verbs, auxiliaries, and elements of the noun phrase as well as to any additional inflected forms such as adverbs inflected for degree. We remind the reader that even in the scenario labeled "None" we break contractions into their component parts. The results of stemming are presented in Figure 1 and Figure 2. For ease of exposition, the axes in the two figures are oriented so that improvements (i.e. reductions) in perplexity correspond to bars projected above the baseline. Bars projected below the baseline have a black top at the point where they meet the base plane. The base pane indicates the model perplexity when no stemming is performed in either language.

As Figure 1 illustrates, E-G perplexity is improved across the board if stemming is performed on the target language (German). If no stemming is done on the German side, stemming on the source language (English) worsens perplexity. Interestingly, the stemming of German verbs causes the largest improvements across all English stemming scenarios.

Figure 2 shows a remarkably different picture. If English is the target language, any stemming on either the German source or the English target yields worse perplexity results than not stemming at all, with the exception of tiny improvements when full stemming or verb stemming is performed on English.

The difference between the two graphs can be interpreted quite easily: when the target language makes fewer distinctions than the source language, it is easier to model the target probability than when the target language makes more distinctions than the source language. This is because a normalized term in the source language will have to align to multiple un-normalized words in the target across the corpus, smearing the probability mass.

In order to assess the impact of these morphological operations on word alignment we manually annotated two sets of reference data. In one set of reference data, no stemming had been performed for either language. In the other set, full stemming had been applied to both languages. The manual annotation consisted of indicating word alignments that were required or permissible (Och and Ney 2000, 2003). We then evaluated the alignments produced by Giza++ for these sentence pairs against the manually annotated gold standard measuring precision, recall and alignment error rate (AER) (Och and Ney 2003). Let A be the set of alignments produced by Giza++, S be the set of sure (i.e. required) alignments and P the set of possible alignments. The definition of precision, recall and AER is then:

$$\text{precision} = \frac{|A \cap P|}{|A|}; \ \text{recall} = \frac{|A \cap S|}{|S|} \qquad (4)$$

$$\text{AER} = \frac{|A \cap P + A \cap S|}{|A + S|}$$

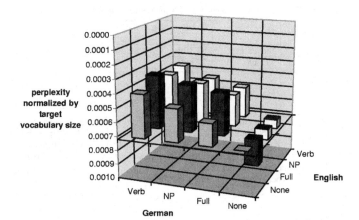

**Fig. 1.** English-to-German alignment

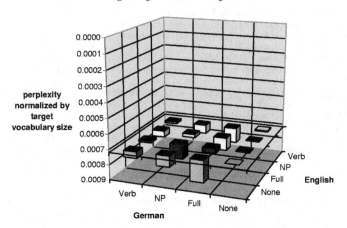

**Fig. 2.** German-to-English alignment

The results are presented in Table 4. Full stemming improves precision by 3.5% and recall by 7.6%. The alignment error rate is reduced from 20.63% to 16.16%, a relative reduction of 21.67%.

**Table 4.** Statistical word alignment accuracy

|  | No stemming | Full stemming |
|---|---|---|
| Precision | 87.10% | 90.24% |
| Recall | 72.63% | 78.15% |
| Alignment error rate | 20.63% | 16.16% |

Note that the alignment error rates in Table 4 are much larger than the ones reported in Och and Ney (2003) for the English-German Verbmobil corpus. For the closest analogue of the Giza++ settings that we use, Och and Ney report an AER of 6.5%. This discrepancy is not surprising, however: Our corpus has approximately three times as many words as the Verbmobil corpus, more than ten times as many singletons and a vocabulary that is nine times larger.

## 6  Discussion

As noted above, the morphological operations that we perform are the complement of those that Nießen and Ney (2000) perform. In future research we intend to combine stemming, which we have demonstrated improves statistical word alignment, with the operations that Nießen and Ney perform. We expect that the effect of combining these morphological operations will be additive.

Additional work remains before the improved word alignments can be applied in an end-to-end statistical machine translation system. It would be most unsatisfactory to present German readers, for example, with only the citation form of words. Now that we have improved the issue of word choice, we must find a way to select the contextually appropriate word form. In many instances in German, the selection of word form follows from other observable properties of the sentence. For example, prepositions govern certain cases and verbs agree with their subjects. One avenue might be to apply a transformation-based learning approach (Brill, 1995) to selecting the correct contextual variant of a word in the target language given cues from the surrounding context or from the source language.

**Acknowledgements.** Our thanks go to Chris Quirk and Chris Brockett for technical assistance with Giza++, and to Ciprian Chelba and Eric Ringger for discussions regarding the normalization of perplexity.

## References

Alshawi, Hiyan, Shona Douglas, Srinivas Bangalore. 2000. Learning dependency translation models as collections of finite-state head transducers. *Computational Linguistics* 26(1): 45-60.

Brill, E. 1995. Transformation-based error-driven learning and natural language processing: A case-study in part of speech tagging. *Computational Linguistics* 21(4):543-565.

Brown, Peter F., Stephen A. Della Pietra, Vincent J. Della Pietra, Robert L. Mercer. The mathematics of statistical machine translation: Parameter estimation. *Computational Linguistics* 19(2):263-311.

Dejean, Herve, Eric Gaussier, Cyril Goutte and Kenji Yamada. 2003. Reducing Parameter Space for Word Alignment. In *Proceedings from the HLT-NAACL 2003 workshop on Building Parallel Texts*. 23-26.

Gamon M., Ringger E., Zhang Z., Moore R., Corston-Oliver S. 2002. Extraposition: A case study in German sentence realization. In *Proceedings of COLING 2002*. 301-307.

Goodman, J. 2001. A Bit of Progress in Language Modeling, Extended Version. Microsoft Research Technical Report MSR-TR-2001-72.

Heidorn, George. 2000. Intelligent Writing Assistance. In R. Dale, H. Moisl and H. Somers, (eds.), *Handbook of Natural Language Processing*. Marcel Dekker.

Marcu, Daniel and William Wong. 2002. A Phrase-Based, Joint Probability Model for Statistical Machine Translation. EMNLP-02.

Nießen, Sonja and Hermann Ney. 2000. Improving SMT quality with morpho-syntactic analysis. COLING '00: The 18th International Conference on Computational Linguistics. 1081-1085.

Nießen, Sonja and Hermann Ney. 2004. Statistical Machine Translation with Scarce Resources Using Morpho-syntactic Information. *Computational Linguistics* 30(2): 181-204.

Och, F. and H. Ney. 2000. Improved statistical alignment models. In Proceedings of the 38th Annual Meeting of the Association for Computational Linguistics. 440-447.

Och, F. and H. Ney. 2003. A systematic comparison of various statistical alignment models. *Computational Linguistics* 29(1):19-52.

Vogel, Stephan, Hermann Ney, Christoph Tillman. HMM-based word alignment in statistical translation. Proceedings of COLING '96: The 16th International Conference on Computational Linguistics. 836-841.

# System Description: A Highly Interactive Speech-to-Speech Translation System

Mike Dillinger and Mark Seligman

Spoken Translation, Inc.
1100 West View Drive
Berkeley, CA 94705 USA
{mike.dillinger, mark.seligman}@spokentranslation.com

Spoken Translation, Inc. (STI) of Berkeley, CA has developed a commercial system for interactive speech-to-speech machine translation designed for both high accuracy and broad linguistic and topical coverage. Planned use is in situations requiring both of these features, for example in helping Spanish-speaking patients to communicate with English-speaking doctors, nurses, and other health-care staff.

The twin goals of accuracy and broad coverage have until now been in opposition: speech translation systems have gained tolerable accuracy only by sharply restricting both the range of topics which can be discussed and the sets of vocabulary and structures which can be used to discuss them. The essential problem is that both speech recognition and translation technologies are still quite error-prone. While the error rates may be tolerable when each technology is used separately, the errors combine and even compound when they are used together. The resulting translation output is generally below the threshold of usability -- unless restriction to a very narrow domain supplies sufficient constraints to significantly lower the error rates of both components.

*STI's approach has been to concentrate on interactive monitoring and correction of both technologies.*

First, users can monitor and correct the speaker-dependent speech recognition system to ensure that the text which will be passed to the machine translation component is completely correct. Voice commands (e.g. **Scratch That** or **Correct <incorrect text>**) can be used to repair speech recognition errors. While these commands are similar in appearance to those of IBM's ViaVoice or ScanSoft's Dragon NaturallySpeaking dictation systems, they are unique in that they remain usable even when speech recognition operates at a server. Thus they provide for the first time the capability to interactively confirm or correct wide-ranging text which is dictated from anywhere.

Next, during the MT stage, users can monitor, and if necessary correct, one especially important aspect of the translation -- lexical disambiguation.

R.E. Frederking and K.B. Taylor (Eds.): AMTA 2004, LNAI 3265, pp. 58–63, 2004.

The problem of determining the correct sense of input words has plagued the machine translation field since its inception. In many cases, the correct sense of a given term is in fact available in the system with an appropriate translation, but for one reason or another it does not appear in the output. Word-sense disambiguation algorithms being developed by research groups have made significant progress, but still often fail; and the most successful still have not been integrated into commercial MT systems. Thus no really reliable solution for automatic word-sense disambiguation is on the horizon for the short and medium term.

STI's approach to lexical disambiguation is twofold: first, we supply a specially controlled *back translation*, or translation of the translation. Using this paraphrase of the initial input, even a monolingual user can make an initial judgment concerning the quality of the preliminary machine translation output. To make this technique effective, we use proprietary facilities to ensure that the lexical senses used during back translation are appropriate.

In addition, in case uncertainty remains about the correctness of a given word sense, we supply a proprietary set of Meaning Cues™ – synonyms, definitions, etc. – which have been drawn from various resources, collated in a unique database (called SELECT™), and aligned with the respective lexica of the relevant machine translation systems. With these cues as guides, the user can select the preferred meaning from among those available. Automatic updates of translation and back translation then follow.

The result is an utterance which has been monitored and perhaps repaired by the user at two levels – those of speech recognition and translation. By employing these interactive techniques while integrating state-of-the-art dictation and machine translation programs – we work with Philips Speech Processing for speech recognition; with Word Magic and Lingenio for MT (for Spanish and German, respectively); and with ScanSoft for text-to-speech – we have been able to build the first commercial-grade speech-to-speech translation system which can achieve broad coverage without sacrificing accuracy.

# 1  A Usage Example

When run on a Motion Computing Tablet PC, the system has four input modes: speech, typing, handwriting, and touch screen. To illustrate the use of interactive correction for speech recognition, we will assume that the user has clicked on the microphone icon onscreen to begin entering text by speaking. The image below shows the preliminary results after pronunciation of the sentence "The old man sat on the bank".

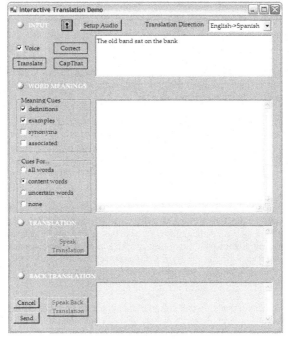

**Fig. 1.**

The results of automatic speech recognition are good, but often imperfect. In this example "man" was incorrectly transcribed as "band"(Fig. 1.). Accordingly, the user can perform voice-activated correction by saying "Correct band". A list of alternative speech recognition candidates then appear, seen in the image below. The user can select the correct alternative in this case by saying "Choose one", yielding a corrected sentence. (If the intended alternative is not among the candidates, the user can supply it manually – by typing on a standard keyboard, by using a touch screen keyboard, or by writing with a stylus for high-accuracy handwriting recognition.)

The spoken (or clicked) "Translate" command (Fig. 2.) provides a translation of the corrected input, seen below in the Translation window (Fig. 3.). Also provided are a Back Translation (the translated sentence re-translated back into the original, as explained above) and an array of Meaning Cues giving information about the word meanings that were used to perform the translation, seen in the Word Meanings list. The user can use these cues to verify that the system has interpreted the input as intended.

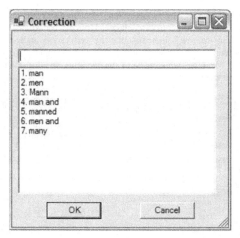

Fig. 2.

Fig. 3.

In this example (Fig. 3.), synonyms are used as Meaning Cues, but definitions, examples, and associated words can also be shown. Here the back-translation ("The old man took a seat in the row") indicates that the system has understood "bank" as meaning "row". Presumably, this is not what the user intended. By clicking on the word in the Word Meanings window, he or she can bring up a list of alternative word meanings, as in the image below.

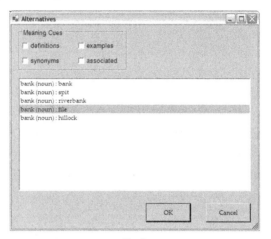

**Fig. 4.**

When a new word meaning has been chosen from this list, e.g. the "riverbank" meaning in this case, the system updates the display in all windows to reflect that change (Fig. 4.). In this example, the updated Spanish translation becomes "El hombre viejo se sentó en la orilla del río". The corresponding back translation is now "The old man took a seat at the bank of the river" – close enough, we can assume, to the intended meaning.

When the user is satisfied that the intended meaning has been correctly understood and translated by the system, the system's Send button can be used to transmit the translation to the foreign-language speaker via instant messaging, chat, or on-screen display for face-to-face interaction. At the same time, synthesized speech can be generated, and if necessary transmitted, thus completing the speech-to-speech cycle.

## 2  Languages

The current version of the system is for English <> Spanish, and a German <> English version is in development. Discussion is also in progress with several vendors of Japanese MT.

## 3  Implementation

The system runs as a stand-alone application on a variety of Windows computers: tablet PC's provide the greatest range of input modes, but the system will run stand-alone on standard current laptops, PCs, etc. With future ports to client-server implementations in mind, it has been programmed with .NET technology.

# A Fluency Error Categorization Scheme to Guide Automated Machine Translation Evaluation

Debbie Elliott, Anthony Hartley, and Eric Atwell

School of Computing and Centre for Translation Studies, University of Leeds, LS2 9JT, UK
{debe,eric}@comp.leeds.ac.uk, a.hartley@leeds.ac.uk,

**Abstract.** Existing automated MT evaluation methods often require expert human translations. These are produced for every language pair evaluated and, due to this expense, subsequent evaluations tend to rely on the same texts, which do not necessarily reflect real MT use. In contrast, we are designing an automated MT evaluation system, intended for use by post-editors, purchasers and developers, that requires nothing but the raw MT output. Furthermore, our research is based on texts that reflect corporate use of MT. This paper describes our first step in system design: a hierarchical classification scheme of fluency errors in English MT output, to enable us to identify error types and frequencies, and guide the selection of errors for automated detection. We present results from the statistical analysis of 20,000 words of MT output, manually annotated using our classification scheme, and describe correlations between error frequencies and human scores for fluency and adequacy.

## 1 Introduction

Automated machine translation evaluation is quicker and cheaper than obtaining human judgments on translation quality. However, automated methods are ultimately validated by the establishment of correlations with human scores. Overviews of both human and automated methods for MT evaluation can be found in [1] and on the FEMTI[1] website [2]. Although existing automated methods such as BLEU [3] and RED [4] can produce scores that correlate with human quality judgments, these methods still require human translations, which are expensive to produce. BLEU requires up to four human 'reference' translations against which MT output is automatically compared and scored according to modified $n$-gram precision. The test corpus used for this research comprised 500 sentences from general news stories, with four human translations of each. RED, on the other hand, automatically ranks MT output based on edit distances to multiple reference translations. In [5], 16 human reference translations of 345 sentences in two language directions were used from the Basic Travel Expression Corpus [6].

To eliminate the expense of producing human translations, and to investigate the potential of a more portable method, our aim is to design an automated MT evaluation system, initially for language pairs in which the target language is English, which does not require human reference translations. The system will detect fluency errors

---

[1] A Framework for the Evaluation of Machine Translation in ISLE.

R.E. Frederking and K.B. Taylor (Eds.): AMTA 2004, LNAI 3265, pp. 64–73, 2004.
© Springer-Verlag Berlin Heidelberg 2004

characteristic of MT output, and will be designed to meet the needs of post-editors, purchasers and developers.

## 2  Texts for Evaluation Research

Many published MT evaluation projects, such as BLEU [3] and the DARPA evaluation series [7] have based their research entirely on newspaper texts. Many subsequent MT evaluation experiments have also made use of the DARPA corpus, such as [8], [9], [10], [11], [12] and [13]. Consequently, we conducted a survey of MT users in 2003 to find out which text types were most frequently translated by MT systems. Responses showed a great difference between the use of MT by companies/organizations and by individuals who machine translated documents for personal use [14]. It was found that companies most frequently machine translated user manuals and technical documents on a large scale. As a result, the decision was taken to collect such texts for our evaluation research, along with a smaller number of legislative and medical documents, which also figured highly among survey responses. The resulting multi-lingual parallel corpus is TECMATE, (a TEchnical Corpus for MAchine Translation Evaluation), comprising source texts, human and machine translations, and human scores for fluency and adequacy for an increasing number of texts [15].

## 3  Designing an Error Categorization Scheme

The decision to devise a classification scheme of fluency errors stemmed from the need to identify error types in MT output to guide automated evaluation. Statistics from the human annotation of MT output using such a scheme would provide information on the frequency of error types in texts produced by different MT systems and would help us select errors for automated detection. Statistics would also enable us to compare error type frequency with human judgments for fluency and adequacy, enabling us to focus on the detection of those error types whose frequency correlated with lower human scores for one or both of those attributes.

Fine-grained error classification schemes are not practical for the black-box evaluation of large numbers of machine translations; such a method is even more time-consuming than, for instance, the evaluation of fluency or fidelity at segment level. Consequently, few MT error classification schemes have been devised, and most have been designed with a particular purpose in mind. The SAE J2450 Quality Metric, developed by the Society of Automotive Engineers [16], and the Framework for Standard Error Marking devised by the American Translators Association [17] were both designed for the evaluation of human translations and are insufficiently fine-grained for our purpose. Correa's typology of errors commonly found in automatic translation [18] was also unsuited to our needs, largely because it was designed for glass-box evaluations during system development. Flanagan's Error Classification for MT Evaluation [19] to allow end-users to compare translations by competing systems, Loffler-Laurian's typology of errors for MT, based on linguistic problems for post-editors [20] and classifications by Roudaud et al. [21], Chaumier and Green in [22] provide a more useful starting point for our work. However, these are still insuf-    •

ficiently fine-grained for our purpose, all rely on access to the source text, and most are based on errors found in translations out of English. As our intention is to design an automated error detection system that does not require access to the original or to any human translation for comparison, it was essential to devise categories based on the analysis of MT output in isolation.

Our classification of errors was progressively developed during the analysis and manual annotation of approximately 20,000 words of MT output, translated from French into English by four systems (Systran, Reverso Promt, Comprendium and SDL's online FreeTranslation[2]). The four machine translations of twelve texts (each of approximately 400 words) from the TECMATE corpus were annotated with error types. The texts comprised three extracts from software user manuals, three FAQs (frequently asked questions) on software applications, three press releases on technical topics and three extracts from technical reports taken from the BAF corpus[3]. All texts were chosen on the basis that they would be understandable to regular users of computer applications.

Annotations were made according to items that a post-editor would need to amend if he/she were revising the texts to publishable quality. Although the source text was not made available, knowledge of the source language was necessary, as the scheme requires untranslated words to be annotated with parts-of-speech. Furthermore, it was important for the annotator to be familiar with the named entities and acronyms (eg. names of software applications) in the texts, to better represent the end-user and code these terms appropriately.

Errors were annotated using the Systemic Coder[4], a tool that supports hierarchical linguistic coding schemes and enables subsequent statistical analyses. Error types were divided according to parts-of-speech, as this would provide more detailed information for analysis and would enable us to make more informed decisions when selecting and weighting errors for our automated system. As the Coder supports the insertion of new nodes into the hierarchy at any time, this facilitated the progressive data-driven refinement of the coding scheme. For example, after annotating around 1,000 words, a decision was taken to sub-divide 'inappropriate' items (see Figure 1) into 'meaning clear', 'meaning unclear' and 'outrageous' (words with an extremely low probability of appearing in a particular text type and subject area). This refinement would enable us to make better comparisons between MT systems, and isolate those errors that have a greater effect on intelligibility.

During these initial stages of analysis, it became clear that, having set out to annotate fluency errors, adequacy errors were also detectable as contributors to disfluency, despite the absence of the source text. Words or phrases that were obviously incorrect in the given context were marked as 'meaning unclear' and can be seen as both fluency and adequacy errors. For this research, we can, therefore, define each annotated error as a unit of language that surprises the reader because its usage does not seem natural in the context in which it appears.

---

[2] http://www.freetranslation.com/
[3] http://www-rali.iro.umontreal.ca/arc-a2/BAF/Description.html
[4] http://www.wagsoft.com/Coder/index.html

| | | | | |
|---|---|---|---|---|
| *Part of speech* | Noun: Compound | Noun string or Named entity | Inappropriate | Meaning clear/unclear |
| | | | | Part meaning clear/unclear |
| | | | Untranslated | Untranslated |
| | | | | Part untranslated |
| | Noun: Acronym | Incorrect | | |
| | Noun: Pronoun | Inappropriate | Incorrect anaphor | |
| | | | Other | |
| | | Untranslated | | |
| | | Unnecessary | | |
| | | Omitted | Direct object pronoun | |
| | | | Relative pronoun | |
| | | | Other | |
| | Noun: Common or Adjective or Adverb or Conjunction | Inappropriate | Meaning clear/unclear | |
| | | | Outrageous | |
| | | Untranslated | | |
| | | Unnecessary | | |
| | | Omitted | | |
| | Preposition | Inappropriate | With noun/verb/adjective | |
| | | Untranslated | | |
| | | Unnecessary | | |
| | | Omitted | | |
| | Determiner | Inappropriate | | |
| | | Untranslated | | |
| | | Unnecessary | Definite article | |
| | | | Indefinite article | |
| | | | Other | |
| | | Omitted | Definite article | |
| | | | Indefinite article | |
| | | | Other | |
| | Verb | Inappropriate | Meaning clear/unclear | |
| | | | Outrageous | |
| | | | Multiword verb structure | |
| | | Untranslated | | |
| | | Unnecessary | | |
| | | Omitted | | |
| *Tense or conjuga-tion* | Tense or mood | | | |
| | Conjugation | | | |
| *Incorrect position* | Acronym / pronoun / common noun / adjective / adverb / conjunction / preposition / determiner / verb / negator / noun string appendage | | | |
| | Compound noun sequence | Noun string or Named entity | Word order | |
| | | | Arrangement | |
| *Other* | Part of speech incorrect / inelegant or inappropriate style / incomprehensible expression / spelling error / incorrect negation / ordinal number untranslated / qualifier unnecessary | | | |
| | Number | Singular should be plural / plural should be singular | | |
| | Case | Upper case required / lower case required | | |

**Fig. 1.** Fluency Error Categorization Scheme

## 4   Organization of Error Categories

The current scheme contains all error types found in the French-English MT output. However, the organization of categories reflects the constraints of the tool to a certain extent. It was noticed during the annotation process that items often involved two and, in rare instances, three error types. For example, a noun could be 'inappropriate', its position within the phrase could be incorrect and it could lack a required capital letter, or a verb could be 'inappropriate' and the tense also incorrect. The scheme was, therefore, organized in such a way that the tool would allow all of these combinations of categories to be assigned to the same word or group of words where necessary.

**Table 1.** Some definitions of categories and examples of annotation

| Error category | Definitions and examples |
|---|---|
| Outrageous | The item has an extremely low probability of appearing in this text type and subject area.<br>Eg. *beach* rather than *time slot, shelterers* rather than *(web) hosts*. |
| Multi-word verb structure | A verb comprising multiple words (in addition to prepositions) is incorrect.<br>Eg. *are more priority than* as opposed to *take priority over*. |
| Noun string / named-entity word order | The constituent parts are ordered incorrectly.<br>Eg. *Properties Internet Connection* rather than *Internet Connection Properties*. |
| Noun string / named-entity arrangement | The constituent parts are ordered incorrectly and additional words are included (common in translations from French into English).<br>Eg. *window of definition of the filter* rather than *filter definition window*. |
| Noun string appendage position | Two noun strings are 'combined' so that when translated into English, the word order is incorrect.<br>Eg. *tabs of options <u>and regulations</u>* should be *options <u>and regulations</u> tabs*.<br>Here *tabs of options* would be marked 'noun string arrangement' and the words underlined would be marked as 'incorrect noun string appendage position'. |
| Noun inappropriate, meaning clear | Eg. *...a cd-rom placed in the <u>reader</u> of the device* |
| Noun inappropriate, meaning unclear | Eg. *...activating the <u>notch</u>, you will see the lunar globe ...* |
| Verb inappropriate, meaning clear | Eg. *...if the open file was already <u>registered</u> in this format ...* |
| Verb inappropriate, meaning unclear | Eg. *...the main window <u>behaves</u> the menu bar...* |
| Adverb position | Eg.   *Francophone users avoid <u>systematically</u> using...* |
| Definite article omitted | Eg.   *Among \*\*\* most frequent, ...* (Three asterisks are inserted to mark the omission of an item.) |

An item can be annotated with up to four main categories: part-of-speech, verb tense or conjugation, incorrect position and 'other', as shown on the left-hand side of Figure 1. Sub-categories must then be selected, moving from left to right, until the final node is reached. The Systemic Coder allows categories to be added, moved or deleted at any time. This will be essential for the analysis of MT output from other source languages, in which we expect to find different error types. Table 1 provides definitions of some of the categories with examples of coded text.

## 5   Capturing the Essence of Fluency and Adequacy

Statistics from our annotations were compared with human evaluation scores to explore correlations between the number of errors annotated and intuitive judgments on fluency and adequacy. Each of the 48 machine translations was evaluated by three different judges for each attribute. Texts were evaluated at segment level on a scale of 1-5, using metrics based on the DARPA evaluations [7]. For fluency, evaluators had access only to the translation; for adequacy, judges compared candidate segments with an aligned human reference translation. A mean score was calculated per segment for each attribute. These scores were then used to generate a mean score per text and per system. Methods and results are described in [15].

Assuming that all error types in the classification scheme affect fluency, we initially compared the total number of errors per system with human fluency scores. We then removed all error categories that were considered unlikely to have an affect on adequacy (such as 'inappropriate' items with a clear meaning, unnecessary items, inappropriate prepositions and determiners, omitted determiners, incorrect positions of words, spelling errors, case errors and incorrect verb tense/mood or conjugation, the majority of these being an inappropriate present tense in English). The remaining classification of adequacy errors was then compared with the adequacy scores from our human evaluations, as shown in Table 2.

Table 2. Human scores and error counts for fluency and adequacy

| System | Mean human fluency score and rank | Number of fluency errors and rank | Mean human adequacy score and rank | Number of adequacy errors and rank |
|---|---|---|---|---|
| Systran | 3.519 (1) | 1015 (1) | 4.136 (2) | 127 (1) |
| Reverso | 3.466 (2) | 1020 (2) | 4.142 (1) | 132 (2) |
| Comprendium | 3.221 (3) | 1195 (3) | 4.013 (3) | 161 (3) |
| FreeTranslation | 2.827 (4) | 1460 (4) | 3.644 (4) | 287 (4) |

Human fluency scores and the number of annotated fluency errors rank all four systems in the same order. The picture is slightly different for adequacy, with Systran and Reverso competing for the top position. We calculated Pearson's correlation coefficient $r$ between the human scores and the number of errors per system for each attribute. A very strong negative correlation was found between values: for fluency the value of $r = -0.998$ and for adequacy $r = -0.997$. Of course, only four pairs of variables are taken into consideration here. Nevertheless, results show that we have managed to capture adequacy as well as fluency by annotating errors without reference to the source text.

## 6   Correlating Error Frequency and Human Scores by Text Type

We computed error frequencies for the four text types. For each of the four systems, user manuals were annotated with the largest number of errors, followed by FAQs, technical reports and finally, press releases. The number of fluency errors and the subset of adequacy errors were then compared with human scores for fluency and adequacy according to text type. No significant correlation was found. In fact, human scores for fluency were highest for user manuals for all systems, yet these texts contained the largest number of annotated errors. It is clear, therefore, that errors must be weighted to correlate with intuitive human judgements of translation quality. The two main reasons for the large number of errors annotated in the user manuals were (i) the high frequency of compound nouns (eg. computer interface items and names of software applications), which, in many cases, were coded with two error types (eg. inappropriate translations and word order) and (ii) the high number of inappropriately translated verbs, which although understandable in the majority of cases, were not correct in the context of software applications (eg. *leave* instead of *quit* or *exit*, *register* or *record* instead of *save* etc.) Furthermore, user manuals were annotated with the largest number of untranslated words, yet many of these were understandable to evaluators with no knowledge of French, having little or no adverse effect on adequacy scores. A further experiment showed that 58% of all untranslated words in this study were correctly guessed in context by three people with no knowledge of French. In fact, 44% of these words, presented in the form of a list, were correctly guessed out of context.

## 7   Selecting Error Types for Automated Detection

The eight most common error types (from a total of 58 main categories) were found to be the same for all four systems, although the order of frequency differed between systems and text types. The frequency of these eight errors represents on average 64% of the total error count per system.

Table 3 shows that only in the case of inappropriate verbs (2) and inappropriate prepositions (6) does the total number of errors correspond to the rank order of the four systems according to human scores for fluency. The number of inappropriate noun string content errors (7) corresponds to human rankings for adequacy. Furthermore, the frequency of very few error types in the entire scheme corresponds to human rankings of the four systems for either fluency or adequacy. It is also clear from Table 3 that the frequency of particular errors within a given text type does not represent system performance as a whole.

Findings show that, while the frequencies of the above eight error types are significant, detecting a small number of errors to predict scores for a particular text type or system is not sufficient. Quality involves a whole range of factors – many of which must be represented in our automated system. Furthermore, our intention is to build a tool that will provide information on error types to help users and developers, rather than merely a mechanism for producing a raw system score. It is clear, therefore, that a number of different error categories should be selected for detection, based on their combined frequencies, and on their computational tractability; we still need to determine which error types could be detected more successfully.

**Table 3.** Top eight error types by system

| Error type | Number of errors annotated | | | |
|---|---|---|---|---|
| | Systran | Reverso | Comprend | FreeTrans |
| (1) Incorrect compound nn sequence | 130 | 145 | 151 | 148 |
| Manuals/FAQs/Press/Reports | 56/21/39/14 | 58/30/42/15 | 64/28/41/18 | 62/30/40/16 |
| (2) Inappropriate verb | 121 | 126 | 135 | 141 |
| Manuals/FAQs/Press/Reports | 51/31/20/19 | 38/42/23/23 | 47/39/22/27 | 48/46/22/25 |
| (3) Unnecessary determiner | 105 | 102 | 137 | 121 |
| Manuals/FAQs/Press/Reports | 31/14/18/42 | 28/15/18/41 | 39/20/24/54 | 31/17/19/54 |
| (4) Inappropriate noun | 77 | 82 | 79 | 105 |
| Manuals/FAQs/Press/Reports | 17/20/22/18 | 16/14/24/28 | 19/18/24/18 | 18/24/29/34 |
| (5) Incorrect verb tense or mood | 76 | 56 | 103 | 90 |
| Manuals/FAQs/Press/Reports | 29/30/11/6 | 12/24/13/7 | 40/42/14/7 | 25/35/13/17 |
| (6) Inappropriate preposition | 73 | 77 | 84 | 89 |
| Manuals/FAQs/Press/Reports | 27/21/8/17 | 23/19/12/23 | 24/22/18/20 | 28/28/15/18 |
| (7) Inappropriate.nn string content | 48 | 38 | 69 | 82 |
| Manuals/FAQs/Press/Reports | 23/9/10/6 | 11/8/17/2 | 26/18/19/6 | 35/13/27/7 |
| (8) Inappropriate adjective | 48 | 37 | 59 | 42 |
| Manuals/FAQs/Press/Reports | 7/8/13/20 | 7/6/8/16 | 8/8/17/26 | 5/11/7/19 |

## 8   Conclusions and Future Work

We have devised an adaptable fluency error categorization scheme for French-English MT output, which also enables the detection of adequacy errors, without access to the source text. Preliminary analyses show that the number of errors annotated per system correlates with human judgments for fluency, and that a sub-set of error categories correlates with human judgments for adequacy. The annotated MT output has provided us with valuable information for the design of an automated MT evaluation system to help users and developers. Statistics are enabling us to identify the weak points of participating systems, and findings show that we must aim to automatically detect a good number of these to represent system performance.

Future work will involve:
- investigating inter-annotator agreement, as error annotation is subjective (for some categories more than others);
- the subsequent investigation and evaluation of methods for automating the detection of selected errors using machine-learning techniques on the annotated and part-of-speech tagged corpus;
- investigating correlations between human judgments and error type/frequency within texts;
- research into error weighting;

- the classification of errors by relative difficulty of correction during post-editing and/or by the possibility of correction by updating user dictionaries (although not appropriate for online MT systems);
- expanding the scheme to accommodate additional source languages translated into English;
- producing detailed documentation on the error categorization scheme, to include a full tag-set with examples;

## References

1. White, J.S.: How to evaluate machine translation. In Somers, H. (ed.): Computers and translation: a translator's guide. J. Benjamins, Amsterdam Philadelphia (2003) 211-244
2. FEMTI: A Framework for the Evaluation of Machine Translation in ISLE: http://www.issco.unige.ch/projects/isle/femti/ (2004)
3. Papineni, K., Roukos, S., Ward, T., Zhu, W.: Bleu: a Method for Automatic Evaluation of Machine Translation. IBM Research Report RC22176. IBM: Yorktown Heights, NY (2001)
4. Akiba, Y., Imamura, K., Sumita, E.: Using multiple edit distances to automatically rank machine translation output. In: Proceedings of MT Summit VIII, Santiago de Compostela, Spain (2001)
5. Akiba, Y., Sumita, E., Nakaiwa, H., Yamamoto, S., Okuno, H.G.: Experimental Comparison of MT Evaluation Methods: RED vs. BLEU. In: Proceedings of MT Summit IX, New Orleans, Louisiana (2003)
6. Takezawa, T., Sumita, E., Sugaya, F., Yamamoto, H., Yamamoto, S.: Toward a broad-coverage bilingual corpus for speech translation of travel conversations in the real world. In: Proceedings of the Third International Conference on Language Resources and Evaluation (LREC), Las Palmas, Canary Islands, Spain (2002)
7. White, J., O'Connell, T., O'Mara, F.: The ARPA MT evaluation methodologies: evolution, lessons, and future approaches. In: Proceedings of the 1994 Conference, Association for Machine Translation in the Americas, Columbia, Maryland (1994)
8. Rajman, M., Hartley, A.: Automatically predicting MT systems rankings compatible with Fluency, Adequacy or Informativeness scores. In: Proceedings of the Fourth ISLE Evaluation Workshop, MT Summit VIII, Santiago de Compostela, Spain (2001)
9. Rajman, M., Hartley, A.: Automatic Ranking of MT Systems. In: Proceedings of the Third International Conference on Language Resources and Evaluation (LREC), Las Palmas, Canary Islands, Spain (2002)
10. Vanni, M., Miller, K.: Scaling the ISLE Framework: Validating Tests of Machine Translation Quality for Multi-Dimensional Measurement. In: Proceedings of the Fourth ISLE Evaluation Workshop, MT Summit VIII, Santiago de Compostela, Spain (2001)
11. Vanni, M., Miller, K.: Scaling the ISLE Framework: Use of Existing Corpus Resources for Validation of MT Evaluation Metrics across Languages. In: Proceedings of the Third International Conference on Language Resources and Evaluation (LREC), Las Palmas, Canary Islands, Spain (2002)
12. White, J., Forner, M.: Predicting MT fidelity from noun-compound handling. In: Proceedings of the Fourth ISLE Evaluation Workshop, MT Summit VIII, Santiago de Compostela, Spain (2001)
13. Reeder, F., Miller, K., Doyon, K., White, J.: The Naming of Things and the Confusion of Tongues. In: Proceedings of the Fourth ISLE Evaluation Workshop, MT Summit VIII, Santiago de Compostela, Spain (2001)

14. Elliott, D., Hartley, A., Atwell, E.: Rationale for a multilingual corpus for machine translation evaluation. In: Proceedings of CL2003: International Conference on Corpus Linguistics, Lancaster University, UK (2003)
15. Elliott, D., Atwell, E., Hartley, A.: Compiling and Using a Shareable Parallel Corpus for Machine Translation Evaluation. In: Proceedings of the Workshop on The Amazing Utility of Parallel and Comparable Corpora, Fourth International Conference on Language Resources and Evaluation (LREC), Lisbon, Portugal (2004)
16. SAE J2450: Translation Quality Metric, Society of Automotive Engineers, Warrendale, USA (2001)
17. American Translators Association, Framework for Standard Error Marking, ATA Accreditation Program, http://www.atanet.org/bin/view/fpl/12438.html (2002)
18. Correa, N.: A Fine-grained Evaluation Framework for Machine Translation System Development. In: Proceedings of MT Summit IX, New Orleans, Louisiana (2003)
19. Flanagan, M.: Error Classification for MT Evaluation. In: Technology Partnerships for Crossing the Language Barrier, Proceedings of the First Conference of the Association for Machine Translation in the Americas, Columbia, Maryland (1994)
20. Loffler-Laurian, A-M.: Typologie des erreurs. In: La Traduction Automatique. Presses Universitaires Septentrion, Lille (1996)
21. Roudaud, B., Puerta, M.C., Gamrat, O.: A Procedure for the Evaluation and Improvement of an MT System by the End-User. In: Arnold D., Humphreys R.L., Sadler L. (eds.): Special Issue on Evaluation of MT Systems. Machine Translation vol. 8 (1993)
22. Van Slype, G.: Critical Methods for Evaluating the Quality of Machine Translation. Prepared for the European Commission Directorate General Scientific and Technical Information and Information Management. Report BR 19142. Bureau Marcel van Dijk (1979)

# Online MT Services and Real Users' Needs: An Empirical Usability Evaluation

Federico Gaspari

Centre for Computational Linguistics - UMIST
PO Box 88, Manchester M60 1QD
United Kingdom
F.Gaspari@postgrad.umist.ac.uk

**Abstract.** This paper presents an empirical evaluation of the main usability factors that play a significant role in the interaction with on-line Machine Translation (MT) services. The investigation is carried out from the point of view of typical users with an emphasis on their real needs, and focuses on a set of key usability criteria that have an impact on the successful deployment of Internet-based MT technology. A small-scale evaluation of the performance of five popular web-based MT systems against the selected usability criteria shows that different approaches to interaction design can dramatically affect the level of user satisfaction. There are strong indications that the results of this study can be fed back into the development of on-line MT services to enhance their design, thus ensuring that they meet the requirements and expectations of a wide range of Internet users.

## 1 Introduction

One of the most interesting areas in the current development of Machine Translation (MT) is the presence on the Internet of a number of on-line services, some of which are available free of charge[1]. MT technology has been available on the Internet for a few years now and since several language combinations are covered at the moment, on-line MT services are becoming increasingly popular and are used on a daily basis by a growing number of people in different ways for a variety of purposes. Due to this interest, recent studies have looked at Internet-based MT technology from a range of perspectives, emphasizing the challenges, potential and versatility of MT applications in the on-line environment ([1], [2], [3], [4], [5], [6], [7], [8], [9], [10]).

Surprisingly, however, to date no attempt has been made to investigate the real users' needs with a view to enhancing the performance of on-line MT services, e.g. by promoting a more usable and user-oriented approach to their design. In order to look

---

[1] The five on-line MT services considered in this study are Babelfish, Google Translate, Freetranslation, Teletranslator and Lycos Translation. They are all available free of charge on the Internet and Table 1 in the Appendix below provides their URLs (this information is correct as of 14 May 2004).

R.E. Frederking and K.B. Taylor (Eds.): AMTA 2004, LNAI 3265, pp. 74–85, 2004.

at this under-researched area, the investigation presented in this paper has considered the performance of five free on-line MT systems[2]. A small-scale evaluation based on some key usability factors has been conducted to assess how successfully users can take advantage of web-based MT technology. Whilst most ordinary people and Internet users today tend to associate MT software with (free) web-based MT services like the ones that have been considered in this study, not much research seems to be geared towards making them more easily accessible and user-friendly. This paper argues that this is a necessity that should be given priority to bridge the gap between the MT industry and researchers on the one hand and end-users on the other.

Section 2 below explains what key web usability factors have been considered in the evaluation and sheds some light on their relevance for on-line MT services. Section 3 presents a few small-scale evaluation procedures that are based on the usability criteria that have been previously introduced and comments on the results of the empirical evaluation, laying particular emphasis on the real needs of people who use on-line MT technology. Finally, Section 4 draws some conclusions and suggests possible lines of practical action for future improvements to the design of on-line MT services on the basis of real users' needs.

## 2  Web Usability and Online MT Services: Set of Key Factors

Web usability has recently received attention as a discipline that offers valuable insights into the subtleties of meeting the needs and expectations of users who interact with on-line applications (see e.g. [11], [12], [13], [14]). In empirical terms a web-site or an Internet-based service (such as any on-line MT system) that is highly usable is easy to interact with and makes it possible for users to achieve their goals effectively and efficiently.

The investigation presented in this paper evaluates the impact of some key web usability criteria on the design of web-based MT systems from the point of view of users, and discusses the extent to which they affect successful interaction and as a result the level of user satisfaction. The assumption behind this approach is that implementing a usability-oriented approach to the design of web-based MT services has a crucial importance for the widespread acceptance and success of on-line MT technology among users.

### 2.1  Guessability and Learnability

Guessability and learnability are two basic notions that fall under the umbrella of web usability and will be explained in more detail in this section. Guessability refers to the effort required on the part of the user to successfully perform and conclude an on-line

---

[2]  All the information presented here regarding the evaluation procedures and the tests referred to later in the paper is based on experiments carried out by the author on the Internet and is correct as of 14 May 2004.

task for the first time, and directly depends on how intuitive and predictable its design is – both in terms of the graphic user interface and of the interaction procedures involved ([15]:11-12).

Learnability, on the other hand, involves the effort and time required on the part of the users to familiarize themselves with the satisfactory operation of a web-based application after they have used it already at least once ([15]:12-13). Learnability, then, is directly linked with how intuitive and memorable completing an on-line task is for users.

Guessability has a crucial importance the first time an Internet user tries to access an on-line MT service, and as a result is of particular interest for novice users who have never been exposed to a particular web-based MT system before. Learnability, on the other hand, has a longer-term relevance since it refers to how easily users of any level of experience can memorise and retain the procedures that are necessary to interact with the on-line MT technology, and accordingly follow them correctly in the future – this applies in particular to returning users. The two interrelated notions of learnability and guessability presented here also allude to the likelihood to make mistakes while users operate an on-line application. As a result, they lay emphasis on the need to provide straightforward ways in which users can recover from errors made during on-line interaction.

Different user profiles obviously require different levels of support and guidance while operating MT systems, as has been argued in [16]:227 with particular reference to the appropriateness of off-line MT software documentation for various types of users. It seems equally desirable that on-line MT services provide support that is useful for users with a range of skills and levels of expertise, from novice to highly experienced.

## 2.2   Parallel Browsing of an Original Web-Page and Its Machine Translation

One function that seems particularly useful when Internet-based MT is applied to entire web-pages[3] is the option to switch back and forth between the original source document (as found on the Internet) and its machine-translated version in the desired target language (as provided by the on-line MT service). This possibility gives great flexibility to users, since it enables them to browse in parallel the original source-language web document and the MT output in the target language; it should be remembered in this respect that thanks to HTML filters, Internet-based MT services normally preserve in the translated web-pages the format and layout of the original, making it fairly easy and straightforward to compare the original and the translation of a particular section of a web-page (say, a title, a paragraph, a hyperlink, a caption under a picture, text shown in a frame, etc.).

---

[3] This function of on-line MT services is of interest here, i.e. when users supply the URL of a whole web-page they would like to translate. The other option usually available in web-based MT systems is the translation of plain text that can be copied and pasted or typed into an appropriate box, but this latter mode of use will not be taken into consideration here. Each of the five free on-line MT services considered in this study offers both these options.

Web-surfers who have only a very poor knowledge of a foreign language may still prefer to read MT output in their own mother tongue (provided this is available), checking the original source document from time to time for a more thorough understanding when necessary. In such cases, Internet users with limited linguistic skills in more than one language may use the machine-translated document as a partial aid to grasp the general information on a web-page, with the option to refer back to the original text, whose contents they may have some ability to read and understand. Under such circumstances users can supplement the inadequacies in the performance of the system, e.g. where the output is of particularly poor quality, and for example some specialized jargon that is not in the MT system's lexicon may be understood by the user in the foreign language.

### 2.3  Continuous Machine Translation of Hyperlinks with Online MT Services

At this stage of the discussion, following [17] a useful distinction should be made between *on-demand* and *on-the-fly* machine translation services that operate on-line. *On-demand* MT "occurs when a user initiates some action to cause a page to be translated. The user interface to receive the user's translation request can be, but is not limited to, a button or a hyperlink" ([17]:3). The so-called *on-the-fly* machine translation, on the other hand, takes place "automatically, meaning there is no explicit user interaction, using the user's browser's language preference or the language preferences defined by the translation system's administrator" (ibid.).

On a similar level, some on-line MT services perform "*one-time translation*", which causes "the page itself to be translated, but any other pages accessed from this page (such as through hyperlinks) will not be translated but displayed in the language in which they were authored" ([17]:4). On the other hand, web-based MT systems performing "*continuous translation*" (in other words, an *implicit on-line MT of hyperlinks*) offer the possibility for "the page itself to be translated as well as all subsequent pages through link modification. [...] With all of the links modified in this manner, continuous translation can be achieved" (ibid.).

Since the reading process in the on-line environment is largely based on hypertextuality, it is essentially non-linear, as opposed to what usually happens with most traditional printed, paper-based texts. The focus of this research is on texts in digital form contained in web-pages (irrespective of their length), since they are typically fed into on-line MT systems to serve as input.

Internet users regularly take advantage of links to navigate the Web, so as to move around from one page to another of the same Internet site, or indeed to visit some external web-sites. As a result, while users read on-line texts, they typically follow non-linear threads with very unsystematic and fragmented browsing patterns that cannot be pre-determined or predicted in any way.

Web-surfers who request on-line MT for a web-page from language A into language B almost certainly prefer to keep on reading MT output in language B, if they click on a hypertext anchor that points them to another web-page whose contents are written in language A. Allowing users to do so is bound to greatly enhance the quality of their browsing experience, but on-line MT services do not always allow continuous translation of linked web-pages, thus somehow contradicting the principle that the reading process mostly follows a non-linear pattern on the Internet. The difference between having access to continuous translation as opposed to one-time translation seems to have a crucial impact on the degree of usability that users experience during their interaction with on-line MT services.

## 3  Empirical Usability Evaluation

The previous section has focused on web usability and in particular on a limited set of key factors (e.g. guessability and learnability) that will be considered here in more detail. This section will in fact try to establish some direct links with on-line MT services, emphasizing the impact of web usability issues on typical users' needs in terms of interaction design. Against this background, the purpose of this section is to examine and evaluate the relevance to web-based MT systems of the web usability factors identified above. A number of small-scale evaluation procedures are proposed mainly on a comparative basis for the benefit of clarity.

The approach to this evaluation of on-line MT services does not aim to establish which are the best solutions or strategies among those reviewed. In other words, there is no explicit or implicit intention to suggest that a particular on-line MT service is ultimately better than another because it seems to offer a more satisfactory performance according to the specific usability criteria that will be looked at. Rather, here it will be sufficient to briefly discuss some crucial features that have a bearing on the use of on-line MT technology, without attempting a real final classification of preferred strategies. This loose approach to evaluation is partially due to the fact that there are no set standards or benchmarks available yet to formally evaluate the level of usability of on-line MT services. As a result, this innovative approach to the evaluation of the users' needs of on-line MT services will inevitably need to be further refined and improved in the future.

It is however interesting to note that [18], a general textbook on Machine Translation, does briefly mention usability when covering the evaluation of MT and computer-assisted translation (CAT) products on the basis of the attention that this concept received in [19], a highly influential report concerning the standards for the evaluation of NLP systems. Even though [18]:262 offers a brief illustration of the main implications of usability in general for PC-based MT and CAT software, it does not cover any aspect of web usability as such that may be related to the design of and interaction with on-line MT services. Similarly, in the context of a discussion devoted to the possibility of automating evaluation procedures for MT, [20]:107 refers to the concept of usability in connection with MT, but again this term is applied to off-line MT software packages.

As a result, care should be taken not to confuse the general concept of *usability* referred to in [18] and [20], which refers to software products in general, with the more specific one of *web usability*, as explained in Section 2 above, which is of particular interest in the present study focusing on Internet-based MT services.

### 3.1  Evaluation of Guessability and Learnability of the Online MT Services

The guessability and learnability factors are most suitable to be measured on a comparative basis in empirical web usability inspections, since it is very hard to find effective ways to evaluate them in absolute terms. As a result, the degree of guessability and learnability would be typically measured by testing and comparing the performance of two or more similar on-line applications on equivalent tasks.

Due to reasons of space, here it seems sufficient to provide a practical appraisal of these factors by briefly showing how they can be greatly enhanced by looking in particular at some features of one free on-line MT service (i.e. Babelfish, see [1], [7]). For the sake of clarity and in order to avoid unwieldy reports that would exceed the purpose of this discussion, Babelfish will be considered here for the purpose of illustrating a simple but successful strategy aimed at increasing the degree of guessability and learnability for the benefit of all its users, and novice or unexperienced users in particular.

The on-line submission forms used by the five popular free web-based MT services considered here seem to be equally intuitive, in that they all request the same type of information from the users by means of similar procedures. It is worth pointing out, though, that Babelfish does seem to offer a clever guessability and learnability advantage if compared to the other free on-line systems, which is crucial in terms of enhancing the overall degree of usability. As a matter of fact, Babelfish shows a series of succinct user tips in the on-line MT request form, just under the field where URLs should be entered.

These practical suggestions are displayed on a rotation basis and aim at familiarising users with procedures or simple tricks that enhance the performance of the MT service, thus maximising its usability in the interest of net-surfers. When a user logs on to the Babelfish web-site, a number of different tips appear on a rotation basis and are visible under one of the two drop-down menus to select the language combination for the translation job (Figures 1, 2 and 3 in the Appendix show three of these tips).

This strategy gives users effective practical advice to improve their interaction with the on-line MT system without requiring too much effort and background knowledge, since the tips are very short, clearly written in plain non-technical language and explicitly goal-oriented. Of the five free on-line MT systems reviewed in this research, Babelfish is the only one that presents this approach to the enhancement of guessability and learnability, thus presumably lending itself to more successful operation, especially by novice, "one-off" and casual users (cf. [16]:223, 225).

### 3.2  Evaluation of Parallel Browsing of Original and Translated Web-Page

This part of the discussion tries to assess the practical implications that the parallel browsing of a machine-translated web-page and its original source document can have from the point of view of on-line MT users. It could well be the case, for instance, that an Internet user who visits a web-site or web-page that is available exclusively in English only has a superficial knowledge of this language.

As a result, in spite of not being very confident with English, they may know or understand words that appear in the original web-pages that they are visiting, and recognise phrases or specialised terms that the on-line MT service may not be able to translate correctly but that the user may be familiar with, if for example they are words belonging to a specific field of interest of the user (e.g. leisure information regarding a hobby or professional content). As a result, in such cases users may want to have a machine-translated version into another language to read, but it may sometimes be helpful for them to go back to the original, so as to check unclear key-words (e.g. those appearing in hyperlinks, if they want to decide whether to click on the hypertext anchor or not), or specific parts of the text on the web-page.

An in-built facility to make such a "parallel" process possible is available only in the environment of Babelfish, Google Translate and Teletranslator, whereas the other web-based MT services that have been reviewed for this evaluation (i.e. Freetranslation and Lycos Translation) do not offer it. Figures 4, 5 and 6 in the Appendix show details of the screenshots of Babelfish, Google Translate and Teletranslator, respectively, i.e. a top frame that is automatically added by these on-line MT services into the browser window to inform users that they can click on a link/button to view the web-page in the original language, while the bottom frame in the rest of the browser window (not included in the figures) shows the translated version.

If users click on the appropriate link/button of the top frame, a new small browser window pops up on the screen, showing the corresponding original source document. As a result, the reader may refer to the original web-page in the source language, whilst the machine-translated web-page is still displayed in the background. In this way the Internet user can easily switch back and forth between the two parallel versions, if they want to do so.

The practice of browsing in parallel an original web-page and its machine-translated version into the target language selected by the user may be an effective strategy for disambiguation purposes, since on-line MT engines are usually designed to cope with general-purpose language and standard vocabulary. However, in spite of having a limited and superficial multilingual knowledge, Internet users may be able to understand in a variety of languages technical terms, acronyms and jargon usage specific to their own field of interest.

Where the MT system's performance is likely to be poor or the output in the target language is unclear or full of blatant errors, users may still in some cases be able to grasp an indication of the gist of on-line texts by also looking at the original language. The link/button in the top frame shown in Figures 4, 5 and 6 in the Appendix offers a straightforward feature to navigate original web-pages and their machine-translated versions in parallel, if users prefer to do so. This neat feature may in some cases greatly benefit multilingual Internet users who find MT useful as an aid to increase their understanding of the contents of web-pages, but are also able to compensate for its shortcomings, and is a clever implementation of usability.

### 3.3  Evaluation of Continuous Machine Translation of Hyperlinks

Taking into consideration the preliminary observations proposed in Section 2.3 above, this part of the evaluation reports on the results of practical tests whose aim was to evaluate the performance of the on-line MT services in terms of continuous machine translation of hyperlinks, which is a crucial feature when Internet-based MT services are used to translate entire web-pages. There is a significant difference between the on-line MT services that have been reviewed in this respect as well, which greatly affects the level of their usability and the extent to which they meet typical users' needs. Whilst Babelfish, Google Translate and Teletranslator enable web-surfers to keep on reading the machine translation into their preferred target language of linked pages, Freetranslation and Lycos Translation simply point users to the original web-page, thus potentially confusing Internet users who are supposedly not familiar with the language in which it is written.

As far as continuous machine translation of hyperlinks is concerned, Babelfish, Google Translate and Teletranslator offer a good user-friendly approach to navigation design. As a matter of fact, whenever users are visiting a web-page that has been machine-translated into their own preferred language, and click on a hyperlink that points them to another web-page that is still written in the same original language, these on-line MT services implicitly do the continuous translation into the preferred target language of the user, without needing any explicit external command (in this respect, cf. the information contained in the user tip provided to users by Babelfish, which is shown in Figure 2 of the Appendix). Freetranslation and Lycos Translation, on the other hand, do not offer this function, since they are on-demand-only on-line MT systems, exclusively providing users with one-time machine translation (cf. [17] and see Section 2.3 above for a more detailed discussion of the relevant differences).

## 4  Conclusions and Future Work

The previous section has attempted to present some simple procedures to evaluate the degree of usability of five of the most popular free on-line MT services, according to the key factors that had been previously identified in Section 2, discussing the main implications of the results. The list of criteria that have been covered is by no means complete, and the evaluation tests were mainly based on superficial observations and brief comparisons.

In spite of this rather informal methodological approach to evaluation, the previous section provides evidence for the fact that usability criteria affect the overall quality of on-line MT services, as well as the extent to which users can successfully interact with them for the purpose of translating entire web-pages.

### 4.1 Conclusions

In summary, two main general conclusions can be drawn on the basis of the evaluation that has been presented here. First of all, different approaches seem to be adopted by various on-line MT services with respect to the role played by single usability criteria, which have a number of implications from the point of view of the users' needs. As a matter of fact, the fragmented picture given above shows that no specific preferences emerge at the moment regarding the design of user interaction for web-based MT systems.

It should be noted, however, that there are some practices that seem to be fairly standardised, as is for instance the case for the procedures that users are expected to follow in order to access and start the on-line MT procedures. At the same time, though, in a number of other areas that play a crucial role for the user interaction with the web-based application, diverging strategies are adopted by different systems.

Secondly, no general consensus or established rules exist at present as to what are the best strategies to successfully offer MT technology in the on-line environment, with special reference to the translation of entire web-pages. This situation seems to emphasize the need for a rapid development of specific reliable evaluation criteria, benchmarks and standards, that may encourage user-centred approaches to the design of on-line MT applications to be implemented in the short term.

### 4.2 Future Work

Along the lines of the approach adopted for this research on a very small scale, empirical data derived from formal usability inspections and a range of more in-depth evaluation tests would provide a solid platform to pursue the enhancement of on-line MT services, focusing on a larger set of key factors that are crucial for users.

As far as the preliminary results presented in this research are concerned, the investigation of a few key usability factors has shown that simple principles and design guidelines greatly enhance the overall performance of on-line MT services. Web usability is quickly reaching a state of maturity in other widespread Internet-based applications, especially those connected with e-commerce web-sites and remotely-managed financial services and business transactions. In these areas user-centred design is at present widely advocated as a major concern.

Web-based MT services, on the other hand, do not currently seem to be adequately designed to meet the specific needs of users in the Internet environment. Web-surfers have demands and priorities that need to be catered for by on-line MT technology, if this is to be successful as a useful resource to navigate the World Wide Web. Looking at how the sample of free on-line MT services considered here are designed today, it is easy to notice that many improvements at various levels are still needed.

This study suggests in conclusion that prompt action should be taken in order to apply usability principles to the design and development of web-based MT services. The previous discussion has identified some important areas that are crucial to the users of Interned-based MT technology, and some of the indications provided by this study may be fed back into the research and development of on-line MT services to enhance their design, thus ensuring that they meet the real needs of their growing population of users.

# References

1. Yang, J., Lange, E.: SYSTRAN on AltaVista: A User Study on Real-Time Machine Translation on the Internet. In: Farwell, D., Gerber, L., Hovy, E. (eds.): Machine Translation and the Information Soup. Lecture Notes in Artificial Intelligence, Vol. 1529. Springer-Verlag, Berlin Heidelberg New York (1998) 275-285
2. Hutchins, J.: The Development and Use of Machine Translation Systems and Computer-based Translation Tools. In: Zhaoxiong, C. (ed.): Proceedings of the International Conference on Machine Translation and Computer Language Information Processing, 26-28 June 1999, Beijing, China (1999) 1-16 [Available on-line at the URL
   http://ourworld.compuserve.com/homepages/WJHutchins/Beijing.htm - Accessed 14 May 2004]
3. Miyazawa, S., Yokoyama, S., Matsudaira, M., Kumano, A., Kodama, S., Kashioka, H., Shirokizawa, Y., Nakajima, Y.: Study on Evaluation of WWW MT Systems. In: Proceedings of the Machine Translation Summit VII. MT in the Great Translation Era, 13-17 September 1999, Singapore (1999) 290-298
4. Macklovitch, E.: Recent Trends in Translation Technology. In: Proceedings of the 2nd International Conference The Translation Industry Today. Multilingual Documentation, Technology, Market, 26-28 October 2001, Bologna, Italy (2001) 23-47
5. O'Connell, T.: Preparing Your Web Site for Machine Translation. How to Avoid Losing (or Gaining) Something in the Translation (2001) [Available on-line at the URL http://www-106.ibm.com/developerworks/library/us-mt/?dwzone=usability - Accessed 14 May 2004]
6. Zervaki, T.: Online Free Translation Services. In: Proceedings of the Twenty-fourth International Conference on Translating and the Computer, 21-22 November 2002, London. Aslib/IMI, London (2002)
7. Yang, J., Lange, E.: Going Live on the Internet. In: Somers, H. (ed.): Computers and Translation. A Translator's Guide. John Benjamins, Amsterdam Philadelphia (2003) 191-210
8. Gaspari, F.: Enhancing Free On-line Machine Translation Services. In: Lee, M. (ed.): Proceedings of the 7th Annual CLUK Research Colloquium, 6'7 January 2004, University of Birmingham (2004) 68-74
9. Gaspari, F.: Integrating On-line MT Services into Monolingual Web-sites for Dissemination Purposes: an Evaluation Perspective. In: Proceedings of the Ninth EAMT Workshop Broadening Horizons of Machine Translation and Its Applications, 26-27 April 2004, Foundation for International Studies, University of Malta, Valletta, Malta (2004) 62-72
10. Gaspari, F.: Controlled Language, Web Usability and Machine Translation Services on the Internet. In: Blekhman, M. (ed.): International Journal of Translation. A Half-Yearly Review of Translation Studies. Special Number on Machine Translation, Vol. 16, No. 1, Jan-June 2004. Bahri Publications, New Delhi (2004) 41-54
11. Nielsen, J.: Designing Web Usability. The Practice of Simplicity. New Riders Publishing, Indiana (2000)

12. Krug, S.: Don't Make Me Think. A Common Sense Approach to Web Usability. New Riders Publishing, Indiana (2000)
13. Nielsen, J., Tahir, M.: Homepage Usability. 50 Websites Deconstructed. New Riders Publishing, Indiana (2002)
14. Brinck, T., Gergle, D., Wood, S.D.: Designing Web Sites That Work. Usability for the Web. Morgan Kaufmann Publishers, San Francisco (2002)
15. Jordan, P.W.: An Introduction to Usability. Taylor & Francis, London (1998)
16. Mowatt, D., Somers, H.: Is MT Software Documentation Appropriate for MT Users? In: White, J.S. (ed.): Envisioning Machine Translation in the Information Age. Lecture Notes in Artificial Intelligence, Vol. 1934. Springer-Verlag, Berlin Heidelberg New York (2000) 223-238
17. Sielken, R.: Enabling a Web Site for Machine Translation Using WebSphere Translation Server (2001) [Available on-line at the URL http://www7b.boulder.ibm.com/wsdd/library/techarticles/0107_sielken/0107sielken.html Accessed 14 May 2004]
18. Trujillo, A.: Translation Engines. Techniques for Machine Translation. Springer-Verlag, Berlin Heidelberg New York (1999)
19. Expert Advisory Group on Language Engineering Standards (EAGLES): Evaluation of Natural Language Processing Systems Final Report. Technical Report EAG-EWG-PR.2 (Version of October 1996). ISSCO University of Geneva (1996) [Available on-line at the URL http://www.issco.unige.ch/projects/ewg96/ewg96.html - Accessed 14 May 2004]
20. White, J.S.: Contemplating Automatic MT Evaluation. In: White, J.S. (ed.): Envisioning Machine Translation in the Information Age. Lecture Notes in Artificial Intelligence, Vol. 1934. Springer-Verlag, Berlin Heidelberg New York (2000) 100-108

# Appendix[4]

**Table 1.** Details of the five free on-line MT services considered in the evaluation

| Free on-line MT services | |
| --- | --- |
| *Name* | *URL* |
| Babelfish | http://world.altavista.com |
| Google Translate | http://www.google.com/language_tools |
| Freetranslation | http://www.freetranslation.com |
| Teletranslator | http://www.teletranslator.com |
| Lycos Translation | http://translation.lycos.com |

---

[4] Disclaimer: the information presented in Table 1 is correct as of 14 May 2004. The screenshots and the figures presented in the Appendix have been downloaded from the Internet by the author of this paper on 14 May 2004.

**Fig. 1.** Screenshot of Babelfish: tip 1[5]

**Fig. 2.** Screenshot of Babelfish: tip 2

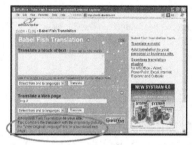

**Fig. 3.** Screenshot of Babelfish: tip 3

**Fig. 4.** Top frame added by Babelfish

**Fig. 5.** Top frame added by Google Translate

**Fig. 6.** Top frame added by Teletranslator

---

[5] It should be noted that this user tip refers to the on-line machine translation of passages of plain text, since otherwise it is impossible for users to add extra characters or symbols to the text contained in a web-page, in order to keep a word or proper name in the source document untranslated (e.g. "Pink Floyd"). In spite of not being directly applicable to the on-line translation of entire web-pages, this tip is shown here to provide a more general idea of the information supplied to users by Babelfish.

# Counting, Measuring, Ordering: Translation Problems and Solutions

Stephen Helmreich and David Farwell

Computing Research Laboratory
New Mexico State University
Las Cruces, NM 88003
{shelmrei, david}@crl.nmsu.edu

**Abstract.** This paper describes some difficulties associated with the translation of numbers (scalars) used for counting, measuring, or selecting items or properties. A set of problematic issues is described, and the presence of these difficulties is quantified by examining a set of texts and translations. An approach to a solution is suggested.

## 1  Introduction

Translation of numbers would seem to be a particularly easy task. After all, 15 is 15, and even if *fifteen* is not *quinze* there is a one-to-one correspondence between them. However, as Tom Lehrer would be quick to point out, $15_{10}$ is not the same as $15_6$. We are lucky that the decimal system is widespread and that representation in other bases is usually explicitly noted.

In this paper, we focus on some difficult cases, where numbers may not be all that they seem, particularly as far as translation goes. We focus on the use of numbers in text, to count, to measure, to order or select. In previous work, we have discussed in detail a particular case of selection (Farwell and Helmreich, 1997, 1999). Two translators decided differently about which floor-naming convention to use in translating into English a Spanish newspaper article that mentioned the "*segundo piso*" and the "*tercero piso*". One translated these phrases as "second floor" and "third floor" while the other translated them as "third floor" and "fourth floor." We argued that both translations were correct, and justified on the basis of default reasoning about the convention likely to be used by the author of the article and the convention likely to be inferred by the audience of the translation.

Section 2 defines the scope of the issue highlighted in that article. Section 3 presents an incomplete list of specific problematic issues that fall within this scope. In Section 4, we examine a set of texts and translations to try to determine the quantitative extent of the issue. We suggest some approaches to the solution in Section 5.

R.E. Frederking and K.B. Taylor (Eds.): AMTA 2004, LNAI 3265, pp. 86–93, 2004.

## 2   The Scope of the Problem

There appear to be three human activities that cover the scope of this problem: counting, measuring, and ordering or selecting. The activities attempt to answer questions such as "How many?" (counting); "How much?" (measuring) and "Which?" (selecting). In each case there is a *domain* which consists of some thing which is counted, measured, or selected. For counting and selecting, it is usually a set of objects, for measuring, a property. There is a *unit of measurement*. For counting and selecting, it is usually an individual in the set. For measuring, the unit of measurement is usually specific to the property. There is a set of *counters*, which may be a finite set, a countably infinite set, or an uncountably infinite set. For counting and selecting, the standard and productive set is the set of positive integers, or the natural numbers. For measuring, it is real numbers (though in practice the rationals are usually sufficient). For each counter, there is a set of *linguistic representations* or *names*. Usually there is more than one linguistic representation for each counter. There is also an *ordering* on the set of counters, which allows for specifying a range or specific subset of the things counted. Finally, there is a *starting point* for the ordering. The order and starting point may be specified by convention, as in the differing floor-naming conventions, or derived from the context, as in (1)

(1)  The people in the picture are listed counterclockwise, starting in the upper left.

For the purposes of this paper, let us call a set consisting of these six elements {domain, unit of measurement, {counters}, {{linguistic representations}}, ordering, starting point} a scalar system. This information is summarized in Table 1.

**Table 1.** Standard Elements of Scalar Systems

|  | Domain | Unit | Counters | Names | Order | Start |
|---|---|---|---|---|---|---|
| Counting/ Selecting | Objects | Individuals | Natural Numbers | {{1, one,..} ,...} | < | 1 |
| Measuring | Property | Property-specific | Real Numbers | {{.5, ½ ...} ,...} | < | 0 |

For the purposes of this paper, we shall regard scalar systems that differ in domain, unit of measurement, counting set, order, or starting point as different scalar systems. Systems that differ only in the names assigned to the set of counters are not regarded as different scalar systems. Scalar systems are thus not restricted to a particular language.

Translation difficulties may arise if there is more than one scalar system in use, particularly if the correlation between the two systems is complex. Problematic cases also arise within a single scalar system if the sets of names are not disjoint, that is, if the same name is connected to more than one counter. We list a number of such difficulties and problematic cases, by no means complete. It is left to the reader to apportion the difficulty to one or more of the elements of the scalar systems.

## 3 Problematic Scalar Systems

**The 10 Commandments.** There are differences between the standard Roman Catholic and Lutheran enumeration of the commandments and the Reformed and Jewish enumeration. The latter adds as the second commandment "Thou shalt make no graven images." The former splits the final commandment into two: "Thou shalt not covet your neighbor's house" and "Thou shalt not covet everything else." Thus, any reference to the second through the tenth commandment is ambiguous.

**The Psalms.** The enumeration of the Psalms differs between the Hebrew Bible and the Greek and Vulgate versions. The latter merge Psalms 9 and 10 together and also Psalms 114 and 115, while dividing 116 and 147. The end result is that between Psalm 10 and 148 the enumerations differ by one.

**Books of the Bible.** The Greek and Vulgate Bibles contain additional books that are not contained in the Hebrew Bible (or most Protestant versions). These books are interspersed among the books of the Hebrew Scriptures. In addition, the ordering of books is quite different in the Hebrew Bible than in the standard Christian ones.

**Monetary systems.** These systems have a dual nature. On the one hand, they enumerate specific amounts of currency that is legal tender in some country. These amounts have equivalents, via the international currency exchange with different amounts in the currency of other nations. This relationship itself changes over time, usually incrementally, but sometimes not.

At a second level, the amount represents a certain amount of goods or services which can be purchased with that amount of currency. The relationship between the value of these goods and services varies also from time to time. In addition, there is no direct connection between the purchasing power of a certain amount of currency and its "equivalent" in another currency. Those are two independent ways of measuring the value of the amount.

**The standard enumeration systems (the natural numbers/rational numbers/real numbers).** Numerical representation of digits is ambiguous with respect to the base. Names for the natural numbers are usually unambiguous, though in English, there is a distinction between the American dialect, in which "billion" = 1,000,000,000. In the English dialect, this counter is named "milliard." This introduces an ambiguity at every succeeding naming level. So, for instance, English "billion" then equals American "trillion" etc.

Other ambiguities in the naming conventions include differences in the use of comma and period as delimiters. For example, in English, a standard representation for "fifteen hundred" would be "1,500" and for "three-fourth", "0.75." European standard representations for these two numbers are "1.500" and "0,75." In addition, as will be seen below, there are differences in what is considered the most informative way of naming.

**The musical key system.** Musical keys (semitones) are labeled with alphabetic characters, starting with A, A-sharp (= B-flat), B, C (= B sharp), C-sharp, (= D-flat), etc. In German, however, B-flat is named B, and B is named H. Thus, Bach's Mass in b minor, is, in German, Messe in H-moll, and Tchaikovsky's Concerto no. 1 in B-flat minor is, in German, in B-moll.

**Calendar systems.** The domain is time, and although it is continuous, there is a natural division into days and years. There are at least four calendar systems in use: Gregorian, Julian, Jewish, and Islamic. All of these have different, but equivalent notation for days, months, and years. Since two calendars are lunar and two are solar, there is not a simple equivalent between the two.

Even within the same calendar system, there may be complications due to the names associated with particular dates. For instance, standard German notation is day/month/year, while standard American notation is month/day/year.

**Time measurement.** There are two standard systems in use: am/pm and military.

**Measures of space: length, area, volume, and weight.** There are two standard systems in use: metric and English. They differ in units of measurement.

**Measures of temperature.** There are three systems in use: Celsius, Fahrenheit, and Kelvin. There is a difference in the size of the measuring unit (degrees) between Celsius and Kelvin on the one hand, and Fahrenheit on the other. The difference between Celsius and Kelvin is a difference in starting point.

**Floor-naming conventions.** Which floor counts as "the first floor" determines the name identify of the other floors. There are also some slight variations in that many US buildings do not have a 13th floor, while Japanese buildings often do not have a 4th floor. Thus the floor name (elevator number name) and the actual floor number may vary as well.

**Alphabetization conventions.** Each language has different conventions for ordering the letters of their alphabet. Thus in Spanish, vowels accented with an acute accent are alphabetized with the vowel itself, while ñ and double ll are given separate status.

**Musical works.** Musical works by a single composer are often enumerated by Opus number, usually assigned by the composer. However, for the works of a number of composers, have been catalogued by scholars and assigned a numerical tag, again usually in chronological order. However, as new works are discovered, other works assigned to other composers, different scholars may propose different enumerations. So, there is the S listing and the BWV listing for Bach's works, The K and the L listing for Scarlatti's works, etc.

**Book cataloguing schemas.** There are two systems in common use: Dewey Decimal and Library of Congress. It is interesting to note that the Dewey Decimal system has a non-standard ordering. A book catalogued as 251.35 is filed *after* a booked catalogued as 251.4.

In addition to the difficulties caused by the scalar systems themselves, additional translation difficulties are caused by two common language strategies: (a) ellipses of repeated material; and (b) omission of shared mutual knowledge. These linguistic strategies make it difficult to identify exactly which scalar system is in use. Examples (2) and (3) illustrate strategy (a). Examples (4) through (6) exemplify strategy (b).

    (1)   John will be four years old in Saturday, and his brother will be two on Tuesday.

    (2)   That long board measures 6 feet long, while the smaller one is only 4.

    (3)   Whew it's hot out there. It must be at least 80 degrees in the shade.

    (4)   In 1960, Kennedy was elected president.

    (5)   In Ottawa, that would cost you $10.

A final translation difficulty arises in selecting an appropriate scalar system for the target audience. In general, there are four translation strategies. Which one is used will depend on knowledge of and inferences about the scalar systems in use by the target audience, decisions about the purpose of the translation, and possibly other pragmatic factors.

(A) A literal translation of the source language scalar system would convey to the reader a more exact understanding of the original text. It may also serve the purpose of highlighting the foreign nature of the original text or setting, as in example (7):

(6)  "I'll give you a thousand ducats for that horse!" cried the Sultan.

(B) A translation into the target language scalar system will communicate more directly the intended content of the source language text, as in (9) as opposed to (8).

(7)  The orchestra played Bach's "Messe in H-moll".

(8)  The orchestra played Bach's "Mass in b minor".

(C) A translation strategy may provide both a literal translation of the original scale and a translation into the target language scalar system, as in (10):

(9)  The shipment cost 43,000 yuans (4,940 dollars).

(D) A final translation strategy tries to overlook the exact scale and provides a general equivalent, if the exact amount or number is not vital to the understanding of the text, as in (11) through (13). Here the original text "decenas" means literally "tens".

(10)(Original) decenas de empresas occidentales

(11)(Translation 1) dozens of Western businesses

(12)(Translation 2) numerous Western businesses

## 4  Empirical Evidence

Given the multiple scalar systems in use as described in Section 3, given the common occurrence of language strategies such as ellipses and omission, and given the omnipresence of four translation strategies, it would seem that translation of scalar system references would be difficult indeed. On the other hand, it is possible that the multiple systems listed above are in infrequent use, and in the vast majority of instances, a simple word-for-word, number-for-number translation is effective and correct.

We examined 100 Spanish newspaper texts each with two professional English translations (provided for the DARPA MT evaluation in 1994) (White et al., 1994). We isolated all the scalar phrases in the texts. These were any phrase that contained a number, whether spelled out or written in numerals, as well as any phrase that specified a member or set of members of a scalar system by reference to that system. That would include phrases like "on Wednesday", "last week," or "the majority of the commission," "both men." We did not include phrases that identified a specific individual through the use of definite or indefinite articles, nor did we include quantified phrases in general. We did more extensive work on the first 15 texts.

The first 15 texts contained a total of 5759 words. We isolated from these texts 222 scalar phrases, containing 796 words, or 13.8% of the total. This is the percentage of text that could, a priori, exhibit translation difficulties due to scalar systems. Of these 222 scalar phrases, 115 exhibited a difference between the two English translation, or about 51.8%. These 115 phrases accounted for 388 words or about 48% of the total. (This last figure may be somewhat misleading, as the 796 words of the scalar phrases were counted in the Spanish original text, while the 388 words of difference were counted from one of the English translations.)

Of the 222 scalar phrases in the original, we identified 44, or 19.8% of the total, where the translation was not a simple. Fifteen of the 44 involved a simple substitution of period for comma or vice versa as in (14) through (17).

(13) Original: 31,47%
(14) Translation: 31.47%
(15) Original: unos 300.000 empleados
(16) Translation: some 300,000 employees

21 cases also involved the period/comma alternation, but in a more complex fashion. Apparently in Spanish, it is standard to speak about thousands of millions of dollars. English standard is to speak of billions of dollars. Thus in these cases, the period was not transposed into a comma. Instead, it was kept and the word "millones" was translated as "billion" as in (18) and (19).

(17) Original: 2.759 millones de dólares
(18) Translation: 2.759 billion dollars

Six additional cases involved scalar phrases using the metric system. In all six, both translators opted for translation strategy (A) – leaving the translation in the metric system as in (20) through (22).

(19) Original: a unos 30 km
(20) (21 Translation1: some 30 km. away
(21) Translation2: about 30 km away

Two final cases involved the floor-naming convention discussed as discussed in Farwell and Helmreich, 1997.

Generalizing, we estimate that about 13.8% of text involves scalar phrases and thus potential translation difficulties, and that 19.8% of those (or about 2.73% of total text) actually does exhibit these difficulties. Furthermore, the languages and cultures involved (Spanish and English) are not too different. One would expect a greater number of difficulties in translation of scalar phrases the more distant the source and target languages and cultures are.

Good translators, of course, can insure that these translation difficulties do not cause translation problems. However, even these professional translators in six cases produced semantically incompatible translations. Two of the cases involved the floor-naming convention, as shown in (23) through (28). This appears to be the result of different decisions about which floor-naming conventions were in use.

(22) Original: tercero piso
(23) Translation1: third floor
(24) Translation2: fourth floor
(25) Original: segundo piso
(26) Translation2: third floor
(27) Translation1: second floor

One case appeared to involve a choice by one translator to use translation strategy (D). This was shown in examples (11)-(13), repeated here as (29) through (31):

(28) (Original) decenas de empresas occidentales
(29) (Translation 1) dozens of Western businesses
(30) (Translation 2) numerous Western businesses

Two more cases appeared to be perhaps the result of interference from the scalar systems involved, resulting in errors, as shown in (32) through (37).

(31) Original: 16 millones de dólares
(32) Translation1: 16 billion dollars
(33) Translation2: 16 million dollars
(34) Original: 2.069 millones de dólares
(35) Translation1: 2.069 billion dollars
(36) Translation2: 2,069 billion dollars

The final case appears to be a simple error on the part of one translator, as shown in (38) through (40).

(37) Original: 8.879 millones de dólares
(38) Translation1: 8.870 billion dollars
(39) Translation2: 8.879 billion dollars

## 5   Solutions

In Helmreich and Farwell (1998), we argued strongly that in all such cases, a deep-pragmatic solution is the "correct" one. That is, the correct solution examines the meaning of the text as a whole, and then based on knowledge of and inference about the intent of the source language author, the understanding of the source language audience, the purpose of the translation activity, and knowledge of the target language audience, determines an appropriate translation. We do not propose to re-argue that case here. Suffice it to point that that scalar systems are clearly culture-specific, which may or may not coincide with linguistic boundaries.

Instead, we attempt to provide some interim solutions that might assist in getting the translation "right" without requiring an intensive knowledge-based translation system that relies on defeasible reasoning.

In this section, however, we provide an algorithm that relies on more readily accessible information and does not require a non-monotonic inferencing engine.

**Step 1: Identify the scalar phrase.** This step is fairly straightforward as these phrases are nearly co-extensive with phrases that include a number.

**Step 2: Identify the domain.** This second step is not quite as easy. Frequently measuring phrases include a unit of measurement, which can be tied to a property. If a whole number is involved, counting may be involved, and the objects counted should be mentioned in the phrase.

**Step 3: Identify the scalar system.** Having identified the domain, a restricted set of scalar systems are connected with each domain. An additional clue may be found in the source language, which may be indicative of certain scalar systems. The linguistic representations of the counters are often unique, or may help narrow the plausible set of scalar systems. For example, "January" would identify the Julian or Gregorian calendar system, and eliminate the Jewish or Arabic ones.

It is at this step that some complexity may be added to the algorithm by hard-coding inferences made on the basis of sets of clues. The clues can be simple, such as the identity of the source language, or the geographical origin of the source text. Or it could be more complex. For example, the object or objects possessing a measured property often have more or less standard ranges for that property, ranges that are dependent on the scale. For instance, the ambient temperature on earth usually ranges between –20 and 120 degrees Fahrenheit, and between –30 say, and 55 degrees Celsius. A temperature between 55 and 120 that is predicated of the ambient temperature is likely to be in degrees Fahrenheit.

**Step 4: Select a scalar system for the target language text.** This is the first step in choosing a translation strategy. The easiest choice is the same as that one used in the source language text. However, that may not be the best choice. Since the target language and presumably the target language audience are known prior to translation, an acceptable list of scalar systems can be chosen beforehand, for each domain.

**Step 5: Select an equivalent counter.** This step needs to be performed only if a different scalar system than that identified in the source language text is chosen for the target language. Otherwise, the counter remains the same.

**Step 6: Select a linguistic representation.** This step is the actual translation step. For each counter there should be an appropriate linguistic representation in the target language. This may or may not be the same linguistic representation (even for numbers) in the source language. The two languages may differ, for example, in which numbers are usually written out in text and which are displayed as numerals. Or, as we saw, the standard representation of certain types of large numbers may differ from language/culture to language/culture.

This algorithm should provide a standard method for translation of phrases involving scalar systems, a method which can avoid some of the pitfalls of this kind of translation, and a method which can be enhanced by making use of as much additional information is available in the context (linguistic or otherwise), yet without requiring sophisticated knowledge bases and inference engines.

# 6   Conclusion

In this paper, we have first provided a framework that describes scalar systems and with which it is possible to classify differences in scalar systems. Second, we have shown that there are a number of such scalar systems, and that in many cases, different scalar systems are in use in different languages and cultures. Third, we have analyzed a number of texts and translations to ascertain the frequency of occurrence of problematic scalar phrases. We discovered that scalar phrases occupy about 13% of text and that 20% of that (about 2.5% of all text) is problematic with respect to translation. Finally, though we believe that the best solution involves knowledge-based inferencing, we offer an algorithm, which, though not fully satisfactory, can help avoid some of the pitfalls of translating phrases involving scalar systems.

# References

1. Farwell, D., and S. Helmreich. 1997. What floor is this? Beliefs and Translation. *Proceedings of the 5th International Colloquium on Cognitive Science*, 95-102.
2. Farwell, D., and S. Helmreich. 1999. Pragmatics and Translation. *Procesamiento de Lenguaje Natural*, 24:19-36.
3. Helmreich, S. and D. Farwell. 1998. Translation Differences and Pragmatics-Based MT. *Machine Translation* 13:17-39.
4. White, J., T. O'Connell and F. O'Mara. 1994. "The ARPA MT Evaluation Methodologies: Evolution, Lessons, and Future Approaches" in *Technology Partnerships for Crossing the Language Barrier: Proceedings of the First Conference of the Association for Machine Translation in the Americas*, Columbia, Maryland, pp. 193-205.

# Feedback from the Field: The Challenge of Users in Motion

L. Hernandez, J. Turner, and M. Holland

Army Research Laboratory
2800 Powder Mill Road
Adelphi, MD 20783
{lhernandez, jturner}@arl.army.mil

**Abstract.** Feedback from field deployments of machine translation (MT) is instructive but hard to obtain, especially in the case of soldiers deployed in mobile and stressful environments. We first consider the process of acquiring feedback: the difficulty of getting and interpreting it, the kinds of information that have been used in place of or as predictors of direct feedback, and the validity and completeness of that information. We then look at how to better forecast the utility of MT in deployments so that feedback from the field is focused on aspects that can be fixed or enhanced rather than on overall failure or viability of the technology. We draw examples from document and speech translation.

## 1 Introduction

The military has developed and tested a variety of systems that include machine translation (MT) and has sent some of these systems to the field. Although we strive to get information about the utility of these systems, feedback is often difficult to obtain and, when it comes, tricky to interpret. Here, we reflect on the process of getting feedback from operators at the "forward edge" – usually mobile and under stress; we look at what kinds of indicators or predictors of field utility are available short of observation and direct feedback; and we discuss the adequacy of these indicators and predictors with examples from the field. On this basis, we consider how to organize user tests of MT to better predict its utility in the field and improve the quality of feedback we get from users on the move. Note that we do not provide references for some of what we talk about, either because a technology deployment is militarily sensitive or because specific vendors are involved or because the data have not yet been officially released.

When we refer to machine translation in the field, we mean end-to-end systems in which MT is an "embedded" component and input undergoes numerous processes that affect translation (Reeder & Loehr, 1998; Voss & Reeder, 1998; Voss & Van Ess-Dykema, 2004; 2000). Thus, feedback from the field must be interpreted in light of how other components perform. Here, we consider the examples of MT embedded in speech translators as well as document processing.

R.E. Frederking and K.B. Taylor (Eds.): AMTA 2004, LNAI 3265, pp. 94–101, 2004.
© Springer-Verlag Berlin Heidelberg 2004

## 2   Obtaining Feedback About Machine Translation in the Field

### 2.1   Obstacles and Benefits

When machine translation goes with troops to the field, it is often deployed in distant, hard-to-access locations with intermittent phone and email connection. These locations may be in developing or less developed countries with limited or damaged infrastructure. Moreover, users become busy with missions, working up to 20 hours a day, seven days a week, leaving little time to send feedback to scientists and developers. Finally, soldiers are highly and often unpredictably mobile, and they are often reassigned to new tasks, making it hard to track those who might provide instructive data. Clearly, being on the ground with soldiers at the time they are using a system is the best way to get feedback. However, on dangerous missions and in theaters where threat to life is imminent, scientific and evaluation teams are typically barred.

Army operators, then, are a special case of users in motion: they are distributed, dynamic, and difficult to locate. Getting their feedback is a challenge. However, as we have pointed out previously, their feedback is precious in part because they are an ideal customer for MT (Holland, Schlesiger, & Turner, 2000): Soldiers tolerate poorer quality translations, and they regularly apply such translations to tasks lower on the Taylor & White text-handling scale (1998), such as relevance screening. Even when soldiers serve as linguists or translators who perform high-level tasks – say, writing complete translations – they often lack the degree of training, experience, and full-time assignment to those tasks that characterizes translators in intelligence agencies. These distinctions may, in fact, account for why soldiers seem disproportionately welcoming of automatic translation. Finally, soldiers who need technology will generally find ways to fix and adapt systems on the fly. Given the value of what soldiers have to teach us, how can we facilitate getting feedback from troops in the field or, alternatively, mitigate the lack of it? What information about MT utility is available, and by what means, short of being on-site or directly linked to users?

### 2.2   The Next Best Thing to Being There?

When we cannot be on site, or be linked to users by email, phone, or fax, there are other sources of impressions about or predictions of the utility of MT in the field:

- Requests for particular systems from users in the field are often taken as an indicator of utility.
- Reports from military system managers who purchase, issue, and track deployed systems provide second-hand feedback.
- Results from formal and informal user tests before systems are fielded are used to predict utility in the field.

How valid and complete are these sources compared with on-site observations or other direct feedback? Below we consider each form of information.

**Requests from the field: Common misinterpretations.** Offices that field equipment may receive requests for translation devices or systems, as well as requests for additional copies to supplement those that have been deployed. It is not uncommon for developers or agencies to cite such requests as evidence of value and effectiveness of an MT system. "Commander X has requested translation systems for 10 teams," a briefing may claim. But we do not know whether these requests result from actually seeing systems being used and rendering value, or from hearing that a technology has arrived in some unit and *might* be helpful, or from active marketing (demos, promotional circulars) by developers or developing agencies.

Deployment itself is sometimes cited as evidence of utility. Developers or agencies may state: "Now being used in Bosnia," or "1500 copies sent to Region X." But without an intimate tie to users, we do not know whether the systems that were sent are in fact used and with what result. Indeed, some of the follow-up information we receive, described below, suggests that MT, even when  installed and trained, is not employed. Failure to send back systems or devices is also sometimes taken as evidence of utility, when in fact there may be practical or logistical reasons for not returning them. Number of hits on a website that provides MT is also a tempting form of data, and is easily obtained, but does not answer questions of utility.

**Second-hand feedback: Filling in blanks.** More instructive than requests for MT are accounts from system managers or from returning troops who, while not themselves users, may have seen the system or talked to users. While we consider these second-hand accounts a reliable reflection of utility, we also view them as incomplete and potentially unrepresentative. They may signify the perspective of a single user, and even if more broadly reflective, they typically leave open questions of how a system was used, for what tasks, and with kinds of data.

For example, in 2003 we at special request provided Falcon (Forward Area Language Converter), a prototype small-scale document translator (Holland & Schlesiger, 1998), to a unit in an undisclosed location that was dealing with documents in a Middle Eastern language. We heard months later that users abandoned machine translation because they found the results indecipherable. Because we did not have an opportunity to communicate with users before, during, or after deployment, we can only speculate about causes. Similarly, we hear from a fielding activity that users of a large-scale document translation and management system, which is set up at an overseas site, avoid the MT component and use the system primarily for electronic tagging and storage of documents. Again, there is little information about why this is the case. A supportable inference, based on what we have seen of documents from that region, is that an obstacle to utility is paper documents whose quality is too poor for commercial OCR (optical character recognition), which these systems are equipped with. However, we need more information from the field to tell what factors are at play, to diagnose problems, and to draw conclusions about the effectiveness of the embedded MT.

Thus, we can get glimpses of aspects of MT at work: whether it is being used, is considered useful, is regarded as desirable, or is laid aside.  These glimpses do not answer but, rather, pave the way for questions that require direct links to users.

**User tests: The gap between rehearsal and reality.** Systems are not officially deployed in the military until they have undergone a series of tests on numerous dimensions. Advanced Concept Technology Demonstrations (ACTDs) are a good way to get prototypes into users' hands quickly in the context of standard large-scale exercises that have operational realism. Such exercises are regularly scheduled both at home and abroad to train and rehearse service members in skills they may need in combat or peacekeeping – such as medical triage, logistics planning, or casualty evacuation. Sometimes new technologies or prototypes can be incorporated into an exercise to assess their suitability and to see where they need improvement. Evaluation dimensions generally include effectiveness, suitability, and usability. Also, outside of standard exercises, "limited utility evaluations" may be built around a particular system that is of critical interest to a set of users.

The results of these assessments are sometimes used to support deployment decisions. How adequately do the results predict whether a system is ready for field operation – or, if a system is not deemed ready, how to prepare it?

*The example of speech translation: What military exercises say.* While flexible two-way speech-to-speech translation is still a research goal (Lavie et al., 2001; Schultz, 2002), more limited speech translation prototypes have been developed in "1 and ½ way" mode. This limited mode allows questions to be spoken in English and limited responses to be spoken in another language. Responses are usually constrained by the phrasing of questions – such as "Why did you come to this clinic? Answer fever, vomiting, or pain" or "Tell me your age: just say a number." In 2003-04 a system in this mode was readied in a Central Asian language needed in the field. A limited utility evaluation was performed at a domestic military post to ensure that the system was ready to send with deploying troops. The results showed that the system was usable, did not crash, usually recognized the English speakers, and often recognized speakers of the other language. The latter speakers were language instructors for whom the English input was masked, allowing them to play validly the role of a non-English speaker.

This evaluation was reinforced by participation of the same 1 and ½ way system in a joint yearly military exercise in 2004, where the system mediated between questions in English and answers in a Pacific Rim language. While no measures of communicative effectiveness were taken, an independent military test center surveyed users on both the interviewer and the interviewee side about their use of and reaction to the system and produced a report.

Thirty English-speaking troops who had acted as interviewers responded to 10 survey questions on translation effectiveness and system usability (for example, "It was easy to conduct the queries for this scenario via the system" and "[system] reduced the time needed to convey or acquire information.") When responses were aggregated, 95% (284/299) were positive. Twenty-eight speakers who had acted as interviewees (and did not speak English) responded to two survey questions on "ease of communication." Summed across their responses, 93% percent were positive.

Thus, the survey responses were overwhelmingly favorable toward the system. The system was concluded to have "garnered the most favorable impressions from the target population" [of 3 different systems tried in the exercise – the other 2 being for text translation]. Conclusions about suitability and usability stated that the platform "was very durable and easy to use...extremely portable and capable of extended battery operation" and that the system "was stable and did not crash" while the translations were "accurate... acceptable and understood by the non-English speakers during the interviews."

A telling limitation, however, showed up in the comments quoted from some users:

"Useful but need to be able to vary in responses and answers."
"It should wait longer for you to speak, a few times it didn't recognize because interviewee was slow to answer."
"Sometimes it made mistakes, especially time or numbers."
"It requires the cooperation of the interviewee. If the person is answering the right thing but in a wrong way, such as too fast or unclear, the device didn't work."

Recognizing these indicators, the report concluded that the scenarios – the question and answer lists – that had been programmed into the system were "functionally limited...[with] too few scenarios available, and the type of questions presented ... did not reflect ... military operations." Indeed, the report acknowledged that because the scenarios did not match the requirements of the exercise, the user test was conducted on the side rather than integrated into the exercise. But this was deemed repairable: "Scenarios need to be expanded" by "coordinating with military professional to create actual scenarios from start to finish in logical order." It was observed that "most users were successful in using the technology to conduct the programmed scenarios."

*The example of speech translation: What the field says.* What happened in the field? An officer from the units deploying with the system reported to the deploying agency that the systems weren't being used; that when they were used, the foreign speaker responses were sometimes not recognized at all and sometimes incorrectly translated. Numbers were a noticeable problem. A respondent might say "35" when asked their own age, or the age of a relative, and the response was translated as "23." Although no data were offered, it appeared that mistranslations happened often enough to lead the troops to put aside the device and to call on human translators when they needed to communicate with local people.

Given the limitations of second-hand feedback noted above, the home agency decided to conduct another assessment to find out what was snagging communication in the field. Maybe the recognizer was timing out too quickly, before respondents completed their answer. Maybe respondents were intoning a dialect variation for which the system had not been trained. Maybe ambient noise was causing misrecognition. Maybe respondents were saying things that had not been included in the response domain. The new assessment pointed to a combination of these factors and suggested that the system had been prematurely fielded.

This suggestion is strengthened by a recent (2004) assessment of other selected speech translators, also in the 1 and ½ way mode, as part of a medical exercise in which use of the systems was an integral part of the larger triage and treatment goals of the exercise. While users' attitudes toward speech translators were favorable, the systems did not work to mediate medic-patient communication. Results of this assessment are being compiled by a military test agency.

Thus, the results of users tests in military exercises or in limited utility assessments can mislead us about system utility and readiness. How can pre-deployment evaluations be organized and designed to provide researchers and developers diagnostic data that is fair and controlled, yet give decision-makers information that better represents the realities of the field? The features of the above assessments furnish pointers.

# 3   Getting More Out of Feedback from the Field: Improving the Predictiveness of Pre-deployment Evaluations

Feedback from missions overseas is sparse and precious. We might hypothesize that some user tests tend to overestimate readiness. This would mean that MT may be deployed before it is ready, making it likely that the feedback we get concerns all-or-nothing function – it works or it fails – rather than specific features that can be adjusted or enhanced or specific observations of efficiency and effectiveness and the conditions that affect them. If pre-deployment evaluations can be organized and designed to better predict utility in the field, or at least to rule out systems with major shortcomings, then we can expect more meaningful feedback from users on the move. At the same time, plunging systems into an exercise that simulates field conditions is wasteful if a system has not already undergone tiers of testing that can pinpoint not only component performance problems but also various levels of user difficulties so that developers can address them.

## 3.1   Tiers of Testing Prior to Deployment

Tests within the developer's lab can isolate component performance problems and permit these to be resolved before users are brought in. Subsequently, constrained tests outside the developer's lab with soldiers and with foreign language documents or speakers can isolate levels of problems prior to integration of a system in a military exercise. Two of the assessments of 1 and ½ way speech translation described above – the limited utility evaluation at a domestic military post and the joint military exercise in 2004 – exemplify constrained tests. What their design allows us to do is determine whether under the best of circumstances – when interviewers and interviewees say what they are supposed to say – the system can recognize and translate the utterances. In both assessments, English speakers were trained on the script (what they can say in English) and the foreign language speakers were well prepared: although they were not given a script, they were allowed to practice with the device, to repeat responses, and to learn as they went both acceptable response length and how to conform answer content to the restrictions assumed by question structure. These, then, were formative evaluations necessary to reveal basic functional gaps in user interaction. If English speakers or speakers of the target language (albeit carefully selected) are not able to learn how to use the device or cannot be recognized, then the developer learns that there is a lot more work to do. But these evaluations cannot substitute for integration into a field exercise that has a larger goal, that scripts only the goals and not the words, and that views translation tools as one of many means to an end.

## 3.2   Insitutionalizing Surprise: Approximating Field Conditions in a Military Exercise

Feedback from the field to date confirms the factor of surprise: The quality of documents and the nature of their noise cannot be predicted – otherwise, OCR and preprocessors could be trained to manage some of that noise. Nor can the behavior and responses of indigenous people be predicted who are faced with a speech translation device and with questions posed in their language, even questions that are very well-structured. The issue of coverage in MT comes to the foreground in the field.

Military exercises are known for being extensively planned, setting up authentic scenarios, using real equipment, and finding experienced role players to interact with soldiers. They also attempt to bring in data that mirrors what is found in the field – although the noise surrounding that data is hard to duplicate. Exercises run off predefined scenarios, with clear goals as in a real mission; but like a real mission, the scenarios are never scripted down to the word.

When MT is well integrated into such an exercise, we have a best chance of realizing surprise and thereby predicting utility in the field. This kind of integration is exemplified by the medical exercise referenced above, where role-players responding to questions mediated by 1 and ½ way speech translation did not have the chance to repeat and practice utterances until they were recognized. As patients in a disaster relief scenario, their time with medics was too limited.

From our experience observing assessments of various kinds, from the lab to the field, we make the following recommendations, especially with regard to speech MT:

- Follow lab tests of MT systems with limited utility evaluations with representative users and data.
- Employ increasing levels of realism in limited utility evaluations, for example,

    o Start with speakers under ideal circumstances – they know what to say and are in a conventional, face-to-face posture.
    o Next, have speakers physically act out the event (by asking "what would you do?" not just "what would you say?") so as to predict encumbered postures that may affect use and recognition.

- Follow limited utility evaluations with participation in realistic military exercises.

    o Train English speakers thoroughly but do not give them scripts.
    o Use novice role players who have not rehearsed with the system.
    o Use role players who are native speakers and broadly sample the target language

- Use independent observers, not developers, in evaluations and exercises, especially when opinion surveys are administered.
- Involve cognitive or human factors psychologists, not just engineers and linguists, to better anticipate factors that may affect performance.

Through these measures, we expect that systems going to the field will be more thoroughly vetted and that feedback from the field, when we can obtain it, will reflect aspects and surprises that can only be discovered there.

# References

1. Holland, M., Schlesiger, C.: High-Mobility Machine Translation for a Battlefield Environment. Proceedings of NATO/RTO Systems Concepts and Integration Symposium, Monterey, CA. Hull, Canada: CCG, Inc. (ISBN 92-837-1006-1) (1998) 15/1-3
2. Lavie A., Levin L., Schultz T., Langley C., Han B., Tribble, A., Gates D., Wallace D., Peterson K.: Domain Portability in Speech-to-speech Translation. Proceedings of the of the First International Conference on Human Language Technology Conference (HLT 2001), San Diego, March 2001.
3. Reeder, F., Loehr, D.: Finding the Right Words: An Analysis of Not-Translated Words in Machine Translation. In: Farwell, D. et al. (eds.), Machine Translation and the Information Soup: Proceedings of the Association for Machine Translation in the Americas Annual Meeting. Springer-Verlag (1998) 356-363
4. Schultz T. GlobalPhone: A Multilingual Speech and Text Database developed at Karlsruhe University. ICSLP2002, Denver, Colorado. (2002)
5. Taylor, K., White, J.: Predicting What MT is Good for: User Judgments and Task Performance. In: Farwell, D. et al. (eds.), Machine Translation and the Information Soup: Proceedings of the Association for Machine Translation in the Americas Annual Meeting. Springer-Verlag (1998) 364-373
6. Voss, C., Reeder, F. (eds.): Proceedings of the Workshop on Embedded Machine Translation: Design, Construction, and Evaluation of Systems with an MT Component. (In conjunction with the Association for Machine Translation in the Americas Annual Meeting, Langhorne, PA). Adelphi, MD: Army Research Lab. (1998)
7. Voss, C., Van Ess-Dykema, C.: When is an Embedded MT System "Good Enough" for Filtering? Proceedings of the Embedded Machine Translation Workshop II. In conjunction with the Applied Natural Language Processing Conference, Seattle (2000)

# The Georgetown-IBM Experiment
# Demonstrated in January 1954

W. John Hutchins

jhutchins@beeb.net;
http://ourworld.compuserve.com/homepages/WJHutchins

**Abstract.** The public demonstration of a Russian-English machine translation system in New York in January 1954 – a collaboration of IBM and Georgetown University – caused a great deal of public interest and much controversy. Although a small-scale experiment of just 250 words and six 'grammar' rules it raised expectations of automatic systems capable of high quality translation in the near future. This paper describes the system, its background, its impact and its implications.

## 1 The Impact

On the 8th January 1954, the front page of the *New York Times* carried a report of a demonstration the previous day at the headquarters of International Business Machines (IBM) in New York under the headline „Russian is turned into English by a fast electronic translator“:

> A public demonstration of what is believed to be the first successful use of a machine to translate meaningful texts from one language to another took place here yesterday afternoon. This may be the cumulation of centuries of search by scholars for „a mechanical translator.“

Similar reports appeared the same day in many other American newspapers (*New York Herald Tribune, Christian Science Monitor, Washington Herald Tribune, Los Angeles Times*) and in the following months in popular magazines (*Newsweek, Time, Science, Science News Letter, Discovery, Chemical Week, Chemical Engineering News, Electrical Engineering, Mechanical World, Computers and Automation*, etc.) It was probably the most widespread and influential publicity that MT has ever received. The experiment was a joint effort by two staff members of IBM, Cuthbert Hurd and Peter Sheridan, and two members of the Institute of Languages and Linguistics at Georgetown University, Leon Dostert and Paul Garvin.

## 2 The Background

Léon Dostert had been invited to the first conference on machine translation two years before in June 1952. He had been invited for his experience with mechanical aids for translation. Dostert had been Eisenhower's personal interpreter during the war, had been liaison officer to De Gaulle, and had worked for the Office of Strategic Services (predecessor of the Central Intelligence Agency). After the war he designed and installed the system of simultaneous interpretation used during the Nuremberg war crimes tribunal, and afterwards at the United Nations. In 1949 he was invited to

R.E. Frederking and K.B. Taylor (Eds.): AMTA 2004, LNAI 3265, pp. 102–114, 2004.
© Springer-Verlag Berlin Heidelberg 2004

Georgetown University to establish the Institute of Languages and Linguistics at the University's School of Foreign Service for training linguists and translators primarily for government service [10].

Dostert went to the conference as a sceptic but returned as an enthusiast determined to explore the possibilities of machine translation. It was his conviction that MT needed to demonstrate its feasibility in a practical experiment. For obvious political reasons Dostert decided that the demonstration should translate from Russian into English; the lack of knowledge about activities in the Soviet Union was already a major concern in US government circles.

Dostert contacted a personal acquaintance, Thomas J. Watson, founder of IBM, and they agreed to collaborate. The project was headed by Cuthbert Hurd, director of the Applied Sciences Division at IBM, and Dostert himself. The linguistic side of the experiment was the work of Garvin, a Czech linguist (associate professor) at the Institute – see Montgomery [6] for a biography. The computer programming was done by Peter Sheridan, staff member of IBM.

The Georgetown pair decided to demonstrate translations on a small number of sentences from organic chemistry and some others on general topics, which would illustrate some grammatical and morphological problems and give some idea of what might be feasible in the future. The experiment was to be small, with a vocabulary of just 250 lexical items (stems and endings) and a limited set of just six rules.

## 3  The Demonstration

Reports of the demonstration appeared under headlines such as „Electronic brain translates Russian", „The bilingual machine", „Robot brain translates Russian into King's English", and „Polyglot brainchild" – at the time computers were commonly referred to as 'electronic brains' and 'giant brains' (because of their huge bulk).

The newspapermen were much impressed:

> In the demonstration, a girl operator typed out on a keyboard the following Russian text in English characters: „Mi pyeryedayem mislyi posryedstvom ryechi". The machine printed a translation almost simultaneously: „We transmit thoughts by means of speech." The operator did not know Russian. Again she types out the meaningless (to her) Russian words: „Vyelyichyina ugla opryedyelyayatsya otnoshyenyiyem dlyini dugi k radyiusu." And the machine translated it as: „Magnitude of angle is determined by the relation of length of arc to radius." (New York Times)

It appears that the demonstration began with the organic chemistry sentences. Some of these were reported, e.g.

> The quality of coal is determined by calory content
> Starch is produced by mechanical method from potatoes.

but the journalists were clearly much more impressed by those on other topics:

> And then just to give the electronics a real workout, brief statements about politics, law, mathematics, chemistry, metallurgy, communications, and military affairs were submitted in the Soviet language... (Christian Science Monitor)

All the reports recognised the small scale of the experiment but they also reported future predictions from Dostert:

„Those in charge of this experiment," the professor continued, „now consider it to be definitely established that meaning conversion through electronic language translation is feasible." [and] the professor forecast that „five, perhaps three, years hence, interlingual meaning conversion by electronic process in important functional areas of several languages may well be an accomplished fact." (Christian Science Monitor)

He made other projections and predictions:

100 rules would be needed to govern 20,000 words for free translation... Eventually, the machine will be able to translate from Russian: „She taxied her plane on the apron and then went home to do housework." In such a sentence with double-meaning words, the machine will be able to tell what meaning of apron and taxi would be needed in that particular context. (New York Herald Tribune)

Whether these were Dostert's words is not known, but obviously expectations were high. Some wider implications, both for linguistics as well as for translation, were also expressed. Neil Macdonald [4] gave a sound assessment:

Linguists will be able to study a language in the way that a physicist studies material in physics, with very few human prejudices and preconceptions... The technical literature of Germany, Russia, France, and the English-speaking countries will be made available to scientists of other countries as it emerges from the presses... But of course, it must be emphasized that a vast amount of work is still needed, to render mechanically translatable more languages and wider areas of a language. For 250 words and 6 syntactical structures are simply a "Kitty Hawk" flight. [4]

A number of reports picked up the observation made by the developers that the expensive 701 computer was „'overdesigned' for language translation; it has too many functions not essential to this task that were built in to solve problems in astronomy and physics" [7]. It was expected that MT would require special-purpose machines.

## 4  The Processes

Most of the reports are illustrated with a photograph of a punched card with a Russian sentence; and many have photographs of the machines and of the Georgetown and IBM personnel. But they gave few hints of how the system worked.

The most common references were to rules for inversion, all using the example of Russian *gyeneral mayor*, which has to come out in English as *major general*. One gave some idea of the computer program:

The switch is assured in advance by attaching the rule sign 21 to the Russian *gyeneral* in the bilingual glossary which is stored in the machine, and by attaching the rule-sign 110 to the Russian *mayor*. The stored instructions, along with the glossary, say „whenever you read a rule sign 110 in the glossary, go back and look for a rule-sign 21. If you find 21, print the two words that follow it in reverse order (Journal of Franklin Institute, March 1954)

A few explained how rules selected between alternative translations:

The word root „ugl" in Russian means either „angle" or „coal" depending upon its suffix. This root is stored in the form of electrical impulses on a magnetic drum together with its English meanings and the Garvin rules of syntax and context which determine its meaning. The code is so set up so that when the machine gets electrical impulses via the punched cards that read „ugla" it translates it as „angle", when „uglya" the translation is „coal". (New York Herald Tribune)

It is doubtful whether newspaper readers would have gained much understanding from these brief explanations. However, some of the weeklies went into much more detail. Macdonald's report [4] included a list of the six rules, a flowchart of the program for dictionary lookup and a table illustrating the operation of the rules on a sample sentence.

## 5   The Computer

An illuminating account of the computational aspects of the experiment is given in the contemporary article by Peter Sheridan [9]. As the first substantial attempt at non-numerical programming, every aspect of the process had involved entering quite unknown territory. Decisions had to be made on how alphabetic characters were to be coded, how the Russian letters were to be transliterated, how the Russian vocabulary was to be stored on the magnetic drum, how the 'syntactic' codes were to operate and how they were to be stored, how much information was to go on each punched card, etc. Detailed flow charts were drawn up for what today would be simple and straightforward operations, such as the identification of words and their matching against dictionary entries.

The IBM 701-type machine had been developed for military applications and was first installed in April 1953. Like other computers of the day its main tasks were the solution of problems in nuclear physics, rocket trajectories, weather forecasting, etc. It was hired out initially at $15,000 per month, and later sold at $500,000 – and was at that time only one of about 100 general-purpose computers in existence. Its huge size was impressive; it was likened to „an assortment of 11 complicated electronic units, not unlike modern kitchen ranges, connected by cables to function as a unit" and „which occupy roughly the same area as a tennis court." [7]. A similar-sized machine, the 702, was also developed for business applications. Its successor in late 1955 was the 704 model, a substantial improvement on the 701 and which sold in large numbers.

The 701 could perform 33 distinct operations: addition, subtraction, multiplication, division, shifting, transfers, etc. – all coded in 'assembly language'. Multiplication was performed at 2,000 per second. It consisted of two types of storage. Electrostatic (high-speed) storage was in the form of a bank of cathode ray tubes; each unit could accommodate up to 2048 „full words", where a „full word" comprised 35 bits (binary digits) and one sign bit – 36 bits in all. Each full word could be split (stored) as two „half words", each of 17 bits and one sign bit. Although the 701 had two electrostatic units, only one was used in the MT experiment. Average access time was 12 microseconds. The second type of storage (with lower access speed, 40 milliseconds) was a magnetic drum unit comprising four 'addressable' drums, each accommodating up to 2048 'full words'. The magnetic drum was used to store dictionary information; the reading and writing rate was 800 words per second.

Input to the 701 was by card reader. Information from 72 column cards (precursor of the familiar IBM 80 column punched cards in use for computer input until the early 1970s) – i.e. each with a maximum capacity of 72 upper case (capital letter) alphabetic or numeric characters – could be read and converted to internal binary code at a rate 150 per minute. Output was by a line printer (also capital letters only) at a rate of 150 lines per minute.

The program used a seven-bit code for characters: six bits for distinguishing 40 alphanumeric and other characters, plus one sign bit used for various tests (see below). This means that each „full word" location could contain up to five characters.

The Russian-English dictionary was input by punched cards and stored on the (low-speed) magnetic drum. The Russian word and the English equivalents (two maximum) were stored on consecutive locations, separated by 'full words' containing zeros. They were followed by the so-called diacritics on consecutive drum locations. Each 'word' included a 'sign bit', either + or -, which indicated whether the entry was for a stem or for an ending, respectively.

Sentences were read into the electrostatic storage, separated by strings of zero-filled 'words'. The input words were then each looked up in the drum storage, first by consultation of a „thumb index" which gave the address (location) of the first word in the dictionary with the same initial letter. The lookup routine searched for the longest matching string of characters (whether complete word or stem plus hyphen), extracted the (two) English equivalents onto a separate area of the store, and copied the diacritics onto another area of the store. A special area was also set aside for the temporary (erasable) location of word-endings. Each of these areas and addresses would have to be specified either directly (specifically by store address) or indirectly (using variables) in the program (called Lexical Syntax Subprogram). Sheridan describes the operations of comparison in terms of successive and repeated processes of logical multiplication, addition and subtraction using 'masks' (sequences of binary digits). When a 'diacritic' indicated that either the first English equivalent or the second English equivalent was to be selected, then the program went back to the addresses to the separate store area, and transferred the one selected to a (temporary) print-out area of the electrostatic store.

## 6  The Six Rules

Before the system was given to Sheridan of IBM for programming, it was tested by hand on a set of cards by people who did not know Russian ([2], [4], [5]). The sentences were written in Russian characters on the cards. The test involved finding the corresponding cards for each word and following the instructions. The instructions for the Operational Syntax Subprogram were formulated in language such as:

Rule 1. Rearrangement.   If first code is '110', is third code associated with preceding complete word equal to '21'? If so, reverse order of appearance of words in output (i.e., word carrying '21' should follow that carrying '110') – otherwise, retain order. In both cases English equivalent I associated with '110' is adopted.

Rule 2. Choice-Following text.   If first code is '121', is second code of the following complete, subdivided or partial (root or ending) word equal to '221' or '222'? If it is '221', adopt English equivalent I of word carrying

'121'; if it is '222', adopt English equivalent II. In both cases, retain order of appearance of output words.

Rule 3. Choice-Rearrangement. If first code is '131', is third code of preceding complete word or either portion (root or ending) of preceding subdivided word equal to '23'? If so, adopt English equivalent II of word carrying '131', and retain order of appearance of words in output – if not, adopt English equivalent I and reverse order of appearance of words in output.

Rule 4. Choice-Previous text. If first code is '141', is second code of preceding complete word or either portion (root or ending) of preceding subdivided word equal to '241' or '242'? If it is '241', adopt English equivalent I of word carrying '141'; if it is '242' adopt English equivalent II. In both cases, retain order of appearance of words in output.

Rule 5. Choice-Omission. If first code is '151', is third code of following complete word or either portion (root or ending) of following subdivided word equal to '25'? If so, adopt English equivalent II of word carrying '151'; if not, adopt English equivalent I. In both cases, retain order of appearance of words in output.

Rule 6. Subdivision. If first code associated with a Russian dictionary word is '***', then adopt English equivalent I of alternative English language equivalents, retaining order of appearance of output with respect to previous word.

According to Sheridan, the rules formulated in this manner were easily converted into program code for the 701 computer. Sheridan's account [9] includes a flowchart of the processes of dictionary lookup and 'operational syntax'.

# 7  The Sentences

The most detailed account of the linguistic operations is given by Garvin [3] in a retrospective evaluation of the experiment and its significance. He includes 137 dictionary entries for words, stems and endings; and 49 of the original Russian sentences (in a transliteration scheme devised for the experiment)

Most of the „more than 60" sentences in the demonstration concerned topics of organic chemistry. These were intended to illustrate the variety of sentence patterns which the rules could deal with, and nouns and verbs occurring in different roles. Some examples are:

(1) (a) They prepare TNT; (b) They prepare TNT out of coal; (c) TNT is prepared out of coal; (d) TNT is prepared out of stony coal; (e) They prepare ammonite; (f) They prepare ammonite out of saltpeter; (g) Ammonite is prepared out of saltpeter.

(2) (a) They obtain gasoline out of crude oil; (b) Gasoline is obtained out of crude oil; (c) They obtain dynamite from nitroglycerine; (d) Ammonite is obtained from saltpeter; (e) Iron is obtained out of ore;  (f) They obtain iron out of ore; (g) Copper is obtained out of ore.

(3) (a) They produce alcohol out of potatoes; (b). Alcohol is produced out of potatoes; (c). They produce starch out of potatoes;  (d). Starch is produced

out of potatoes; (e) Starch is produced by mechanical method from potatoes.

(4) (a) The quality of coal is determined by calory content; (b). The price of potatoes is determined by the market; (c). Calory content determines the quality of coal; (d) Calory content determines the quality of crude oil; (e) The quality of crude oil is determined by calory content; (f) The quality of saltpeter is determined by chemical methods.

There were also, as the newspapers reported, a number (about 20) of sentences of relative greater complexity on other topics. It is notable that the journalists picked on these sentences in their reports rather than the less interesting chemistry examples.

(5) Magnitude of angle is determined by the relation of length of arc to radius.

(6) Angle of site is determined by optical measurement.

(7) We transmit thoughts by means of speech.

(8) Military court sentenced the sergeant to deprival of civil rights.

(9) A commander gets information over a telegraph.

(10) Penal law constitutes an important section of legislation.

(11) Vladimir appears for work late in the morning.

(12) International understanding constitutes an important factor in decision of political questions.

## 8  The Dictionary and the Linguistic Operations

Dictionary entries (for both stems and endings) included three codes. The first code, Program Initiating Diacritic (PID) was one of '110', '121', '131', '141'or '151'. The second and third codes were Choice Determining Diacritics (CDD). The second code ($CDD_1$) was one of '221', '222', '241', '242'. The third code ($CDD_2$) was one of '21', '23', '25'.

The operations can be illustrated with the following table for one of the journalists' favourite sentences: *Magnitude of angle is determined by the relation of length of arc to radius* (5: translation of величина угла определяется отношением длины дуги к радиусу). The table is adapted from [9]; it was reproduced in [4], and [7].

| Russian input | English equivalents | | 1st code | 2nd code | 3rd code | rule |
|---|---|---|---|---|---|---|
| | Eng₁ | Eng₂ | (PDD) | (CDD₁) | (CDD₂) | |
| vyelyichyina | magnitude --- | *** | *** | ** | | 6 |
| ugl- | coal | angle | 121 | *** | 25 | 2 |
| -a | of | --- | 131 | 222 | 25 | 3 |
| opryedyelyayetsya | is determined | --- | *** | *** | ** | 6 |
| otnoshyenyi- | relation | the relation | 151 | *** | ** | 5 |
| -yem | by | --- | 131 | *** | ** | 3 |
| dlyin- | length | --- | *** | *** | ** | 6 |
| -i | of | --- | 131 | *** | 25 | 3 |
| dug- | arc | --- | *** | *** | ** | 6 |
| -i | of | --- | 131 | *** | 25 | 3 |
| k | to | for | 121 | *** | 23 | 2 |
| radyius- | radius | --- | *** | 221 | ** | 6 |
| -u | to | --- | 131 | *** | ** | 3 |

The first word величина ('vyelyichyina') has just one English equivalent (*magnitude*) and its PID (***) refers to rule 6 – i.e. the result is simply copied out and there is no change of word order. The second entry is the stem 'ugl-', which initiates rule 2 by PID '121' searching for code '221' or'222' in the CDD₁ of the following entry; it finds '222', therefore the second equivalent (Eng2) of 'ugl-' is chosen (*angle*). The next entry, the suffix '-a' (of угла) with PID '131', triggers rule 3 searching for '23' in the CDD₂ of the preceding entry, which since it is not there prompts selection of the first equivalent (Eng₁ *of*) and reversal of word order (i.e. *of angle*). The next entry is the verb form 'opryedyelyayetsya' with PID '***', hence rule 6, selection of first equivalent (*is determined*) and no change of word order. The next word (отношением) has been subdivided: the stem ('otnoshyenyi-') initiates rule 5 (PID '151') searching for code '25' in the CDD₂ of the following entry (i.e. its ending) or of the next following word (stem or ending). The '25' is found in the ending '-i' of the word (длины), so the second equivalent (Eng₂) of 'otnoshyenyi-' is selected (*the relation*) and the word order is retained. The process now continues with the next entry after 'otnoshyenyi-', i.e. its instrumental ending (-yem), where the PID '131' initiates rule 3, a search for '23' in preceding entries. None is found so the first equivalent (Eng₁: *of*) is chosen and word order is reversed (i.e. *producing of the relation*). Next comes the entry 'dug-' (stem of дуги) with PID '***', i.e. selection of Eng₁ (*arc*), and no change of order; then its ending ('-i') with PID '131' (rule 3) searching for '23' in preceding entries and failing, so Eng₁ (*of*) is chosen and word order is reversed (i.e. *of arc*). The process now comes to the preposition 'k' which has two equivalents – out of the many possible translations of the Russian word – viz. *to* and *for*. Rule 2 (PID '121') searches for '221' or '222' in the CDD₁ of the following stem or ending, and finds '221' in the relevant CDD of 'radyius-'; thus, the first equivalent (Eng₁: *to*) is selected. The entry for 'radyius-' (PID '***') initiates no change. Finally, the PID '131' of its ending '-u' searches for '23' in one of the two preceding entries, finds it in the entry for the preposition 'k', selects the second equivalent (Eng₂), i.e. blank, and retains word order.

This detailed explication of the process gives rise to contradictory impressions. On the one hand there is the complexity of coding for maintaining or inverting word order. On the other there is the care to establish rules and codes of some generality, i.e. not specific to particular sentences and constructions. More specific comments follow.

Firstly, the inclusion of the full verb ('opryedyelyayetsya') was followed by Garvin for all the sentences listed above (1)-(4) which have similar Russian reflexive forms translated in English by passives ('is prepared', 'is obtained', 'is produced', 'is determined') – each occurring only in the singular. The same option is made for their corresponding non-reflexive forms (translated as 'they prepare', 'they obtain', 'they produce' – all plural – and 'determines'). Thus problems of verb morphology and choice of translation are avoided.

Russian has no articles, so the insertion of *the*, *a* and *an* in English are problems for any MT system. Garvin has reduced them by including very few in the sample sentences. They are 'the price' and 'the quality' in several sentences, which, as in this example, are derived by rule '151' and a search for '25' in a following entry. The other example is 'the science', which however initiates rule '141' and a search for code '23'. The different treatment does not reveal a clear methodology.

The example above illustrates also the method of distinguishing homonyms which newspapers reported, namely the selection of *angle* or *coal* for 'ugl-'. Rule 2 (initiated by PID '121') searches for '221' or '222' in the following entry. When it is '-a', '221' is found and the result is the choice of *angle*; when it is '-ya', '222' is found and the choice is *coal*. In fact, the original Russian is not strictly a homonym, there are two separate words: угол (*corner* or *angle*) and уголь (*coal*). Garvin's procedure is based on the fact that the genitive for угол is угола and the genitive for уголь is угля.

The example also illustrates Garvin's approach to the ambiguity (or rather multiple possible translations) of prepositions. Garvin reduces the problem by providing just two equivalents, which are selected by occurrences of '221' or '222' in the ending of the following noun – which can certainly be justified linguistically.

A number of sentences contain instrumental phrases (*by chemical process, by mechanical method*). Each are generated by the production of the preposition *by* from the case ending of the adjective and then translating the following noun as if it had no case ending. This would be regarded then and now as abnormal, since adjectival forms are held to be dependent on the nouns they are modifying, so we would expect *by* to be generated from the noun ending. For example, the phrase *by optical measurement*:

| Russian word | Eng$_1$ | Eng$_2$ | PID | CDD$_1$ | CDD$_2$ |
|---|---|---|---|---|---|
| optichesk- | optical | | *** | *** | ** |
| -yim | by | --- | 131 | *** | 23 |
| yizmyeryenyi- | measurement | | *** | *** | ** |
| -yem | by | --- | 131 | *** | ** |

The entry 'optichesk-' with PID '***' is printed out (*optical*); the suffix '-yim' initiates rule '131', fails to find CDD$_2$ '23', outputs Eng$_1$ (*by*) and inverts word order (i.e. *by optical*). The next entry 'yizmyeryenyi-' has one equivalent (*measurement*); and its suffix '-yim' invokes rule '131', finds a CDD$_2$ '23' in the preceding subdivided word (the entry for '-yim'), selects Eng$_2$ ('---') and retains word order.

From these descriptions it is apparent that much of the variety of sentences is derived from a fairly restricted set of interlocking rules and codes operating on fixed patterns into which nouns and phrase constructions are slotted.

Many of the operations are quite clearly specific to the particular words and sentences in the sample, and the rules are applied as appropriate in specific instances – this is particularly obvious in the non-chemistry sentences. There was no attempt to align rules with specific linguistic features. In particular, there was no analysis in terms of grammatical categories (noun, verb, adjective) and no representation of either agreement relations, or dependency relations, or phrase/clause structures.

## 9  The Consequences

The Russians had seen reports of the January event and the time was propitious (after the 'thaw' following Stalin's death) for the Russians to engage in the development of computers and their applications. The Institute of Precise Mechanics and Computer Technology had just completed development of BESM, the first working Russian computer, and machine translation was to be among its first applications, under the direction of Yurij Panov. By early 1956 it was ready to demonstrate a prototype system, which in many respects followed the design of the IBM-Georgetown system, with a basic set of rules for substitution, movement and morphological splitting [8].

At Georgetown itself, however, despite the widespread publicity there was no official support for further research until a grant in June 1956 from the National Science Foundation, stimulated, as it seemed at the time, by the Soviet interest [5]. The funds were in fact from the Central Intelligence Agency – Dostert had worked for its predecessor (Office for Strategic Services) and was a good friend of its director Allen Dulles. A full-scale project for Russian-English translation was organized with more than twenty researchers [5]. Initially two groups were set up: one for developing a dictionary, the other for linguistic analysis. After examining the coding of the 1954 experiment for a few months, the group decided to abandon continuation on these lines – a fact often forgotten by later critics of the Georgetown activity. There emerged a considerable divergence of opinions, and Dostert decided to give each of the proposed methods a chance to show its capability in 'free competition'. By January 1957 there were four groups, known as 'code-matching', 'syntactic analysis', 'general analysis', and 'sentence-by-sentence'. The first group, headed by Ariadne Lukjanow, assigned codes to dictionary entries which indicated grammatical and association functions and which were compared and matched during analysis. The second group under Garvin developed a method of dependency syntactic analysis later known as 'fulcrum method'. The third group under Michael Zarechnak formulated a method of sentence analysis at various levels (morphological, syntagmatic, syntactic), i.e. a variant of 'phrase structure' analysis. The fourth 'group' was a one-man project of French-English translation by A.F.R.Brown where procedures developed first for one sentence were tested on another, more procedures were added, tested on another sentence, further procedures were added, tested, and so forth. In due course, Lukjanow and Garvin left the Georgetown project to continue elsewhere, and the 'general analysis' method was adopted together with Brown's computational techniques [5], [10], [11].

## 10 The Assessments

A year after the demonstration, Dostert [2] gave an assessment of the significance of the experiment, and suggested future ideas for MT development. In his opinion, the experiment (a) „has given practical results by doing spontaneous, authentic, and clear translation", (b) showed that „the necessity of pre- and post-editing has not been verified", (c) demonstrated that „the primary problem in mechanical translation… is a problem of linguistic analysis…", (d) formulated „the basis for broader systematic lexical coding", defining „four specific areas of meaning determination… from which fruitful results may be expected", (e) developed a „functional coding system, permitting the preparation of functional, subfunctional and technical lexicons… reducing the magnitude of the coding requirements and thereby… the extent of storage needs", and (f) provided a „theory for the development of a general code for the mechanical formulation of multilingual syntax operations". These were major claims, and clearly not justified on the basis of this first small-scale experiment. Rather these were expectations Dostert had for later research.

The retrospective assessment by Garvin [3] was much more modest than Dostert's. In this somewhat defensive account of his early essay in MT research,

Garvin freely admitted the shortcomings of the experiment. The limitations were the consequence of restricting the algorithm to „a few severely limited rules, each containing a simple recognition routine with one or two simple commands." Nevertheless, in Garvin's view, the experiment was „realistic because the rules dealt with genuine decision problems, based on the identification of the two fundamental types of translation decisions: selection decisions and arrangement decisions."

Garvin summarised the limitations as of two principal types: the restriction of the search span to immediately adjacent items, the restriction of target words to just two possibilities, and the restriction of rearrangements to two immediately adjacent items. The choice of target language equivalents was restricted to those which were idiomatic for the selected sentences only. The limitation of the procedure for Russian case endings was severe: either a case suffix was not translated at all or it was translated by one „arbitrarily assigned" English preposition. Further limitations were highlighted by Michael Zarechnak [11], a member of the Georgetown group. None of the Russian sentences had negative particles; all were declaratives; there were no interrogatives or compound sentences (coordinate or subordinate clauses); and nearly all the verbs were in the third person.

Does this mean that the experiment was fixed, a deception? Naturally members of the Georgetown group deny it – pointing out that the program „was thoughtfully specified and implemented; the program ran, the translation was generated according to the program, which was developed based on... linguistic principles." [6]. This was basically true, however, only for the chemistry sentences and the rules and dictionary entries which were applied for their translation. Further chemistry sentences could clearly have been treated, with an expansion of the dictionary – but only as long as the sentences conformed to the patterns of those in the sample. There are many chemistry sentences that would obviously not be covered by the rules. Although organic chemistry might constitute a sublanguage and its vocabulary might be captured in a 'micro-glossary' (as others advocated at the time) with few ambiguities, this program in 1954 did not cover all of the field, nor indeed a substantial proportion of it. As for the non-chemistry sentences, these were clearly produced by dictionary entries and codes specifically designed for this particular demonstration; and there could have been no question of expanding general coverage on the lines of this program – as indeed was found in the later research at Georgetown.

The limitations of the experiment made it possible for the output to be impressively idiomatic, and would have suggested to many observers (not only reporters) that continued experiments on the same lines would lead to systems with larger vocabularies and even better quality. On the other hand, the experiment drew attention to the importance of the linguistic problems, and in particular that translation was not a trivial task even for the largest computer, as a contemporary commentator, Ornstein [7], remarked:

> the formulation of the logic required to convert word meanings properly, even in a small segment of two languages, necessitated as many instructions to the computer as are required to simulate the flight of a guided missile.

In truth, neither Dostert nor Garvin claimed much more than that it was a first effort (a „Kitty Hawk" experiment) – not even a prototype system. In later years, they might well have agreed that the demonstration had been premature; certainly it was made public at a stage much earlier than other contemporary MT researchers would have contemplated. However, there was another probably more important aim for Dostert; it was to attract funds for further research at Georgetown, and it succeeded.

## 11  The Implications

Undoubtedly, the wrong impression had been given that automatic translation of good quality was much closer than was in fact the case. Sponsorship and funding of MT research in the following years were more liberal (and unquestioning) than they ought to have been. The results in the next 10 years were inevitably disappointing, and as a consequence, the funders set up an investigation committee, ALPAC [1]. One of the principal arguments used by ALPAC was that MT output had to be extensively post-edited. They pointed out that the Georgetown-IBM output was of a quality that had no need of editing while that of later Georgetown systems did. The mistake of ALPAC was to ignore the preliminary nature of the 1954 experiment, that it had been specifically designed for a small sample of sentences, that it had not been a 'prototype' system but a 'showcase' intended to attract attention and funds, and that comparisons with full-scale MT systems were invalid.

In 1954, when other MT groups saw reports of Dostert's demonstration they were disparaging or dismissive. They disliked three things. One was the conduct of research through newspapers; another was the exaggerated publicity given by journalists to an obviously incomplete system; and a third was the passing-off as true 'translations' sentences which could only have been extracted as wholes from computer memories. Other MT groups were far from even thinking of demonstrating their results – and were unprepared to do so for many years to come.

It was only the first of demonstrations by the Georgetown group. Later ones were undoubtedly more genuine – systems had not been 'doctored' – but the suspicion of other MT groups was that they were not all they appeared. Such suspicions continued to haunt the Georgetown group throughout its existence and have coloured the judgements of later commentators.

It does have to be admitted, however, that the Georgetown-IBM demonstration has not been the only example of a MT system being 'doctored' for a particular occasion. In subsequent years it was not uncommon for demonstrated systems to introduce grammar and vocabulary rules specifically to deal with the sentences of a particular text sample, with the aim of showing their system in the best possible light.

In recent years MT researchers have been much more circumspect when demonstrating experimental systems and have been less willing to indulge in speculations for journalists. The painful lessons of the Georgetown-IBM demonstration seem to have been learned by MT researchers. On the other hand, some vendors of systems have a more 'liberal' attitude: many MT systems are being publicised and sold (particularly on the internet) with equally exaggerated claims and perhaps with equally damaging impact for the future of machine translation.

The historical significance of the Georgetown-IBM demonstration remains that it was an actual implementation of machine translation on an operational computer. Before 1954, all previous work on MT had been theoretical. Considering the state of the art of electronic computation at the time, it is remarkable that anything resembling automatic translation was achieved at all. Despite all its limitations, the demonstration marked the beginning of MT as a research field seen to be worthy of financial support.

## References

1.   ALPAC: *Languages and machines: computers in translation and linguistics*. A report by the Automatic Language Processing Advisory Committee, Division of Behavioral Sciences, National Academy of Sciences, National Research Council. Washington, D.C.: National Academy of Sciences – National Research Council. (1966)
2.   Dostert, Leon E. : 'The Georgetown-I.B.M. experiment', in Locke, W.N. and Booth, A.D. (eds.) *Machine translation of languages*. Cambridge, Mass.: M.I.T.Press (1955), 124-135.
3.   Garvin, Paul: 'The Georgetown-IBM experiment of 1954: an evaluation in retrospect', *Papers in linguistics in honor of Dostert*. The Hague: Mouton (1967), 46-56; reprinted in his *On machine translation* . The Hague: Mouton (1972), 51-64.
4.   Macdonald, Neil: 'Language translation by machine - a report of the first successful trial', *Computers and Automation* 3 (2), 1954, 6-10.
5.   Macdonald, R.R.: 'The history of the project' in: *General report 1952-1963*, ed. R.R.Macdonald. Washington, DC: Georgetown University Machine Translation Project (1963), 3-17. (Georgetown University Occasional Papers on Machine Translation, 30)
6.   Montgomery, Christine A.: 'Is FAHQ(M)T impossible? Memoirs of Paul Garvin and other MT colleagues', in: W. John Hutchins (ed.) *Early years in machine translation: memoirs and biographies of pioneers*. Amsterdam/Philadelphia: John Benjamins (2000), 97-110.
7.   Ornstein, Jacob: 'Mechanical translation: new challenge to communication', *Science* 122, 21 (October 1955), 745-748.
8.   Panov, Yu.N.: *Automatic translation*. Translated by R.Kisch. London: Pergamon. (1960)
9.   Sheridan, Peter: 'Research in language translation on the IBM type 701', *IBM Technical Newsletter* 9, 1955, 5-24.
10.  Vasconcellos, Muriel: 'The Georgetown project and Leon Dostert: recollections of a young assistant', in: W. John Hutchins (ed.) *Early years in machine translation: memoirs and biographies of pioneers*. Amsterdam/Philadelphia: John Benjamins (2000), 87-96.
11.  Zarechnak, Michael: 'The history of machine translation', in: Bozena Henisz-Dostert, R. Ross Macdonald and Michael Zarechnak, *Machine translation*. The Hague: Mouton (1979), 20-28.

# Pharaoh:
# A Beam Search Decoder for Phrase-Based Statistical Machine Translation Models

Philipp Koehn

Computer Science and Artificial Intelligence Laboratory
Massachusetts Institute of Technology
koehn@csail.mit.edu

**Abstract.** We describe Pharaoh, a freely available decoder for phrase-based statistical machine translation models. The decoder is the implementation of an efficient dynamic programming search algorithm with lattice generation and XML markup for external components.

Statistical machine translation has emerged as a very active research field, which has already spawned a number of commercial systems that define the state of the art translation performance for some language pairs.

Recently, phrase-based methods have been shown to produce the best translation performance. Systems that follow this approach have been developed at RWTH Aachen [Zens et al., 2002], CMU [Vogel et al., 2003], IBM [Tillmann, 2003], ISI [Koehn et al., 2003], and JHU [Kumar and Byrne, 2004].

The field's active research community has been nurtured by the availability of standard tools, most notably GIZA++ [Och and Ney, 2003] and the Rewrite Decoder [Germann, 2003], the training and decoding tools for IBM Model 4 word-based translation models. Here, we describe Pharaoh, a freely available[1] translation engine for phrase-based statistical machine translation models.

## 1 Phrase-Based Standard Model

We will now define the phrase-based statistical machine translation standard model that covers roughly all cited phrase-based approaches.

Figure 1 on the following page illustrates the process of phrase-based translation. The input is segmented into a number of sequences of consecutive words (so-called "phrases"). Each phrase is translated into an English phrase, and English phrases in the output may be reordered.

Or, more formally: During decoding, the foreign input sentence $f$ is segmented into a sequence of $I$ phrases $\bar{f}_1^I$. Each foreign phrase $\bar{f}_i$ in $\bar{f}_1^I$ is translated into an English phrase $\bar{e}_i$. The English phrases may be reordered. Phrase translation is modeled by a translation model $p(\bar{f}_i, \bar{e}_i)$.

---

[1] available at http://www.isi.edu/licensed-sw/pharaoh/

R.E. Frederking and K.B. Taylor (Eds.): AMTA 2004, LNAI 3265, pp. 115–124, 2004.

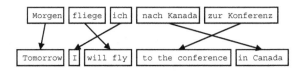

**Fig. 1.** Phrase-based machine translation: input is segmented in phrases, each phrase is translated and may be reordered.

Originally, the definition of machine translation models was motivated by the noisy channel model. The application of the Bayes rule $\text{argmax}_e p(e|f) = \text{argmax}_e p(f|e)p(e)$ allows the reformulation of the translation process from a source language (or "foreign", f) into a target language (or "English", e) into a translation component $p(f|e)$ and a separate language model component $p(e)$.

Recent empirical results do not always justify the mathematical inversion of the translation direction — $p(e|f)$ into $p(f|e)$ — and also suggest that a number of additional feature functions may be helpful [Och and Ney, 2002].

The standard model of phrase-based statistical machine translation is a log-linear model $\text{argmax}_e p(e|f) = exp(\sum_i \lambda_i h_i(e, f))$ that uses a number of feature functions $h_i$ with weights $\lambda_i$. The feature functions are typically a language model, reordering model, word penalty, and various translation models (phrase translation probability, lexical translation probability, etc.).

There is currently no agreement on what is the best method to train such phrase-translation models. Typically, given a large (10-150 million words) parallel corpus of translated material, first a word alignment is established (with GIZA++), then phrase translations are extracted, and finally a scoring function is defined – which could be derived from maximum likelihood phrase translation probability estimation, lexical translation probabilities, etc. Alternatively, a parallel corpus could be directly phrase-aligned [Marcu and Wong, 2002].

## 2    Decoder

We will now describe the search algorithm of Pharaoh. More detailed information is given by Koehn [2003]. The decoder implements a beam search and is roughly similar to work by Tillmann [2001] and Och [2002]. In fact, by reframing Och's alignment template model as a phrase translation model, the decoder is also suitable for his model (without the use of word classes).

We start with defining the concept of translation options, describe the basic mechanism of beam search, and its necessary components. We continue with details on word lattice generation and XML markup as interface for external components.

**Translation Options** — Given an input string of words, a number of phrase translations could be applied. We call each such applicable phrase translation a *translation option*. This is illustrated in Figure 2, where a number of phrase

| Maria | no | daba | una | bofetada | a | la | bruja | verde |
|---|---|---|---|---|---|---|---|---|
| Mary | not | give | a | slap | to | the | witch | green |
|  | did not |  | a slap |  | by |  | green witch |  |
|  | no |  | slap |  | to the |  |  |  |
|  | did not give |  |  |  | to |  |  |  |
|  |  |  |  |  | the |  |  |  |
|  |  | slap |  |  |  | the witch |  |  |

**Fig. 2.** Some translation options for the Spanish input sentence *Maria no daba una bofetada a la bruja verde*

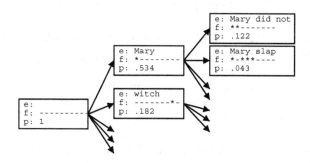

**Fig. 3.** State expansion in the beam decoder: in each expansion English words are generated, additional foreign words are covered (marked by *), and the probability cost so far is adjusted. In this example the input sentence is *Maria no daba una bofetada a la bruja verde.*

translations for the Spanish input sentence *Maria no daba una bofetada a la bruja verde* are given.

Translation options are collected before any decoding takes place. This allows a quicker lookup than consulting the phrase translation table during decoding.

**Core Algorithm** — The phrase-based decoder we developed employs a beam search algorithm, similar to the one by Jelinek [1998] for speech recognition. The English output sentence is generated left to right in form of hypotheses.

This process is illustrated in Figure 3. Starting from the initial hypothesis, the first expansion is the foreign word *Maria*, which is translated as *Mary*. The foreign word is marked as translated (marked by an asterisk). We may also expand the initial hypothesis by translating the foreign word *bruja* as *witch*.

We can generate new hypotheses from these expanded hypotheses. Given the first expanded hypothesis we generate a new hypothesis by translating *no* with *did not*. Now the first two foreign words *Maria* and *no* are marked as being covered. Following the back pointers of the hypotheses we can read of the (partial) translations of the sentence.

Given this algorithm, the size of the search space of possible translation is exponential to the length of the sentence. To overcome this, we prune out hypotheses using hypothesis recombination and by heuristic pruning.

**Recombining Hypotheses** — Recombining hypothesis is a risk-free way to reduce the search space. Two hypotheses can be recombined if they agree in (i) the foreign words covered so far, (ii) the last two English words generated, and (iii) the end of the last foreign phrase covered.

If there are two paths that lead to two hypotheses that agree in these properties, we keep only the cheaper hypothesis, e.g., the one with the least cost so far. The other hypothesis cannot be part of the path to the best translation, and we can safely discard it. We do keep a record of the additional arc for lattice generation (see below).

**Beam Search** — While the recombination of hypotheses as described above reduces the size of the search space, this is not enough for all but the shortest sentences. Let us estimate how many hypotheses (or, states) are generated during an exhaustive search. Considering the possible values for the properties of unique hypotheses, we can estimate an upper bound for the number of states by $N \simeq 2^{n_f} |V_e|^2 n_f$ where $n_f$ is the number of foreign words, and $|V_e|$ the size of the English vocabulary. In practice, the number of possible English words for the last two words generated is much smaller than $|V_e|^2$. The main concern is the exponential explosion from the $2^{n_f}$ possible configurations of foreign words covered by a hypothesis. Note this causes the problem of machine translation decoding to be NP-complete [Knight, 1999] and thus dramatically harder than, for instance, speech recognition.

In our beam search we compare the hypotheses that cover the same *number* of foreign words and prune out the inferior hypotheses. We could base the judgment of what inferior hypotheses are on the cost of each hypothesis so far. However, this is generally a very bad criterion, since it biases the search to first translating the easy part of the sentence. For instance, if there is a three word foreign phrase that easily translates into a common English phrase, this may carry much less cost than translating three words separately into uncommon English words. The search will prefer to start the sentence with the easy part and discount alternatives too early.

So, our measure for pruning out hypotheses in our beam search does not only include the cost so far, but also an estimate of the future cost. This future cost estimation should favor hypotheses that already covered difficult parts of the sentence and have only easy parts left, and discount hypotheses that covered the easy parts first. For details of our future cost estimation, see [Koehn, 2003].

Given the cost so far and the future cost estimation, we can prune out hypotheses that fall outside the beam. The beam size can be defined by threshold and histogram pruning. A relative threshold cuts out a hypothesis with a probability less than a factor $\alpha$ of the best hypotheses (e.g., $\alpha = 0.001$). Histogram pruning keeps a certain number $n$ of hypotheses (e.g., $n = 1000$).

Note that this type of pruning is not risk-free (opposed to the recombination). If the future cost estimates are inadequate, we may prune out hypotheses on the

```
initialize hypothesisStack[0 .. nf];
create initial hypothesis hyp_init;
add to stack hypothesisStack[0];
for i=0 to nf-1:
  for each hyp in hypothesisStack[i]:
    for each new_hyp that can be derived from hyp:
      nf[new_hyp] = number of foreign words covered by new_hyp;
      add new_hyp to hypothesisStack[nf[new_hyp]];
      prune hypothesisStack[nf[new_hyp]];
find best hypothesis best_hyp in hypothesisStack[nf];
output best path that leads to best_hyp;
```

**Fig. 4.** Pseudo code for the beam search algorithm

path to the best scoring translation. In a particular version of beam search, A*
search, the future cost estimate is required to be *admissible*, which means that
it never overestimates the future cost. Using best-first search and an admissible
heuristic allows pruning that is risk-free. In practice, however, this type of pruning does not sufficiently reduce the search space. See more on search in any good
Artificial Intelligence text book, such as the one by Russel and Norvig [1995].

Figure 4 describes the algorithm we used for our beam search. For each number of foreign words covered, a hypothesis stack in created. The initial hypothesis
is placed in the stack for hypotheses with no foreign words covered. Starting with
this hypothesis, new hypotheses are generated by committing to phrasal translations that covered previously unused foreign words. Each derived hypothesis
is placed in a stack based on the number of foreign words it covers.

We proceed through these hypothesis stacks, going through each hypothesis
in the stack, deriving new hypotheses for this hypothesis and placing them into
the appropriate stack (see Figure 5 for an illustration). After a new hypothesis is
placed into a stack, the stack may have to be pruned by threshold or histogram
pruning, if it has become too large. In the end, the best hypothesis of the ones
that cover all foreign words is the final state of the best translation. We can
read off the English words of the translation by following the back links in each
hypothesis.

**Generating Word Lattices** — Usually, we expect the decoder to give us
the best translation for a given input according to the model. But for some
applications, we might be interested in the top $n$ best translations.

A common method in speech recognition, that has also emerged in machine
translation [Koehn and Knight, 2003; Och et al., 2003], is: First, use a machine
translation system as a base model to generate a set of candidate translations for
each input sentence. Then, use additional features to rescore these translations.

To enable this type of work, our decoder outputs a word lattice of possible
translations for each input sentence. This lattice is taken from the search graph
of the heuristic beam search. Recall the process of state expansions, illustrated
in Figure 3. The generated hypotheses and the expansions that link them form

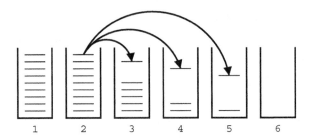

**Fig. 5.** Hypothesis expansion: Hypotheses are placed in stacks according to the number of foreign words translated so far. If a hypothesis is expanded into new hypotheses, these are placed in new stacks.

a graph. Paths branch out when there are multiple translation options for a hypothesis from which multiple new hypotheses can be derived. Paths join when hypotheses are recombined.

The graph of the hypothesis space (See Figure 3) can be viewed as a probabilistic finite state automaton. The hypotheses are states, and the records of back-links and the additionally stored arcs are state transitions. The added probability scores when expanding a hypothesis are the costs of the state transitions.

Finding the n-best path in such a probabilistic finite state automaton is a well-studied problem. In our implementation, we store the information about hypotheses, hypothesis transitions, and additional arcs in a file that can be processed by the finite state toolkit Carmel[2], which we use to generate the n-best lists. This toolkit uses the $n$ shortest paths algorithm by Eppstein [1994]. Our method is related to work by Ueffing et al. [2002] for generating n-best lists for IBM Model 4.

## 3    XML-Markup

While statistical machine translation methods cope well with many aspects of translation of languages, there are a few special problems for which better solutions exist. One example is the translation of named entities, such as proper names, dates, quantities, and numbers.

Consider the task of translating numbers, such as *17.55*. In order for a statistical machine translation system to be able to translate this number, it has to observed it in the training data. But even if it has been seen a few times, it is possible that the translation table learned for this "word" is very noisy.

Translating numbers is not a hard problem. It is therefore desirable to be able to tell the decoder up front how to translate such numbers. To continue our example of the number 17.55, this may take the following form:

```
Er erzielte <NUMBER english='17.55'> 17,55 </NUMBER> Punkte .
```

---

[2] available at http://www.isi.edu/licensed-sw/carmel/

This modified input passes to the decoder not only the German words, but also that the third word, the number *17,55*, should be translated as *17.55*.

**Phrase-Based Translation with XML Markup** — Marking a sequence of words and specifying a translation for them fits neatly into the framework of phrase-based translation. In a way, for a given phrase in the sentence, a translation is provided, which is in essence a phrase translation with translation probability 1. Only for the other parts of the sentence, translation options are generated from the phrase translation table.

Since the first step of the implementation of the beam search decoder is to collect all possible translation options, only this step has to be altered to be sensitive to specifications via XML markup. The core algorithm remains unchanged.

**Passing a Probability Distribution of Translations** — Making the hard decision of specifying the translation for parts of the sentence has some draw-backs. For instance, the number *1* may be translated as *1, one, a,* and so on into English. So we may want to provide a set of possible translations.

Instead of passing one best translation choice to the decoder, we may want to pass along a probability distribution over a set of possible translations. Given several choices, the decoder is aided by the language model to sort out which translation to use. We extend the XML markup scheme by allowing the specification of multiple English translation options along with translation probabilities.

Example: `Es ist <NPPP english='a small house|a little house' prob='0.6|0.4'> ein kleines Haus </NPPP>` .

Here, both *a small house* and *a little house* are passed along as possible translations, with the translation probabilities 0.6 and 0.4, respectively.

The scores that are passed along with the translations do not have to be probabilities in a strict sense, meaning, they do not have to add up to 1. They also do not include language model probabilities, but only the phrase translation probability for the marked part of the sentence.

**Multi-Path Integration** — By specifying a set of possible translations, we can deal with uncertainty which of the translations is the right one in a given context. But there is also the uncertainty, when to use specified translations at all. Maybe the original model has a better way to deal with the targeted words.

Recognizing that the hard decision of breaking out certain words in the input sentence and providing translations to them may be occasionally harmful, we now want to relax this decision. We allow the decoder to use the specified translations, but also to bypass them and use its own translations.

We call this multi-path integration, since we allow two pathways when translating. The path may go through the specified translations, or through translation options from the regular translation model.

## 4    Experiments

In this section, we will report on a few experiments that illustrate the speed and accuracy of the decoder at different beam sizes.

**Table 1.** Threshold pruning: hypothesis that score worse by a threshold factor than the best hypothesis in the same stack (see Figure 5) are discarded. A threshold of 0.1 gives a good trade-off between speed (15 seconds) and search errors (+1% over baseline).

| Threshold | 0.0001 | 0.001 | 0.01 | 0.05 | 0.08 | 0.1 | 0.15 | 0.2 | 0.3 |
|---|---|---|---|---|---|---|---|---|---|
| Time per Sentence | 149 sec | 119 sec | 70 sec | 27 sec | 18 sec | 15 sec | 13 sec | 10 sec | 7 sec |
| Search Errors | - | +0% | +0% | +0% | +0% | +1% | +3% | +6% | +12% |

**Table 2.** Histogram pruning: maximum number of hypothesis kept in a stack (see Figure 5). A beam size of 100 gives a good trade-off between speed (14 seconds) and search errors (+2% over baseline). Threshold pruning with factor 0.1 is applied.

| Beam Size | 1000 | 200 | 100 | 50 | 20 | 10 | 5 |
|---|---|---|---|---|---|---|---|
| Speed | 15 sec | 15 sec | 14 sec | 10 sec | 9 sec | 9 sec | 7 sec |
| Search Errors | +1% | +1% | +2% | +4% | +8% | +20% | +35% |

The translation mode has been trained on a 30 million word German-English parallel corpus extracted from European Parliament proceedings. The model uses various phrase scoring methods, e.g. maximum likelihood phrase translation, lexical translation, and word penalty. The test set used consists of 1500 sentence of average length 28.9. Translation direction is German to English.

**Threshold Pruning** — If we do not limit the beam size, the number of hypotheses in each stack grows exponentially (or polynomially when a fixed reordering limit is used).

Recall that there are two criteria to limit the number of hypotheses in each stack. One is threshold pruning, where hypotheses that are worse by a certain ratio in respect to the best hypothesis in the stack are discarded. Table 1 displays the effect of different thresholds on the speed and the accuracy of the decoder. Speed is given in translation time per sentence (excluding the start-up time for the decoder). Accuracy is given in the percentage of search errors.

Since we are dealing with some very long sentences, computing the best translation according to the model without any restrictions on the search is prohibitively expensive. We therefore report on relative search errors in respect to the translations generated by the decoder with the threshold 0.0001 and maximum beam size 1000. Table 1 reveals that search time is almost linear with the threshold. With a threshold of 0.1 we can achieve a ten-fold increase in speed with only 1% more search errors.

**Histogram Pruning** — The second pruning method, histogram pruning, limits the maximum number of hypothesis per stack. Results are given in Table 2. Using now a threshold of 0.1, noticeable changes to speed and accuracy can only be observed with very small beam size: a beam size of 10 increases the number of search errors by +20%, while barely doubling the speed.

**Limits on Translation Table** — A final strategy to increase the speed of the decoder is to reduce the number of translation options. By limiting the num-

**Table 3.** Size of translation table per input phrase: Fewer translation options speeds up the search. A beam size of 100 and a pruning threshold of 0.1 is used.

| T-Table Limit | 1000 | 500 | 200 | 100 | 50 | 20 | 10 | 5 |
|---|---|---|---|---|---|---|---|---|
| Speed | 15.0 sec | 7.6 sec | 3.8 sec | 1.9 sec | 0.9 sec | 0.4 sec | 0.2 sec | 0.1 sec |
| Search Errors | +1% | +1% | +1% | +1% | +1% | +2% | +7% | +18% |

ber of translation table entries that are used for each foreign phrase, the number of generated hypotheses can be reduced – not just the number of hypotheses that are entered into the stack.

Table 3 shows the linear increase in speed in respect to the translation table limit. If we limit the number of translation options to, say, 50, we can drop the translation time per sentence to under a second, with the same 1% relative search error.

In conclusion, using the beam threshold 0.1, maximum stack size 1000, and translation table limit 50, we can dramatically increase the speed of the decoder – by a factor of 1000 in respect to the original setting – with only limited cost in terms of search errors.

## 5   Conclusions

We described Pharaoh, a beam search decoder for phrase-based statistical machine translation models. Our experiments show that the decoder can achieve very fast translation performance (one sentence per second).

The decoder also allows the generation word lattices and n-best lists, which enable the exploration of reranking methods. An XML interface allows the integration of external knowledge, e.g., a dedicated name translation module.

We hope that the availability of the decoder fosters research in training phrase translation models and the integration of machine translation into wider natural language applications.

**Acknowledgments** — The development of the decoder was aided by many helpful hints by Franz Och. The XML markup owes much to Ulrich Germann, who developed a similar scheme for his greedy decoder for IBM Model 4 [Germann, 2003].

# References

Eppstein, D. (1994). Finding the $k$ shortest paths. In *Proc. 35th Symp. Foundations of Computer Science*, pages 154–165. IEEE.

Germann, U. (2003). Greedy decoding for statistical machine translation in almost linear time. In *Proceedings of HLT-NAACL*.

Jelinek, F. (1998). *Statistical Methods for Speech Recognition*. The MIT Press.

Knight, K. (1999). Decoding complexity in word-replacement translation models. *Computational Linguistics*, 25(4):607–615.

Koehn, P. (2003). *Noun Phrase Translation*. PhD thesis, University of Southern California, Los Angeles.

Koehn, P. and Knight, K. (2003). Feature-rich translation of noun phrases. In *41st Annual Meeting of the Association of Computational Linguistics (ACL)*.

Koehn, P., Och, F. J., and Marcu, D. (2003). Statistical phrase based translation. In *Proceedings of HLT-NAACL*.

Kumar, S. and Byrne, W. (2004). Minimum bayes-risk decoding for statistical machine translation. In *Proceedings of HLT-NAACL*.

Marcu, D. and Wong, D. (2002). A phrase-based, joint probability model for statistical machine translation. In *Proceedings of EMNLP*, pages 133–139.

Och, F. J. (2002). *Statistical Machine Translation: From Single-Word Models to Alignment Templates*. PhD thesis, RWTH Aachen, Germany.

Och, F. J., Gildea, D., Sarkar, A., Khudanpur, S., Yamada, K., Fraser, A., Shen, L., Kumar, S., Smith, D., Jain, V., Eng, K., Jin, Z., and Radev, D. (2003). Syntax for machine translation. Technical report, John Hopkins University Summer Workshop http://www.clsp.jhu.edu/ws2003/groups/translate/.

Och, F. J. and Ney, H. (2002). Discriminative training and maximum entropy models for statistical machine translation. In *Proceedings of ACL*.

Och, F. J. and Ney, H. (2003). A systematic comparison of various statistical alignment models. *Computational Linguistics*, 29(1):19–52.

Russel, S. and Norvig, P. (1995). *Artificial Intelligence: A Modern Approach*. Prentice Hall, New Jersey.

Tillmann, C. (2001). *Word Re-Ordering and Dynamic Programming based Search Algorithm for Statistical Machine Translation*. PhD thesis, RWTH Aachen, Germany.

Tillmann, C. (2003). A projection extension algorithm for statistical machine translation. In *Proceedings of EMNLP*, pages 1–8.

Ueffing, N., Och, F. J., and Ney, H. (2002). Generation of word graphs in statistical machine translation. In *Proceedings of EMNLP*, pages 156–163, Philadelphia. Association for Computational Linguistics.

Vogel, S., Zhang, Y., Huang, F., Tribble, A., Venugopal, A., Zhao, B., and Waibel, A. (2003). The CMU statistical machine translation system. In *Proceedings of the Ninth Machine Translation Summit*.

Zens, R., Och, F. J., and Ney, H. (2002). Phrase-based statistical machine translation. In *Proceedings of the German Conference on Artificial Intelligence (KI 2002)*.

# The PARS Family of Machine Translation Systems for Dutch System Description/Demonstration

Edward A. Kool[1], Michael S. Blekhman[1], Andrei Kursin[2], and Alla Rakova[2]

[1] Lingvistica b.v.
109-11115Cavendish Blvd., Montreal, H4R 2M9, QC, Canada
Tel: 1 514 331 0172
www.lingvistica.nl
[2] Lingvistica '98 Inc., Ukrainian affiliation
Tel: 1 514 331 0172
ling98@videotron.ca; ling98@canada.com
www.ling98.com,

**Abstract.** Lingvistica is developing a family of MT systems for Dutch to and from English, German, and French. PARS/H, a Dutch⇔English system, is a fully commercial product, while PARS/HD, for Dutch⇔German MT, and PARS/HF, for Dutch⇔French, are under way. The PARS/Dutch family of MT systems is based on the rule-based Lingvistica's Dutch morphological-syntactic analyzer and synthesizer dealing with vowel and consonant alterations in Dutch words, as well as Dutch syntactic analysis and synthesis. Besides, a German analyzer and synthesizer have been developed, and a similar French one is being constructed. Representative Dutch and German grammatical dictionaries have been created, comprising Dutch and German words and their complete morphological descriptions: class and subclass characteristics, alteration features, and morphological declension/conjugation paradigms. The PARS/H dictionary editor provides simple dictionary updating. Numerous specialist dictionaries are being and have been created. The user interface integrates PARS/H with MS Word and MS Internet Explorer, fully preserving the corresponding formats. Integrating with MS Excel and many other applications is under way.

In order to build up an efficient machine translation system for Dutch, it is necessary, first of all, to solve the following tasks:

- develop an efficient morphological analyzer for Dutch, which will be able to recognize the word forms in the source text, when translating from Dutch into another language;
- create an equally efficient morphological synthesizer for generating correct Dutch word forms in the target text when translating into Dutch.

Dutch is one of the languages of the Germanic group, and, although it is mainly analytical, unlike Slavic languages, it, as our experience shows, poses a lot of challenges that make its formalized representation a task far from trivial.

The PARS family of MT systems embraces the following languages:

- Slavic: Polish, Russian, Ukrainian [1]; Bulgarian is under way;
- Germanic: English, German [2], Dutch.

R.E. Frederking and K.B. Taylor (Eds.): AMTA 2004, LNAI 3265, pp. 125–129, 2004.
© Springer-Verlag Berlin Heidelberg 2004

For Dutch, we are developing the following systems:

- English⇔Dutch – PARS/H, which is now commercially available;
- German⇔Dutch (under way)
- French⇔Dutch (under way)

## 1  PARS Dictionary Editor

The dictionary editor is user friendly: in particular, it lets the lexicographer have a Dutch verb semi-automatically tagged. For tagging the Dutch words entered into the English⇔Dutch dictionaries in the PARS/H English⇔Dutch MT system, we use several tools, one of them being the automatic verb encoding mechanism. It is based on the Dutch morphology description developed in the framework of the PARS project, and recognizes the Dutch verb conjugation paradigm and alteration(s).

For example, after the Dutch verb *aandringen* has been entered into the dictionary, and the POS = Verb selected, the dictionary editor prompts that *aan* is a separable prefix. The dictionary officer confirms this and selects Irregular for the Conjugation type. After that, the dictionary editor automatically assigns the conjugation paradigm to the verb including the alterations. The paradigm is not displayed for the dictionary officer but is used by the program for morphological analysis and synthesis.

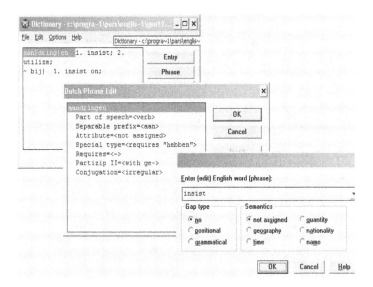

**Fig. 1.**

When tagging Dutch nouns, the lexicographer selects the relevant values for the corresponding noun features, such as Gender, endings, and alteration type.

It is important to note that creating a dictionary, one, in fact, builds two of them: an English to Dutch one as well as a Dutch to English one. This is achieved by activating the so-called *Mirror* option in the Dictionary Editor. When this option is ON, both dictionary parts are created, but, when it is OFF, the reverse correspondence is not entered into the dictionary.

Another option lets the lexicographer transpose the translations in the dictionary entry to place the most "relevant" one at the top. By doing so, the lexicographer predicts which of the translations should be used by the translation program and put into the target text, while the others will be provided as translation variants – a characteristic feature of the PARS MT systems.

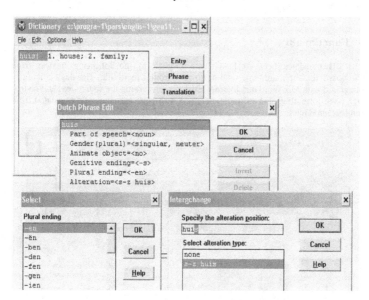

**Fig. 2.**

## 2   Grammar Rules

The PARS/H morphological analyzer and synthesizer make use of the English⇔Dutch dictionaries based on the above-mentioned grammatical features of Dutch words. This makes it possible for the analyzer to recognize any Dutch word-form in the source Dutch text, and synthesize the correct Dutch word-form in the target Dutch text. Besides, a special set of rules is aimed at decomposing the Dutch composite nouns.

This Dutch analysis and synthesis apparatus can and will be laid in the foundation of a family of Dutch MT systems, such as Dutch⇔German, Dutch⇔French (both under way), and others.

In addition to the morphological analyzer for translating to and from the Dutch language, two grammar books are used to specify and test the PARS English⇔Dutch MT program [3, 4].

Those grammar books have 1250 rules altogether, covering various issues ranging from spelling to irregular verbs in Dutch, and Present Indefinite to phrasal verbs. We are developing a translation program that would translate between English and Dutch according to those rules. Implementing the rules makes it possible to get what is usually called "draft translation".

## 3  Functionality

PARS/H translates between Dutch and English in the following modes: from Clipboard to Clipboard, drag-and-drop, and from file to file. Besides, it is fully integrated with MS Word and Internet Explorer, preserving the source text and source web page formatting. For example, here is a web page automatically translated from English into Dutch:

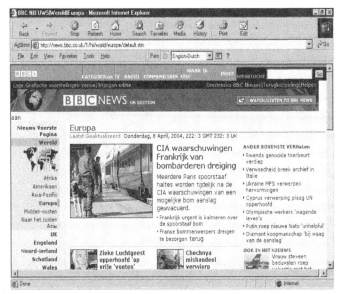

Fig. 3.

# References

1. Michael S. Blekhman. Slavic Morphology and Machine Translation. Multilingual. Volume 14, Issue 4, 2003, 28-31.
2. Michael Blekhman et al. A New Family of the PARS Translation Systems. In: Machine Translation: From Research to Real Users, 5th Conference of the Association for Machine Translation in the Americas, AMTA 2002 Tiburon, CA, USA, October 6-12, 2002, Proceedings. Lecture Notes in Computer Science 2499 Springer 2002, 232-236.
3. Nederlandse grammatica voor anderstaligen. (Dutch grammar for non-native speakers). ISBN 90 5517 014 3.
4. English Grammar in Use. Cambridge University Press. ISBN 0 521 43680 X.

# Rapid MT Experience in an LCTL (Pashto)

Craig Kopris

Senior Linguist
Applications Technology, Inc.

## 1 Introduction

A year ago we were faced with a challenge: rapidly develop a machine translation
(MT) system for written Pashto with limited resources. We had three full-time native
speakers (one with a Ph.D. in general linguistics, and translation experience) and one
part-time descriptive linguist with a typological-functional background. In addition,
we had a legacy MT software system, which neither the speakers nor the linguist was
familiar with, although we had the opportunity to occasionally confer with
experienced system users. There were also dated published grammars of varying
(usually inadequate) quality available.

Here we will describe some of our experiences in developing a grammatical
analysis, corpus, and lexicon in an implementable fashion, despite the handicaps.

## 2 Morphology and Syntax

Initial morphological analysis proceeded in a traditional manner. Pashto is a typical
inflecting language, and the basic morphology is relatively straightforward. Nouns
inflect for number (singular, plural) and case (direct, oblique). They also have
grammatical gender (masculine, feminine). Adjectives agree with nouns in number,
gender, and case. Verbs inflect for tense (present, past), aspect (perfective,
imperfective), person (first, second, third), number, and, in the third person, gender.

The speakers divided the three inflecting parts of speech into conjugation classes
and prepared paradigms of prototypical members of each conjugation class. The
paradigms were placed in tables in Word documents, following an inherited format
for which Word macros had previously been designed. These macros read the tables
and converted them into a series of morphological rules in a format that could be
compiled into the translation program. Due to difficulties with the macros, new Perl
scripts were written to create the desired output format using the same Word table
input.

Additional Perl scripts were written to generate inflected forms based on the rules
formed in the previous step. These were used to verify that the rules performed
correctly and that lexical entries were put in the proper conjugation class, so that, for
instance, (to use English examples for ease of explanation) 'say' was not incorrectly
put in the past as *'sayed' parallel to 'played', or that the alternation 'ring-rang-rung,
sing-sang-sung, drink-drank-drunk' was not used to create *'think-thank-thunk'.
Output was in the same Word table format as the original paradigms.

These rules were then compiled into the MT program, along with a small test
lexicon. Test documents consisting of inflected nouns, verbs and adjectives were

R.E. Frederking and K.B. Taylor (Eds.): AMTA 2004, LNAI 3265, pp. 130–133, 2004.
© Springer-Verlag Berlin Heidelberg 2004

translated automatically. Untranslated forms were used to diagnose problems in analysis or rule writing: in some instances, for example, verbs had been assigned to the wrong conjugation class. The morphological rules for the wrong class did not allow base forms to be parsed out, hence the forms were not found in the lexicon. When the correct conjugation class was specified, those inflected forms did of course translate.

Syntactic development followed a different tack. The MT program was designed with a Lexical-Functional Grammar (LFG) formalism in mind, and MT systems for English and Arabic had been created in that format. Pashto, however, is typologically different from English and Arabic; whereas English and Arabic are typical accusative languages, Pashto is accusative only in the present tense, following an ergative alignment in the past. Other syntactic complexities of Pashto include endoclitics and frequent discontinuous constituents.

Fortunately, the original developers of the translation software designed the program such that the users could define rules and features, rather than locking them into just the analytical framework the developers had in mind at the time. We added concepts from Role and Reference Grammar (RRG), a functional theory stressing a typological approach, to handle Pashto on its own terms. For instance, traditional concepts like 'subject' or 'object' have no descriptive value for many languages. Instead of rules for Pashto designed to force a unitary concept of 'subject', we switched to concepts from RRG. A traditional rule for verb agreement in Pashto might be stated thus:

(1) The verb agrees with the subject in the present, the transitive object in the past

Note that this rule has to mention both tense and transitivity, and leaves it unclear why some (but not all) subjects trigger agreement. Typologically, this rule could be restated more simply:

(2) The verb agrees with the nominative argument in the present, the absolutive in the past

Only tense has to be addressed in a typological perspective. An RRG-inspired rule would be:

(3) When there is more than one argument to choose from, the verb agrees with the Actor in the present, the Undergoer in the past

Again, only tense needs to be mentioned.[1] In addition to controlling verb agreement, traditional subjects can also be dropped in conjoined clauses. Thus, the English sentence,

(4) The cat saw the dogs and ran away

lacks an overt argument for the intransitive 'run away'. The unstated argument, as the subject of the intransitive, must be identical to the subject of the preceding transitive, and thus we know 'the cat' rather than 'the dogs' ran away. The dropped argument can be called the pivot. Thus, the traditional subject is both controller of verb agreement and pivot.

In Pashto, these two functions are separate. In the Pashto equivalent of 'the cat saw the dogs and ran away',

(5)   دلـﻪﻲﺗﺒﺮﻮﺕ ﺍﻭ ﻭﻠﻴــﺪﻝ ﺳــﭙﻲ ﭙﺸـــﻮ

---

[1] Technically in RRG, intransitives also have an Actor or Undergoer. However, as there is only one argument available, the choice, or rather lack thereof, is irrelevant.

pišu spi   wəlidəl aw    wətəštedəla
cat dogs saw    and   ran away

the transitive verb *wəlidəl* 'saw' agrees with the Undergoer *spi* 'dogs' since it is in the past. The intransitive *wətəštedəla* 'ran away' agrees with its sole argument. However, that argument is not *spi* 'dogs', but rather *pišu* 'cat'. In Pashto, the pivot follows an accusative pattern, like English. Thus, the traditional European-based concept of subject is not what is actually found here in Pashto.

RRG breaks these two functions of the traditional subject into separate entities. The controller of agreement and the pivot are separate functions, and need not go together. While English merges the concepts of controller and pivot, Pashto keeps them separate.

Although Pashto normally employs a word order that would traditionally be called Subject-Object-Verb, for emphatic purposes the order Object-Subject-Verb is frequently found. Note that the traditional immediate syntactic constituent 'Verb Phrase' is defined as a verb and its adjacent object. In these Pashto constructions, the verb and object are separated by the subject, and hence do not form an immediate constituent. Since the MT program was originally inspired by LFG, which lacks transformations, we could not postulate an 'underlying' different word order that gets changed through movement rules. RRG, however, lacks the concept of verb phrase. RRG constituent structures are based on the layered structure of the clause, which in turn is based on universal syntactic distinctions between predicate and argument on the one hand, and between argument and non-argument on the other. The predicate (verb) and the 'object' argument do not form a constituent. Thus, the variable word order preventing a valid verb phrase is irrelevant.

Using non-traditional concepts adapted from RRG has allowed a more straightforward analysis of Pashto syntax on its own terms. A continuing challenge has been to portray the RRG concepts in an LFG format, in order to be understood by the MT program. Additionally, the Pashto-English transfer system is challenging in the need to find equivalents between the two orientations used in the language-specific analyses.

## 3  Corpus

Our corpus started off with sentences elicited to answer typical fieldwork questions about the general nature of the language, such as word order, alignment, and clause combining techniques. These were extended at first with a set of artificial sentences showing interesting phenomena, starting relatively simple and building towards greater complexity. After the first few hundred such test sentences, we moved on to genuine texts, especially covering newspaper and journal articles.

Sentences from all sources were analyzed in a format inherited from previous work on other languages. Excel spreadsheets were set up containing each example sentence in a column, followed by each word of that sentence in rows in the next column. Additional columns were used for coding morphosyntactic and semantic features of each word, such as case, number, gender, tense, and aspect. These could thus be later used as additions to the lexicon, if not already present. Perl scripts were also developed to take raw original texts and reformat them into separate sentences and words so that only the morphosyntactic and semantic tagging needed to be added.

## 4  Lexicon

Lexicon development began with compilation by native speakers of various public domain dictionaries, further amplified by lexical items from the corpus not already part of the dictionaries. The lexicon was prepared in an Excel spreadsheet format, with each entry on a separate row. Homographs were each given their own entry. Columns were used to indicate various morphosyntactic and semantic features, not to mention the translations, similarly to the feature coding of individual words in the corpus. Pashto speakers then went through the lexicon, correcting entries. For instance, in many cases dictionaries gave obsolete terms, or forms limited to specific dialects. Some information, such as conjugation class, was not part of the original lexical sources (whether dictionary or corpus), and had to be added. Translations were checked with English speakers.

Excel macros which had previously been developed for the Arabic MT system were then used to convert the lexicon into the specific formalism used by the MT software.

## 5  Putting It All Together

The morphosyntactic rules on the one hand and the lexicon on the other are both linked to the corpus. The corpus provides it's own vocabulary list, complete with morphological and semantic features. This vocabulary can be compared directly with the lexicon, and any items not in the lexicon (and not derivable through typical rules of inflection) can be easily added. Features of words in the corpus vocabulary can also be compared with features of the same words in the lexicon. It is common, for instance, for words in corpora to primarily be used in a sense secondary to that given by traditional lexicographers.

More interesting is the relationship between the corpus and the grammar. Rules can be automatically acquired from a properly organized corpus. For instance, in an English corpus, the frequency of adjective-noun pairs will greatly exceed that of noun-adjective pairs, while a French corpus would show the reverse.

Our Pashto corpus is tagged primarily morphologically and syntactically. Although the morphological tags are standard (as mentioned at the beginning of section 2), the syntactic tagging followed a typological-functional orientation. Concepts taken from RRG, which addresses the interaction of syntax, semantics, and pragmatics, while assuming a cross-linguistic starting point, were used in developing a Four-Dimensional Matrix Approach. These matrices are usable as semantic-syntactic templates that can be filled with constituent structures.

Tagging a corpus using the Four-Dimensional Matrix provides a handle for automatic acquisition of rules. When applied to parallel corpora, equivalent structures can be pulled from both source and target languages, enabling transfer rules to be inferred.

The rules developed in the slower traditional method and those acquired automatically need not be in conflict. Rather, they provide two perspectives on the same phenomena, and the end results can be merged to improve MT performance.

# The Significance of Recall in Automatic Metrics for MT Evaluation

Alon Lavie, Kenji Sagae, and Shyamsundar Jayaraman

Language Technologies Institute
Carnegie Mellon University
{alavie,sagae,shyamj}@cs.cmu.edu

**Abstract.** Recent research has shown that a balanced harmonic mean (F1 measure) of unigram precision and recall outperforms the widely used BLEU and NIST metrics for Machine Translation evaluation in terms of correlation with human judgments of translation quality. We show that significantly better correlations can be achieved by placing more weight on recall than on precision. While this may seem unexpected, since BLEU and NIST focus on n-gram precision and disregard recall, our experiments show that correlation with human judgments is highest when almost all of the weight is assigned to recall. We also show that stemming is significantly beneficial not just to simpler unigram precision and recall based metrics, but also to BLEU and NIST.

## 1  Introduction

Automatic Metrics for machine translation (MT) evaluation have been receiving significant attention in the past two years, since IBM's BLEU metric was proposed and made available [1]. BLEU and the closely related NIST metric [2] have been extensively used for comparative evaluation of the various MT systems developed under the DARPA TIDES research program, as well as by other MT researchers. Several other automatic metrics for MT evaluation have been proposed since the early 1990s. These include various formulations of measures of "edit distance" between an MT-produced output and a reference translation [3] [4], and similar measures such as "word error rate" and "position-independent word error rate" [5], [6].

The utility and attractiveness of automatic metrics for MT evaluation has been widely recognized by the MT community. Evaluating an MT system using such automatic metrics is much faster, easier and cheaper compared to human evaluations, which require trained bilingual evaluators. In addition to their utility for comparing the performance of different systems on a common translation task, automatic metrics can be applied on a frequent and ongoing basis during system development, in order to guide the development of the system based on concrete performance improvements.

In this paper, we present a comparison between the widely used BLEU and NIST metrics, and a set of easily computable metrics based on unigram precision and recall. Using several empirical evaluation methods that have been proposed

R.E. Frederking and K.B. Taylor (Eds.): AMTA 2004, LNAI 3265, pp. 134–143, 2004.
© Springer-Verlag Berlin Heidelberg 2004

in the recent literature as concrete means to assess the level of correlation of automatic metrics and human judgments, we show that higher correlations can be obtained with fairly simple and straightforward metrics. While recent researchers [7] [8] have shown that a balanced combination of precision and recall (F1 measure) has improved correlation with human judgments compared to BLEU and NIST, we claim that even better correlations can be obtained by assigning more weight to recall than to precision. In fact, our experiments show that the best correlations are achieved when recall is assigned almost all the weight. Previous work by Lin and Hovy [9] has shown that a recall-based automatic metric for evaluating summaries outperforms the BLEU metric on that task. Our results show that this is also the case for evaluation of MT. We also demonstrate that stemming both MT-output and reference strings prior to their comparison, which allows different morphological variants of a word to be considered as "matches", significantly further improves the performance of the metrics.

We describe the metrics used in our evaluation in Section 2. We also discuss certain characteristics of the BLEU and NIST metrics that may account for the advantage of metrics based on unigram recall. Our evaluation methodology and the data used for our experimentation are described in section 3. Our experiments and their results are described in section 4. Future directions and extensions of this work are discussed in section 5.

## 2    Evaluation Metrics

The metrics used in our evaluations, in addition to BLEU and NIST, are based on explicit word-to-word matches between the translation being evaluated and each of one or more reference translations. If more than a single reference translation is available, the translation is matched with each reference *independently*, and the best-scoring match is selected. While this does not allow us to simultaneously match different portions of the translation with different references, it supports the use of recall as a component in scoring each possible match. For each metric, including BLEU and NIST, we examine the case where matching requires that the matched word in the translation and reference be identical (the standard behavior of BLEU and NIST), and the case where stemming is applied to both strings prior to the matching[1]. In the second case, we stem both translation and references prior to matching and then require identity on stems. We plan to experiment in the future with less strict matching schemes that will consider matching synonymous words (with some cost), as described in section 5.

### 2.1    BLEU and NIST

The main principle behind IBM's BLEU metric [1] is the measurement of the overlap in unigrams (single words) and higher order n-grams of words, between a

---

[1] We include BLEU and NIST in our evaluations on stemmed data, but since neither one includes stemming as part of the metric, the resulting BLEU-stemmed and NIST-stemmed scores are not truly BLEU and NIST scores. They serve to illustrate the effectiveness of stemming in MT evaluation.

translation being evaluated and a set of one or more reference translations. The main component of BLEU is n-gram precision: the proportion of the matched n-grams out of the total number of n-grams in the evaluated translation. Precision is calculated separately for each n-gram order, and the precisions are combined via a geometric averaging. BLEU does not take recall into account directly. Recall – the proportion of the matched n-grams out of the total number of n-grams in the reference translation, is extremely important for assessing the quality of MT output, as it reflects to what degree the translation covers the entire content of the translated sentence. BLEU does not use recall because the notion of recall is unclear when simultaneously matching against multiple reference translations (rather than a single reference). To compensate for recall, BLEU uses a *Brevity Penalty*, which penalizes translations for being "too short". The NIST metric is conceptually similar to BLEU in most aspects, including the weaknesses discussed below:

- **The Lack of Recall:** We believe that the brevity penalty in BLEU does not adequately compensate for the lack of recall. Our experimental results strongly support this claim.
- **Lack of Explicit Word-matching Between Translation and Reference:** N-gram counts don't require an explicit word-to-word matching, but this can result in counting incorrect "matches", particularly for common function words. A more advanced metric that we are currently developing (see section 4.3) uses the explicit word-matching to assess the grammatical coherence of the translation.
- **Use of Geometric Averaging of N-grams:** Geometric averaging results in a score of "zero" whenever one of the component n-gram scores is zero. Consequently, BLEU scores at the sentence level can be meaningless. While BLEU was intended to be used only for aggregate counts over an entire test-set (and not at the sentence level), a metric that exhibits high levels of correlation with human judgments at the sentence level would be highly desirable. In experiments we conducted, a modified version of BLEU that uses equal-weight arithmetic averaging of n-gram scores was found to have better correlation with human judgments at both the sentence and system level.

## 2.2   Metrics Based on Unigram Precision and Recall

The following metrics were used in our evaluations:

1. **Unigram Precision:** As mentioned before, we consider only exact one-to-one matches between words. Precision is calculated as follows:

$$P = \frac{m}{w_t}$$

where $m$ is the number of words in the translation that match words in the reference translation, and $w_t$ is the number of words in the translation. This may be interpreted as *the fraction of the words in the translation that are present in the reference translation.*

2. **Unigram Precision with Stemming:** Same as above, but the translation and references are stemmed before precision is computed.
3. **Unigram Recall:** As with precision, only exact one-to-one word matches are considered. Recall is calculated as follows:

$$R = \frac{m}{w_r}$$

where $m$ is the number of matching words, and $w_r$ is the number of words in the reference translation. This may be interpreted as *the fraction of words in the reference that appear in the translation.*
4. **Unigram Recall with Stemming:** Same as above, but the translation and references are stemmed before recall is computed.
5. $F_1$: The harmonic mean [10] of precision and recall. $F_1$ is computed as follows:

$$F_1 = \frac{2PR}{P+R}$$

6. $F_1$ **with Stemming:** Same as above, but using the stemmed version of both precision and recall.
7. **Fmean:** This is similar to $F_1$, but recall is weighted nine times more heavily than precision. The precise amount by which recall outweighs precision is less important than the fact that most of the weight is placed on recall. The balance used here was estimated using a development set of translations and references (we also report results on a large test set that was not used in any way to determine any parameters in any of the metrics). Fmean is calculated as follows:

$$Fmean = \frac{10PR}{9P+R}$$

## 3   Evaluating MT Evaluation Metrics

### 3.1   Data

We evaluated the metrics described in section 2 and compared their performances with BLEU and NIST on two large data sets: the DARPA/TIDES 2002 and 2003 Chinese-to-English MT Evaluation sets. The data in both cases consists of approximately 900 sentences with four reference translations each. Both evaluations had corresponding human assessments, with two human judges evaluating each translated sentence. The human judges assign an Adequacy Score and a Fluency Score to each sentence. Each score ranges from one to five (with one being the poorest grade and five the highest). The adequacy and fluency scores of the two judges for each sentence are averaged together, and an overall average adequacy and average fluency score is calculated for each evaluated system. The total human score for each system is the sum of the average adequacy and average fluency scores, and can range from two to ten. The data from the 2002 evaluation contains system output and human evaluation scores for seven systems. The 2003 data includes system output and human evaluation scores for six systems. The 2002 set was used in determining the weights of precision and recall in the Fmean metric.

### 3.2  Evaluation Methodology

Our goal in the evaluation of the MT scoring metrics is to effectively quantify how well each metric correlates with human judgments of MT quality. Several different experimental methods have been proposed and used in recent work by various researchers. In our experiments reported here, we use two methods of assessment:

1.  **Correlation of Automatic Metric Scores and Human Scores at the System-level:** We plot the automatic metric score assigned to each tested system against the average total human score assigned to the system, and calculate a correlation coefficient between the metric scores and the human scores. Melamed et al [7], [8] suggest using the Spearman rank correlation coefficient as an appropriate measure for this type of correlation experiment. The rank correlation coefficient abstracts away from the absolute scores and measures the extent to which the two scores (human and automatic) similarly rank the systems. We feel that this rank correlation is not a sufficiently sensitive evaluation criterion, since even poor automatic metrics are capable of correctly ranking systems that are very different in quality. We therefore opted to evaluate the correlation using the Pearson correlation coefficient, which takes into account the distances of the data points from an optimal regression curve. This method has been used by various other researchers [6] and also in the official DARPA/TIDES evaluations.

2.  **Correlation of Score Differentials between Pairs of Systems:** For each pair of systems we calculate the differentials between the systems for both the human score and the metric score. We then plot these differentials and calculate a Pearson correlation coefficient between the differentials. This method was suggested by Coughlin [11]. It provides significantly more data points for establishing correlation between the MT metric and the human scores. It makes the reasonable assumption that the differentials of automatic metric and human scores should highly correlate. This assumption is reasonable if both human scores and metric scores are linear in nature, which is generally true for the metrics we compare here.

As mentioned before, the values presented in this paper are Pearson's correlation coefficients, and consequently they range from -1 to 1, with 1 representing a very strong association between the automatic score and the human score. Thus the different metrics are assessed primarily by looking at which metric has a higher correlation coefficient in each scenario.

In order to validate the statistical significance of the differences in the scores, we apply a commonly used bootstrapping sampling technique [12] to estimate the variability over the test set, and establish confidence intervals for each of the system scores and the correlation coefficients.

**Table 1.** Correlation coefficients with human judgments for each metric on the DARPA/TIDES 2002 Chinese data set

| Metric | Pearson's Coefficient | Confidence Interval |
|---|---|---|
| NIST | 0.603 | +/- 0.049 |
| NIST-stem | **0.740** | +/- 0.043 |
| BLEU | 0.461 | +/- 0.058 |
| BLEU-stem | 0.528 | +/- 0.061 |
| P | 0.175 | +/- 0.052 |
| P-stem | 0.257 | +/- 0.065 |
| R | 0.615 | +/- 0.042 |
| R-stem | **0.757** | +/- 0.042 |
| F1 | 0.425 | +/- 0.047 |
| F1-stem | 0.564 | +/- 0.052 |
| Fmean | 0.585 | +/- 0.043 |
| Fmean-stem | **0.733** | +/- 0.044 |

## 4   Metric Evaluation

### 4.1   Correlation of Automatic Metric Scores and Human Scores at the System-Level

We first compare the various metrics in terms of the correlation they have with total human scores at the system level. For each metric, we plot the metric and total human scores assigned to each system and calculate the correlation coefficient between the two scores. Tables 1 and 2 summarize the results for the various metrics on the 2002 and 2003 data sets. All metrics show much higher levels of correlation with human judgments on the 2003 data, compared with the 2002 data. The 2002 data exhibits several anomalies that have been identified and discussed by several other researchers [13]. Three of the 2002 systems have output that contains significantly higher amounts of "noise" (non ascii characters) and upper-cased words, which are detrimental to the automatic metrics. The variability within the 2002 set is also much higher than within the 2003 set, as reflected by the confidence intervals of the various metrics.

The levels of correlation of the different metrics are quite consistent across both 2002 and 2003 data sets. Unigram-recall and F-mean have significantly higher levels of correlation than BLEU and NIST. Unigram-precision, on the other hand, has a poor level of correlation. The performance of F1 is inferior to F-mean on the 2002 data. On the 2003 data, F1 is inferior to Fmean, but stemmed F1 is about equivalent to Fmean. Stemming improves correlations for all metrics on the 2002 data. On the 2003 data, stemming improves correlation on all metrics except for recall and Fmean, where the correlation coefficients are already so high that stemming no longer has a statistically significant effect. Recall, Fmean and NIST also exhibit more stability than the other metrics, as reflected by the confidence intervals.

**Table 2.** Correlation coefficients with human judgments for each metric on the DARPA/TIDES 2003 Chinese data set

| Metric | Pearson's Coefficient | Confidence Interval |
|---|---|---|
| NIST | 0.892 | +/- 0.013 |
| NIST-stem | 0.915 | +/- 0.010 |
| BLEU | 0.817 | +/- 0.021 |
| BLEU-stem | 0.843 | +/- 0.018 |
| P | 0.683 | +/- 0.041 |
| P-stem | 0.752 | +/- 0.041 |
| R | **0.961** | +/- 0.011 |
| R-stem | **0.940** | +/- 0.014 |
| F1 | 0.909 | +/- 0.025 |
| F1-stem | **0.948** | +/- 0.014 |
| Fmean | **0.959** | +/- 0.012 |
| Fmean-stem | **0.952** | +/- 0.013 |

### 4.2   Correlation of Score Differentials Between Pairs of Systems

We next calculated the score differentials for each pair of systems that were evaluated and assessed the correlation between the automatic score differentials and the human score differentials. The results of this evaluation are summarized in Tables 3 and 4. The results of the system pair differential correlation experiments are very consistent with the system-level correlation results. Once again, Unigram-recall and F-mean have significantly higher levels of correlation than BLEU and NIST. The effects of stemming are somewhat less pronounced in this evaluation.

### 4.3   Discussion

It is clear from these results that unigram-recall has a very strong correlation with human assessment of MT quality, and stemming often strengthens this correlation. This follows the intuitive notion that MT system output should contain as much of the system output should contain as much of the meaning of the input as possible. It is perhaps surprising that unigram-precision, on the other hand, has such low correlation. It is still important, however, to factor precision into the final score assigned to a system, to prevent systems that output very long translations from receiving inflated scores (as an extreme example, a system that outputs every word in its vocabulary for every translation would consistently score very high in unigram recall, regardless of the quality of the translation). Our Fmean metric is effective in combining precision and recall. Because recall is weighted heavily, the Fmean scores have high correlations. For both data sets tested, recall and Fmean performed equally well (differences were statistically insignificant), even though precision performs much worse. Because we use a weighted harmonic mean, where precision and recall are multiplied, low

**Table 3.** Correlation coefficients for pairwise system comparisons on the DARPA/TIDES 2002 Chinese data set

| Metric | Pearson's Coefficient | Confidence Interval |
|---|---|---|
| NIST | 0.679 | +/- 0.042 |
| NIST-stem | 0.774 | +/- 0.041 |
| BLEU | 0.498 | +/- 0.054 |
| BLEU-stem | 0.559 | +/- 0.058 |
| P | 0.298 | +/- 0.051 |
| P-stem | 0.325 | +/- 0.064 |
| R | 0.743 | +/- 0.032 |
| R-stem | **0.845** | +/- 0.029 |
| F1 | 0.549 | +/- 0.042 |
| F1-stem | 0.643 | +/- 0.046 |
| Fmean | 0.711 | +/- 0.033 |
| Fmean-stem | **0.818** | +/- 0.032 |

levels of precision properly penalize the Fmean score (thus disallowing the case of a system scoring high simply by outputting many words).

One feature of BLEU and NIST that is not included in simple unigram-based metrics is the approximate notion of word order or grammatical coherence achieved by the use of higher-level n-grams. We have begun development of a new metric that combines the Fmean score with an explicit measure of grammatical coherence. This metric, METEOR (Metric for Evaluation of Translation with Explicit word Ordering), performs a maximal-cardinality match between translations and references, and uses the match to compute a coherence-based penalty. This computation is done by assessing the extent to which the matched words between translation and reference constitute well ordered coherent "chunks". Preliminary experiments with METEOR have yielded promising results, achieving similar levels of correlation (but so far not statistically significantly superior) as compared to the simpler measures of Fmean and recall.

## 5   Current and Future Work

We are currently in the process of enhancing the METEOR metric in several directions:

*Expanding the Matching between Translation and References:* Our experiments indicate that stemming already significantly improves the quality of the metric by expanding the matching. We plan to experiment with further expanding the matching to include synonymous words, by using information from synsets in WordNet. Since the reliability of such matches is likely to be somewhat reduced, we will consider assigning such matches a lower confidence that will be taken into account within score computations.

**Table 4.** Correlation coefficients for pairwise system comparisons on the DARPA/TIDES 2003 Chinese data set

| Metric | Pearson's Coefficient | Confidence Interval |
|---|---|---|
| NIST | 0.886 | +/- 0.017 |
| NIST-stem | 0.924 | +/- 0.013 |
| BLEU | 0.758 | +/- 0.027 |
| BLEU-stem | 0.793 | +/- 0.025 |
| P | 0.573 | +/- 0.053 |
| P-stem | 0.666 | +/- 0.058 |
| R | **0.954** | +/- 0.014 |
| R-stem | 0.923 | +/- 0.018 |
| F1 | 0.881 | +/- 0.024 |
| F1-stem | **0.950** | +/- 0.017 |
| Fmean | **0.954** | +/- 0.015 |
| Fmean-stem | 0.940 | +/- 0.017 |

*Combining Precision, Recall and Sort Penalty:* Results so far indicate that recall plays the most important role in obtaining high-levels of correlation with human judgments. We are currently exploring alternative ways for combining the components of precision, recall and a coherence penalty with the goal of optimizing correlation with human judgments, and exploring whether an optimized combination of these factors on one data set is also persistent in performance across different data sets.

*The Utility of Multiple Reference Translations:* The metrics described use multiple reference translations in a weak way: we compare the translation with each reference separately and select the reference with the best match. This was necessary in order to incorporate recall in our metric, which we have shown to be highly advantageous. We are in the process of quantifying the utility of multiple reference translations across the metrics by measuring the correlation improvements as a function of the number of reference translations. We will then consider exploring ways in which to improve our matching against multiple references. Recent work by Pang, Knight and Marcu [14] provides the mechanism for producing semantically meaningful additional "synthetic" references from a small set of real references. We plan to explore whether using such synthetic references can improve the performance of our metric.

*Matched Words are not Created Equally:* Our current metrics treats all matched words between a system translation and a reference equally. It is safe to assume, however, that matching semantically important words should carry significantly more weight than the matching of function words. We plan to explore schemes for assigning different weights to matched words, and investigate if such schemes can further improve the sensitivity of the metric and its correlation with human judgments of MT quality.

**Acknowledgments.** This research was funded in part by NSF grant number IIS-0121631.

# References

1. Papineni, Kishore, Salim Roukos, Todd Ward, and Wei-Jing Zhu. 2002. BLEU: a Method for Automatic Evaluation of Machine Translation. In *Proceedings of 40th Annual Meeting of the Association for Computational Linguistics (ACL)*, pages 311–318, Philadelphia, PA, July.
2. Doddington, George. 2002. Automatic Evaluation of Machine Translation Quality Using N-gram Co-Occurrence Statistics. In *Proceedings of the Second Conference on Human Language Technology (HLT-2002)*. San Diego, CA. pp. 128–132.
3. K.-Y. Su, M.-W. Wu, and J.-S. Chang. 1992. A New Quantitative Quality Measure for Machine Translation Systems. In *Proceedings of the fifteenth International Conference on Computational Linguistics (COLING-92)*. Nantes, France. pp. 433–439.
4. Y. Akiba, K. Imamura, and E. Sumita. 2001. Using Multiple Edit Distances to Automatically Rank Machine Translation Output. In *Proceedings of MT Summit VIII.* Santiago de Compostela, Spain. pp. 15–20.
5. S. Niessen, F. J. Och, G. Leusch, and H. Ney. 2000. An Evaluation Tool for Machine Translation: Fast Evaluation for Machine Translation Research. In *Proceedings of the Second International Conference on Language Resources and Evaluation (LREC-2000)*. Athens, Greece. pp. 39–45.
6. Gregor Leusch, Nicola Ueffing and Herman Ney. 2003. String-to-String Distance Measure with Applications to Machine Translation Evaluation. In *Proceedings of MT Summit IX.* New Orleans, LA. Sept. 2003. pp. 240–247.
7. I. Dan Melamed, R. Green and J. Turian. 2003. Precision and Recall of Machine Translation. In *Proceedings of HLT-NAACL 2003.* Edmonton, Canada. May 2003. Short Papers: pp. 61–63.
8. Joseph P. Turian, Luke Shen and I. Dan Melamed. 2003. Evaluation of Machine Translation and its Evaluation. In *Proceedings of MT Summit IX.* New Orleans, LA. Sept. 2003. pp. 386–393.
9. Chin-Yew Lin and Eduard Hovy. 2003. Automatic Evaluation of Summaries Using N-gram Co-occurrence Statistics. In *Proceedings of HLT-NAACL 2003.* Edmonton, Canada. May 2003. pp. 71–78.
10. C. van Rijsbergen. 1979. Information Retrieval. Butterworths. London, England. 2nd Edition.
11. Deborah Coughlin. 2003. Correlating Automated and Human Assessments of Machine Translation Quality. In *Proceedings of MT Summit IX.* New Orleans, LA. Sept. 2003. pp. 63–70.
12. Bradley Efron and Robert Tibshirani. 1986. Bootstrap Methods for Standard Errors, Confidence Intervals, and Other Measures of Statistical Accuracy. *Statistical Science, 1(1)*. pp. 54–77.
13. George Doddington. 2003. Automatic Evaluation of Language Translation using N-gram Co-occurrence Statistics. Presentation at DARPA/TIDES 2003 MT Workshop. NIST, Gathersberg, MD. July 2003.
14. Bo Pang, Kevin Knight and Daniel Marcu. 2003. Syntax-based Alignment of Multiple Translations: Extracting Paraphrases and Generating New Sentences. In *Proceedings of HLT-NAACL 2003.* Edmonton, Canada. May 2003. pp. 102–109.

# Alignment of Bilingual Named Entities in Parallel Corpora Using Statistical Model

Chun-Jen Lee[1,2], Jason S. Chang[2], and Thomas C. Chuang[3]

[1] Telecommunication Labs., Chunghwa Telecom Co., Ltd.,
Chungli, Taiwan, ROC
cjlee@cht.com.tw

[2] Department of Computer Science, National Tsing Hua University,
Hsinchu, Taiwan, ROC
jschang@cs.nthu.edu.tw

[3] Vanung University,
Chungli, Taiwan, ROC
tomchuang@msa.vnu.edu.tw

**Abstract.** Named entities make up a bulk of documents. Extracting named entities is crucial to various applications of natural language processing. Although efforts to identify named entities within monolingual documents are numerous, extracting bilingual named entities has not been investigated extensively owing to the complexity of the task. In this paper, we describe a statistical phrase translation model and a statistical transliteration model. Under the proposed models, a new method is proposed to align bilingual named entities in parallel corpora. Experimental results indicate that a satisfactory precision rate can be achieved. To enhance the performance, we also describe how to improve the proposed method by incorporating approximate matching and person name recognition. Experimental results show that performance is significantly improved with the enhancement.

## 1 Introduction

Named Entities (NEs) make up a bulk of text documents. Extracting and translating NE is vital for research areas in natural language processing-related topics, including machine translation, cross-language information retrieval, and bilingual lexicon construction. At the 7th Message Understanding Conference (MUC-7), the NE task [6] consisted of three subtasks: entity names (organizations (ORG), persons (PER), and locations (LOC)), temporal expressions (dates, times), and number expressions (monetary values, percentages). We will focus on extracting the first type of NE phrases, i.e. entity names.

Although many investigators have reported on the NE identification within monolingual documents, the feasibility of extracting interlingual NEs has seldom been addressed owing to the complexity of the task. Al-Onaizan and Knight [1] proposed an algorithm to translate NEs from Arabic to English using monolingual and bilingual

R.E. Frederking and K.B. Taylor (Eds.): AMTA 2004, LNAI 3265, pp. 144–153, 2004.

resources. Huang and Vogel [8] proposed an iterative approach to extract English-Chinese NE pairs from bilingual corpora using a statistical NE alignment model. Chen et al. [5] investigated formulation and transformation rules for English-Chinese NEs. Moore [13] proposed an approach to choose English-French NE pairs in parallel corpora using a multiple progressively refined models. Kumano et al. [9] presented a method for acquiring English-Japanese NE pairs from parallel corpora. In our previous work, Lee et al. [11] proposed an approach using a phrase translation model and a transliteration model to align English-Chinese NE pairs in parallel corpora. In this paper, we improve on that previous work by integrating statistical models with approximate matching and additional knowledge source to align English-Chinese NE pairs in parallel corpora. Experimental results show greatly improved performance.

## 2   Baseline Method

For the sake of comparison, we first describe a baseline method that directly utilizes a phrase translation model and a transliteration model to align bilingual NE pairs in parallel corpora. Then, we describe a modified phrase translation model and a scoring formula to determine the alignment scores of NE pairs.

### 2.1   Our Previous Work

In our previous work, Chang et al. [4] proposed a statistical translation model to perform noun phrase translation and Lee and Chang [10] proposed a statistical transliteration model to conduct machine transliteration. We briefly describe the above models in this subsection.

**Statistical Phrase Translation Model (SPTM)**
In the noisy channel approach to machine translation proposed by Brown et al. [3], a source sentence $e$ is fed into a noisy channel and translated to a target sentence $f$. Following Brown et al [3], we model the probability of translating an English phrase $e$ with $l$ words into a Mandarin Chinese phrase $f$ with $m$ words by decomposing the channel function into two independent probabilistic functions: (a) lexical translation probability function $P(f_{a_i} | e_i)$ where $e_i$ is the $i$-th word in $e$ and $e_i$ is aligned with $f_{a_i}$ in $f$ under the alignment $a$, and (b) alignment probability function $P(a | l, m) = P(a_1, a_2, ..., a_l | l, m)$.

Based on the above model, finding the best translation $f^*$, for a given $e$, is the following:

$$f^* = \arg\max_f P(f | e) = \arg\max_f \sum_a P(f, a | e).  \tag{1}$$

For simplicity, the best alignment with the highest probability is chosen to decide the most probable translation $f^*$, instead of summing all possible alignments $a$. Thus, we have:

$$f^* = \operatorname*{arg\,max}_{f} \max_{a} P(f,a \mid e) = \operatorname*{arg\,max}_{f} \max_{a} P(a \mid l,m) \times \prod_{i=1,l} P(f_{a_i} \mid e_i). \tag{2}$$

In the original formulation, Brown et al decompose probability of alignment for a sentence as the product of the alignment of $i$-th word for $i = 1$ to $l$. Since the number $l$ is usually quite small for phrase to phrase translation, it might be better to compute the phrase alignment probability as a whole instead of the product of individual word alignment $P(a_i \mid i, l, m)$. Therefore, we have:

$$P(a \mid l,m) \equiv P(a_1,a_2,...,a_l \mid l,m). \tag{3}$$

For example, consider the case where the source phrase, $E$ = "Ichthyosis Concern Association" and its Chinese phrase of translation, $F$ = "關懷 魚鱗癬 協會". The correct alignment is ($a_1 = 2$, $a_2 = 1$, $a_3 = 3$). Thus, the phrase translation probability is represented as:

$$P(關懷 \ 魚鱗癬 \ 協會 \mid Ichthyosis\,Concern\,Association) \approx \tag{4}$$
$$P(魚鱗癬 \mid Ichthyosis) \times P(關懷 \mid Concern) \times P(協會 \mid Association) \times P(2,1,3 \mid 3,3).$$

Based on the modified formulation for alignment probability, the best translation $f^*$, for a given $e$, is performed by Eq. (5):

$$f^* = \operatorname*{arg\,max}_{f} \max_{a} P(f,a \mid e) = \operatorname*{arg\,max}_{f} \max_{a} P(a_1 a_2 ... a_n \mid l,m) \times \prod_{i=1,l} P(f_{a_i} \mid e_i) \tag{5}$$

The integrated score function for the target phrase $f$, given $e$, is defined as follows, by regarding the score function as a log probability function.

$$Score_{SPTM}(f \mid e) \equiv \log(P(a \mid l,m) \prod_{i=1,l} P(f_{a_i} \mid e_i)) \tag{6}$$
$$= \log P(a \mid l,m) + \sum_{i=1,l} Score_{lex}(f_{a_i} \mid e_i),$$

$$Score_{lex}(f_a \mid e) \equiv \sum_{i=1,l} Score_{lex}(f_{a_i} \mid e_i). \tag{7}$$

**Estimating Lexical Translation Probability (LTP) Based on Parallel Corpus**

Although, in bilingual NE translation, a general bilingual dictionary contains translations for many common words, many domain-specific words are usually not covered, such as terminology and proper nouns. However, manually constructing bilingual lexicons is a labor-intensive and time-consuming process. Therefore, the development of methods for automatically exploiting domain-specific bilingual lexicons from the relevant bilingual corpus is essential. To do so, we adopt a word alignment module based on syntactic and statistical analyses [14]. Firstly, we develop a list of preferred part-of-speech (POS) patterns of collocation in both languages. We then conduct collocation candidates matching to the preferred POS patterns and apply N-gram statistics for both languages. The log likelihood ratio statistics is employed for two consecutive words in both languages. Finally, we deploy content word alignment based on the Competitive Linking Algorithm [12].

For the purpose of not introducing too much noise, only bilingual phrases with high probabilities are considered. The integrated lexical translation probability $P(f_{a_i} \mid e_i)$ is estimated using the linear interpolation strategy:

$$P(f_{a_i} \mid e_i) = \lambda_2 P_{gen}(f_{a_i} \mid e_i) + (1 - \lambda_2) P_{cor}(f_{a_i} \mid e_i), \tag{8}$$

where $P_{gen}(f_{a_i} \mid e_i)$ and $P_{cor}(f_{a_i} \mid e_i)$ are estimated from a general bilingual diction-ary and a domain-relevant corpus, respectively, and $\lambda_2$ is an interpolation constant. $P_{gen}(f_{a_i} \mid e_i)$ and $P_{cor}(f_{a_i} \mid e_i)$ are weighted according to their contribution to the discrimination power. Currently, $\lambda_2$ is empirically set to 0.3.

### Estimating Lexical Translation Probability Based on Transliteration Model (TM)

Since each of the nouns in the phrase being translated may be a common noun or a proper noun. For common nouns, we rely on previous work in word alignment to estimate lexical translation probability. For proper nouns, we consider machine trans-literation for estimation of LTP. Mandarin Chinese and English are disparate lan-guages and no simple rules are available for direct mapping between them based on sounds, one possible solution is to adopt a Chinese Romanization system to represent the pronunciation of each Chinese character and then find the mapping rules between them. In the following discussion, $E$ and $F$ are assumed to be an English word and a Romanized Chinese character sequence, respectively. The transliteration probability $P(F|E)$ can be approximated by decomposing $E$ and $F$ into transliteration units (TUs). A TU is defined as a sequence of characters transliterated as a group.

A word $E$ with $l$ characters and a Romanized word $F$ with $m$ characters are denoted by $e_1 e_2 \ldots e_l$ and $f_1 f_2 \ldots f_m$ respectively. We can represent the mapping of $(E, F)$ as a sequence of matched $n$ TUs, $\{(u_1, v_1), (u_2, v_2), \ldots (u_n, v_n) \}$:

$$\begin{cases} E = e_1 e_2 \ldots e_l = u_1 u_2 \ldots u_n \\ T = f_1 f_2 \ldots f_m = v_1 v_2 \ldots v_n, \end{cases} \tag{9}$$

Hence, the alignment $a$ between $E$ and $F$ can be represented as a sequence of match type $(m_1 m_2 \ldots m_n)$ where $m_i$ denotes as a pair of lengths of $u_i$ and $v_i$. Therefore, the probability of $F$ given $E$, $P(F|E)$, is formulated as follows:

$$P(F|E) = \sum_a P(F, a \mid E). \tag{10}$$

From the above definitions and independent assumptions, Eq. (10) is rewritten as:

$$P(F \mid E) = \sum_a P(v_1 v_2 \ldots v_n \mid u_1 u_2 \ldots u_n) P(m_1 m_2 \ldots m_n) = \sum_a \prod_{i=1}^n P(v_i \mid u_i) P(m_i). \tag{11}$$

However, to reduce the amount of computation, the process of finding the most probable transliteration $F^*$, for a given $E$, can be approximated as:

$$F^* = \arg \max_F \max_a P(F, a \mid E) = \arg \max_F \max_a \prod_{i=1}^n P(v_i \mid u_i) P(m_i). \tag{12}$$

Then, by regarding the score function as a log probability function, the transliteration score function for $F$, given $E$, is defined as

$$Score_{tm}(F \mid E) = \max_a \log(\prod_{i=1}^n P(v_i \mid u_i) P(m_i)). \tag{13}$$

## 2.2  Named Entity Alignment

To tackle the insertion and the deletion problems frequently happening to English-Chinese NE phrase translation, we are motivated to apply the approximate phrase matching method similar to the method proposed by Damerau [7]. We assume that $l$ and $m$ are the number of words of $e$ and $f$, respectively. Then the best match $g(l,m)$ between $e$ and $f$ is calculated using the recurrence relation shown as follows:

Step 1 (Initialization):

$$g(0,0) = 0. \tag{14}$$

Step 2 (Recursion):

$$g(i, j) = \max \begin{cases} g(i-1, j) - c_{\gamma 1}, \\ g(i, j-1) - c_{\gamma 2}, \\ g(i-1, j-1) + Score_{lex}(f_{a_i} \mid e_i) \end{cases}, 0 \le i \le l, \ 0 \le j \le m. \tag{15}$$

Step 3 (Termination):

$$Score_{lex}(f_a \mid e) = g(l, m), \tag{16}$$

where $c_{\gamma 1}$ and $c_{\gamma 2}$ are penalty score values for a insertion operation and a deletion operation on the word level.

Suppose that there is an entry $(e_i, w_f)$ with probability $p$ (or score $c_p = \log p$) in the bilingual dictionary. $Score_{lex}(f_{a_i} \mid e_i)$ is formulated as:

$$Score_{lex}(f_{a_i} \mid e_i) = \begin{cases} c_p, & \text{if } f_{a_i} = w_f \quad (17) \\ Score_{tm}(R(f_{a_i}) \mid e_i), & \text{if } f_{a_i} \neq w_f \text{ and} \\ & \qquad Score_{tm}(R(f_{a_i}) / e_i) \geq Thr_l \\ c_{\gamma 3}, & \text{otherwise} \end{cases}$$

where $R(f_{a_i})$ is the Romanization of $f_{a_i}$, and $c_{\gamma 3}$ and $Thr_l$ denote a floor score value and a threshold, respectively.

## 3   Improvement

In this section, we incorporate multiple knowledge sources to improve on Phrase Translation Model and Transliteration Model, including approximate matching and Chinese personal name recognition.

### 3.1   Approximate Matching (AM)

In practice, the transformation of NEs from English to Chinese is more complicated than the transformation process mentioned above. Usually, an English NE phrase may have several equally acceptable Chinese NE variations. For example, the NE "International Commercial Bank of China" can be translated into "中國國際商業銀行", "中國商業銀行", or "中國商銀". It is advisable to measure the similarity between two Chinese NE variations when estimating phrase translation probability. For example, high probabilistic value for $P$("中國商業銀行" | "International Commercial Bank of China") and high similarity between "中國商業銀行" and "中國商銀" imply that we should also give high probabilistic value for $P$("中國商銀" | "International Commercial Bank of China"). We enhance the lexical score function by incorporating the approximate string matching approach [7]. To do that, the lexical score function $Score_{lex}(f_{a_i} \mid e_i)$ in Eq. (17) is modified as follows:

$$Score_{lex}(f_{a_i} \mid e_i) = \begin{cases} c_p, & \text{if } f_{a_i} = w_f \quad (18) \\ c_p \times (1 + \dfrac{J-I}{J}) - c_{\gamma 4}, & \text{if } 0 < I < J \\ Score_{tm}(R(f_{a_i}) \mid e_i), & \text{if } I = 0 \text{ and} \\ & \qquad Score_{tm}(R(f_{a_i}) \mid e_i) \geq Thr_l \\ c_{\gamma 3}, & \text{otherwise} \end{cases}$$

where $J$ is the number of Chinese characters in $w_f$, $I$ is the number of matched Chinese characters between $f_{a_i}$ and $w_f$, and $c_{\gamma 4}$ denotes a penalty score value.

## 3.2  Chinese Personal Name Recognition (CPNR)

To deal with the mapping between the foreign name and the Chinese name in parallel corpora, we apply a Chinese personal name recognizer to extract the Chinese part of the PER-typed NE. Chinese personal names consist of surnames and given names. Chinese surnames and given names are single or two characters. The Chinese personal name recognizer is automatically trained from a large personal name corpus consisting of one million Chinese personal names. We use Chinese surnames as anchor points, and then determine the likelihood of the one or two characters following the surname being a Chinese given name. Suppose that $c_1 c_2$ is the two subsequent Chinese characters. The likelihood function $d(c_1 c_2)$ for the two-character given name is defined as follows:

$$d(c_1 c_2) = \begin{cases} true, & if \quad P(c_1 c_2 / GN_{12}^2) > Thr_2 \quad or \\ & \quad P(c_1 / GN_1^2) \times P(c_2 / GN_2^2) > Thr_3, \\ false, & otherwise. \end{cases} \tag{19}$$

where $GN_{12}^2$, $GN_1^2$, and $GN_2^2$ stand for the two-character given name, the first character of the two-character given name, and the second character of the two-character given name, respectively, and $Thr_2$ and $Thr_3$ are constants.

The decision function $d(c_1)$ for the single-character given name is defined as follows:

$$d(c_1) = \begin{cases} true, & if \quad P(c_1 \mid GN^1) > Thr_4, \\ false, & otherwise. \end{cases} \tag{20}$$

where $GN^1$ stands for the one-character given name, and $Thr_4$ is a constant.

The threshold values $Thr_2$, $Thr_3$, and $Thr_4$ were empirically determined to let 95% of the training set pass through the verification test. Since the bilingual sentences are well aligned and given names are used as the anchor points, this approach works quite well on aligning a foreign name with its corresponding Chinese names.

The Chinese personal name recognizer is applied only on the case that the given NE is a named person and $Score_{tm}(R(f_{a_i}) \mid e_i)$ in Eq. (18) is less than $Thr_1$. Then, given a named person, the transliteration score function is reformulated as

$$Score_{tm}(R(f_{a_i}) \mid e_i) = \tag{21}$$
$$\begin{cases} \max \{\log(P(c_1 c_2 \mid GN_{12}^2)), \log(P(c_1 \mid GN_1^2) \times P(c_2 \mid GN_2^2))\}, \\ \qquad\qquad\qquad\qquad if \ d(c_1 c_2) \text{ is true,} \\ \log(P(c_1 \mid GN^1)), \qquad\qquad otherwise \ if \ d(c_1) \text{ is true.} \end{cases}$$

## 4   The Unified Framework

This section describes the unified framework that integrates the proposed statistical models with multiple knowledge sources to align bilingual NEs. A sentence alignment procedure is thus applied first to align parallel texts at the sentence level. An English NE identifier is then developed that utilizes capitalization information, keywords, and contextual information to approximately label NE candidates in an English text. Next, the labels are corrected manually. With many studies having already identified mono-language NE, especially for identifying English NEs, this study does not focus on investigating an English NE identifier. Finally, an NE transformation procedure, which combines SPTM, TM and other knowledge features, is applied to identify the corresponding NEs in the target text.

The overall process is summarized as follows:

I.   Preprocess:
    (I.1).   Perform sentence alignment.
    (I.2).   Label English named entities.

II.   Main process:
    For each given English named entity $NE_E$ in the aligned English sentence $S_E$, align the corresponding Chinese named entity $NE_C$ in the aligned Chinese sentence $S_C$.
    (II.1).   Generate all possible Chinese named-entity candidates by the proposed SPTM model using general-purpose and domain-relevant lexicons. To describe more specifically, for each labeled $NE_E$, apply SPTM and AM to find Chinese named-entity candidates $\{NE_A\}$ in $S_C$.
    (II.2).   For any word $W_E$, in $NE_E$, that cannot find the corresponding Chinese translation in $S_C$, apply the proposed STM, enhanced with CPNR to extracting the corresponding Chinese transliterations $\{NE_B\}$, in $S_C$, with scores above a predefined threshold.
    (II.3).   Merge $\{NE_A\}$ with $\{NE_B\}$ into possible candidates $\{NE_C\}$.
    (II.4).   Rank $\{NE_C\}$ by the cost scores. The candidate with the maximum score is chosen as the answer.

## 5   Experiments

Several corpora were collected to estimate the parameters of the proposed models. Noun phrases of the BDC Electronic Chinese-English Dictionary [2] were used to train PTM. The LDC Central News Agency Corpus was used to extract keywords of entity names for identifying NE types. We collected 117 bilingual keyword pairs from the corpora. In addition, a list of Chinese surnames was also gathered to help to identify and extract the PER-type of NEs. To train the transliteration model, 2,430 pairs of English names together with their Chinese transliterations and Chinese Romanization were used. The parallel corpus collected from the *Sinorama* Magazine was used to construct the corpus-based lexicon and estimation of LTP. Test cases were also drawn from the *Sinorama* Magazine to evaluate the performance of bilingual NE alignment.

Performance on the alignment of NEs is evaluated according to the precision rate at the NE phrase level. To analyze and scrutinize the performance of the proposed methods for NE alignment, we randomly selected 275 aligned sentences from *Sinorama* and manually prepared the answer keys. Each chosen aligned sentence contains at least one NE pair. Currently, we restrict the lengths of English NEs to be less than 6. In total, 830 pairs of NEs are labeled. The numbers of NE pairs for types PER, LOC, and ORG are 208, 362, and 260, respectively. Several experiments were conducted to analyze relevant contributions of corresponding enhancements to the performance with respective to the baseline. We add each feature individually to the baseline method and then combine all features altogether to the baseline to examine their effects on performance. Experimental results are shown in Table 1.

**Table 1.** Performance of bilingual NE alignment

| Method | PER | LOC | ORG | Average |
|---|---|---|---|---|
| Baseline | 88.94% | 95.58% | 80.00% | 89.04% |
| Baseline+AM | 88.46% | 96.98% | 87.98% | 92.05% |
| Baseline+CPNR | 95.67% | 95.33% | 79.84% | 90.60% |
| Baseline+AM+CPNR | 96.15% | 96.96% | 88.85% | 94.22% |

In Table 1, the results reveal that each knowledge feature has different contributions to different NE types. As shown in Table 1, the performance of the enhanced method is much better than that of the baseline. Furthermore, experimental results indicate that the LOC-type test has the best performance and ORG ones are the worst. The reason for lower performance of ORG is largely due to its highly complex structure and variation.

## 6  Conclusions

In this paper, a new method for bilingual NE alignment is proposed. Experiments show that the baseline method aligns bilingual NEs reasonably well in parallel corpora. Moreover, to improve performance, a unified framework has investigated to perform the task by incorporating proposed statistical models with multiple knowledge sources, including approximate matching and Chinese personal name recognition. Experimental results demonstrate that the unified framework can achieve a very significant improvement.

**Acknowledgements.** We would like to thank Yuan Liou Publishing for providing data for this study. We acknowledge the support for this study through grants from National Science Council and Ministry of Education, Taiwan (NSC 92-2524-S007-002, NSC 91-2213-E-007-061 and MOE EX-91-E-FA06-4-4) and MOEA under the Software Technology for Advanced Network Application Project of the Institute for Information Industry.

# References

1.  Al-Onaizan, Yaser, Kevin Knight: Translating named entities using monolingual and bilingual resources. In Proceedings of ACL 40 (2002) 400-408.
2.  BDC: The BDC Chinese-English electronic dictionary (version 2.0). Behavior Design Corporation, Taiwan (1992).
3.  Brown, P. F., Della Pietra S. A., Della Pietra V. J., Mercer R. L.: The mathematics of statistical machine translation: parameter estimation. Computational Linguistics, 19 (2) (1993) 263-311.
4.  Chang, Jason S., David Yu, Chun-Jen Lee: Statistical Translation Model for Phrases. Computational Linguistics and Chinese Language Processing, 6 (2) (2001) 43-64.
5.  Chen, Hsin-Hsi, Changhua Yang, Ying Lin: Learning formulation and transformation rules for multilingual named entities. In Proceedings of the ACL Workshop on Multilingual and Mixed-language Named Entity Recognition (2003), 1-8.
6.  Chinchor, Nancy: MUC-7 Named entity task definition. In Proceedings of the 7th Message Understanding Conference (1997).
7.  Damerau, F.: A technique for computer detection and correction of spelling errors. Comm. of the ACM, 7(3), (1964), 171-176.
8.  Huang, Fei, Stephan Vogel: Improved Named Entity Translation and Bilingual Named Entity Extraction. In Proceedings of Int. Conf. on Multimodal Interfaces (2002), 253-260.
9.  Kumano, Tadashi, Hideki Kashioka, Hideki Tanaka, Takahiro Fukusima: Acquiring Bilingual Named Entity Translations from Content-aligned Corpora. In Proceedings of the First International Joint Conference on Natural Language Processing (2004).
10. Lee, Chun-Jen, Jason S. Chang: Acquisition of English-Chinese transliterated word pairs from parallel-aligned texts using a statistical machine transliteration model. In Proceedings of HLT-NAACL 2003 Workshop on Building and Using Parallel Texts: Data Driven Machine Translation and Beyond (2003), 96-103.
11. Lee, Chun-Jen, Jason S. Chang, Jyh-Shing Roger Jang: Bilingual named-entity pairs extraction from parallel corpora. In Proceedings of IJCNLP-04 Workshop on Named Entity Recognition for Natural Language Processing Applications, (2004), 9-16.
12. Melamed, I. Dan: A Word-to-Word Model of Translational Equivalence. In Proceeding of ACL 35, (1997) 490-497.
13. Moore, Robert C.: Learning Translations of Named-Entity Phrases from Parallel Corpora. In Proceedings of the 10th Conference of the European Chapter of the Association for Computational Linguistics (2003) 259-266.
14. Wu, Chien-Cheng, Jason S. Chang: Bilingual Collocation Extraction Based on Syntactic and Statistical Analyses. In Proceedings of ROCLING XV (2003) 33-55.

# Weather Report Translation Using a Translation Memory

Thomas Leplus, Philippe Langlais, and Guy Lapalme

RALI/DIRO
Université de Montréal
C.P. 6128, succursale Centre-ville
H3C 3J7, Montréal, Québec, Canada
http://www.rali-iro.umontreal.ca

**Abstract.** We describe the use of a translation memory in the context of a reconstruction of a landmark application of machine translation, the Canadian English to French weather report translation system. This system, which has been in operation for more than 20 years, was developed using a classical symbolic approach. We describe our experiment in developing an alternative approach based on the analysis of hundreds of thousands of weather reports. We show that it is possible to obtain excellent translations using translation memory techniques and we analyze the kinds of translation errors that are induced by this approach.

## 1 Introduction

In the mid seventies, a group of linguists and computer scientists of Université de Montréal (*TAUM* group) developed an English to French weather report machine translation system which became known as TAUM-MÉTÉO, described in [8, chap12]. It involves three major steps: a dictionary look-up, a syntactic analysis and a light syntactic and morphological generation step.

The transfer from English to French is encoded at the word level in three special purpose lexicons: idioms (e.g. *blowing snow* ↔ *poudrerie*) , locations (e.g. *Newfoundland* ↔ *Terre Neuve*) and a general dictionary containing syntactic and semantic features (e.g. *amount*=N((F,MSR),*quantite*) which means that *amount* translates into the feminine F French noun N *quantite* which is a measure MSR noun).

The syntactic stage is the result of a detailed analysis that was done by hand at the early stage of the prototype. [3] reports that MÉTÉO-2, a subsequent system that became operational at Environment Canada, used fifteen different grammars categorised into five major types from which the syntactic analysis chooses the most appropriate one.

The third and last step performs French word reordering (e.g. adjectives are placed after the noun they modify), preposition selection (e.g. we say *à Montréal* but *en Nouvelle-Écosse* and *au Manitoba*) plus a few morphological adjustments (e.g. *le été* → *l'été*).

R.E. Frederking and K.B. Taylor (Eds.): AMTA 2004, LNAI 3265, pp. 154–163, 2004.

This system has been in continuous use since 1984, translating up to 45,000 words a day. [7] argues that one of the reasons for the success of the MÉTÉO system is the nature of the problem itself: a specific domain, with very repetitive texts that are particularly unappealing to translate for a human (see for example the reports shown in Figure 1). Furthermore, the life of a weather report is, by nature, very short (approximatively 6 hours), which makes them an ideal candidate for automation.

Professional translators are asked to correct the machine output when the input English text cannot be parsed, often because of spelling errors in the original English text. MÉTÉO is one of the very few machine translation systems in the world from which the unedited output is used by the public in everyday life without any human revision.

Some alternatives to machine translation (MT) have been proposed for weather reports, namely multilingual text generation directly from raw weather data: temperatures, winds, pressures etc. Such generation systems also need some human template selection for organising the report. Generating text in many languages from one source is quite appealing from a conceptual point of view and has been cited as one of the potential applications for natural language generation [15]; some systems have been developed [9,6,4] and tested in operational contexts. But thus far, none has been used in everyday production to the same level as the one attained by MT. One of the reasons for this is that meteorologists prefer to write their reports in natural language rather than selecting text structure templates.

Our goal in this study was to determine how well a simple memory-based approach would fit in the context of the weather report translation. We describe in section 2 the data we received from Environment Canada and what preprocessing we performed to obtain our MÉTÉO bitext. We present in section 4 the first prototype developed and then report on the results obtained in section 5. We analyse in section 6 the main kinds of errors that are produced by this approach. In section 7, we conclude with a general discussion of this study and propose some possible extensions.

## 2  The Corpus

We obtained from Environment Canada forecast reports in both French and English produced during 2002 and 2003. The current reports are available on the web at http://meteo.ec.gc.ca/forecast/textforecast_f.html.

We used this corpus to populate a bitext i.e. an aligned corpus of corresponding sentences in French and English weather reports. Like all work on real data, this conceptually simple task proved to be more complicated than we had initially envisioned. This section describes the major steps of this stage.

We received files containing both French and English weather forecasts. Both the source report, usually in English, and its translation, produced either by a human or by the current MÉTÉO system, appear in the same file. One file contains all reports issued for a single day. A report is a fairly short text, on

```
FPCN18 CWUL 312130                    FPCN78 CWUL 312130

SUMMARY FORECAST FOR WESTERN QUEBEC   RESUME DES PREVISIONS POUR L'OUEST
ISSUED BY ENVIRONMENT CANADA          DU QUEBEC EMISES PAR ENVIRONNEMENT
                                      CANADA


MONTREAL AT 4.30 PM EST MONDAY 31     MONTREAL 16H30 HNE LE LUNDI 31
DECEMBER 2001 FOR TUESDAY 01 JANUARY  DECEMBRE 2001 POUR MARDI LE 01
2002. VARIABLE CLOUDINESS WITH        JANVIER 2002. CIEL VARIABLE AVEC
FLURRIES. HIGH NEAR MINUS 7.          AVERSES DE NEIGE. MAX PRES DE MOINS
                                      7.


END/LT                                FIN/TR
```

**Fig. 1.** An example of an English weather report and its French translation.

average 304 words, in a telegraphic style. All letters are capitalised and non accented and almost always without any punctuation except for a terminating period.

As can be seen in the example in Figure 1, there are few determiners such as articles (*a* or *the* in English, *le* or *un* in French). A report usually starts with a code identifying the source which issued the report. For example, in FPCN18 CWUL 312130, 312130 indicates that the report was produced at 21h30 on the 31st day of the month; CWUL is a code corresponding to Montreal and the western area of Quebec. A report (almost always) ends with a closing markup: END or FIN according on the language of the report. If the author or the translator is a human, his or her initials are added after a slash following the markup.

Our first step is to determine the beginning and end of each weather forecast using regular expressions to match the first line of a forecast, which identifies the source which issued it, and the last line which usually starts with END or FIN.

Then we distinguish the English forecasts from the French ones according to whether they ended with END or FIN. Given the fact that we started with a fairly large amount of data, we decided to discard any forecast that we could not identify with this process. We were left with 273 847 reports.

Next, we had to match English and French forecasts that are translations of each other. As we see in fig. 1, the first line of the two reports is almost the same except for the first part of the source identifier which is FPCN18 in English and FPCN78 in French. After studying the data, we determined that this shift of 60 between English and French forecast identifiers seemed valid for identifiers from FPCN10 through FPCN29. These identifiers being the most frequent, we decided to keep only these into our final bitext.

This preprocessing stage required about 1 500 lines of Perl code and few weeks of monitoring. Of the 561 megabytes of text we originally received, we were left with *only* 439 megabytes of text, representing 89 697 weather report pairs.

To get a bitext out of this selected material, we first automatically segmented the reports into words and sentences using an in-house tool that we did not try to adapt to the specificity of the weather forecasts.

We then ran the Japa sentence aligner [11] on the corpus (this took around 2 hours running on a standard P4 workstation), to identify 4,4 million pairs of sentences, from which we removed about 28 000 (roughly 0.6%) which were not one-to-one sentence pairs.

We divided this bitext into three non-overlapping sections, as reported in Table 1: TRAIN (January 2002 to October 2003) for populating the translation memory, BLANC (December 2003) for tuning a few meta-parameters, and TEST (November 2003) for testing.

The TEST section was deliberately chosen so as to be different from the TRAIN period in order to recreate as much as possible the working environment of a system faced with the translation of new weather forecasts.

**Table 1.** Main characteristics of the subcorpora used in this study in terms of number of pairs of sentences, English and French words and tokens. Figures are reported in thousands.

| corpus | pairs | English words | toks | French words | toks |
|---|---|---|---|---|---|
| TRAIN | 4 211 | 30 493 | 10.0 | 37 542 | 11.1 |
| BLANC | 122 | 888 | 3.0 | 1 092 | 3.2 |
| TEST | 36 | 269 | 1.9 | 333 | 2.0 |
| total | 4 370 | 31 383 | 10.1 | 38 968 | 11.3 |

A quick inspection of the bitext reveals that sentences are fairly short: an average of 7.2 English and 8.9 French words. Most sentences are repeated: only 8.6% of the English sentences unique. About 90% of the sentences to be translated can be retrieved verbatim from the memory with at most one edit operation i.e. insertion, suppression and substitution of a word. These properties of our bitext naturally suggest a memory-based approach for translating weather reports.

## 3   The Translation Memory

Our translation memory is organised at the sentence level. We define a memory ($\mathcal{M}$) as a set of ($M$) triplets, where a source sentence ($e_i$) is associated to its $N$ most frequent translations ($f_1^i, \ldots, f_N^i$), each translation $f_j^i$ being associated with its count ($n_j^i$) of cooccurrence with $e^i$ in the memory:

$$\mathcal{M} = \left\{ \left(e^i; f_1^i, \ldots, f_N^i; n_1^i, \ldots, n_N^i\right) \right\}_{i \in [1,M]}$$

Two parameters could significantly affect the performance of the memory: its size ($M$) and the number ($N$) of French translations kept for each English sentence.

The size of the translation memory affects our system in two ways. If we store only the few most frequent English sentences and their French translations, the time for the system to look for entries in the memory will be short. But, on the

other hand, it is clear that the larger the memory, the better our chances will
be to find sentences we want to translate (or ones within a short edit distance),
even if these sentences were not frequent in the training corpus.

The percentage of sentences to translate found verbatim in the memory grows
logarithmically with the size of the memory until it reaches approximately 20 000
sentence pairs. With the full memory (about 300 000 source sentences), we obtain
a peek of 87% of sentences found into the memory.

The second parameter of the translation memory is the number of French
translations stored for each English sentence. Among the 488 792 different English sentences found in our training corpus, 437 418 (89.5%) always exhibit the
same translation. This is probably because most of the data we received from
Environment Canada is actually machine translated and has not been edited by
human translators. In practice, we found that considering a maximum of $N = 5$
translations for a given English sentence was sufficient for our purposes.

## 4   The Translation Procedure

The overall scenario for translating a sentence is the following. The source sentence is first preprocessed in order to handle more easily entities such as dates,
hours or numbers. Note that this process has been done as well for the sentences
populating the memory. The source sentences which are closest to this processed
source sentence are then retrieved from the translation memory. This leaves us
with a set of target sentences from which we select the best ones . The chosen
translation is then postprocessed to remove the meta-tokens introduced by the
preprocessing phase. We now briefly discuss each of these steps.

Eight classes of tokens (*punctuation, telephone numbers, months, days, time,
numeric values, range of values* and *cardinal coordinates*) are identified via regular expressions at the character level and replaced by a corresponding tag (num-
bered if there are more than one of the same class in a sentence). This process
is quite different from the creation of specialised lexicons used in the current
MÉTÉO system. In particular, we did not explicitly encode place names.

For a given sentence to translate $e$, a set of the 10 closest source sentences (in
terms of edit distance) in the memory is first computed: $\mathcal{E} = \{\overline{e}_1, \ldots, \overline{e}_{10}\}$. Since
each of these source sentences is associated with at most $N = 5$ translations,
we retrieve from the memory a set $\mathcal{F}$ of at most 50 candidate translations and
their associated count. Note that several target sentences might be identical in
the set:
$$\mathcal{F} = \left\{ \langle (f_1^c, \ldots, f_N^c), (n_1^c, \ldots, n_N^c) \rangle_{c \in [1,10]} \right\}$$
The target sentences $f_j^c$ are then ranked in increasing order of edit distance
between their associated English sentence $e^c$ and the source sentence $e$. Ties in
this distribution are broken by prefering larger counts $n_j^c$.

The translations produced are finally postprocessed in order to transform the
meta-tokens introduced during preprocessing into their appropriate word form.
We observed on a held-out test corpus that this cascade of pre- and postprocess-
ing clearly boosted the coverage of the memory.

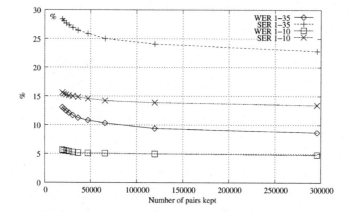

**Fig. 2.** Performance of the engine as a function of the number of pair of sentences kept in the memory. Each point corresponds to a frequency threshold (from 10 to 1) we considered for filtering the training sentences. These rates are reported for sentences of 10 words or less (1-10) and for 35 words of less (1-35).

## 5   Results

We report in Figure 2 the performance of the engine measured on the TEST corpus in terms of Word Error Rate (WER) and Sentence Error Rate (SER) as a function of the number ($M$) of pairs retained in the memory.

Clearly the larger the memory is, the better the performance. The sentence error rate flattens at 23% (13% if measured on short sentences only), while the word error rate approaches 9% (around 5% for short sentences).

In Table 2, we report the best results (obtained for the full memory) that we observed in terms of WER, SER, NIST and BLEU scores. The last two scores were computed on a single reference by the mteval program (version v11a), available at http://www.nist.gov/speech/tests/mt/resources/scoring.htm. Performances were evaluated on all the sentences of the TEST corpus (FULL column), as well as on the subset consisting of only the sentences that were not found verbatim in the memory (SUBSET column).

We provide the performance as a function of the number of translations returned by the system. When more than one translation is considered, we assume an oracle selecting the best one; in our case, the oracle was choosing the translation with the lowest WER in relation to the reference translation.

Not surprisingly, the performance measured on the full test corpus (FULL) is much better than that measured on previously unseen source sentences (SUBSET). The difference is especially noticable on the SER metric, where 75% of the trans-

**Table 2.** Performance of the engine as a function of the number of translations returned by the system for the full test corpus (FULL) as well as on the subset of the 4641 sentences not seen verbatim in the memory (SUBSET).

| $n$-best | FULL | | | | SUBSET | | | |
|---|---|---|---|---|---|---|---|---|
| | WER% | SER% | NIST | BLEU | WER% | SER% | NIST | BLEU |
| 1 | 9.18 | 23.56 | 10.8983 | 0.8695 | 22.78 | 86.80 | 9.3587 | 0.6811 |
| 2 | 5.93 | 16.56 | 11.1463 | 0.9071 | 18.58 | 84.51 | 9.7498 | 0.7211 |
| 3 | 5.02 | 12.57 | 11.2740 | 0.9168 | 17.13 | 83.17 | 9.8823 | 0.7350 |
| 4 | 4.69 | 12.04 | 11.3055 | 0.9202 | 16.26 | 82.54 | 9.9664 | 0.7437 |
| 5 | 4.54 | 11.94 | 11.3213 | 0.9219 | 15.76 | 81.87 | 10.0225 | 0.7493 |

lations produced in the former case were identical with the reference, while only 15% were in the latter case.

More surprisingly, these figures tell us that our simple approach is a fairly accurate way to translate MÉTÉO sentences, a WER of 9 being several times lower than what we usually observe in "classical" translation tasks. However, we are still below the performance that has been reported in [13]. The author manually inspected a sample of 1257 translations produced by the MÉTÉO2 system and determined that around 11% of them required a correction (minor or not). In our case, and although the SER we measure does not compare directly, we observed on a sample of 36228 translations, that around 24% of them are not verbatim the reference ones.

We analyse in the following section the major errors produced by our approach.

## 6   Error Analysis

We analysed semi-automatically the most frequent errors produced by our process for the 25% of the translations that differed from the reference. We (arbitrarily) selected one of the alignments with the minimum edit distance between the reference translation and the erroneous candidate translation. From this alignment, we identified locus of errors. This process is illustrated in Figure 3 in which an error is indicated by the following notation *SOURCE ⤳ TARGET*.

As the classical edit distance between two sequences behaves poorly in the case of word reordering, some errors might not have been analyzed correctly by our process (see the alignment in the last line of Figure 3). However, casual inspection of the errors did not reveal severe problems.

Out of the 8900 errors found at the word level, we manually inspected the 100 most frequent ones (the first ten are reported in Table 3), covering 42.6% of the errors. We found that more than 53% of the errors at the word sequence level were replacement errors, such as the production of the word LEGER (*light*) instead of the expected word FAIBLE (*light*). Around 30% were suppression errors, i.e. portions of text that have not been produced, but that should have

```
SRC ... FLURRIES THIS AFTERNOON
REF ... AVERSES DE NEIGE  CET  APRES-MIDI
CAN ... AVERSES DE NEIGE CETTE     NUIT
ALI        =    =   =    S         S
```

CET APRES-MIDI⤳CETTE NUIT

```
SRC  WINDS BECOMING LIGHT __DAY1__ MORNING AND THEN ...
REF  VENTS DEVENANT FAIBLES    EN    MATINEE __DAY1__ PUIS      ...
CAN  VENTS DEVENANT LEGERS __DAY1__ MATIN              PUIS      ...
ALI  =        =      S        S       S         D      =
```

FAIBLES EN MATINÉE -DAY-⤳LEGERS -DAY- MATIN

```
SRC ... AND THEN TO SOUTHWEST __INT2__ THIS EVENING
REF ... PUIS           DU SUD-OUEST A __INT2__ CE      SOIR
CAN ... PUIS DIMINUANT DU SUD-OUEST A __INT2__ EN      SOIREE
ALI      =    I        =    =   =   =    S         S
```

⤳DIMINUANT, CE SOIR⤳EN SOIREE

```
SRC ... APPROACHES FROM THE WEST ...
REF ... A  L APPROCHE D  UN CREUX VENANT      DE        ...
CAN ...              UN CREUX   S    APPROCHANT PAR ...
ALI ... D D   D    D =   =    S       S         I
```

A L APPROCHE D⤳, VENANT DE⤳S APPROCHANT PAR

**Fig. 3.** Illustration of the error detection process on four sentences making use of the edit distance alignment between the reference and the candidate translations. **I** indicates an insertion, **S** a substitution, **D** a deletion, and = the identity of two words. Errors detected are noted as `reference sequence⤳candidate sequence`.

been according to the reference (see `A L APPROCHE D⤳` in the fourth alignment of figure 3); the rest (17%) were insertion errors, i.e. a portion of text not found in the reference translation (see `⤳DIMINUANT` in the third alignment of figure 3)).

Among the replacement errors, more than 40% are cardinal point substitutions such as *SUD-EST* (*southeast*) instead of *SUD-OUEST* (*southwest*), and more than 7% involve time code substitutions such as `HNP/HAP`, `HNR/HAR`, `HNE/HAE` and `HNT/HAT`. This means that roughly half of replacement errors could be handled simply by maintaining a small special-purpose lexicon. This also goes for place names that were not dealt with specially in this experiment.

Note that replacement errors are not always synonyms: some are not unrelated `CET APRÈS-MIDI⤳CE SOIR` (*this afternoon⤳tonight*), but others are antonymic as in `DIMINUANT⤳AUGMENTANT` (*diminishing⤳increasing*). This clearly shows the need for post-processing the translation retrieved from the memory. Similarly some insertions and suppressions often modify the semantics of a sentence, as is the case in the fourth error of Figure 3.

**Table 3.** The 10 most frequent word-sequence errors found with their translation with their number of occurrences in the corpus. The insertion ⤳TOTALE is likely to be an artefact of our TEST corpus, since it often appears in the form ACCUMULATION TOTALE DE ⎵INT⎵⎵ CM., translated as ACCUMULATION ⎵INT⎵ CM.

| |
| --- |
| 150 CM. ⤳MM. |
| 138 ⤳POSSIBILITÉ DE (⤳*chance of*) |
| 134 DE PROBABILITÉ⤳ (*chance of*⤳) |
| 131 TÔT⤳ (*early*⤳) |
| 117 TARD⤳ (*late*⤳) |
| 92 NEIGE⤳PLUIE (*snow*⤳*rain*) |
| 90 DE⤳A |
| 87 SUD-OUEST⤳NORD-OUEST(*southwest*⤳*northwest*) |
| 80 D'OUEST⤳DU NORD-OUEST (*west*⤳*northwest*) |
| 76 ⤳TOTALE |

## 7  Discussion

In this paper, we have described a translation memory based approach for the *recreation* of the MÉTÉO system nearly 30 years after the birth of the first prototype at the same university. The main difference between these two systems is the way they were developed. The original system is a carefully handcrafted one based on a detailed linguistic analysis, whilst ours simply exploits a memory of previous translations of weather forecasts that were, of course, not available at the time the original system was designed. Computational resources needed for implementing this corpus-based approach are also much bigger than what was even imaginable when the first MÉTÉO system was developed.

This paper shows that a simple-minded translation memory system can produce translations that are comparable (although not as good) in quality with the ones produced by the current system. Clearly, this prototype can be improved in many ways. We have already shown that many errors could be handled by small specific bilingual lexicons (place names, cardinals, etc.). Our translation memory implementation is fairly crude compared to the current practice in example-based machine translation [2], leaving a lot of room for improvements. We have also started to investigate how this memory-based approach can be coupled with a statistical machine translation system in order to further improve the quality of the translations [12].

**Acknowledgements.** We thank Rick Jones and Marc Besner from the Dorval office of Environment Canada who provided us with the corpus of bilingual weather reports. We are also indebted to Elliot Macklovitch who provided us with articles describing the MÉTÉO system that we could not have found otherwise. This work has been funded by NSERC and FQRNT.

# References

1. Peter F. Brown, Stephen A. Della Pietra, Vincent J. Della Pietra, and Robert L. Mercer. 1993. The mathematics of statistical machine translation: Parameter estimation. *Computational Linguistics*, 19(2):263–311.
2. Michael Carl and Andy Way, editors. 2003. *Recent Advances in Example-Based Machine Translation*, volume 21 of *Text, Speech and Language Technology*. Kluwer Academic.
3. John Chandioux. 1988. Meteo (tm), an operational translation system. In *RIAO*.
4. J. Coch. 1998. Interactive generation and knowledge administration in multimeteo. In *Ninth International Workshop on Natural Language Generation*, pages 300–303, Niagara-on-the-lake, Ontario, Canada.
5. G. Foster, S. Gandrabur, P. Langlais, E. Macklovitch, P. Plamondon, G. Russell, and M. Simard. 2003. Statistical machine translation: Rapid development with limited resources. In *Machine Translation Summit IX*, New Orleans, USA, sep.
6. E. Goldberg, N. Driedger, and R. Kittredge. 1994. Using natural language processing to produce weather forecasts. *IEEE Expert 9*, 2:45–53, apr.
7. Annette Grimaila and John Chandioux, 1992. *Made to measure solutions*, chapter 3, pages 33–45. J. Newton, ed., Computers in Translation: A Practical Appraisal, Routledge, London.
8. W. John Hutchins and Harold L. Somers, 1992. *An introduction to Machine Translation*, chapter 12, pages 207–220. Academic Press.
9. R. Kittredge, A. Polguère, and E. Goldberg. 1986. Synthesizing weather reports from formatted data. In *11th. International Conference on Computational Linguistics*, pages 563–565, Bonn, Germany.
10. Philipp Koehn, Franz Josef Och, and Daniel Marcu. 2003. Statistical phrase-based translation. In *Proceedings of the Second Conference on Human Language Technology Reasearch (HLT)*, pages 127–133, Edmonton, Alberta, Canada, May.
11. Philippe Langlais, Michel Simard, and Jean Véronis. 1998. Methods and practical issues in evaluating alignment techniques. In *Proceedings of the 36th Annual Meeting of the Association for Computational Linguistics (ACL)*, Montréal, Canada, August.
12. Thomas Leplus, Philippe Langlais, and Guy Lapalme. 2004. A corpus-based Approach to Weather Report Translation. *Technical Report*, University of Montréal, Canada, May.
13. Elliott Macklovitch. Personnal communication of results of a linguistic performance evaluation of METEO 2 conducted in 1985.
14. S. Nießen, S. Vogel, H. Ney, and C. Tillmann. 1998. A dp based search algorithm for statistical machine translation. In *Proceedings of the 36th Annual Meeting of the Association for Computational Linguistics (ACL) and 17th International Conference on Computational Linguistics (COLING) 1998*, pages 960–966, Montréal, Canada, August.
15. Ehud Reiter and Robert Dale. 2000. *Building Natural Language Generation Systems*. Cambridge University Press. 270 p.

# Keyword Translation from English to Chinese for Multilingual QA

Frank Lin and Teruko Mitamura

Language Technologies Institute
Carnegie Mellon University
{frank,teruko}@cs.cmu.edu

**Abstract.** The Keyword Translator is a part of the Question Analyzer module in the JAVELIN Question-Answering system; it translates the keywords, which are used to query documents and extract answers, from one language to another. Much work has been in the area of query translation for CLIR or MLIR, however, many have focused on methods using hard-to-obtain and domain-specific resources, and evaluation is often based on retrieval performance rather than translation correctness. In this paper we will describe methods combining easily accessible, general-purpose MT systems to improve keyword translation correctness. We also describe methods that utilize the question sentence available to a question-answering system to improve translation correctness. We will show that using multiple MT systems and the question sentence to translate keywords from English to Mandarin Chinese can significantly improve keyword translation correctness.

## 1   Introduction

Query translation plays an important role in Cross-Language Information Retrieval (CLIR) and Multilingual Information Retrieval (MLIR) applications. Any application that involves CLIR or MLIR requires translation; either the translation of the query (usually a set of keywords) used to retrieve the documents or the translation of the documents themselves. Since translating documents is more expensive computationally, most CLIR and MLIR systems chose query translation over document translation. Similarly, the translation of keywords (words used to retrieve relevant documents and extract answers) in a multilingual question-answering system is crucial when the question is in one language and the answer lies within a document written in another language.

### 1.1   JAVELIN Question-Answering System

The Keyword Translator is not a stand-alone system; rather, it is a part of the Question Analysis module, which is part of the JAVELIN (Justification-based Answer Valuation through Language Interpretation) multilingual open-domain question-answering system [1]. The Question Analysis module is responsible for analyzing (syntactically and semantically) the question given by the user, classifying the question, parsing the question, and identifying the keywords within the question sentence. The question analysis output is passed on to the Retrieval Strategist module to retrieve relevant documents, then to the Information Extractor module to extract possible answer candidates within the retrieved

R.E. Frederking and K.B. Taylor (Eds.): AMTA 2004, LNAI 3265, pp. 164–176, 2004.
© Springer-Verlag Berlin Heidelberg 2004

documents, and then to Answer Generator module, which generates an answer to the question according to the information extracted. The keywords given by the Question Analysis module are used both in retrieving documents and extracting information from documents. Therefore, in multilingual question-answering, the Keyword Translator, as a sub-module within the Question Analysis module, translates keywords produced by the module into other languages so that the Retrieval Strategist module and the Information Extractor module may use these keywords to find answers in these languages.

Typically, the quality of query translation in CLIR and MLIR is measured by the performance of the CLIR or MLIR system as a whole (precision and recall). However, rather than looking at the overall information retrieval or question-answering performance, in this paper we will focus on the translation correctness of keywords for the following reasons:

1. We want to isolate the translation problem from problems such as query expansion, which can be dealt with separately in the Retrieval Strategist module.
2. We want to isolate the performance of the Keyword Translator so that each module within the question-answering system can be evaluated individually.
3. In CLIR or MLIR systems, often many documents are retrieved for review, so it may not be as important that all parts of the query be correct as that the correct parts are weighed more heavily. Whereas in a question-answering system, often one or few answers are produced for review, so it is crucial that each keyword is translated correctly in the correct sense according to the context.

## 1.2  Previous Work

In this section we will briefly survey previous work that is relevant to the Keyword Translator.

Query translation, or keyword translation, are typically done using machine-readable dictionaries (MRD), ready-to-use MT systems, parallel corpora, or any combination of the three. Since JAVELIN is an open-domain question-answering system, we do not consider methods that mainly use parallel corpora for query translation. Although comparisons have been made between simple dictionary-based approach and MT-based approach [2] with MT-based having better performance in CLIR, we will consider improved versions to both approaches.

Dictionary-based approaches are popular since the bilingual dictionaries are easily obtained for highdensity language pairs; however, dictionary-based methods must overcome the problem of limited coverage and sense disambiguation [3].

Chen et al. [4] described a technique using a combination of dictionaries and search engine to provide adequate coverage, but the results were disappointing due to low coverage. Gao et al. [5] described a method which tries to solve the low-coverage problem by using corpus statistics. They built a noun-phrase translation model and tried to solve the sense-disambiguation problem by using words within the same query as the contextual information and calculating the correlation using the target corpora. Their method showed significant improvement over simple dictionary translation. However, this method requires the building of parallel corpora, and, in a multilingual setting, multilingual parallel corpora are difficult to obtain. Jang et al. [6] experimented with sense-disambiguation using a bilingual dictionary and statistics from a collection of documents in the target language with good results, but this method and others [7] that similarly use corpus statistics do not generally solve the low-coverage problem. Seo et al. [8] presented a solution to this problem by using two bilingual dictionaries, a general dictionary and a biographical dictionary (for translating proper names not covered by the general dictionary). Pirkola [9] combined a general dictionary with a domain-specific dictionary, together with structured queries, to achieve CLIR performance almost as good as monolingual IR. However, the methods described by Seo et al. and Pirkola both need a special, domain-dictionary, which are not practical in a multilingual open-domain setting.

Generally, MT-based approaches have wider coverage than dictionary-based approaches, since many MT systems available translate common proper names and phrases. However, the quality of translation and sense disambiguation is fully dependent upon the MT system employed. Therefore, people generally do not rely on a single MT system for CLIR translation.

Lam-Adesina and Jones [10] merged results from two MT systems, together with term weighing and query expansion, which improved retrieval performance. Work has also been done in concatenating query translation results from MT systems and dictionaries [11] and in merging documents retrieved by dictionary-translated keywords and documents retrieved by MT-translated keywords [12]. However, since these approaches focus on concatenation of query translations provided by different sources and their performance measure is based on document retrieval, it is difficult to measure in isolation the performance of these approaches in translating queries.

For the Keyword Translator in JAVELIN question-answering system, we chose a MT-based approach based on the following observations:

1. Dictionary-based approaches often require special resources that are either difficult to obtain or domain-specific. On the other hand, general-purpose MT systems are more available and accessible, and many can be accessed through the web for free.
2. Many general-purpose MT's can translate from one language to many other languages, whereas dictionary-based approaches require a bilingual dictionary for each language pair and can differ greatly in quality and coverage.
3. General-purpose MT provides better word and phrase coverage than general dictionaries.

## 2   The Keyword Translator

The Keyword Translator is an open-domain, MT-based word (or phrase) translator for a question-answering system. We choose the MT-based approach for reasons noted in the previous section. The Keyword Translator has two distinguishing features: 1) it uses multiple MT systems and tries to select one correct translation candidate for each keyword and 2) it utilizes the question sentence available to a question-answering system as a context in which to translate the word in the correct sense.

We choose to use multiple MT systems and to utilize the question sentence based on the following assumptions:

- Using more than one MT system gives us a wider range of keyword translation candidates to choose from, and the correct translation is more likely to appear in multiple MT systems than a single MT system, and
- Using the question sentence available to a Question-Answering system gives us a context in which to better select the correct translation candidate.

Given the above assumptions, the Keyword Translator, follow these steps:

1. Get the question sentence and the keywords from the Question Analysis module.
2. Get keyword translation candidates for each keyword from multiple MT systems.
3. Use combinations of algorithms to score and/or penalize translation candidates from each MT system.
4. Return a best-scoring translation for each keyword.
5. Send translated keywords back to the Question Analysis module.

Our focus in this paper is on step 3, where the translation candidates are scored so that a correct translation can be selected in step 4. Based on our assumption, we conducted an experiment to study ways to score translation candidates that would result in correct keyword translations.

## 3   The Experiment

In this experiment we use three free web-based MT systems. We choose to use free web-based MT systems because 1) They are easily accessible, and 2) They are free. We study the performance (translation correctness) of the Keyword Translator using one, two, and three MT systems with different keyword scoring algorithms, from English to Chinese.

### 3.1   Data Sets

For building the models and tuning the parameters, we compiled a list of 50 English questions by selecting different types of questions from TREC-8, TREC-9, and TREC-10. Then we ran the Question Analyzer module over these questions to get the English keywords. The English question sentences and keywords are the input to the Keyword Translator.

For testing the translator, we randomly selected another set of 50 English questions from the same source, making sure that no questions on the training set appears on this testing set. The Question Analyzer module was also used to produce the keywords for input to the Keyword Translator.

### 3.2   Evaluation Criteria

The correctness of the translation is evaluated by hand; a translated keyword is considered correct if: 1) it is a valid translation of the original according to the context of the question sentence, and, 2) it is fully translated.

| Vesuvius → Vesuvius |
| Lou Gehrig's disease → 楼 · Gehrig 's 疾病 |

**Fig. 1.** Examples of keywords not fully translated.

In the above example (Figure 1), "Vesuvius" is not translated as "维苏威," which is the correct translation of "Vesuvius." Instead, "Vesuvius" is returned un-translated. In this case the translation is incorrect. However, there is an exception when an English word's Chinese counterpart is the English word itself. For example, "Photoshop" is a valid Chinese translation of the English word "Photoshop" because Photoshop is never transliterated or translated into Chinese characters in Chinese documents. For evaluating translation correctness, we consider all keywords to be equal. Some keywords are naturally more important than others, so in a question-answering setting it is more important to translate these correctly. Some keywords may not be as important, and some keywords, due to the incorrect analysis of the English question sentence by the Question Analysis module, may even degrade the translation and question-answering performance. In this experiment, however, we will consider all keywords to be equal. The translation correctness will be evaluated based on the percentage of keywords translated correctly. The performance of the different models and combinations of models will be evaluated based on both the percentage of keywords translated correctly and the improvement over the baseline model.

### 3.3    MT Systems and Baseline Model

We do keyword translation using three general-purpose MT systems freely available on the internet1; we will refer to them as S12, S23, and S34.

We first test the three systems independently on the training set, with following results:

**Table 1.** Performance of independent MT systems.

|                        | $S^1$    | $S^2$    | $S^3$   |
|------------------------|----------|----------|---------|
| **Correct/ Total Keywords** | 104/125  | 102/125  | 92/125  |
| **Accuracy**           | 83.20%   | 81.60%   | 73.60%  |

The scoring algorithm of the baseline model is simply to score keywords which appear in two or more MT systems higher than those appear in only one MT system. In the case where all three have the same score (in the baseline model, this happens when all three MT systems give different translations), the translation given by the best-performing individual system, S1, would be selected. And in the case where S2 and S3 tie for the highest scoring keyword, S2 is chosen over S3. This is so that the accuracy of multiple MT's would be at least as good as the best individual MT when there is a tie in the scores. Table 2 shows the MT systems we choose for 1, 2, and 3-MT system models for comparing the improvement of multiple MT systems over individual MT systems. Note that we choose the MT systems to use for evaluating one- MT and two-MT performance based on Table 1, using the best MT first. This way the improvement made by adding more MT's is not inflated by adding MT's with higher performance.

**Table 2.** MT systems used for 1, 2, and 3-MT models

| 1-MT model | 2-MT model | 3-MT model |
|------------|------------|------------|
| $S^1$ | $S^1S^2$ | $S^1S^2S^3$ |

English Sentence: How rich is Bill Gates?
English Keywords: rich/Bill Gates/
S1:  rich -> 富有
      Bill Gates -> 比尔·格茨
S2:  rich -> 丰富
      Bill Gates -> 比尔盖茨
S3:  rich -> 富有
      Bill Gates -> 比尔盖茨
***Final Keywords***
富有/比尔盖茨/

**Fig. 2.** An example of the baseline model.

In the above example, both 富有 and 比尔盖茨 appear in two MT systems, so they were selected instead of 丰富 and 比尔·格茨. However, with the baseline model, using more MT systems may not give us improvement over the 83.2% accuracy of the best individual system. This is due to the following reasons: 1) For many keywords MT systems all disagree with one another, so S1 is chosen by default, and 2) MT systems may agree on the wrong translation. The results from the baseline model show that there is much room for improvement in the scoring algorithm.

## 4   Keyword Scoring Metrics

In this section we describe the metrics used to score or penalize keywords to improve over the baseline model.

### 4.1   Segmented Word-Matching with Partial Word-Matching

Many incorrect translations are incorrect due to sense ambiguity. For sense disambiguation we propose segmented word-matching with partial word-matching. This method is based on our assumption that question sentences provide a "context" in which to translate the keywords in the correct sense.

First we translate the question sentences using the same MT systems used to translate the keywords. Then we segment the sentence (since in written Chinese word boundaries are not marked by spaces) using a combination of forward-most matching and backward-most matching. Forward-most matching (FMM) is a greedy string matching algorithm that starts from left to right and tries to find the longest substring of the string in a word list (we use a word list of 128,455 Mandarin Chinese words compiled from different resources). Backward-most matching (BMM) does the same thing from right to left. We keep the words segmented from FMM and BMM in an array that we call "the segmented sentence." See Figure 3.

---

Sentence: 什么是高尔夫球的直径
FMM: 什么是/高尔夫球/的/直径/
BMM: 什么是/高/尔/夫/球/的/直径/
Segmented Sentence: 什么是/夫/尔/球的/的/直径/高/高尔夫球/

---

**Fig. 3.** An example of segmentation.

After we have the segmented Chinese sentence, we try to match the translated keywords to the segmented sentence, and keywords that match the segmented sentence are scored higher, since they are more likely to be translated in the context of the question sentence.

A feature of the Chinese language is that words sharing the characters are often semantically related. Using this idea, a translated keyword is considered to "partially match" the segmented sentence if the keyword have characters in common with any word in the segmented sentence (i.e. there exists a string that is both a substring of the keyword and a substring of any word in the segmented sentence). A partially matched keyword does not get as high a score as a fully matched word. So a fully matched word would score higher than a partially matched word, and a partially matched word would score higher than a word that does not match at all. As we have mentioned previously, if keywords words have the same score, then by default, S1 is selected over S2 or S3, and S2 is selected over S3. When a keyword translation partially matches a word in the segmented sentence, *it is the word in the segmented sentence that is used as the keyword.* Figure 4 shows examples of fully matched and partially matched words.

---

| 非洲 fully matches 非洲 | – because these two strings are identical |
| 加利福尼亚 partially matches 加州 | – because "加" is a common substring of both words |
| 猎犬 partially matches金黄猎犬 | – because "猎犬" is a common substring of both words |

---

**Fig. 4.** Examples of partial word-matching.

Figure 5 shows a full example of segmented word-matching with partial word-matching. We see from the example that 最高的 is chosen over 高 since a fully matched word scores higher than a partially matched word. In both S1 and S2, "山" partially matches "山的" and "山的" is selected as the translation instead of "山."

```
English Sentence: What is the name of the highest mountain in Africa?
English Keywords: highest/mountain/name/Africa/
S1:   Sentence Translation: 高山的名字是什么在非洲?
        Segmentation: 什么/名字/在/山的/是/的/非洲/高/高山/
        Keyword Translations:
        最高 (highest) partially matches 高
        山 (mountain) partially matches 山的
        名字 (name) matches 名字
        非洲 (Africa) matches 非洲
S2:   Sentence Translation: 在非洲的最高的山的名字是什么？
        Segmentation: 什么/名字/在/山的/是/最高的/非洲的/
        Keyword Translations:
        最高的 (highest) matches 最高的
        山 (mountain) partially matches 山的
        名字 (name) matches 名字
        非洲 (Africa) partially matches 非洲的
***Final Keywords***
最高的/山的/名字/非洲/
```

**Fig. 5.** An example of segmented word-matching with partial word-matching.

## 4.2   Full Sentence Word-Matching (With or Without Fall Back to Partial Word-Matching)

One potential problem with the previous (3.2.1) algorithm is that the word list we used may not provide adequate coverage to properly segment the question sentence. For example, since the Chinese word "棱镜" ("prism") is not in the word list, the segmentation results in two single-character words that do not carry the same meaning:

棱镜 [prism] -> 棱/镜/ [angular/mirror/]

In order to solve the problem with the limited coverage of the word list, we also tried word-matching on the entire un-segmented sentence. This is a simple string matching to see if the translated keyword is a substring of the translated question sentence. There are two variations to this metric; in the case where word-matching on the entire un-segmented question sentence fails, we can either fall back to partial word-matching on the segmented sentence or not fall back to partial word-matching. Figures 6 shows full sentence word-matching with fall back to partial word-matching and Figure 7 shows full sentence word-matching without fall back to partial word-matching:

In both Figure 6 and 7, "山", "名字", and "非洲" matches the question sentence but "最高" does not. In Figure 6, partial-matching is used to match "最高" to "高" therefore "高" is considered to be the partial-matched translation and is scored as a partial matched keyword. In Figure 7, "最高" does not go through partial matching so no score is added to the keyword.

## 4.3   Penalty for Keywords Not Fully Translated

As we explained in section 3.2, keywords that are not fully translated are usually considered incorrect. So we put a penalty on the score of keywords that are not fully translated.

English Sentence:
What is the name of the highest mountain in
Africa?
English Keywords:
highest/mountain/name/Africa/
Sentence Translation:
高山的名字是什么在非洲?
Segmentation:
什么/名字/在/山的/是/的/非洲/高/高山/
Keyword Translations:
最高 (highest) partially matches 高
山 (mountain) matches question sentence
名字 (name) matches question sentence
非洲 (Africa) matches question sentence

English Sentence:
What is the name of the highest mountain in
Africa?
English Keywords:
highest/mountain/name/Africa/
Sentence Translation:
高山的名字是什么在非洲?
Keyword Translations:
最高 (highest) does not match sentence
山 (mountain) matches sentence
名字 (name) matches sentence
非洲 (Africa) matches sentence

**Fig. 6.** An example of full sentence word-matching with fall back to partial word-matching.

**Fig. 7.** An example of full sentence word-matching without fall back to partial word-matching.

English Keywords:
Maria Theresa/
S1:  玛丽亚 · Theresa
S2:  玛利亚·特立莎
***Final Keywords***
玛利亚·特立莎/

**Fig. 8.** An example of penalty for keywords not fully translated.

This is done by simply checking if [A-Z][a-z] appear in the keyword string. In Figure 8, the score for the translation candidate "玛丽亚 · Theresa" is penalized because it is not a full translation. So "玛利亚·特立莎" is selected instead.

### 4.4  Scoring

Each keyword starts with an initial score of 0.0, and as different metrics are applied, numbers are added to or subtracted from the score. Table 3 shows actual numbers used for this experiment; the same scoring scheme is used by all scoring metrics when applicable.

**Table 3.** Scoring scheme.

| A | B | C | D |
|---|---|---|---|
| Full Match | Partial Match | Support by >1 MT | Not Fully Translated |
| +1.0 | +0.5 | +0.3 | -1.3 |

The general strategy behind the scoring scheme is as follows: keywords with full match (A) receive the highest score, keywords with partial match (B) receive the second highest score, keywords supported by more than one MT system (C) receive the lowest score, and keywords not fully translated (D) receive a penalty to their score. All of the above can be applied to the same keyword except for A and B, since a keyword cannot be both a full match and a partial match at the same time. Support by more than one MT system receives the least score because in our experiment it has shown

**Table 4.** Abbreviation for scoring metrics and the scoring that is applied

| | Description (section) | Scoring |
|---|---|---|
| **B** | Baseline (3.3) | C |
| **S** | Segmented Word-Matching and Partial Word-Matching (4.1) | A,B |
| **F¹** | Full Sentence Word-Matching without Fall Back to Partial Word-Matching (4.2) | A |
| **F²** | Full Sentence Word-Matching with Fall Back to Partial Word-Matching (4.2) | A,B |
| **P** | Penalty for Partially Translated or Un-Translated Keywords (4.3) | D |

**Table 5.** Keyword translation accuracy of different models on the training set.

| Model | $S^1$ | $S^1S^2$ | $S^1S^2S^3$ |
|---|---|---|---|
| **B** | 83.20% | 83.20% | 83.20% |
| **B+S** | 58.40% | 64.80% | 66.40% |
| **B+F¹** | 83.20% | 85.60% | 87.20% |
| **B+F²** | 80.80% | 84.00% | 86.40% |
| **B+P** | 83.20% | 83.20% | 83.20% |
| **B+F¹+P** | **83.20%** | **89.60%** | **90.40%** |
| **B+F²+P** | 80.80% | 88.00% | 89.60% |

**Table 6.** Improvement of different models over the baseline model on the training set.

| Model | $S^1$ | $S^1S^2$ | $S^1S^2S^3$ |
|---|---|---|---|
| **B+S** | -29.81% | -22.12% | -20.19% |
| **B+F¹** | 0.00% | 2.88% | 4.81% |
| **B+F²** | -2.88% | 0.96% | 3.85% |
| **B+P** | 0.00% | 0.00% | 0.00% |
| **B+F¹+P** | **0.00%** | **7.69%** | **8.65%** |
| **B+F²+P** | -2.88% | 5.77% | 7.69% |

to be the least reliable indication of a correct translation. Full match has shown to be the best indicator of a correct translation, therefore it receives the highest score and it is higher than the combination of partial match and support by more than one MT system. Keywords not fully translated should be penalized heavily, since they are generally considered incorrect; therefore the penalty is set equal to the highest score possible, the combination of A and C. This way, another translation that is a full translation has the opportunity to receive a higher score. With the above general strategy in mind, the numbers were manually tuned to give the best result on the training set.

# 5   Results

We construct different 7 models (including the baseline model) by combining various scoring metrics. In all models we use the baseline metric that adds score to keyword translation candidates that are supported by more than one MT system. Table 4 shows the abbreviation for each metric, the description of each metric, the section of this paper that describe each metric, and the scoring (refer to Table 3 column headings to look up scoring) that applies to each metric:

Table 5 shows the percentage of keywords translated correctly using different models on the training set, which consists of 125 keywords from 50 questions. Table 6 shows the improvement of different models over the baseline model based on Table5:

Table 7 shows the percentage of keywords translated correctly using different models on the test set, which consists of 147 keywords from 50 questions. Table 8 shows the improvement over the baseline:

Note that all models which use only one MT system does not improve over the baseline model because no improvement can be made when there is no alternative translations to choose from. However, single-MT models can degrade due to partial word-matching using segmented sentence. We will discuss problems with using segmented sentence and other issues in the next section.

**Table 7.** Keyword translation accuracy of different models on the test set.

| Model | $S^1$ | $S^1S^2$ | $S^1S^2S^3$ |
|---|---|---|---|
| B | 78.23% | 78.23% | 78.91% |
| B+S | 59.86% | 61.90% | 64.63% |
| B+F¹ | 78.23% | 80.27% | 80.95% |
| B+F² | 76.19% | 75.51% | 78.91% |
| B+P | 78.23% | 78.23% | 78.91% |
| B+F¹+P | 78.23% | 82.99% | 85.71% |
| B+F²+P | 76.19% | 78.23% | 83.67% |

**Table 8.** Improvement of different models over the baseline model on the test set.

| Model | $S^1$ | $S^1S^2$ | $S^1S^2S^3$ |
|---|---|---|---|
| B+S | -23.48% | -20.87% | -18.10% |
| B+F¹ | 0.00% | 2.61% | 2.59% |
| B+F² | -2.61% | -3.48% | 0.00% |
| B+P | 0.00% | 0.00% | 0.00% |
| B+F¹+P | 0.00% | 6.08% | 8.62% |
| B+F²+P | -2.61% | 0.00% | 6.95% |

**Table 9.** Pros and cons of the scoring metrics.

|   | Pros | Cons |
|---|---|---|
| B | Can be a tie-breaker when two MT systems have the same score | Provides little improvement |
| S | May work well with an adequate word list is for segmentation* | Very poor without adequate word list |
| F¹ | Provides contextual disambiguation; does not need segmentation | Does not do partial matching |
| F² | Provides contextual disambiguation | Needs adequate word list |
| P | Good for selecting translation when individual MT systems lack word coverage | |

## 6  Discussions

From the results of different models on the training set and test set, we make the following observations:

1. In almost all models, increasing the number of MT systems used either increase the performance of the model or does nothing to the model; in other words, additional MT systems do not seem to degrade translation correctness but has the potential to improve translation correctness.
2. As shown in model B+F1, using word-matching on the translated question sentence for sense disambiguation does improve translation correctness.
3. From results of models with S and F2 we see that scoring metrics requiring word list segmentation not only does not improve the translation, they can degrade the translation beyond the baseline model. Upon observation we see that this method, though intuitively sound, relies on the word list to do the segmentation, and word lists' limited coverage degrades the translation greatly.
4. Full sentence word-matching (F1) with penalty for partially or un-translated keywords (P) yields the best results. Although P does not improve the baseline by itself, it boosts the performance of F1 greatly when combined.

From the above four points and other observations, we briefly describe the pros and cons of using the different scoring metrics in Table 9. The asterisk (*) indicates that this experiment does not validate the statement due to the limited coverage of the word list we used.

From Table 9 we can see why model B+F1+P with all three MT systems out performs the others. It 1) uses three MT systems, 2) penalizes keywords that are not fully translated, and 3) does word sense disambiguation without relying on segmentation which needs a word list with adequate coverage, and such a word list may be difficult to obtain. Thus for translating keywords using general MT systems, we can suggest that 1) it is better to use more MT systems if they are available, 2) always penalize un-translated words because different MT systems have different word coverage, and 3) in a setting where resources are limited (small word lists), it is better not to use methods involving segmentation.

## 7   Conclusion

In this paper, we first present the general problem of keyword translation in a multilingual open-domain question-answering system. Then based on this general problem, we chose an MT-based approach using multiple free web-based MT systems. And based on our assumption that using multiple MT systems and the question sentence can improve translation correctness, we present several scoring metrics that can be used to build models that choose among keyword translation candidates. Using these models in an experiment, we show that using multiple MT system and using the question sentence to do sense disambiguation can improve the correctness of keyword translation.

**Acknowledgements.** This work was supported in part by the Advanced Research and Development Activity (ARDA)'s Advanced Question Answering for Intelligence (AQUAINT) Program.

## References

1. Nyberg, E., Mitamura, T., Callan, J., Carbonell, J., Frederking, R., Collins-Thompson, K., Hiyakumoto, L., Huang, Y., Huttenhower, C., Judy, S., Ko, J., Kupse, A., Lita, L., Pedro, V., Svoboda, D., and Van Durme, B.: The JAVELIN Question-Answering System at TREC 2003: A Multi-Strategy Approach with Dynamic Planning. In: Proceedings of the 12th Text REtrieval Conference (2003).
2. Yang, Y. and Ma, N.: CMU in Cross-Language Information Retrieval at NTCIR-3. In: Proceedings of the Third NTCIR Workshop (2003).
3. Chen, H-H., Bian, G-W. and Lin, W-C.: Resolving Translation Ambiguity and Target Polysemy in Cross-Language Information Retrieval. In: Proceedings of the Third NTCIR Workshop (2002).
4. Chen, A., Jiang, H. and Gey, F.: Combining Multiple Sources for Short Query Translation in Chinese- English Cross-Language Information Retrieval. In: Proceedings of the Fifth International Workshop Information Retrieval with Asian Languages (2000).
5. Gao, J., Nie, J-Y., Xun, E., Zhang, J., Zhou, M. and Huang, C.: Improving Query Translation for Cross- Language Information Retrieval using Statistical Models. In: Proceedings of the 24th annual international ACM SIGIR conference on Research and development in information retrieval (2001).
6. Jang, G. M., Kim, P., Jin, Y., Cho, S-H. and Myaeng, S. H.: Simple Query Translation Methods for Korean-English and Korean-Chinese CLIR in NTCIR Experiments. In: Proceedings of the Third NTCIR Workshop (2003).
7. Lin, W-C. and Chen, H-H.: Description of NTU Approach to NTCIR3 Multilingual Information Retrieval. In: Proceedings of the Third NTCIR Workshop (2003).
8. Seo, H-C., Kim, S-B., Kim, B-I., Rim, H-C. and Lee, S-Z.: KUNLP System for NTCIR-3 English- Korean Cross-Language Information Retrieval. In: Proceedings of the Third NTCIR Workshop (2003).

9.  Pirkola, A.: The Effects of Query Structure and Dictionary Setups in Dictionary-Based Cross-Language Information Retrieval. In: SIGIR 98 (1998).
10. Lam-Adesina, A. M. and Jones, G. J. F.: EXETER AT CLEF 2002: Experiments with Machine Translation for Monolingual and Bilingual Retrieval. In: Advances in Cross-Language Information Retrieval, Third Workshop of the Cross-Language Evaluation Forum, CLEF 2002 (2002).
11. Kwok, K. L.: NTCIR-3 Chinese, Cross Language Retrieval Experiments Using PIRCS. In: Proceedings of the Third NTCIR Workshop (2003).
12. Zhang, J., Sun, L., Qu, W., Du, L., Sun, Y., Fan, Y. and Lin, Z.: ISCAS at NTCIR-3: Monolingual, Bilingual and MultiLingual IR Tasks. In: Proceedings of the Third NTCIR Workshop (2003).

# Extraction of Name and Transliteration in Monolingual and Parallel Corpora

Tracy Lin[1], Jian-Cheng Wu[2], and Jason S. Chang[2]

[1] Department of Communication Engineering
National Chiao Tung University
1001, Ta Hsueh Road, Hsinchu, Taiwan, ROC
tracylin@mail.nctu.edu.tw

[2] Dept of Computer Science, National Tsing Hua Univ.
101, Sec. 2, Kuang Fu Rd.
Hsinchu, Taiwan, ROC
jschang@cs.nthu.edu.tw

**Abstract.** Named-entities in free text represent a challenge to text analysis in Machine Translation and Cross Language Information Retrieval. These phrases are often transliterated into another language with a different sound inventory and writing system. Named-entities found in free text are often not listed in bilingual dictionaries. Although it is possible to identify and translate named-entities on the fly without a list of proper names and transliterations, an extensive list of existing transliterations certainly will ensure high precision rate. We use a seed list of proper names and transliterations to train a *Machine Transliteration Model*. With the model it is possible to extract proper names and their transliterations in monolingual or parallel corpora with high precision and recall rates.

## 1 Introduction

Multilingual named entity identification and (back) transliteration are important for machine translation (MT), question answering (QA), cross language information retrieval (CLIR). These transliterated names are not usually found in existing bilingual dictionaries. Thus, it is difficult to handle transliteration only via simple dictionary lookup. The effectiveness of CLIR hinges on the accuracy of transliteration since proper names are important in information retrieval.

Handling transliterations of proper names is not as trivial as one might think. Transliterations tend to vary from translator to translator, especially for names of less known persons and unfamiliar places. That is exacerbated by different Romanization systems used for Asian names written in Mandarin Chinese or Japanese. Back transliteration involves conversion of transliteration back to the unique original name. So there is one and only solution for most instances of the back transliteration task. Therefore, back transliteration is considered more difficult than transliteration. Knight and Graehl [4] pioneered the study of automatic transliteration by the computer and proposed a statistical transliteration model to experiment on converting Japanese

R.E. Frederking and K.B. Taylor (Eds.): AMTA 2004, LNAI 3265, pp. 177–186, 2004.
© Springer-Verlag Berlin Heidelberg 2004

transliterations back to English. Following Knight and Graehl, most previous work on machine transliteration [1, 2, 6, 8, 9, 10, 11] focused on the tasks of machine transliteration and back-transliteration. Very little has been touched on the issue of extracting names and their transliterations from corpora [5, 7].

The alternative to phoneme-by-phoneme machine (back) transliteration is simple table lookup in *transliteration memory* automatically acquired from corpora. Most instances of names and transliteration counterparts can often be found in large monolingual or parallel corpora that are relevant to the task. In this paper, we propose a new method for extraction names and transliterations based on a statistical model trained automatically on a bilingual proper name list via unsupervised learning. We also carried out experiments and evaluation of training and applying the proposed model to extract names and translations from two parallel corpora and a Mandarin translation corpus. The remainder of the paper is organized as follows. Section 2 lays out the model and describes how to apply the model to align word and transliteration. Section 3 describes how the model is trained on a set of proper names and transliterations. Section 4 describes experiments and evaluation. Section 5 contains discussion and we conclude in Section 6.

## 2   Machine Transliteration Model

We will first illustrate our approach with examples. Consider transliterating the English word "*Stanford*," into Mandarin Chinese. Although there are conceivably many acceptable transliterations, the most common one is "史丹福." (Romanization: "shi-dan-fo"). We assume that transliteration is done piecemeal, converting one to six letters as a transliteration unit (TU) to a Mandarin character (transliteration character, TC). For instance, in order to transliterate "Stanford," we break it up into four TU's: "*s*," "*tan*," "*for*," and "*d*." We assume that each TU is converted to zero to two Mandarin characters independently. In this case, the "*s*" is converted to "史," "*tan*" to "丹," "*for*" to "佛," and "*d*" to the empty string λ. In other words, we model the transliteration process based on independence of transliteration of TU's. Therefore, we have the *transliteration probability* of getting the transliteration "史丹佛" given "*Stanford*," $P(史丹佛 \mid Stanford)$,

$$P(史丹佛 \mid Stanford) = \Sigma_a \Pi_i P(a) \, P(a(e_i) \mid e_i) = \Sigma_a \Pi_i P(a) \, P(f_i \mid e_i)$$
$$\approx P(史 \mid s) P(丹 \mid tan) P(佛 \mid for) P(\lambda \mid d)$$

where $a$ is the alignment between English transliteration units (mostly syllables) $e_i$ and Mandarin Chinese characters $f_i$.

It might appear that using Chinese phonemes instead of characters will be more effective to cope with data sparseness. However, there is a strong tendency to use a limited set of characters for transliteration purposes. By using characters directly, we can take advantage of lexical preference and obtain tighter estimates (see Figure 1).

There are several ways such a machine transliteration model (MTM) can be applied, including (1) *Transliteration* of proper names (2) *Back Transliteration* to the original proper name (3) *Name-transliteration Extraction* in a corpus. We will focus on the third problem of name-transliteration extraction in this study.

| τ | ω | P(τ\|ω) | τ | ω | P(τ\|ω) | τ | ω | P(τ\|ω) | τ | ω | P(τ\|ω) | τ | ω | P(τ\|ω) |
|---|---|---|---|---|---|---|---|---|---|---|---|---|---|---|
| a | 亞 | .458 | | 厄 | .034 | | 依 | .043 | | 奈 | .500 | | 游 | .053 |
| | 阿 | .271 | | 伊 | .034 | | 義 | .043 | o | 奧 | .357 | | 爾 | .053 |
| | 艾 | .059 | | 依 | .034 | | 綺 | .043 | | 俄 | .143 | | 歐 | .053 |
| | λ | .051 | | 埃 | .034 | io | 奧 | .500 | | 歐 | .143 | | 優 | .053 |
| | 安 | .017 | | 因 | .017 | | 歐 | .500 | | λ | .071 | v | 夫 | .588 |
| | 拉 | .017 | | 衣 | .017 | je | 傑 | .375 | | 阿 | .036 | | 維 | .176 |
| | 埃 | .017 | | 亞 | .017 | | 杰 | .250 | | 約 | .036 | | 伏 | .059 |
| | 奧 | .017 | | 阿 | .017 | | 耶 | .250 | | 渥 | .036 | | 佛 | .059 |
| an | 安 | .923 | | 耶 | .017 | | 潔 | .125 | | 霍 | .036 | | 芙 | .059 |
| | 恩 | .077 | | 爾 | .017 | ju | 朱 | .500 | oa | 瓦 | .333 | vo | 弗 | .400 |
| ar | 阿 | .750 | en | 恩 | .833 | | 菊 | .500 | | 奧 | .333 | | 佛 | .400 |
| | 亞 | .250 | | 英 | .167 | k | 克 | .797 | | 歐 | .333 | | 沃 | .200 |
| b | 布 | .700 | f | 夫 | .300 | | λ | .145 | p | 普 | .839 | w | λ | .500 |
| | λ | .133 | | 佛 | .300 | | 庫 | .014 | | λ | .065 | | 夫 | .250 |
| | 伯 | .033 | | 弗 | .250 | | 桂 | .014 | | 布 | .032 | wa | 華 | .500 |
| | 柏 | .033 | | λ | .075 | | 珂 | .014 | | 卑 | .032 | | 瓦 | .250 |
| | 普 | .033 | | 孚 | .025 | kan | 肯 | .333 | | 培 | .032 | | 威 | .100 |
| | 比 | .017 | | 法 | .025 | | 康 | .333 | por | 波 | .500 | | 沃 | .050 |
| | 白 | .017 | | 福 | .025 | | 堪 | .333 | | 坡 | .250 | | 韋 | .050 |
| | 勃 | .017 | for | 福 | .714 | l | 爾 | .800 | | 葡 | .250 | woo | 伍 | .857 |
| berg | 堡 | .800 | | 佛 | .143 | | λ | .080 | q | 克 | 1.000 | | 塢 | .143 |
| | 柏 | .200 | g | 格 | .500 | | 耳 | .020 | que | 克 | .667 | x | 克斯 | .591 |
| can | 坎 | .429 | | 葛 | .196 | | 羅 | .020 | | 魁 | .333 | | 克士 | .091 |
| | 加 | .143 | | λ | .179 | li | 利 | .658 | r | 爾 | .741 | | 斯 | .091 |
| | 岡 | .143 | | 平 | .018 | | 里 | .105 | | 耳 | .074 | | 克思 | .046 |
| | 堅 | .143 | | 克 | .018 | | 來 | .079 | | λ | .056 | | 克 | .046 |
| | 堪 | .143 | | 哥 | .018 | | 立 | .026 | | 勒 | .037 | | λ | .046 |
| chi | 奇 | .200 | ge | 奇 | .231 | | 李 | .026 | | 洛 | .019 | xa | 克 | .500 |
| | 基 | .200 | | 格 | .231 | | 律 | .026 | | 奧 | .019 | | 克薩 | .500 |
| | 齊 | .133 | | 吉 | .154 | | 賴 | .026 | | 盧 | .019 | y | 伊 | .462 |
| | 支 | .067 | | 日 | .115 | m | 姆 | .800 | ren | 倫 | .846 | | 依 | .154 |
| | 吉 | .067 | | 及 | .077 | | λ | .080 | | 阮 | .077 | | λ | .077 |
| | 西 | .067 | | 蓋 | .077 | | 木 | .040 | | 藍 | .077 | | 以 | .077 |
| | 芝 | .067 | | 戈 | .038 | | 曼 | .040 | run | 倫 | .500 | | 灣 | .077 |
| | 契 | .067 | | 芝 | .038 | | 梅 | .040 | | 隆 | .500 | ye | 耶 | .667 |
| | 蚩 | .067 | | 基 | .038 | mun | 孟 | .500 | s | 斯 | .704 | | 葉 | .333 |
| | 智 | .067 | h | λ | .833 | | 蒙 | .500 | | λ | .092 | z | 茲 | .476 |
| d | 德 | .526 | | 合 | .083 | my | 米 | .500 | | 史 | .078 | | λ | .286 |
| | λ | .299 | | 赫 | .083 | | 美 | .500 | | 士 | .031 | | 士 | .095 |
| | 特 | .013 | han | 漢 | .500 | n | λ | .457 | sun | 桑 | .500 | | 芝 | .048 |
| da | 戴 | .095 | | 韓 | .300 | | 恩 | .326 | | 森 | .500 | | 斯 | .048 |
| | 大 | .071 | | 汗 | .100 | | 尼 | .043 | t | 特 | .627 | | | |
| | 丹 | .048 | | 翰 | .100 | | 昂 | .043 | | λ | .262 | | | |
| | 代 | .024 | i | 伊 | .348 | | 安 | .022 | tz | 茲 | .444 | | | |
| | 答 | .024 | | 易 | .174 | nar | 那 | .500 | | 茨 | .444 | | | |
| e | λ | .254 | | λ | .087 | | 納 | .500 | | 實 | .111 | | | |
| | 艾 | .237 | | 以 | .087 | ny | 尼 | .500 | u | 烏 | .474 | | | |
| | 愛 | .102 | | 艾 | .043 | | | | | λ | .105 | | | |

**Fig. 1.** TU τ and TC ω mappings; Low probability mappings are removed for clarity.

**Name and Transliteration Extraction Problem**

Given a pair of sentence and translation counterpart, align the words and transliterations therein. For instance, given (1) and (2)

(1) Paul Berg, professor emeritus of biology at Stanford University and a Nobel laureate ...
    史丹佛大學生物系的榮譽教授，諾貝爾獎得主伯格，

We should obtain the alignment results with three name-transliteration pairs: (*Stanford*, 史丹福), (*Nobel*, 諾貝爾), (*Berg*, 伯格).

On the other hand, it is also possible to extract name-transliteration pairs from a monolingual corpus of original or translation text. The common practice of showing source term in brackets (STIB) following the translation gives us lots of instances of name-transliteration pairs in a translation text or document written in a language other than English. For instance, consider the following sentence from the Britannica Concise Encyclopedia, Taiwanese Edition written in Traditional Chinese (BCE/TE):

(3) 德國西部城市(1995年人口約247,000)，位於科隆(Cologne)西北方...
    (City (pop., 1995 est.: 247,000) Western Germany, southwest of Cologne ...)

We should be able to obtain the name-transliteration pair (*Cologne*, 科隆).

The memory-based alternative to machine transliteration is very attractive, considering the ever increasing availability of machine readable texts of original work and translation.

## 2.1  The Statistical Model

We propose a new way for modeling transliteration of an English word $W$ into Chinese characters $T$ via a Machine Transliteration Model. We assume that transliteration is carried out by splitting $W$ into $k$ units (TUs), $\omega_1, \omega_2, ..., \omega_k$ which are subsequently converted independently into $k$ characters (TCs), $\tau_1, \tau_2, ..., \tau_k$ respectively. Finally, $\tau_1, \tau_2, ..., \tau_k$ are put together to produce the transliteration output $T$. Therefore, the probability of converting $W$ into $T$ can be expressed as

$$P(T \mid W) = \max_{k, \omega_1 ... \omega_k, \tau_1 ... \tau_k} \prod_{i=1,k} P(\tau_i \mid \omega_i) \quad , \tag{1}$$

where $W = \omega_1 \omega_2 ... \omega_k$, $T = \tau_1 \tau_2 ... \tau_k$, $|T|$   $k$   $|T| + |W|$, $\tau_i \omega_i$   $\lambda$.

Given a list of proper names and transliterations, it is possible to break up names and transliterations into pairs of matching TUs and TCs. With these matching TUs and TCs, it is then possible to estimate the parameters for the machine transliteration model. That process of applying model to decompose names and their transliterations and train the model can be carried out in a self organized fashion by using the Expectation Maximization (EM) algorithm [3].

## 2.2 Training

In the training phase, we estimated the transliteration probability function $P(\tau|\omega)$, for any given TU $\omega$ and TC $\tau$, based on a given list of names and transliterations. Based on the EM algorithm with Viterbi decoding, the iterative parameter estimation procedure on a set of $n$ training data $(W_k, T_k)$, $k = 1$, to $n$, is described as follows:

**Initialization Step:** Initially, we have a simple model $P_0(\tau|\omega)$

$$P_0(\tau|\omega) = \text{similarity } (R(\tau) \mid \omega) = \text{dice } (t_1 t_2 \ldots t_a, w_1 w_2 \ldots w_b) = \frac{2 \times c}{a+b}, \qquad (2)$$

where $R(\tau)$ = Romanization of Mandarin character $\tau$,
$R(\tau) = t_1 t_2 \ldots t_a$, $\omega = w_1 w_2 \ldots w_b$,
$c$ = number of common letters between $R(\tau)$ and $\omega$

For instance, Consider the case where $W$ = '*Nayyar*' and $T$ = '納雅.' We have $R(\tau_1)$ = $R$('納') = 'na' and $R(\tau_2)$ = $R$('雅') = 'ya' under the Yanyu Pinyin Romanization System. Therefore, breaking up $W$ into two TUs, $\omega_1$ = 'nay' $\omega_2$ = 'yar' lead to the following probabilistic values:

$$P_0(\tau_1 \mid \omega_1) = \text{similarity } (\mathbf{na} \mid nay) = \frac{2 \times 2}{2+3} = 0.8, \text{ and}$$

$$P_0(\tau_2 \mid \omega_2) = \text{similarity } (\mathbf{ya} \mid yar) = \frac{2 \times 2}{2+3} = 0.8$$

**Expectation Step:** In the expectation step, the best way to describe how a proper name gets transliterated is revealed via decomposition into TU's which amounts to calculating the maximum probability $P(T, W)$ in Equation 3:

$$P(T,W) = \max_{k, \omega_1 \ldots \omega_k, \tau_1 \ldots \tau_k} \prod_{i=1,k} P(\tau_i \mid \omega_i), \qquad (3)$$

where $W = \omega_1 \omega_2 \ldots \omega_K$, $T = \tau_1 \tau_2 \ldots \tau_K$, $|T|$   $k$   $|W| + |T|$, $\omega_i \tau_i \neq \lambda$

That also amounts to finding the best Viterbi path matching up TU's in $W$ and TC's in $T$. This can be done by using Equation (3). For that to be done efficiently, we need to define and calculate the *forward probability* $\alpha(i, j) = P(T_{1:i-1}, W_{1:j-1})$ via dynamic programming, $\alpha(i, j)$ denotes the probability of aligning the first $i$-1 Chinese characters[1] $T_{1:i-1}$ and the first $j$-1 English letters $W_{1:j-1}$.

$$\alpha(1, 1) = 1, \qquad (4)$$
$$\alpha(i, j) = \max_{a=0,2, b=1,6} \alpha(i-a, j-b) \, P(\tau \mid \omega), \text{ where } \tau = T_{i-a:i-1} \text{ and } \omega = W_{j-b:j-1}.$$

---

[1] The cases involving two Mandarin characters are rare. The "x" as in "Marx" is transliterated into two TCs, "克斯," while "xa" as in "Texas" is transliterated as "克薩."

**Table 1.** The results of using $P_0(\tau|\omega)$ to align TUs and TCs

| W | T | $\omega$–$\tau$ matches on the Viterbi path |
|---|---|---|
| Kohn | 孔恩 | koh-孔 n-恩 |
| Nayyar | 納雅 | nay-納 yar-雅 |
| Alivisatos | 阿利維撒托斯 | a-阿 li-利 vi-維 sa-撒 to-托 s-斯 |
| Rivard | 里瓦德 | ri-里 var-瓦 d-德 |
| Nechayev | 納卡耶夫 | ne-納 cha-卡 ye-耶 v-夫 |
| Hitler | 希特勒 | hi-希 t-特 ler-勒 |
| Hunt | 杭特 | hun-杭 t-特 |
| Germain | 杰曼 | ger-杰 main-曼 |
| Gore | 高爾 | go-高 re-爾 |
| Laxson | 拉克森 | la-拉 x-克 son-森 |

After calculating $P(T, W)$ via dynamic programming, we also obtained the matching TUs on the Viterbi path. After all pairs were processed and TU's and TC's were found, we then re-estimated the transliteration probability $P(\tau \mid \omega)$ in the Maximization Step.

**Maximization Step:** With all the $(\omega, \tau)$ pairs obtained for a list of names and transliteration $(W_i, T_i)$ in the Expectation Step, we update the maximum likelihood estimates (MLE) of model parameters using Equation (5).

$$P_{MLE}(\tau \mid \omega) = \frac{\sum_{i=1}^{n} \sum_{(\omega,\tau) \text{ in } (W_i, T_i)} \text{count}(\tau, \omega)}{\sum_{i=1}^{n} \sum_{(\omega,*) \text{ in } (W_i, T_i)} \text{count}(\omega)}. \tag{5}$$

The EM algorithm iterates between the Expectation and Maximization Steps, until $P(\tau \mid \omega)$ converges. The maximum likelihood estimates is generally *not* suitable since it does not capture the fact that there are other transliteration possibilities that we may have not encountered. Based on our observations, we used the linear interpolation (LI) of MLE and Romanization-based estimates of Equation (2) to approximate the parameters in Machine Transliteration Model. Therefore, we have $P_{LI}(\tau \mid \omega) = 0.5$ $P_{MLE}(\tau \mid \omega) + 0.5 \, P_0(\tau \mid \omega)$

## 3   Extraction of Name-Transliteration Pairs

There are two ways in which the machine transliteration model can be applied to extract proper names and their transliterations. In this section, we describe the two cases of transliteration extraction: extracting proper names and their transliterations from a parallel corpus and monolingual corpus.

## Name-Transliteration Extraction from a Parallel Corpus

The name-transliteration extraction process from an aligned sentence pair in a parallel corpus is handled in two steps: First, we identify the proper names in the English sentence. Subsequently, we identify the transliteration for each proper name. For instance, consider the following aligned sentences in the Sinorama Magazine Corpus:

(4) 「當你完全了解了太陽、大氣層以及地球的運轉，你仍會錯過了落日的霞輝，」西洋哲學家<u>懷海德</u>說。

(5) "When you understand all about the sun and all about the atmosphere and all about the rotation of the earth, you may still miss the radiance of the sunset." So wrote English philosopher Alfred North <u>Whitehead</u>.

It is not difficult to build part of speech tagger and named entity recognizer for finding the proper nouns, "Alfred," "North," and "Whitehead." We then use the same process of Viterbi decoding described in Section 2 to identify the transliteration in the target language sentence $S$. All substrings of $S$ are considered as transliteration candidates.

## Name-Transliteration Extraction from a Monolingual Corpus

The strategy of extracting name-transliteration from a monolingual corpus is based on the following observations:

- A translation document tends to have source terms in brackets (STIB) following a translation. This practice is also part of an ISO standard for preparing a translated document (ISO 2384).
- Syllabus-based transliteration model can be used to identify the translation associated with a STIB by matching the transliteration characters predicted by the first transliteration unit of the source term.

For instance, we may find instances of STIB for "Charlemagne," as in the following sentences in a monolingual corpus such as the Britannica Concise Encyclopedia, Taiwanese Edition:

(6) 後成爲查理曼帝國(Charlemagne Empire)第二大城 …
    (… and the second city of Charlemagne's Empire …).

By consulting the transliteration probability table for $P(\tau|c)$, $P(\tau|ch)$, $P(\tau|cha)$ or $P(\tau|char)$ for some Mandarin Chinese character $\tau$. It turned out the most likely Chinese TC is "查" for the English TU "char." We can subsequently extract the string between TC "查" and left bracket as the transliteration for the STIB.

For instance, we obtain the transliteration "查理曼帝國" for STIB "Charlemagne Empire" in (6). Table 2 shows more example sentences in BCE/TE containing STIBs that follow a transliteration. It was observed that by favoring the longer matching TU and leftmost TC, one can obtain the best results. We simply ignored the instances of STIB when no plausible TC is found. We subsequently extracted the string between the matched character and left bracket as the transliteration for the STIB. Table 3 shows some examples and results of transliteration extraction.

**Table 2.** Example sentences containing source terms in brackets following transliterations

| Source sentence containing STIB | Source Term in Bracket |
|---|---|
| 波斯薩非王朝(Safavid Dynasty) | Safavid Dynasty |
| 反對祖父穆罕默德‧阿里(Muhammad Ali) | Muhammad Ali |
| 但不准法國人策劃興建蘇伊士運河(Suez Canal) | Suez Canal |
| 最早的大修道院位於義大利的卡西諾山(Monte Cassino) | Monte Cassino |

**Table 3.** The examples of matching the first TUs of words in STIBs and extracted transliterations

| STIB | Name | 1$^{st}$ TU | 1$^{st}$ TC | Candidate | Output |
|---|---|---|---|---|---|
| Safavid Dynasty | Safavid | s | 斯 | 斯薩非王朝 | |
| Safavid Dynasty | Safavid | sa | 薩 | 薩非王朝 | 薩非王朝 |
| Muhammad Ali | Ali | al | 阿 | 阿里 | |
| Muhammad Ali | muhammad | mu | 穆 | 穆罕默德‧阿里 | 穆罕默德‧阿里 |
| Suez Canal | suez | s | 士 | 士運河 | |
| Suez Canal | suez | s | 蘇 | 蘇伊士運河 | |
| Suez Canal | suez | su | 蘇 | 蘇伊士運河 | 蘇伊士運河 |
| Monte Cassino | cassino | ca | 卡 | 卡西諾山 | 卡西諾山 |

## 4   Experiments and Evaluation

We have carried out rigorous evaluation on an implementation of the method proposed in this paper. Close examination of the experimental results revealed that the machine transliteration is general effective in extracting proper names and their transliterations from a parallel corpus or monolingual corpus. We used a bilingual list of some 1,700 proper names in Scientific American, US and Taiwan Editions to train a statistical machine transliteration model via unsupervised learning. The model was subsequently tested on three sets of data, including bilingual sentences from the Sinorama Magazine and Scientific American (US and Taiwanese Editions), and monolingual sentences with STIBs from Britannica Concise Encyclopedia.

Admittedly, some transliterations were not extracted due to data sparseness of proper TUs and TCs. There are also cases where the STIB consists of common nouns and adjectives therefore is not transliterated; "…1956 年加入民族解放陣線 (National Liberation Front; FLN)" is a case in point. We select 200 source terms each from three different sources to evaluate the performance of the proposed method. The source terms are named entities that are normally transliterated. We adopted a rigid standard of judgments where extracted transliterations must completely match the answer key for them to be judged as correct. As shown in Table 4, for the SA/TE and BCE/TE test sets, the precision rates are over 90%, while for the SM test set is the precision rate is 75%. The articles in Sinorama Magazine contains translation from Mandarin Chinese to English while the model is trained with English name list with Mandarin transliteration. That might account for the lower rate for the SM set.

The success of the proposed method for the most part has to do with the capability to balance two conflicting goals of capturing lexical preference of transliterations and the need for smoothing and coping with data sparseness. Although we experimented with a model trained on English to Chinese transliteration, the model seemed to perform reasonably well even with situations in the opposite direction, Chinese to English transliteration. This indicates that the model with the parameter estimation method is very general in terms of dealing with unseen events and bi-directionality.

**Table 4.** The experimental results of word-transliteration alignment

| Test Data | # names | # correct transliterations | Precision Rate |
|---|---|---|---|
| Sinorama Magazine | 200 | 151 | 75.5% |
| Scientific American (SA/TE) | 200 | 180 | 90.0% |
| Britannica Concise Encyclopedia (BCE /TE) | 200 | 193 | 96.5% |

There are several kinds of errors in our results. Inevitably, some errors are due to data sparseness, leading to erroneous identification. Most errors however have to do with translation not covered by the machine transliteration model such as the translation "舊金山" for "San Francisco." Some are part translation part transliteration; such as the mapping between "北伊斯頓" and "North Easton." We found out that "east," "west," "south," "north," "long," "big," "new," "nova," and "St." tend not to be transliterated, leading to errors in applying machine transliteration model to extract name-translation pairs. These errors can be easily fixed by added these as TU with literal translations to the table of transliteration probability. We have restricted our discussion and experiments to transliteration of proper names. Transliterations of Chinese common nouns into lower case English word are not considered.

## 5   Conclusion

In this paper, we propose a new statistical machine transliteration model and describe how to apply the model to extract words and transliterations in a monolingual and parallel corpus. The model was first trained on a modest list of names and transliterations. The training resulted in a set of 'syllable' to character transliteration probabilities, which were subsequently used to extract proper names and transliterations in a corpus. These named entities are crucial for the development of named entity identification module in CLIR and QA.

We carried out experiments on an implementation of the word-transliteration alignment algorithms and tested on three sets of test data. The evaluation showed that very high precision rates were achieved.

A number of interesting future directions present themselves. First, it would be interesting to see how effectively we can port and apply the method to other language pairs such as English-Japanese and English-Korean. We are also investigating the advantages of incorporating a machine transliteration module in sentence and word alignment of parallel corpora.

**Acknowledgements.** We would like to thank Yuan Liou Publishing for providing data for this study. We acknowledge the support for this study through grants from National Science Council and Ministry of Education, Taiwan (NSC 92-2524-S007-002, NSC 91-2213-E-007-061 and MOE EX-91-E-FA06-4-4) and MOEA under the Software Technology for Advanced Network Application Project of the Institute for Information Industry.

# References

1.  Al-Onaizan, Y. and K. Knight. 2002. Translating named entities using monolingual and bilingual resources. In Proceedings of the 40th Annual Meeting of the Association for Computational Linguistics (ACL), pages 400-408.
2.  Chen, H.H., S-J Huang, Y-W Ding, and S-C Tsai. 1998. Proper name translation in cross-language information retrieval. In *Proceedings of 17th COLING and 36th ACL*, pages 232-236.
3.  Dempster, A.P., N.M. Laird, and D.B. Rubin. 1977. Maximum likelihood from incomplete data via the EM algorithm. *Journal of the Royal Statistical Society*, 39(1):1-38.
4.  Knight, K. and J. Graehl. 1998. Machine transliteration. *Computational Linguistics*, 24(4):599-612.
5.  Lee, C.J. and Jason S. Chang. 2003. "Acquisition of English-Chinese Transliterated Word Pairs from Parallel- Aligned Texts using a Statistical Machine Transliteration Model," In Proceedings of HLT-NAACL 2003 Workshop, pp. 96-103.
6.  Lee, J.S. and K-S Choi. 1997. A statistical method to generate various foreign word transliterations in multilingual information retrieval system. In *Proceedings of the 2nd International Workshop on Information Retrieval with Asian Languages (IRAL'97)*, pages 123-128, Tsukuba, Japan.
7.  Lin, T., CJ Wu, and J.S. Chang. 2003 Word Transliteration Alignment, Proceedings of the fifteenth Research on Computational Linguistics Conference, ROCLING XV, Hsinchu.
8.  Lin, W-H Lin and H-H Chen. 2002. Backward transliteration by learning phonetic similarity. In *CoNLL-2002, Sixth Conference on Natural Language Learning*, Taiwan.
9.  Oh, J-H and K-S Choi. 2002. An English-Korean transliteration model using pronunciation and contextual rules. In *Proceedings of the 19th International Conference on Computational Linguistics (COLING)*, Taiwan.
10. Stalls, B.G. and K. Knight. 1998. Translating names and technical terms in Arabic text. In *Proceedings of the COLING/ACL Workshop on Computational Approaches to Semitic Languages*.
11. Tsujii, K. 2002. Automatic extraction of translational Japanese-KATAKANA and English word pairs from bilingual corpora. *International Journal of Computer Processing of Oriental Languages*, 15(3):261-279.

# Error Analysis of Two Types of Grammar
# for the Purpose of Automatic Rule Refinement*

Ariadna Font Llitjós, Katharina Probst, and Jaime Carbonell

Language Technologies Institute
Carnegie Mellon University
{aria,kathrin,jgc}@cs.cmu.edu

**Abstract.** This paper compares a manually written MT grammar and a grammar learned automatically from an English-Spanish elicitation corpus with the ultimate purpose of automatically refining the translation rules. The experiment described here shows that the kind of automatic refinement operations required to correct a translation not only varies depending on the type of error, but also on the type of grammar. This paper describes the two types of grammars and gives a detailed error analysis of their output, indicating what kinds of refinements are required in each case.

## 1 Introduction and Motivation

Due to the recent spread of electronic information to minority populations and their languages, the interest of MT has expanded to language pairs that have previously been untackled because of the lack of large parallel corpora and the lack of human experts that could design translation grammars.

This poses a new challenge to the MT community, and requires to research different MT approaches which, given very little data, are able to build a working MT system and, most importantly, are able to improve this initially small system in a semi-automatic way, not requiring either computer experts or linguists that know the language.

Our approach is to carefully elicit user feedback about MT system output correctness, and use it to automatically refine the translation grammar and lexicon as required to accommodate the changes made by users. Translation grammars in our transfer-based MT system can be both hand-crafted and automatically learned, thus it is interesting to see what are the differences between them in terms of coverage, parsimony, ambiguity, error rate and translation quality.

This paper describes an experiment with these two types of grammars designed to explore whether the automatic rule refinement operations that need to be applied in each case are going to be different and, if so, how.

After a brief description of our MT system focusing on the Rule Learning and Rule Refinement modules, the two grammars used in the experiment are described in detail and the error analysis indicating what kinds of refinements are required in each case follows.

---

* This research was funded in part by NSF grant number IIS-0121631.

R.E. Frederking and K.B. Taylor (Eds.): AMTA 2004, LNAI 3265, pp. 187–196, 2004.

## 2   MT Approach

Our MT research group at Carnegie Mellon has been working on a new MT approach, under the AVENUE project, that is specifically designed to enable rapid development of MT for languages with limited amounts of online resources. Our approach assumes the availability of a small number of bilingual speakers of the two languages, but these need not be linguistic experts. The bilingual speakers create a comparatively small corpus of word aligned phrases and sentences (on the order of magnitude of a few dozen to a few thousand sentence pairs) using a specially designed elicitation tool [7].

From this data, the learning module of our system automatically infers hierarchical syntactic transfer rules, which encode how constituent structures in the source language (SL) transfer to the target language (TL). The collection of transfer rules, which constitute the translation grammar, is then used in our run-time system to translate previously unseen SL text into the TL [6].

The AVENUE transfer-based MT system consists of four main modules: elicitation of a word aligned parallel corpus; automatic learning of translation rules; the run time transfer system, and the interactive and automatic refinement of the translation rules.

### 2.1   The Transfer Rule Formalism

In our system, translation rules have 6 components: a) the type information, which in most cases corresponds to a syntactic constituent type; b) part-of-speech/constituent sequence for both the SL and the TL; c) alignments between the SL constituents and the TL constituents; d) x-side constraints, which provide information about features and their values in the SL sentence; e) y-side constraints, which provide information about features and their values in the TL sentence, and f) xy-constraints, which provide information about which feature values transfer from the source into the target language.

For illustration purposes, Figure 1 shows an example of an English to Spanish translation rule for noun-phrases containing a noun and an adjective. This translation rule swaps the original English word order, from adjective-noun to noun-adjective, enforces their agreement in Spanish and ensures that the noun is the head of the NP. The feature unification equations used in the rules follow a typical unification grammar formalism. For more details about the rule formalism, see [6].

## 3   Learning Rules

For the experiment described in this paper, the translation direction is English to Spanish, and the latter is used for illustration purposes to simulate a resource-poor language. In the following discussion of the learning procedure, the x-side always refers to English, whereas the y-side refers to Spanish.

```
{NP,9}  ;;; Rule identifier ;;;
  NP::NP : [ADJ N] -> [N ADJ]
  ((x1::y2) (x2::y1) ; set constituent alignments
  ((x0 mod) = x1) ; the adjective is the modifier
  (x0 = x2)      ; the noun is the head
  (y2 == (y0 mod)) ; building Spanish sentence f-structure
  (y1 = y0)
  ((y2 agr) = (y1 agr)))
```

**Fig. 1.** Sample Translation Rule. x means source (here: English) and y, target (here: Spanish).

The first step in the Rule Learning (RL) module is Seed Generation. For each training example, the algorithm constructs at least one 'seed rule', i.e. a flat rule that incorporates all the information known about this training example, producing a first approximation to a valid transfer rule. The transfer rule parts can be extracted from the available information or are projected from the English side.

After producing the seed rule, compositionality is added to it. Compositionality aims at learning rules that can combine to cover more unseen examples. The algorithm makes use of previously learned rules. For a given training example, the algorithm traverses through the parse of the English sentence or phrase. For each node, the system checks if there exists a lower-level rule that can be used to correctly translate the words in the subtree. If this is the case, then an element of compositionality is introduced.

In order to ensure that the compositionality algorithm has already learned lower-level rules when it tries to learn compositional rules that use them, we learn rules for simpler constituents first. Currently, the following order is applied: adverb phrases, adjective phrases, noun phrases, prepositional phrases, and sentences. While this improves the availability of rules for the compositionality module at the right time, the issue of co-embedding still needs to be resolved. For more details, see [6].

## 4   Refining Rules

Instead of having to pay a human translator to correct all the sentences output by an MT system, we propose the use of bilingual speakers to obtain information about translation errors and use this information to correct the problems at their root. Namely, by refining the translation rules that generated the errors.

The refinement process starts with an interactive step, which elicits information about the correctness of the translations from users with the Translation Correction Tool (TCTool). This tool allows bilingual users to correct the output of an MT system and to indicate the source of the error. Users can insert words, change the order of words, or specify that an agreement was violated.

To find more about the reliability of translation correction feedback given by bilingual speakers, we ran an English to Spanish user study using the manually written grammar described in 5.1. We found that users can detect translation errors with reasonably high accuracy (89%), but have a harder time determining what type of error it is. Given our MT error classification, users identified the error correctly 72% of the time. For more details about the TCTool and the English-Spanish user study, see [3].

The second step of the refinement process is to do the actual refinement. The Rule Refinement (RR) module modifies the translation grammar according to what user feedback suggests.

The first goal of the RR module is to search the feature space to determine which set of features triggered a particular correction. To do this, the RR module needs to rely on active learning methods to try to discover the underlying principles and constraints of the TL language grammar, which were not elicited at the first stage of the development process, or which were not learned by the RL module.

For RR purposes, we define the difference between two TL minimal pair sentences as the intersection of the set of feature attributes for which they have different values, not taking into consideration the user correction we are seeking to account for. We call this the feature delta function ($\delta$) and, in the general case, it can be written as follows:

$$\delta(\text{T1,T2}) = \bigcap_{i=1}^{n} \delta(\text{wT1}_i, \text{wT2}_i) \tag{1}$$

for all the *relevant* words that are different in T1 and T2 ($\text{wT1}_i \neq \text{wT2}_i$) and where n is the length of the sentence.

The resulting delta set is used as a guidance to explore the feature space of potentially relevant attributes, until the RR module finds the ones that triggered the correction, and can add the appropriate constraints to the relevant rules.

Suppose we are given the English sentence Juan is a great friend, and the translation grammar has the following general rule for noun phrases NP::NP : [ADJ N] -> [N ADJ] (see Figure 1 for the complete rule), then the translation output from the MT system will be Juan es un amigo *grande* (T1), since that is what the general rule for nouns and adjectives in Spanish dictates. However, this sentence instantiates an exception to the general rule, and thus, the user will most likely correct the sentence into Juan es un *gran* amigo (T1').

Now, the RR module needs to find a minimal pair (T2) that illustrates the linguistic phenomenon that accounts for the MT error. Let's assume that Juan is a smart friend is also in the elicitation corpus and it gets correctly translated as Juan es un amigo inteligente.

The delta function of these two TL sentences evaluated is shown below:

$\delta((\text{Juan es un amigo grande}),(\text{Juan es un amigo inteligente})) =$
$$= \delta(\text{grande,inteligente}) = \{\}$$

Since we are comparing minimal pairs, the delta function is reduced to comparing just words that are different between the two TL sentences but are aligned to the same SL word, or are in the same position and have the same POS, and we do not need to calculate the delta functions for differing words that are not relevant, such as $\delta(\texttt{un},\texttt{amigo})$.

If the delta set had contained one feature attribute that, when changed in T2, users would correct it in the same way they corrected T1, then we would hypothesize that it accounts for the correction and would bifurcate the NP rule based on that attribute.

Since both adjectives are singular and undefined with respect to gender, the delta set is empty and thus the RR module determines that the existing feature set is insufficient to explain the difference between prenominal and postnominal adjectives, and therefore it postulates a new binary feature, `feat_1`.

Once the RR module has determined what are the triggering features, it proceeds to refine the relevant grammar and lexical rules to include prenominal adjectives by adding the appropriate feature constraints. In this case, the RR module creates a duplicate of the NP rule shown in Figure 1, switches `N ADJ` to `ADJ N` on the target side and adds the the following constraint to it: (`feat_1 = +`). The original rule also needs to be refined to include the same constraint with the other feature value (`feat_1 = -`). The lexicon will later need to code for the new feature as well.

More detailed examples of minimal pair comparison and the feature space exploration algorithm can be found in [2].

## 5   English-Spanish Experiment

We ran an experiment with two different grammars, a manually written one and an automatically learned one using the RL module described in section 3.

The training set contains the first 200 sentences of the AVENUE elicitation corpus, and the test set contains 32 sentences drawn from the next 200 sentences in the corpus (the same that was used for the English-Spanish user study [3]). Both MT systems used a lexicon with 442 entries, developed semi-automatically seeking to cover the training and the test sets (400 sentences), so that the effectiveness of rules can be measured abstracting away from lexical gaps in the translation system. The description of the two types of grammar follow.

### 5.1   Hand-Crafted Translation Grammar

The manually written grammar contains 12 translation rules: 2 S rules, 7 NP rules, 3 VP rules. It took a grammar writer about two weeks to develop and debug the grammar. Examples of translation rules in this grammar are given below.

```
{S,0} ;;; Rule identifier ;;;        {VP,3}
  S::S : [NP VP] -> [VP]               VP::VP : [VP NP] -> [VP NP]
```

```
; x0 y0   x1 x2      y1                 ((X1::Y1)  (X2::Y2)
((X2::Y1) ; set constituent alignments   ((x2 case) = acc)
  ((x1 agr pers) = (*OR* 1 2))           ((x0 obj) = x2)
  ((x1 agr num) = sg)                    ((x0 agr) = (x1 agr))
  ((x1 case) = nom)                      (y2 == (y0 obj))
  (x0 = x2)                              ((y0 tense) = (x0 tense))
  ((y1 agr) = (x1 agr)))                 ((y0 agr) = (y1 agr)))
```

Spanish is a pro-drop language, so the S rule above causes the subject to be dropped when the subject NP is a 1st or 2nd singular personal pronoun (since this is what the translator of the elicitation corpus did), and it also ensures agreement between the Spanish verb and the English subject. The VP rule illustrates the common syntactic structure were the direct object follows the verb, both in English and Spanish. Figure 1 shows an example of a manually written NP rule.

## 5.2  Automatically Learned Translation Grammar

The RL module described in section 3 can produce a basic and an enhanced grammar fully automatically in about a minute, as it is exactly learned from the elicitation corpus examples [6]. In general, the automatic learning method described in this paper is linear in the input size.

The enhanced version essentially expands the training corpus by traversing the English parse tree from the top down. For each internal node, the enhancement algorithm extracts the subtree rooted at this node. Then, using the word alignments provided by the bilingual user, it forms a new training example for the English and Spanish chunks covered by the subtree. The rule learning algorithm can then be run as is on the expanded training set, resulting in a larger grammar.

For the present experiment, the English training data was parsed using the Charniak parser [1]. A few feature constraints extracted from morphological analyzers for both English and Spanish (gender, number, person and tense) where input to the Rule Learner and the final grammar was able to learn some feature constraints. The enhanced version of the grammar with constraints contains 316 translation rules (194 S, 43 NP, 78 VP and 1 PP), 223 more than the learned grammar with no constraints.

Examples from the final learned grammar (enhanced and with features) are shown below.

```
{S,90}                               {VP,46}
S::S [NP VP] -> [NP VP]              VP::VP [V NP] -> [V NP]
((X1::Y1)(X2::Y2)                    ((X1::Y1)(X2::Y2)
((X1 def) = +)                       ((X2 def) = -)
((X2 def) = -)                       ((X2 agr num) = sg)
((X2 agr num) = (X1 agr num))        ((Y1 agr pers) = 2)
((X2 tense) = past)                  ((Y2 agr gen) = masc)
((Y2 agr gen) = (Y1 agr gen))        ((Y2 agr num) = (Y1 agr num)))
((Y2 agr num) = (Y1 agr num)))
```

Overall, the enhanced grammar rules learned by the Rule Learner make useful generalizations and are quite close to what a linguist might write, however they often contain constraints that are either too specific or too general. In the rules above, the constraint about the tense of the verb in S,90 is too specific; ideally we would like this rule to apply to all VPs regardless of their tense.

On the other hand, the Rule Learner can overgeneralize; when it finds that a feature value match occurs often enough, it will decide that there is a correlation, and thus an agreement constraint gets added to the rule. This is illustrated by the number agreement constraint in rule VP,46. Because enough examples in the training data had the verb and the object coincide in number, it assumes that a generalization can be made. In Spanish, however, verbs and their objects do not always agree.

## 5.3   Grammar Ambiguity

The reason there are many more rules in the learned grammar is that the current implementation of the RL module does not throw away rules that are too specific and that are subsumed by rules which have achieved a higher level of generalization during the learning process.

When running our transfer system on a test set of 32 sentences, it was observed that the manually written grammar results in less ambiguity (on average 1.6 different translations per sentence) than the automatically learned grammar (18.6 different translations per sentence). At the same time, the final version of the learned grammar results in less ambiguity than the learned grammar with no constraints. This is to be expected, since relevant constraints will restrict the application of general rules to the appropriate cases.

Additional ambiguity is not necessarily a problem; however, the goal of the transfer engine should be to produce the most likely outputs first, i.e. with the highest rank. In experiments reported elsewhere [4], we have used a statistical decoder with a TL language model to disambiguate between different translation hypotheses. We are currently investigating methods to prioritize rules and partial analyses within the transfer engine, so that we can rank translation hypotheses also when no TL language model is available.

While this work is under investigation, we emulated this module with a simple reordering of the grammar: we reordered three rules (2 NPs and 1 S rule) that had a high level of generalization (namely containing agreement constraints instead of the more specific value constraints) to be at the beginning of the grammar. This in effect gives higher priority to the translations produced with these rules.

## 5.4   Comparing Grammar Output

Most of the translation errors produced by the manual grammar can be classified into lack of subj-pred agreement, wrong word order of object pronouns (clitic), wrong preposition and wrong form (case) and out-of-vocabulary word. On top of the errors produced by the manual grammar, the current version of the learned grammar also had errors of the following types: missing agreement constraints, missing preposition and overgeneralization.

An example of differences between the errors produced by the two types of grammar can be seen in the translation of John and Mary fell. The manual grammar translates it as *Juan y Maria cayeron, whereas the learned grammar translated it as **Juan y Maria cai. The learned grammar does have an NP rule that covers [Juan y Maria], however it lacks the number constraint that indicates that the number of an NP with this constituent sequence ([NP CONJ NP]) has to be plural. The translation produced by the manual grammar, *Juan y Maria cayeron, is also ungrammatical, but the translation error in this case is a bit more subtle and thus much harder to detect. The correct translation is Juan y Maria se cayeron.

Another example to illustrate this is the translations of John held me with his arm. The MT system with the manual grammar outputs *Juan sujetó me con su brazo, whereas the one with the learned grammar outputs **A Juan sujetó me con su brazo.

Sometimes the output from the learned grammar is actually better than the manual grammar output. An example of this can be seen in the translations of Mother, can you help us?. The manual grammar translated this as **Madre, puedo ayudar nos? and the learned grammar translates is as *Madre, puedes tu ayudar nos?. The number of corrections required to fix both translations is the same, but the one produced by the learned grammar is clearly better.

## 5.5   Error Analysis

The 32 sentences used in the English-Spanish user study described in [3] were translated using both grammars described above. We looked at the 5 first translations only, and found that both grammars translated the same 4 SL sentences correctly. Even though the final number of SL sentences correctly translated by the two grammars is the same, overall, the quality of the translations produced by the learned grammar was worse.

We looked at the best translation for each source language sentence in the user study for one grammar and compared it with the best translation for the other grammar. The results can be seen in Table 1 below.

**Table 1.** Error analysis comparing a learned grammar with a manually written grammar. See Section 6 for examples.

|  | number of sentences (over 32) |
| --- | --- |
| same translation | 17 (3 correct) |
| manual grammar better | 10 |
| learned grammar better | 2 |
| different error type | 3 (1 correct) |

## 6   Rule Refinements Required for Each Type of Grammar

Since 15 out of 32 sentences contained different translation errors for each grammar, the refinement operations required by the translations rules of one grammar and by the other grammar might not be the same for a given SL sentence. Following are a few examples of the cases listed in Table 1.

**Same Translation**

In many cases, the sentences were translated in the same way by the two grammars, and thus they need the same refinements to be corrected. Sentences that only differ in the optional subject pronoun are included in this category. These are two examples from the test set that illustrate this:

SL: I saw you yesterday - TL: *(Yo) vi *tu* ayer

SL: It was a small ball - TL: eso era un balón pequeño

**Different Translation**

For 10 sentences in the test set, even though both translations are wrong, the manual grammar output requires less changes to be correct:

SL: I'm proud of you - TL-l: **Yo estoy orgulloso *tu* - TL-m: *Yo estoy orgulloso de *tu*

besides changing the **tu** into **ti** in both cases, the learned grammar needs an extra refinement, the addition of "de" in front of the second person pronoun.

In addition to the example given section 5.4, the learned grammar output requires less amount of refinement for the following SL sentence:

SL: I like you - TL-l: *Yo me gustas tu - TL-m: **Me *gusta* tu

In a few cases, both grammars output equally bad translations, but with different kinds of errors:

SL: He looked at me - TL-l: *él *miraron* me - TL-m: * él miró *en me*

The current experiment reveals a couple of main interesting differences between the refinements required by hand-crafted grammars and automatically learned grammars. Several rule refinements required to correct sentences translated by the hand-crafted grammar involve bifurcating a rule to encode an exception, whereas a larger portion of the refinements necessary to refine the learned grammar involve adding or deleting agreement constraints. More details on the refinement operations can be found in [2].

In general, the biggest differences between the hand-crafted and the learned grammar is that the learned grammar has a higher level of lexicalization and, currently, it can make good use of the Rule Refinement module to make adjustments to the feature and agreement constraints to achieve the appropriate level of generalization.

## 7   Conclusions and Future Work

The Rule Refinement module, together with the Translation Correction Tool, can improve both hand-crafted and automatically learned translation grammars.

The addition of feature constraints to the automatically learned grammar brings the two types of grammar and their output closer. However, with the current implementation of the learned grammar, the Rule Refinement module will still give the most leverage when combined with an automatically learned grammar.

Given translations for the same SL sentence, both the types of translation rules and the kind of errors they produce differ almost 50% of the time depending on the type of grammar, thus the Rule Refinement module will need to detect the difference in the translation rules and perform the appropriate refinement operations, accordingly.

In general, manually-written grammar rules will need to be refined to encode exceptions, whereas automatically-learned grammars will need to be refined so that they achieve the right level of generalization.

We would like to do some experiments to check whether using a user-corrected pair as new training data for the Rule Learning module and using the user feedback to refine the rules with the Rule Refinement module yield identical or similar results, and what is the best way to improve translation quality over a corpus, once there is an initial grammar, which can be either manually written or automatically learned.

Finally, we would also like to look into using reference translations created to evaluate MT system output [5] to improve our grammar and lexicon automatically. We might be able to do this by applying some minimal edited distance metric, and running a morphological analyzer for at least the target language.

## References

1. Charniak, E.: A Maximum-Entropy-Inspired Parser, North American chapter of the Association for Computational Linguistics (NAACL), 2000.
2. Font Llitjós, A.: Towards Interactive and Automatic Refinement of Translation Rules, PhD Thesis Proposal, Carnegie Mellon University, forthcoming in August 2004 (www.cs.cmu.edu/~aria/ThesisProposal.pdf).
3. Font Llitjós, A., Carbonell, J.: The Translation Correction Tool: English-Spanish user studies, 4th International Conference on Language Resources and Evaluation (LREC), 2004.
4. Lavie, A., Vogel, S., Levin, L., Peterson, E., Probst, K, Font Llitjós, A., Reynolds, R., Carbonell, J., Cohen, R.: Experiments with a Hindi-to-English Transfer-based MT System under a Miserly Data Scenario, ACM Transactions on Asian Language Information Processing (TALIP), 2:2, 2003.
5. Papineni, K., Roukos, S., Ward, T.: Maximum Likelihood and Discriminative Training of Direct Translation Models, Proceedings of the International Conference on Acoustics, Speech, and Signal Processing (ICASSP-98), 1998.
6. Probst, K., Levin, L., Peterson, E., Lavie, A., Carbonell J.: MT for Resource-Poor Languages Using Elicitation-Based Learning of Syntactic Transfer Rules, Machine Translation, Special Issue on Embedded MT, 2003.
7. Probst, K., Brown, R., Carbonell, J., Lavie, A., Levin, L., Peterson, E.: Design and Implementation of Controlled Elicitation for Machine Translation of Low-density Languages, Workshop MT2010 at Machine Translation Summit VIII, 2001.

# The Contribution of End-Users
# to the TransType2 Project

Elliott Macklovitch[1]

RALI Laboratory, Université de Montréal
C.P. 6128, succursale Centre-ville
Montréal, Canada  H3C 3J7
macklovi@iro.umontreal.ca

**Abstract.** TransType2 is a novel kind of interactive MT in which the system and the user collaborate in drafting a target text, the system's contribution taking the form of predictions that extend what the translator has already typed in. TT2 is also an international research project in which end-users are represented by two translation firms. We describe the contribution of these translators to the project, from their input to the system's functional specifications to their participation in quarterly user trials. We also present the results of the latest round of user trials.

## 1    Introduction

The goal of the TransType2 project (Foster et al. 2002) is to develop a novel type of *interactive* machine translation system. The system observes the user as s/he types a translation, attempts to infer the target text the user has in mind and periodically proposes extensions to the prefix which the user has already keyed in. The user is free to accept these completions, modify them as desired or ignore them by simply continuing to type. With each new character the user enters, the system revises its predictions in order to make them compatible with the user's input.

In itself, interactive machine translation (IMT) is certainly not novel; in fact, the first attempts at IMT go back to the MIND system, which was developed by Martin Kay and Ron Kaplan at the RAND Corporation in the late 1960's.[2] There have been numerous subsequent attempts to implement IMT, some of which gave rise to commercial systems, like ALPS' ITS system, while others have been embedded in controlled language systems, like the KANT system developed at CMU (Nyberg et al. 1997).[3] What all of these previous efforts share in common is that the focus of the interaction between the user and the system is on the *source text*. In particular, whenever the system is unable to disambiguate a portion of the source text, it requests assistance from the user. This can be to help resolve various types of source language ambiguity, such as the correct morpho-syntactic category of a particular word, syntactic dependencies between phrases, or the referent of an anaphor. In principle, once the user has provided the system with the information necessary to disambiguate

---

[1]  The work described in this article is the fruit of a sustained collaborative effort, and I want to express my gratitude to all the participants in the TT2 Consortium, particularly to the translators who are testing successive versions of the system.

[2]  For more on MIND, see (Hutchins 1986), pp.296-297.

[3]  Other IMT systems specifically focus on multi-target translation; see for example (Blanchon and Boitet 2004 ) and (Wehrli 1993).

R.E. Frederking and K.B. Taylor (Eds.): AMTA 2004, LNAI 3265, pp. 197–207, 2004.
© Springer-Verlag Berlin Heidelberg 2004

the source text, the system can then complete its analysis and continue to properly translate the text into the target language.

This is not the place to enumerate all the difficulties that have dogged this classic approach to interactive MT; however, there are a few important differences with TransType which we should point out. Suppose that the user of the system is a translator, as was often the case in the early decades of MT. Notice that the kind of information being solicited from the user by these classic IMT systems does not focus on translation knowledge per se, but instead involves formal linguistic analysis, of a kind that many translators have not been trained to perform. In contrast, the focus of the interaction between the user and the system in TransType is squarely on the drafting of the target text. After reading the current source text segment, the translator begins to type his/her desired translation. Based on its analysis of the same source segment and using its statistical translation and language models, TransType immediately proposes an extension to the characters the user has keyed in. The user may accept all or part of the proposed completion, or s/he may simply go on typing; in which case, the system continues trying to predict the target text the user has in mind. When the system performs well, the user will normally accept these machine-generated completions, thereby diminishing the number of characters s/he has to type and hopefully reducing overall translation time. But the important point is that in this paradigm both the user and the system contribute in turn to the drafting of the *target* text, and the translator is not solicited for information in an area in which s/he is not an expert.

Another important difference between classic IMT systems and the target-text mediated approach of TransType may be formulated in this way: Who leads? In the classic IMT approach, it is the system that has the initiative in the translation process; the system decides when and what to ask of the user, and once it has obtained the required information from the user, the system will autonomously generate its translation, much like any other fully automatic MT system. In the best of circumstances, the system will succeed in producing a grammatical and idiomatic sentence in the target language which correctly preserves the meaning of the source sentence. But even in this ideal situation, it would mistaken to believe that this is the *only* correct translation of the source sentence; for as every translator knows, almost any source text admits of multiple, equally acceptable target language renditions. As (King et al. 2003) put it:

> "There is no one right translation of even a banal text, and even the same translator will sometimes change his mind about what translation he prefers."
> (p.227)

What happens if the translation generated by the system does not correspond to the one which the user had in mind? One of two things: either the user changes his/her mind and accepts the machine's proposal; or the user post-edits the system's output, changing it so that it conforms to the translation s/he intended. But in either case, it is the user who is responding to, or following the system's lead. In TransType, on the other hand, it is entirely the other way round. The user guides the system by providing prompts in the form of target text input, and the system reacts to those prompts by trying to predict the rest of the translation which the user is aiming for. Moreover, the system must *adapt* its predictions to changes in the user's input. Here, quite clearly, it is the user who leads and the system which must follow.

This target-text mediated interactive MT is certainly a intriguing idea – but will it work? Only the system's intended end-users, i.e. professional translators, can answer that question. The TransType2 (henceforth TT2) Consortium includes two translation firms, one in Canada (Société Gamma Inc.) and one in Spain (Celer Soluciones S.L.). These partners play a very important role in the TT2 project, serving to balance its ambitious research program with the concrete needs of real end-users. The project provides for various channels through which the end-users can interact with the research teams who are developing the translation engines. One of the most important of these are the user trials that begin about half-way through the project and continue right up to its conclusion, at month thirty-six.

In the following section, we describe in more detail the role of these end-users in the TransType2 project. In section 3, we present the protocol for the latest round of user evaluations, which have just been completed at Société Gamma and at Celer Soluciones. In section 4, we report on the main results obtained in those trials – results which are necessarily tentative, since the project still has more than a year to run. In the final section, we draw some conclusions about the future of IMT.

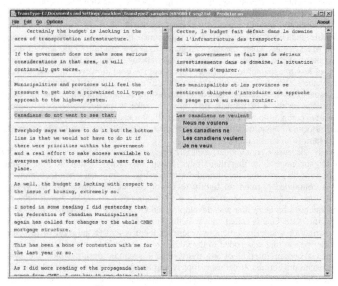

**Fig. 1.** Snapshot of a TransType session

## 2    The Role of End-Users in the TT2 Project

TransType2 is a three-year research project that was officially launched in March 2002. In Europe, it is funded under the EC's Fifth Framework Program, and in Canada by both the federal government (through NSERC) and by the Quebec government's Department of Research, Science and Technology. One of the basic goals of TT2 is to provide a framework in which leading-edge research can be conducted in the area of data-driven methods in NLP and, more specifically, in machine translation. But TT2 also has another major objective, which is to provide a practical application for that research which will hopefully help solve a pressing social problem, to wit: how to meet the ever-growing demand for high-quality translation. Our research in TT2 is aimed at developing an innovative machine-aided translation system which should facilitate the task of producing high-quality translations and make that task more cost-effective for human translators.

As mentioned above, the TT2 Consortium includes two translation firms, and the participating translators at Société Gamma and Celer Soluciones have been directly and actively involved in the project right from the outset. In particular, the translators played a key role in the drafting of the system's functional specifications and in helping to design its graphical user interface (GUI). As an example of their input on the functional specs, the translators insisted on the fact that the system needs to be open to terminological input from the user, in the form of glossaries that would contain client- or domain-specific terminology. Any system that could not be customized in this way, they told us, would be seriously handicapped, because it would force the user to repeatedly correct terminology in the target text that was available in his/her glossary. Such a requirement may not be problematic in rule-based MT systems, where the user can generally add a specialized glossary or modify the content of the system's dictionaries, these being formalized in a manner that is more or less transparent to a human. This is not the case, however, in most statistical MT systems, where there is no user interface to a distinct lexical component. Hence, the translators' requirement raised an interesting research problem for the engine developers on the TT2 project: first, how to make these declarative, user-supplied glossaries compatible with the system's statistical translation engine, and then how to grant priority to the entries in the glossary over the translations previously inferred by the system from its training corpus.

As a (somewhat paradoxical) example of user input on the specs for TT2's GUI, the translators told us that there must be an easy way to shut off the system's predictions. In particular, they found during pre-trial testing that when they went back into a completed segment to lightly revise or correct the translation, the system's predictions cluttered up the screen and proved more of a hindrance than a help. As a consequence, the team that was developing the GUI added a number of new options to the interface. One is called "never-within-text" and, as its name suggests, it blocks the display of system completions whenever there is text to the right of the cursor. Another option that was added to the GUI is a delay setting which allows the user to specify a certain interval of inactivity, e.g. 3 seconds, during which the system displays no predictions. If the user stops typing for more than the specified interval, as when s/he is searching for a solution to a particular translation problem, only then does the system display its predictions. Of course, the user can always summon up a completion by hitting a keyboard short-cut, even when the prediction engine is turned off.

The other major contribution of the users in the TT2 project involves their participation in the quarterly trials that began in month eighteen. These are intended to evaluate the *usability* of successive system prototypes and, in this respect, are quite different from the internal technology evaluations, which also form part of the project work plan. The aim of the latter is to gauge progress in the core technology, i.e.

improvements in the statistical translation engines; and to do this, the principal means employed are automatic metrics such as word error rate or methods like BLEU. The usability evaluation, on the other hand, inescapably involves the intended end-users of TransType, i.e. professional translators; and here, the goal is to evaluate, not so much the performance of the system in vitro (as it were), but its actual impact on the productivity of working translators and the ease (or difficulty) with which they adapt to the system. An equally important objective of the user trials is to provide a channel of communication through which the participating translators can furnish feedback and suggestions to the system developers, so that the latter can continue to make improvements to the system.[4]

We have just completed the third round of user evaluations in the TT2 project, and the first in which the participating translators at Gamma and at Celer have actually had the opportunity to work with the system in a mode that approximates their real working conditions. In the following section, we present our objectives for this round of user trials and the protocol which governed its organization.

## 3     The Protocol for Evaluation Round 3 (ER3)

The corpus selected for ER3 came from a Xerox User Guide for a large commercial printer; it is part of an approximately one million word collection provided by XRCE, one of the partners in the TT2 consortium. Each of the labs developing prediction engines in the project – RWTH in Aachen, ITI in Valencia, and RALI in Montreal – trained its system on this Xerox corpus, excluding of course the chapters that were to be translated during the user trial. For our test corpus, we decided to use the same chapters at the two translation firms. At Celer in Madrid, these would be translated from English into Spanish; at Gamma in Ottawa, they would be translated from English into French. Because these manua ∟ are relatively technical in nature, XRCE also provided a terminology glossary with about 750 entries, as well as a PDF version of the original English manual containing tables and graphics.[5]

One of our sub-objectives for ER3 was to try to determine if users had a marked preference for a single lengthy completion versus multiple predictions (which may or may not be shorter than the single prediction, depending on the engine). To this end, the participants at each site were asked to translate chapters from the Xerox printer manual using two different prediction engines. At Gamma, the participants would translate two test chapters into French with the RWTH engine, configured to provide single full-sentence length predictions, without alternate choices; and they would translate two other chapters with the RALI engine, configured to provide five alternate predictions of shorter length.[6] At Celer, the participants would also use the

---

[4] To encourage users to provide such feedback, TT2 includes a pop-up notepad, with entries that are automatically time-stamped and identified with the user's name.
[5] Currently, TT2 only accepts plain text files as input. By consulting the PDF original, the participants could situate certain segments extracted from tables or graphics within their proper context.
[6] At the time of the ER3 trial, the RALI's maximum entropy engine could not provide completions longer than five words. ITI's engine, which was the other system configured to provide multiple predictions, was able to provide longer predictions, up to full-sentence length.

RWTH engine, configured to provide single full-sentence completions; and instead of the RALI's engine, they would use ITI's engine, configured to provide multiple completions of varying length. All three engines were embedded within the same GUI, which is shown in Figure 1 above.

In order to obtain a baseline comparison of their productivity on this kind of technical material, we also asked the translators to translate one chapter of the Xerox manual using TT2, but with the prediction engine turned off. As can be seen from the snapshot in Figure 1, TransType's GUI takes the form of a two-paned text editor in which the source text appears in the left-hand pane, divided into sentence-like segments. As soon as the user selects a given segment, the system responds by inserting a proposed translation for it in the corresponding cell in the right-hand pane. In this first "dry-run", the prediction engine was turned off and the users simply typed their own translation in the right-hand pane. What isn't evident from the snapshot in Figure 1 is that the GUI also generates a detailed trace file, which records every one of the user's actions and all the system's predictions, including their precise times. To determine each participant's baseline productivity, we had only to consult the trace file, determine how many words the user had translated and divide it by the time expired.

In the remaining four half-day sessions of this evaluation round, the system's prediction engine was turned back on and the participants were asked not to modify the interface parameters, in order to facilitate the comparison of their results.

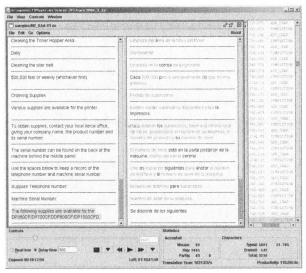

**Fig. 2.** Snapshot of TT-Player

# 4    TT-Player and the Analysis of the Trace Files

We mentioned in the previous section that every interaction between the user and the system is recorded in the trace file, making these files very detailed, lengthy and rather onerous to consult by hand. In order to facilitate the evaluation process, the RALI has developed a utility program called TT-Player which is designed to read the trace file of a TT2 session and play it back, much like a VCR player plays back a video tape. Moreover, TT-Player also produces a statistical summary of the session, highlighting whatever statistics we wish to bring out.

Figure 2 above contains a snapshot of TT-Player taken in replay mode. In this session, the English source text appears in the left-hand pane and, in the middle pane of the main window, the Spanish translation in progress. The narrow pane on the right contains the trace, showing both the actions performed by the user and the completions proposed by the system, including their precise times. This is what is being automatically played back and, like a VCR, the replay can be controlled via the arrow buttons on the bottom of the main frame. In the translation pane, sequences typed by the user appear in black, while those that derive from system predictions appear in red (or are pale if this page isn't printed in colour). At the bottom right of the main frame, certain statistics are provided which are automatically updated with each action. A complete statistical analysis of the session is also available via the View menu.

Given a trace file of this detail, it is possible to extract a broad variety of measurements and statistical indicators from the raw data. In the TT2 research project, there are basically two things that we want to measure: first, the impact that our IMT system has on translators' productivity; and second, the manner in which the translators actually make of use the system, i.e. which features they take advantage of and which they ignore. The latter kind of data should help the developers improve the design of the system, while the former should inform us of the general viability of this novel approach to IMT. Although the NLP literature is replete with methodologies for evaluating MT systems, the great majority of these have been designed for fully automatic MT systems and hence are not entirely appropriate for an interactive system like TransType.[7] The ISLE project developed a particularly thorough and rigorous MT evaluation taxonomy, which is now available online.[8] Here is what we find there on metrics for interactive translation:

> Metric: Steps for translation – method: Count the number of times system requires assistance when translating a test corpus. – Measurement: Number of steps needed or number of steps as percentage of test corpus size.

> Metric: Time for interactive translation – Method: Measure the amount of time it takes to perform interactive translation on test corpus. – Measurement: Amount of time for interactive translation on test corpus.

---

[7] In the context of its work on the original TransType project, the RALI did elaborate an evaluation methodology specifically designed for interactive MT; see (Langlais et al. 2002). Needless to say, we drew heavily on this experience.

[8] C.f. http:// www.issco.unige.ch/projects/isle/femti/

The first metric, notice, betrays a certain bias toward classic IMT systems; the tacit assumption seems to be that the fewer times the system requires the user's assistance, the better. Our bias in target-text mediated IMT is quite different. What we want to count is the number of times that the user accepts the system's proposals in drafting his/her translation; and in principle, the more often s/he does this, the better. As for the second FEMTI metric, this is precisely the way we have adopted to measure our participants' productivity. The following table lists the parameters that TT-Player was programmed to extract from the trace files on ER3. It also summarizes the results of one of the participants on the "dry-run", when the prediction engine was turned off, and on a second session, with one of the two prediction engines turned on.

**Table 1.** Partial results of one participant on ER3

| G-TR3 <br> (English to French) | Chapter M2_4 <br> ("dry-run") | Chapter M2_2 <br> (RWTH Engine) |
|---|---|---|
| date of translation | March 8, 2004 | March 10, 2004 |
| # words / segments in source | 1170 w / 115 seg | 3514 w / 278 seg |
| # words in target / # segments translated | 867 w / 81 seg | 2773 w / 192 seg |
| translation time | 60.1 min | 147 min |
| **Productivity** | **14.4 w/min** | **18.9 w/min** |
| # system predictions | | 5961 |
| % accepted predictions | | 6.4 % |
| average length of accepted predictions | | 4.3 w |
| average time to accept a completion | | 11.4 sec |
| # entire predictions accepted via keyboard | | 95 |
| # partial completions accepted via keyboard | | 22 |
| # entire completions accepted via mouse | | 0 |
| # partial completions accepted via mouse | | 267 |
| % of first completions accepted | | N/A* |
| % of entire first completions accepted | | 25% |
| Ratio: words accepted / words in target | | 0.59 |
| Ratio: chars typed / chars in target | | 0.52 |
| Ratio: deleted chars / chars in target | | 0.09 |
| Ratio: mouse & kb actions per target word | 8.6 actions / w | 3.8 actions / w |

From the table, we see that by using the predictions provided by the RWTH engine, the translator was actually been able to increase her productivity from 14.4 words per minute on the dry-run to an impressive 18.9 words per minute on Chapter M2_2. During this two and a half hour session, the system proposed 5961 completions, of which the translator accepted 6.4%.[9] The average length of an accepted completion was 4.3 words, and the average time required to accept a completion was 11.4 seconds. The next six lines provide information on the manner in which the user accepted the system's proposals: in whole or in part, using the keyboard or the mouse. The final four lines furnish various ratios between the length of the participant's target text (in words or in characters) and different types of actions, e.g. the number of characters typed or deleted during the session. In the final line, we see that translating Chapter 2_4 on her own, the translator required an average of 8.6 keystrokes or mouse-clicks per word, whereas on Chapter M2_2, with the benefit of the system's predictions, the number of actions per word dropped to 3.8.

## 5     The Results

Before presenting a synthesis of the results we obtained on ER3, a number of caveats are definitely in order. As we mentioned above, this was the first time that the participants at Gamma and at Celer were actually translating with TT2 in a mode that resembles their real working conditions; but "resembles" is the operative word here. TransType remains its research prototype and as such its editing environment does not offer all the facilities of a commercial word processor, e.g. automatic spell checking or search-and-replace. Moreover, this was a very small-scale test, involving only four texts and less than ten thousand words of translation. Hence, the results we present below must be viewed as tentative. At least two other evaluation rounds are planned before the end of the TT2 project, during which the participants will be asked to work with the system for longer periods. Finally, there is another important caveat which should cause us to be cautious, and it has to do with quality controls, of which there were none in this round. During the preparatory sessions at the two agencies, the participants were asked to produce translations of "deliverable" quality; but in fact, we did nothing to ensure that this was the case, relying only on the translators' sense of professionalism. Hence, there was nothing to prevent one participant from rushing through his/her translation, without attempting to reread or polish it, while another might well invest significant time and effort in improving the quality of the final text, even though this would have a negative impact on his/her productivity.

With these caveats in mind, let us now turn to the "bottom-line" quantitative results on ER3. Assuming that the baseline figures provided on the dry-run are reliable, three of the four participants succeeded in increasing their productivity on at least one of the four texts they translated with TransType. If they were able to do so, it was largely owing to the performance of certain of the prediction engines. In particular, the participants at Celer were able to achieve impressive productivity gains using ITI's English-to-Spanish prediction engine. One translator at Celer more than doubled his/her word-per-minute translation rate using the ITI engine on one of the texts; on

---

[9] This number of predictions may appear at first to be very high; but then it must be remembered that TransType revises its predictions with each new character the user enters.

another text, the second Celer translator logged the highest productivity of all the participants on the trial, again using ITI's English-to-Spanish prediction engine.

However, when we examine more closely the manner in which the some of the participants actually used the completions proposed by TT2, there is somewhat less cause for jubilation. It seems quite clear that in certain sessions the translators opted for a strategy that is closer in spirit to classic MT post-editing than it is to interactive MT. Instead of progressively guiding the system via prompts toward the translation that they had in mind, the users would often accept the first sentence-length prediction in its entirety, and then edit to ensure its correctness. That the participants were able to increase their productivity by post-editing in this manner certainly speaks well for the translation engines involved. However, our fundamental goal in the TT2 project is to explore the viability of *interactive* machine translation, and this strategy which certain participants adopted – and which is confirmed, incidentally, by replaying the sessions in TT-Player – cannot really be viewed as true IMT.

Still, in our research project as elsewhere, the customer is always right. If the participants at Celer and at Gamma did not make more extensive use of the system's interactive features, it can only be because they felt it was not useful or productive (or perhaps too demanding) for them to do so. Thus, the challenge for the engine developers in the remainder of the TT2 project is to enhance the system's interactive features so that the users will freely choose to exploit them to greater advantage.

In addition to the translations they produced, the participants also provided us with a number of insightful comments about their experience in working with TT2. One user told us, for example, that five alternate completions may be too many, particularly when the differences between them are minimal. The participants also pointed out a number of irritants in the GUI, e.g. the fact that the text does not automatically scroll up when the user reaches the bottom-most segment on the screen; or the occasional incorrect handling of capitalization and spacing around punctuation marks. Although none of these are major, they are a source of frustration for the users and do cause them to lose production time. Finally, the trial appears to validate the decision to base a large part of our usability evaluations on the automatic analysis of the trace files generated in each translation session. Not only is TT-Player able to produce a detailed statistical analysis of each session; it also allows us to verify certain hypotheses by replaying the session, as though we were actually present and looking over the translator's shoulder.

## 6    Conclusions

It remains to be seen whether fully interactive, target-text mediated MT like that offered by TransType will prove to be a productive and a desirable option for professional translators who are called on to produce high-quality texts. The TT2 project still has more than a year to run and there are many improvements we plan to implement and many avenues that we have yet to explore. One thing is already certain, however, and that concerns the essential role that end-users can play in orienting an applied research project like this one. The translators at Gamma and at Celer have already made important contributions to TT2, both in preparing the system's functional specifications and in helping to design its graphical user interface. And through their participation in the remaining evaluation rounds, it is they who will have the last word in deciding whether this novel and intriguing approach to interactive MT is worth pursuing.

# References

Blanchon, H., and Boitet, C.: Deux premières étapes vers les documents auto-explicatifs. In: Actes de TALN 2004, Fès, Morocco (2004) pp. 61-70

Foster, G., Langlais, P., Lapalme, G.: User-Friendly Text Prediction for Translators. In: Proceedings of the 2002 Conference on Empirical Methods in Natural Language Processing (EMNLP), Philadelphia (2002) pp. 148-155

Hutchins, W. John: Machine Translation: Past, Present, Future. Ellis Horwood Limited, Chichester, United Kingdom (1986)

King, M., Popescu-Belis, A., Hovy, E.: FEMTI: creating and using a framework for MT evaluation. In: Proceedings of MT Summit IX, New Orleans (2003) pp. 224-231

Langlais, P., Lapalme, G., Loranger, M.: TRANSTYPE: Development–Evaluation Cycles to Boost Translator's Productivity. Machine Translation 17 (2002) pp. 77-98

Nyberg, E., Mitamura, T., Carbonell, J.: The KANT Machine Translation System: From R&D to Initial Deployment. LISA Workshop on Integrating Advanced Translation Technology, Washington D.C., (1997)

Wehrli, E.: Vers un système de traduction interactif. In Bouillon, P., Clas, A. (eds.): La Traductique. Les presses de l'Université de Montréal, AUPELF/UREF (1993) pp. 423-432

# An Experiment on Japanese-Uighur Machine Translation and Its Evaluation

Muhtar Mahsut[1], Yasuhiro Ogawa[2], Kazue Sugino[2],
Katsuhiko Toyama[2], and Yasuyoshi Inagaki[3]

[1] Graduate School of International Development, Nagoya University,
Furo-cho, Chikusa-ku, Nagoya 464-8601, JAPAN
muhtar@gsid.nagoya-u.ac.jp
[2] Graduate School of Information Science, Nagoya University,
Furo-cho, Chikusa-ku, Nagoya 464-8601, JAPAN
{yasuhiro, toyama}@is.nagoya-u.ac.jp
sugino@kl.i.is.nagoya-u.ac.jp
[3] Faculty of Information Science and Technology,
Aichi Prefectural University,
1522-3 Ibaragabasama, Kumabari, Nagakute-cho,
Aichi-gun, Aichi, 480-1198, JAPAN
inagaki@ist.aichi-pu.ac.jp

**Abstract.** This paper describes an evaluation experiment on a Japanese-Uighur machine translation system which consists of verbal suffix processing, case suffix processing, phonetic change processing, and a Japanese-Uighur dictionary including about 20,000 words. Japanese and Uighur have many syntactical and language structural similarities. For these reasons, it is considered that we can translate Japanese into Uighur in such a manner as word-by-word aligning after morphological analysis of the input sentences without complicated syntactical analysis. From the point of view of practical usage, we have chosen three articles and conducted a full-text translation experiment on the articles with our MT system, for clarifying our argument. As a result of the experiment, 84.8% of precision has been achieved.

## 1 Introduction

Machine translation(MT) has been a very challenging field in the area of natural language processing for many years. The very early approaches were largely unsuccessful, not only for lack of computing resources and/or machine readable language resources, but also because the complexity of the interaction effects in natural language phenomena had been underestimated. On the other hand, machine translation is an applied area which benefit from advances in the area of theoretical artificial intelligence(AI) and natural language processing(NLP) – in spite of some partial results which have been achieved, we are still far from a satisfying treatment of natural language. Recently, the computing resources seem no longer to be critical problem, and machine readable language resources like

R.E. Frederking and K.B. Taylor (Eds.): AMTA 2004, LNAI 3265, pp. 208–216, 2004.
© Springer-Verlag Berlin Heidelberg 2004

corpora have been available (for some major languages like English, Japanese, Spanish and so on). And consequently, seeking ways of avoiding the need for massive knowledge acquisition by rejecting the entire established NLP paradigm in favor of knowledge-free, linguistics- and AI-independent approaches have become a modest approach for MT. For example, statistical MT [1] , which seeks to carry out translation based on complex cooccurrence and distribution probability calculations over very large aligned bilingual text corpora, and example-based MT [2] , which involves storing translation examples in a database, and then matching the input sentence against these examples, finding the best matching translation example.

Japanese and Uighur have many syntactical and language structural similarities, including word order, existence and same functions of case suffixes and verbal suffixes[1], morphological structure, etc. More importantly, syntactical structure and language structure depend on case suffixes and verbal suffixes in the two languages. For these reasons, we have a suggestion that we can translate Japanese into Uighur in such a manner as word-by-word aligning after morphological analysis of the input sentences, without complicated syntactical analysis, i.e. we can align an appropriate Uighur case suffix correspondent to each Japanese case suffix in the input sentences, instead of doing syntactical analysis, and we can avoid the need for massive knowledge acquisition.

However, there is some divergence on the treatment of the verbal suffixes between the two languages from the point of view of traditional Japanese grammar. For resolving the divergence, we utilized a Japanese-Uighur machine translation approach[3,4], which based on the derivational grammar[5].

On the other hand, there is few one-to-one correspondences between Japanese and Uighur nominal suffixes, especially the case suffixes that specify the role of noun phrases in the sentences. For resolving this problem, we utilized the case pattern based approach[6,7], and the common characteristics that dependent relations between nominal suffixes and verbal phrases in the two languages.

In the process of Japanese-Uighur machine translation, we also have to resolve the phonetic change problem due to the vowel harmony phenomena in Uighur. For this purpose, we formalized a phonetic change rules and achieved a morpheme synthesizing system in high precision.

And furthermore, we have incorporated a Japanese-Uighur dictionary[8,9], including about 20,000 words for our Machine Translation system. Thus, we have accomplished a nearly practical Japanese-Uighur machine translation system which consists of verbal suffix processing, case suffix processing, phonetic change processing, and a Japanese-Uighur dictionary.

From the point of view of pragmatical usage, we have chosen three articles about environmental issue appeared in the Nippon Keizai Shinbun, and conducted a translation experiment on the articles with our system. As a results of our experiment, 84.8% of precision has been achieved. Here, we counted the correctness of a phrase in the output sentences to be the evaluating criterion.

---

[1] Also say case particles and auxiliary verbs respectively in traditional Japanese grammar.

**Table 1.** Arabic based and Roman based Uighur alphabets

| 1 | 2 | 3 | 4 | 5 | 6 | 7 | 8 | 9 | 10 | 11 |
|---|---|---|---|---|---|---|---|---|---|---|
| ئا | ب | د | ئې | ف | گ | خ | ئى | ج | لـ | ل |
| A,a | B,b | D,d | E,e | F,f | G,g | H,h | I,i | J,j | K,k | L,l |

| 12 | 13 | 14 | 15 | 16 | 17 | 18 | 19 | 20 | 21 | 22 |
|---|---|---|---|---|---|---|---|---|---|---|
| م | ن | ئو | پ | چ | ر | س | ت | ئۇ | ۋ | ش |
| M,m | N,n | O,o | P,p | Q,q | R,r | S,s | T,t | U,u | W,w | X,x |

| 23 | 24 | 25 | 26 | 27 | 28 | 29 | 30 | 31 | 32 |
|---|---|---|---|---|---|---|---|---|---|
| ي | ز | غ | ھ | ق | ئە | ئۆ | ئۈ | ژ | ڭ |
| Y,y | Z,z | Ğ,ğ | Ḥ,ḥ | Ķ,ķ | É,é | Ö,ö | Ü,ü | Ƶ,ƶ | NG,ng |

This is because almost sentences in practical use are long sentences, and the less appearances of incorrect phrases in the output sentences are very desired in translation process, especially in the situation that a machine translation system acts as a "computer aided translation system."

In this paper, we will illustrate the similarities between Japanese and Uighur, and point out of the problems we have to resolve in the process of machine translation. Then, describe an implementation of our machine translation system based on derivational grammar and case suffixes replacement approaches. Finally, we will do an experiment and evaluation on the system to show validity of our argument that we can achieve a Japanese-Uighur machine translation system in high precision without syntactical analysis.

Note that, in this paper, we have transcribed Uighur characters in Roman based alphabet. But in modern Uighur, an Arabic based alphabet, as shown in Table 1 , is rather being used.

## 2    Similarities Between Japanese and Uighur

### 2.1    Syntactical Similarities

Japanese and Uighur are agglutinative languages belong to the same language family, and they are often referred to be the languages such as free word order languages. In Japanese, for example, we can say "karega tobirawo aketa" as well as "tobirawo karega aketa". Both sentences have the same meaning of "He opened the door" in English. What does allow keeping the equivalent meaning? The reason should be found in the function of those case suffixes. The dependent relation of a nominal to other words, or role of a nominal which plays in a sentence is identified by the case suffixes following the nominals.

The Japanese case suffix '-ga' indicates the subjective in a sentence, and '-wo' indicates the objective in a sentence. So, the case suffixes make it possible to keep and understand as identical meaning even if the positions of "karega" and "tobirawo" are changed.

The same case can be found in Uighur Language. Here, the case suffixes '-ø'(nominative case) and '-ni'(accusative case) in Uighur are respectively corresponding to the case suffixes '-ga' and '-wo' in Japanese. But in Uighur, the nominative case is often indicated by the 'zero-form', and we show it by 'ø'. So, we can say the same thing about the word order, i.e., the Uighur case suffixes make it possible to change the word order in a sentence without change of the meaning of the sentence.

Thus, we can translate both of Japanese sentences "karega tobirawo aketa" and "tobirawo karega aketa" into Uighur sentences "Uø ixikni aqti." and "Ixikni uø aqti." respectively in the manner of word-by-word alignment.

This observation means that the case suffixes play the essential roles on the syntactical structures in Japanese and Uighur, and we can find that Japanese-Uighur machine translation can be achieved without complicated syntactical analysis. The detailed observation can be found in [6] and [7].

### 2.2 Morphological Similarities

It has been considered that there is a morphological difference between Japanese and Uighur. This is due to the divergence of views between Japanese Traditional grammar and Uighur grammar on how to deal with the formation of verbal variants. In fact, there is no any difference on the formation of verbal variants in both languages from standpoint of derivational grammar, which claims that Japanese verbs do not conjugate, and that appending certain suffixes to verbal stems makes Japanese verbal variants. The situation about the verbal variant formation in Uighur grammar fits the standpoint of the derivational grammar one. The detailed formation rule of the verbal variants can be find in [3] and [4].

## 3   Problems in Japanese-Uighur Machine Translation

Although there are many critical similarities between the two languages, we have also some problems to resolve in our machine translation system. In this section, we will illustrate these problems with some examples.

### 3.1   Problems of Verbal Suffixes

Table 2 shows the correspondences between Japanese and Uighur syntactical suffixes. As we see, Japanese participle suffixes are the same form as finite suffixes while the Uighur ones are not. For example, Japanese perfective syntactical suffix '-(i)ta' is used for both of finite and participle forms. In Uighur however, there are different forms as shown in Table 3. For this reason, to translate '-(i)ta' into Uighur, we have to decide which of '-di' and '-ǧan' is the correct one.

### 3.2   Problems of Case Suffixes

We have already explained that Japanese and Uighur case suffixes specify the role of nominals in the sentences. This feature allows the flexible word order in the

**Table 2.** Syntactical Suffixes in Japanese and Uighur

| form | meaning | Japanese | Uighur |
|------|---------|----------|--------|
| finite form | non-perfective | -(r)u | *-(i)du* |
|  | perfective | -(i)ta | *-di* |
| participle form | non-perfective | -(r)u | *-(i)diğan* |
|  | perfective | -(i)ta | *-ğan* |
| converb form | perfective copulative | -(i)te | *-(i)p* |
|  | provisional conditional | -(r)eba | *-sa* |
|  | negative copulative | -(a)zu | *-mastin* |
|  | simultaneous | -(i)nagara | *-gaq* |
| imperative form | affirmative | -e, -ro | *-ğin* |
|  | negative | -(r)una | *-mağin* |

**Table 3.** The difference of finite and participle form in Japanese and Uighur

| form | Japanese | Uighur | Meaning |
|------|----------|--------|---------|
| finite form | "karega tobirawo ake<u>ta</u>" | "*u ixikni aqdi*" | he opened the door |
| participle form | "karega ake<u>ta</u> tobira" | "*u aqğan ixik*" | the door he opened |

sentences of the two languages. However, there is few one-to-one correspondences between case suffixes of Japanese and those of Uighur. For example, "gomi<u>wo</u> suteru" is translated into "*ehlet<u>ni</u> tökidu*", where Japanese case suffix 'wo' is translated into Uighur case suffix '*ni*'. On the other hand, "hashi<u>wo</u> wataru" is translated into "*köwrük<u>din</u> ötidu*". Japanese case suffix 'wo' is translated into '*din*'. The suffix 'wo' usually indicates the object, but sometimes it indicates the place, while Uighur case suffixes '*ni*' and '*din*' indicate the object and the place respectively. So we have to choose '*ni*' or '*din*' according to the role of 'wo' in the Japanese sentence. In a fact, the case suffix 'wo' that indicates a place often appears together with such the motional verbs like "tooru"(pass) and "wataru"(cross). This suggests we can choose '*ni*' or '*din*' according to the verbs which the nominals with 'wo' depends on.

## 4   Suffix Adjustment

Now let us proceed to our discussions on realization of our word-by-word translation from Japanese to Uighur. The facts we revealed so far show that the problems to be resolved here is how to decide verbal and case suffix correspondences correctly. To overcome these problems, we adopt a method to assign the default Uighur suffix to each Japanese suffix and then to substitute a well-fitted suffix for an unnatural one under replacement rules. Since a verbal stem and a following verbal suffix affect each other, we can choose an appropriate suffix by knowing the right and left words. On the other hand, the verb which the nominal with a case suffix depends on affects the suffix. So we need to decide the correct

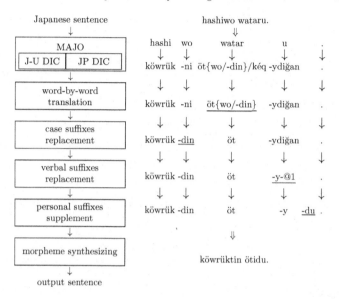

**Fig. 1.** Outline of Japanese-Uighur machine translation system, and a translation example

case suffix considering the verbs depended. About this subject we can refer [7] and [4].

## 5    Implementation of Japanese-Uighur Machine Translation System

We have implemented a Japanese-Uighur Machine Translation system based on the approaches we have proposed. Our system consists of four modules: MAJO, the two replacement modules and the morpheme synthesizing system. MAJO is a Japanese morphological analyzer based on the derivational grammar, and its dictionary consists of 3-tuples (Japanese morpheme, part-of-speech, meaning). For the translation, we replace the 3-tuples with (Japanese morpheme, part-of-speech, Uighur morpheme). Therefore outputs of MAJO become word-by-word translations for input sentences.

Here, a Japanese input sentence is "hashiwo wataru." (cross the bridge) shown in Figure 1. Firstly, MAJO divides it into Japanese words and yield a sequence of equivalent Uighur words. Secondly, replacement rules of verbal suffixes are

環境問題の原点は，人類が自然界の一員であることを自覚し，自然を征服するこ
とでつくり上げた文明のあり方を問い直し，見直すことから始まる．言い換えれ
ば自然の破壊・開発をもって文明としてきた人類の歴史を，自然との共生・調和
の方向につくり変えていくことにほかならない．人間中心主義とも言える自然観，
文明観を転換し，宇宙船地球号の一員として自らを律し，その知恵と能力を自然
との共栄共存のために使うことでなければならない．

**Fig. 2.** A sample Japanese passage from first article which used for our translation
experiment. From the point of view of practical usage, we have chosen three articles
about environmental issue appeared in Nihon Keizai Shimbun, and conducted a full-
text translation experiment on the articles with our MT system

muḩit mésilésining baxlinixi, insanlar méwjudatning bir ézasi ikénligini angḳap,
tébi'étni beḳindurux arḳiliḳ ḳurup qiḳḳan médiniyétning méwjut bolux xékilni ḳayta
oylap, ḳayta duruslaxtin baxlinidu. baxḳiqé eytḳanda tébiétni wéyran ḳilix, eqixni
médiniyét dép kélgén insanlarning tarihini, tébi'ét bilén bolğan ortaḳ yaxax, maslixixning téripigé özgértip berixtin baxḳisi bolmaydu. adémzat özék mésliki dépmu
diyéléydiğan tébiétḳarax, médiniyét ḳaraxni özgértip, além kemisi yér xari nomurining bir ézasi süpitidé özligidin tertipké kelip, uning éḳil bilén iḳtidarni tébi'ét
bilén bolğan ortaḳ güllinix ortaḳ yaxax üqün ḳollinidiğan ix bolmisa bolmaydu.

**Fig. 3.** An Uighur passage correspondent to Japanese passage in Figure 2 which translated by an Uighur native speaker

applied to those Uighur suffixes if they match the conditions on the replacement
table.

Thirdly, case suffixes are replaced if the verbs that they depend have the
replacement rules satisfied the condition. In the example, the first step translates '-wo' into '-*ni*'. But the verb 'watar' on which the noun phrase "hashiwo"
depends has a replacement rule (watar, consonant verb, *öt*{wo/*din*}). So, '-*ni*'
is replaced with '-*din*'. Finally, the morpheme synthesizing system synthesizes
Uighur morphemes according to the context of personal suffix and the phonetic
change rule and generates a Uighur output sentence.

## 6    Evaluation Experiment

From the point of view of pragmatical usage, we have chosen three articles about
environmental issue appeared in the Nihon Keizai Shimbun, and conducted a
translation experiment on the articles with our system which includes about
20,000 words of Japanese-Uighur Dictionary. The articles have 136 Japanese
sentences and include 306 verbal phrases(254 different patterns). We show a
portion of those sentences and its translations in Figure 2, 3, and 4.

We compared each phrase in the system translated sentences against the
correspondent phrase in the native Uighur speaker translated sentences. Thus,

muḥit mésilésining baxlinixi, insanlar méwjudatning bir ézasisi ixni angḳap, tébi'étni beḳindurux arḳiliḳ ḳurup qiḳḳan médini méwjut bolux xékilni ḳayta oylap, ḳayta duruslaxtin baxlinidu. baxḳiqé eytḳanda tébiétlik wéyran ḳilix, eqix bilén médiniyét süpitidé kélgén insanlarning tarihini, tébi'ét bilén bolǧan ortaḳ yaxax, maslixixning téripigé özgértip berixtin baxḳisi bolmaydu. adémzat özék mésliki bilénmu diyéléydiǧan tébiétḳarax, médiniyét ḳaraxni özgértip, além kemisi yér xari nomurining bir ézasisi süpitidé ḳolmu-ḳolni tertipké selip, uning éḳil bilén iḳtidarni tébi'ét bilén bolǧan ortaḳ güllinix ortaḳ yaxixi üqün ḳollinix arḳiliḳ bolmisa bolmaydu.

**Fig. 4.** An Uighur passage correspondent to Japanese passage in Figure 2 which translated with our system. Each underlined–wrong–phrase in the passage correspondent to those underlined–correct–phrase in the passag in Figure 3

**Table 4.** The failure case of the experiment

| case of failure | case suffix replacement | verbal suffix replacement | morpho-logical analysis | morpheme synthesiz-ing | meaning processing | others | total |
|---|---|---|---|---|---|---|---|
| number | 70 | 29 | 8 | 71 | 155 | 2 | 335 |

we counted 1,799 correct phrases in the total of 2,122 phrases. As a results of our experiment, 84.8% of precision has been achieved. In this evaluation, we counted the correctness of a phrase in the output sentences to be a evaluating criterion. This is because that the numbers of phrases in sentences are varying extremely, and we can not say a longer sentence and a shorter sentence including a wrong phrase have the same incorrectness. Furthermore, in the situation that a machine translation system acts as a "computer aided translation system," the more appearances of correct phrases in the output (long) sentences are desired. In the first sentence in Figure 4, we can see there are 23 phrases, and there are 3 wrong phrases. In this case, we only need to correct those 3 wrong phrases manually, and we can obtain a correct output sentence, that is the first sentence in Figure 3. Here, we show the failure case of the experiment in Table 4.

## 7   Conclusion and Future Work

In this paper, we illustrated the similarities between Japanese and Uighur, and pointed out of the problems we have to resolve in the process of machine translation. Then, we described the basic structure of our machine translation system based on derivational grammar and case suffixes replacement approaches. The translation system has succeeded in systematic word-by-word translation. In addition, it can generate nearly natural Uighur sentences by using replacement rules. So, we can say that, by utilizing of similarities between Japanese and

Uighur, a practical high precision Japanese-Uighur machine translation system can be achieved without complicated syntactical analysis.

However, our machine translation system does not take account of ambiguities of word meaning. This is beyond of our purpose in this paper. Because, the syntactical structures in Japanese and Uighur depend on case suffixes, and we can ignore the dependencies between syntactical analysis and word selection in machine translations between the two languages. But as a future work, we need to develop a mechanism for word selection.

Here, we have discussed only case suffixes, but there are other suffixes in Japanese. Some of them corresponds to certain Uighur suffixes and the other ones do not correspond to Uighur suffixes exactly. We are now making bigger size of experiments on our translation system, and collecting more replacement rules. We are aiming to make our system fit for practical use.

# References

1. Brown, P., Cocke, J., Della Pietra, S., Della Pietra, V., Jelinek, F., Mercer, R.L. and P.S. Roossin: A statistical approach to language translation. Computational Linguistics. vol 16, (1990) 79–85
2. Nagao, M.: A framework of a mechanical translation between Japanese and English by analogy principle. In: A. Elithorn and R. Banerji (eds.) Artificial and Human Intelligence. NATO Publications(1984).
3. Ogawa, Y., Muhtar M., Sugino, K., Toyama, K. and Inagaki, Y.: Generation of Uighur Verbal Phrases Based on Derivational Grammar. Journal of Natural Language Processing(in Japanese), Vol.7, No.3 (2000) 57–77
4. Muhtar, M., Ogawa, Y., Sugino, K. and Inagaki, Y.: Utilizing Agglutinative Features in Japanese-Uighur Machine Translation. In: Proceedings of the MT Summit VIII, Santiago de Compostela, Galicia, Spain (2001) 217–222
5. Kiyose, G. N.: Japanese grammar –A new approach–. Kyoto University Press (1995)
6. Muhtar, M., Casablanca, F., Toyama, K. and Inagaki, Y.: Particle-Based Machine Translation for Altaic Languages: the Japanese-Uighur Case. In: Proceedings of the 3rd Pacific Rim International Conference on Artificial Intelligence, Vol.2. Beijing, China (1994) 725–731
7. Muhtar, M., Ogawa, Y. and Inagaki, Y.: Translation of Case suffixes on Japanese-Uighur Machine Translation. Journal of Natural Language Processing(in Japanese), Vol.8, No.3 (2001) 123–142
8. Muhtar, M., Ogawa, Y., Sugino, K. and Inagaki, Y.: Semiautomatic Generation of Japanese-Uighur Dictionary and Its Evaluation. Journal of Natural Language Processing(in Japanese), Vol.10, No.4 (2003) 83–108
9. Muhtar, M., Ogawa, Y., Sugino, K. and Inagaki, Y.: Semiautomatic Generation of Japanese-Uighur Dictionary and Its Evaluation. In: Proceedings of the 4th Workshop On Asian Language Resources (2004) 103–110

# A Structurally Diverse Minimal Corpus for Eliciting Structural Mappings Between Languages*

Katharina Probst and Alon Lavie

Language Technologies Institute
Carnegie Mellon University
{kathrin,alavie}@cs.cmu.edu

**Abstract.** We describe an approach to creating a small but diverse corpus in English that can be used to elicit information about any target language. The focus of the corpus is on *structural* information. The resulting bilingual corpus can then be used for natural language processing tasks such as inferring transfer mappings for Machine Translation. The corpus is sufficiently small that a bilingual user can translate and word-align it within a matter of hours. We describe how the corpus is created and how its structural diversity is ensured. We then argue that it is not necessary to introduce a large amount of redundancy into the corpus. This is shown by creating an increasingly redundant corpus and observing that the information gained converges as redundancy increases.

## 1   Introduction and Motivation

Field linguistics has long recognized elicitation as an important means to documenting languages [2], [1]. In our work, we address a similar problem: we elicit data for the purpose of creating bilingual corpora that can be used for natural language processing tasks. The problem of gathering bilingual data by eliciting a carefully constructed corpus has also been addressed by a small number of projects, e.g. by [9], [4]. In our work, we use the elicited data to learn transfer rules for Machine Translation that capture how structures and features map from one language into another. The learned rules function at run-time the same way a hand-written transfer grammar is used [7], [3].

Elicitation focuses on gathering information about different structures and different linguistic features. An elicitation corpus is then a set of sentences and phrases that a bilingual speaker translates, so that information about the target language (TL) can be gathered from the corpus. Why is this worthwhile? In our work, we aim at building MT systems for language pairs where an abundance of information is given for one of the languages (such as English), while we have access to neither a large bilingual corpus nor to other resources such as a parser for the other language. In such a case, elicitation can be used to obtain

---

* This research was funded in part by NSF grant number IIS-0121631.

R.E. Frederking and K.B. Taylor (Eds.): AMTA 2004, LNAI 3265, pp. 217–226, 2004.
© Springer-Verlag Berlin Heidelberg 2004

information about this language. However, we do not simply elicit *any* data: A naturally occurring corpus exhibits all the structure and feature phenomena of a language; the disadvantage of using a naturally occurring corpus for elicitation is that it is highly redundant, especially in the most frequent phenomena (e.g. NP→ DET ADJ N). An elicitation corpus, on the other hand, is a condensed set of sentences, where each sentence pinpoints a different phenomenon of interest. Because the elicitation will contain some noise, a certain amount of redundancy should be built into the corpus.

In our previous work on elicitation, we focused mainly on feature information [6], [8]. The resulting corpus contains sequences such as He has one daughter, He has one son, He has two daughters, and He has two sons. Clearly, such a sequence of sentences will be crucial in detecting the marking of gender, number, case, and other features. It will however be redundant if the goal is to learn how the structure S→NP VP is expressed in the target language. Redundancy in itself is not necessarily detrimental and can actually help in learning exceptions to general rules. However, redundancy will come at the expense of diversity. Precisely because in feature elicitation it is important to hold as many other factors as possible constant (i.e. elicit gender differences by comparing two sentences that differ *only* in gender), a very different elicitation corpus is needed when eliciting structures. For this reason, the most important design criterion for the corpus described in this paper is that it should be diverse by including a wide variety of structural phenomena. Further, it should be sufficiently small for a bilingual user to translate it within a matter of hours.

As was noted before [8], one inherent challenge of automatic language elicitation is a bias towards the source language (SL). The user is simply presented with a set of sentences to translate. Phenomena that might occur only in the TL not easily captured without explanations, pictures, or the like. In parallel work, we are addressing the issue; meanwhile, we must be aware of this elicitation bias. We handle it in our rule learning module by only conservatively proposing TL structures. Structures that are not mirrored in the SL are not learned explicitly. For more details on the rule learning, refer to [7].

## 2    Creating a Structurally Diverse Elicitation Corpus

To create a structurally diverse minimal elicitation corpus, we begin with 122176 sentences from the Brown section of the Penn Treebank [5].Each of the sentences is annotated with a full parse. We map the tagset used in the Penn Treebank to a tagset that is more suitable to our task, e.g. different verb forms (VBD for past and VB for non-past) are collapsed. Our algorithm then traverses the parses from the top down, splitting each of them into multiple subparses and thereby creating a substantially larger training corpus. For each interior node, i.e. a node that does not pertain to only one specific word, the enhancement algorithm extracts the subtree rooted at this node. This allows us to obtain examples of NPs of different make-up and context, e.g. with adjectives, series of modifying PPs, etc. It also allows us to model the distribution of types of structures other than full sentences. In our experiment, the enhanced Penn Treebank training corpus contains 980120 sentences and phrases. Elicited examples of different types are used by the rule learner to transfer rules for different structures, so that the rules can compositionally combine to cover larger input chunks.

The next step is to represent each parse by a meaningful identifier. This is done in order to determine how many different structures are present in the corpus, and how often each of these structures occurs. Consider the following two examples sentences:

```
The jury talked.
(<S>
  (<NP> (DET the-1) (N jury-2))
  (<VP> (V talked-3)))
```

```
Robert Snodgrass , state GOP chairman , said a meeting held Tuesday night
in Blue Ridge brought enthusiastic responses from the audience.
(<S>
  (<NP> [Robert Snodgrass ... chairman , ])
  (<VP> [said ... audience]))
```

We can see that they essentially instantiate the same high-level structure of a sentence, namely S→ NP VP. For this reason, we chose to represent each parse as an instance of its *component sequence*, which describes the parse's general *pattern*. Since a pattern is always uniquely represented by a component sequence, the two terms are essentially used interchangeably in the remainder of the paper. The component sequence of a parse is defined as a context-free rule whose left-hand side is the label of the parse's top node, and whose right-hand side is the series of node labels *one level down* from the parse's top node, S→ NP VP in the examples above.

The resulting training corpus contains a list of sentences and phrases, together with their parses and corresponding component sequences. We then create a list of all the unique patterns (component sequences) encountered in the training data and a count of how many times each such sequence occurred. The sequences are sorted by *types*, i.e. the label of the parse's top node. The elicitation corpus we want to create should contain example patterns from each type. We chose to focus on the following types: ADVP, ADJP, NP, PP, SBAR, and finally S, as we believe these to be stable constituents for transfer between many language pairs. Future work may address other types of structures, such as VP or WHNP (e.g. 'in what'). Some pattens occur frequently, whereas others are rarely encountered. For example, NPs can exhibit different patterns, e.g. NP→PRO, or NP→DET N, both of which are very frequent patterns, but also, less frequently, NP→ DET ADJP N N. Table 1 shows the five most frequent patterns for each type, together with their frequency of occurrence in the training corpus.

In order to maximize the time effectiveness of the bilingual speaker who will translate the corpus, we wish to focus on those patterns that occur frequently. At the same time, we would like to know that we have covered most of the probability mass of the different patterns of a given type. We chose to use the following method: for each pattern, we plot a graph depicting the cumulative probability with the addition of each pattern. An example of such a graph can be seen in Figure 1 below. The y-axis in this graph is the cumulative probability

**Table 1.** Most frequent patterns for different types

| AdvP: | | AdjP: | |
|---|---|---|---|
| Frequency | Component Sequence | Frequency | Component Sequence |
| 27930 | ADVP→ ADV | 14046 | ADJP→ ADJ |
| 1631 | ADVP→ ADV ADV | 2650 | ADJP→ ADV ADJ |
| 1468 | ADVP→ PREP | 2186 | ADJP→ ADJ PP |
| 910 | ADVP→ ADV PP | 1057 | ADJP→ ADJ CONJ ADJ |
| 448 | ADVP→ ADV ADV PP | 848 | ADJP→ V |
| **NP:** | | **PP:** | |
| Frequency | Component Sequence | Frequency | Component Sequence |
| 48337 | NP→ N | 106864 | PP→ PREP NP |
| 45424 | NP→ PRO | 2279 | PP→ PREP S |
| 40560 | NP→ DET N | 1407 | PP→ PREP PP |
| 15412 | NP→ DET N PP | 876 | PP→ PREP ADJP |
| 11797 | NP→ DET ADJ N | 838 | PP→ ADVP PREP NP |
| **SBAR:** | | **S:** | |
| Frequency | Component Sequence | Frequency | Component Sequence |
| 6993 | SBAR→ SUBORD S | 26813 | S→ NP VP |
| 2649 | SBAR→ WHADVP S | 11622 | S→ NP AUX VP |
| 771 | SBAR→ WHPP S | 1535 | S→ NP AUX NEG VP |
| 239 | SBARQ→ WHADVP SQ | 1361 | S→ PP PUNCT S |
| 205 | SBAR→ DET S | 1246 | S→ NP AUX ADVP VP |

covered (i.e. what portion of the occurences of this type in the training corpus are covered), and the x-axis is the cumulative number of patterns. In other words, the highest-ranking NP pattern accounts for about 17.5% of all occurrences of NPs in the training data; the highest and second highest ranking patterns together account for about 30% of NPs. We then linearly interpolate the data points in the graph, and choose as a cutoff the relative addition of probability mass by a pattern: We compute for each pattern the amount of probability that is added when adding a pattern. This can be computed by $\delta_{p_i} = \frac{c_{p_i}}{\sum_{j=1}^{n} c_{p_j}}$ where $c_{p_i}$ is the number of times pattern $p_i$ occurred in the training data and $n$ is the number of unique patterns for a specific type. We include in the corpus all patterns whose $\delta_{p_i}$ falls above a threshold. For the experiments presented here, we chose this threshold at 0.001. This allows us to capture most of the relevant structures for each type, while excluding most idiosyncratic ones. For instance, the lowest-ranking NP pattern included in the corpus still occurred more than 300 times in the original corpus.

For each of the patterns that is to be included in the elicitation corpus, we would like to find an example that is both representative and as simple as possible. For instance, consider again the two sentences presented above: `The jury talked.` and `Robert Snodgrass , state GOP chairman , said a meeting held Tuesday night in Blue Ridge brought enthusiastic responses from the audience.` Clearly, the first sentence could be a useful

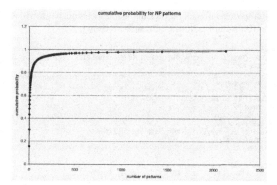

**Fig. 1.** An example of a cumulative probability graph

elicitation sentence, while the second sentence introduces much more room
for error: a number of reasons (such as lexical choice, the complex SBAR
structure, etc.) could prevent the user from translating this sentence into a
similar structure. We therefore would like to create a corpus with representative
yet simple examples. In order to automate this process somewhat, we extract
for each pattern one of the instantiations with the fewest number of parse
nodes. This heuristic can help create a full elicitation corpus automatically.
It is however advisable to hand-inspect each of the automatically extracted
examples, for a variety of reasons. For instance, the automatic selection process
cannot pay attention to lexical selection, resulting in sentences that contain
violent or otherwise inappropriate vocabulary. It can also happen that the
automatically chosen example is in fact an idiomatic expression and would
not easily transfer into the a TL, or that the structure, taken out of context,
is ambiguous. Some patterns are also not appropriate for elicitation, as they
are idiosyncratic to English, e.g. determiners can make up NPs (e.g the 'this'
in This was a nice dinner), but this does not necessarily hold for other
languages. Finally, the Penn Treebank contains some questionable parses. In all
these problematic cases, we manually select a more suitable instantiation for
the pattern, or eliminate the pattern altogether.

The resulting corpus contains 222 structures: 25 AdvPs, 47 AdjPs, 64 NPs, 13
PPs, 23 SBARs, and 50 Ss. Some examples of elicitation sentences and phrases
can be seen in listing below. The examples are depicted here together with
their parses and component sequences. The bilingual user that will translate
the sentences is only optionally presented with the parses and/or component
sequences. Since not all bilingual users of our system can be expected to be
trained in linguistics, it may be appropriate to present them simply with the
phrase or sentence to translate. Other context information, such as the parse as

well as the complete sentence (if eliciting a phrase), can be provided. This can help the user to disambiguate the phrase if necessary.

```
SL: to the election
C-Structure:(<PP> (PREP to-1) (<NP> (DET the-2) (N election-3)))
CompSeq: PP-> PREP NP

SL: the chair in the corner
C-Structure:(<NP> (DET the-1) (N chair-2) (<PP> (PREP in-3)
  (<NP> (DET the-4) (N corner-5))))
CompSeq: NP-> DET N PP

SL: attorneys for the mayor
C-Structure:(<NP> (N attorneys-1) (<PP> (PREP for-2) (<NP>
  (DET the-3) (N mayor-4))))
CompSeq: NP-> N PP

SL: I can not run
C-Structure:(<S> (<NP> (PRO I-1)) (<AUX> (AUX can-2)) (<NEG>
  (ADV not-3)) (<VP> (V run-4)))
CompSeq: S-> NP AUX NEG VP
```

## 3   Multiple Corpora

In this section, we argue that an elicitation corpus as small as the one we describe can be useful without losing important information. This is shown by creating an increasingly redundant corpus and observing that the information gained converges as redundancy increases, as described below.

One common problem is that lexical selection in the elicitation language can lead to unexpected or non-standard translations. For example, when eliciting the pattern NP→ DET ADJ N with a TL such as Spanish or French, depending on the adjective in the example, it will occur either before or after the noun in the TL. The ultimate goal of elicitation is to learn both the general rule (i.e. adjective after the noun) as well as the exceptions; it is however more important that we not miss the more general rule. This would happen if the elicitation instance will contain an adjective that represents an exception. Redundancy in the corpus can serve as a safeguard against this issue. We have therefore created three corpora, each of which contain different examples for the *same* list of SL patterns. Whenever possible, the structure of the training example was slightly altered; the high-level structure, i.e. the component sequence, however, always remained the same. For instance, each of the corpora contains an example of the high-level structure (type and component sequence) NP→ DET N PP.

```
SL: the size of this city
C-Structure:(<NP> (DET the-1) (N size-2) (<PP> (PREP of-3) (<NP> (DET this-4) (N city-5))))
CompSeq: NP-> DET N PP

SL: a dispute with the school board
C-Structure:(<NP> (DET a-1) (N dispute-2) (<PP> (PREP with-3) (<NP> (DET the-4) (N school-5)
  (N board-6))))
CompSeq: NP-> DET N PP

SL: the chair in the corner
C-Structure:(<NP> (DET the-1) (N chair-2) (<PP> (PREP in-3) (<NP> (DET the-4) (N corner-5))))
CompSeq: NP-> DET N PP
```

For evaluation purposes, we have translated the three corpora into German and have word-aligned the parallel phrases and sentences by hand. Two of the corpora were also translated into Hebrew by an informant. Below, we evaluate our structural elicitation corpus based on the translations obtained for German and Hebrew.

### 3.1   Results on Component Alignments

We elicited examples with different component sequences in the hope of obtaining information about similar structures in in the TL. In order to measure how much more information we gather by adding additional corpora, we seek to determine how the component sequences are mapped into the other language. For example, we may find that the sequence NP→ DET ADJ N maps to the TL structure NP→ DET N ADJ with the alignments $((1,1),(2,3),(3,2))$, i.e. the second component in the SL maps to the third component in the TL, etc. The basic premise of designing a small elicitation corpus is that these component alignments would mostly stay constant for different instantiations of the same pattern. It can always happen that the instance for a specific pattern exhibits an exception to a more general rule, in which case the general mapping rule would not be learned. Redundancy in the corpus can overcome this problem. As was said above, however, the redundancy in our corpus must be kept to a minimum in order to keep the translation task relatively small for the bilingual informant. A balance must be struck between these two competing interests.

We can measure how many different component alignments are added with the addition of each corpus. This is done by comparing the component alignment for each pattern between corpora. For instance, we check whether the elicitation resulted in the same or different component alignments for 'the new management', 'a favorable report', and 'the first year', all instances of the pattern NP→ DET ADJ N.

The component alignments can be determined with high confidence from the word alignments. They represent the order in which the SL components are transferred to the TL. In the simplest case, the word alignments contain only one-to-one alignments. In this case, we can simply gather all the indices under each component into one index on the SL side. On the TL side, we use the word alignments to create sets of TL components (i.e. all indices that align to all SL indices of a specific SL component). For example:

```
;;SL: that he would not sleep ;;TL(Hebrew): $ HWA LA II$N
ConstSeq: SBAR-> SUBORD S
word alignment: ((1,1),(2,2),(4,3),(5,4))
component alignment: ((1,1)(2,2))
```

In this case, the S 'he would not sleep' is a component, so that SL indices 2-5 together form a component. The aligned TL indices form a set with no alignments to any other component (other than the SL S), so that it can be postulated that they form a TL component. However, things are not always this simple. For instance, it can happen that there are 0-1 or 1-0 word alignments,

1-many or many-1 word alignments, discontinuous constituents, or boundary
crossings. Discontinuous constituents result in splitting the sets for one component into two. Many-1 or 1-many word alignments are handled by gathering
them in one set of indices to form a component. For instance, if SL index 1 aligns
to TL indices 3 and 4, then we create a TL component containing indices 3 and
4, as in the pattern below.

```
;;SL: federal aid to education ;;TL: staatliche Ausbildungshilfe
CompSeq: NP-> ADJ N PP
word alignment: ((1,1),(2,2),(4,2))
component alignment: ((1,1)(2,2)(3,2))
```

Each corpus contains 222 SL patterns. When adding a second corpus for German, we obtained an additional 52 patterns. The addition of the third corpus
resulted in only an additional 25 patterns. For Hebrew, we only have translations for two of the corpora available. It was found that in the first corpus, 209
unique component sequences and alignments were elicited. Some patterns (15)
were not translated; others (10) had more than one translation, while not all
translations resulted in different component analyses. The second corpus added
55 new patterns with unique component alignments, and an additional 15 that
were not translated in the first corpus. In the second corpus, 9 patterns were not
translated. It can be seen from the results in the below table that the addition
of corpora does add patterns that had not been observed before. However, each
additional corpus adds less to the number of patterns observed, as expected. The
main conclusion is that the number of additional patterns drops off very quickly.
With the third German corpus, only 11% of the patterns in the corpus result in a
component sequence that was previously unobserved. This leads us to argue that
we have good evidence that in the case of German, the most common structure
mappings appear to be covered already by the first two instances. The addition
of a third corpus adds additional redundancy and protection from information
loss. Hebrew is a more difficult case for elicitation, so that a third (and maybe
fourth) corpus appears to be advisable.

| | German | Hebrew |
|---|---|---|
| $corpus_1$ | 222 | 209 |
| $corpus_1 + corpus_2$ | 52 | 55+15 |
| $corpus_1 + corpus_2 + corpus_3$ | 25 | n/a |

## 3.2   Results on Learned Grammars

The previous evaluation metric is important because it allows us to gain insight
into how different the elicited structures are between different corpora. The ultimate purpose of elicitation for our work is however to learn structural transfer
rules. In this section, we describe and discuss the rules that were learned from
the three German and two Hebrew corpora.

In our rule learning system, we pay special attention to not overgeneralize
the learned rules. This is achieved in part by leaving unaligned words lexicalized.
Similarly, words that are not aligned one-to-one are often left lexicalized, so
as to not postulate structures in the TL that are merely caused by specific

lexical choices. Thus some of the rules contain lexical items and are thus not as general as they would be if a human grammar writer had designed them. This means that we will often learn different rules for the same pattern, even if the component alignment as described above is the same. This indicates a measure of safeguarding in the training corpus. In order to determine how effective our elicitation corpus is for learning rules, we trained our system on the three German and two Hebrew corpora separately and measured how many unique rules are learned in each case. The results can be seen in the table below.

| | German | Hebrew |
|---|---|---|
| $corpus_1$ | 222 | 209 |
| $corpus_1 + corpus_2$ | 96 | 134 |
| $corpus_1 + corpus_2 + corpus_3$ | 73 | n/a |

As expected, there is more overlap in the rules learned for German between the different corpora, because English and German are more closely related than English and Hebrew. In particular, it was observed that many words in the English-Hebrew rules are left lexicalized due to word alignments that were not one-to-one. This again leads us to conclude that it would be useful to obtain additional data.

Some examples of learned rules can be seen below. As was mentioned above, the rules are learned for different types, so that they can combine compositionally at run time.

```
;;SL: MOST RURAL AREAS ;;TL(German): DIE MEISTEN LAENDLICHEN GEGENDEN
NP::NP [ADJ ADJ N] -> ["DIE" ADJ ADJ N]
((X1::Y2)(X2::Y3)(X3::Y4))

;;SL: I WILL SOON READ THE BOOK ;;TL(German): ICH WERDE DAS BUCH BALD LESEN
S::S [NP AUX ADVP V NP] -> [NP AUX NP ADVP V]
((X1::Y1)(X2::Y2)(X3::Y4)(X4::Y5)(X5::Y3))

;;SL: THE CITY EXECUTIVE COMMITTEE ;;TL(Hebrew): H W&DH H MNHLT $L H &IRIH
NP::NP ["THE" N N N] -> ["H" N "H" N "$L" "H" N]
((X2::Y7)(X3::Y4)(X4::Y2))

;;SL: A SPECIAL CONSTITUTIONAL QUESTION ;;TL(Hebrew): $ALH XWQTIT MIWXDT
NP::NP ["A" ADJ ADJ N] -> [N ADJ ADJ]
((X2::Y3)(X3::Y2)(X4::Y1))
```

## 4   Conclusions and Future Work

We have presented an approach to designing a very small elicitation corpus that covers a large portion of the probability mass of English patterns that of interest to our work. Because of the structural diversity of the corpus, we can utilize the time of a bilingual user efficiently: translating and hand-alignining a corpus of 222 sentences or phrases is a task of one or two hours, as reported by a bilingual speaker who translated the corpus into Hebrew. One or more additional corpora of the same size add additional TL (i.e. elicited) patterns and introduce important redundancy into the corpus, so that is unlikely that only exceptions, not general rules are learned.

We observed that for closely related languages, such as English and German, a smaller corpus is sufficient for learning rules, while for not closely related languages, such as English and Hebrew, more data collection is appropriate. We observed however that even for Hebrew there is significant overlap between the rules and TL structures observed from the first and the second corpus. Additional examples for each pattern are expected to yield even fewer new rules and structures.

Future work in this area can be divided into two different areas. First, we have already begun investigating methods to identify elicitation examples that are not appropriate for a given TL. Some structures are heavily biased towards English, and might only be interesting for closely related languages such as German. Others can result in overgeneralized transfer rules. Second, we plan to expand the corpus. With a bilingual informant available for more than a few hours, we can elicit additional information. In such a case, we can begin to focus on eliciting important exceptions to general rules, and to infer the cases in which these exceptions occur. The ultimate goal is for this structural corpus to be integrated with our elicitation corpus that focuses on linguistic features. An online navigation algorithm will help the system elicit only pertinent sentences or phrases, and eliminate phenomena that are not relevant to a given TL.

# References

1. Bouquiaux, Luc and J.M.C. Thomas. Studying and Describing Unwritten Languages, The Summer Institute of Linguistics, Dallas, TX, 1992.
2. Comrie, Bernard and N. Smith. Lingua Descriptive Series: Questionnaire, Lingua, 42, 1-72, 1977.
3. Lavie, Alon, S. Vogel, L. Levin, E. Peterson, K. Probst, A. Font Llitjos, R. Reynolds, J. Carbonell, R. Cohen. Experiments with a Hindi-to-English Transfer-based MT System under a Miserly Data Scenario, ACM Transactions on Asian Language Information Processing (TALIP), 2:2, 2003.
4. Jones, Douglas and R. Havrilla. Twisted Pair Grammar: Support for Rapid Development of Machine Translation for Low Density Languages, Third Conference of the Association for Machine Translation in the Americas (AMTA-98), 1998.
5. Marcus, Mitchell, A. Taylor, R. MacIntyre, A. Bies, C. Cooper, M. Ferguson, A. Littmann. The Penn Treebank Project, http://www.cis.upenn.edu/ treebank/home.html, 1992.
6. Probst, Katharina, R. Brown, J. Carbonell, A. Lavie, L. Levin, E. Peterson. Design and Implementation of Controlled Elicitation for Machine Translation of Low-density Languages, Workshop MT2010 at Machine Translation Summit VIII, 2001.
7. Probst, Katharina, L. Levin, E. Peterson, A. Lavie, J. Carbonell. MT for Resource-Poor Languages Using Elicitation-Based Learning of Syntactic Transfer Rules, Machine Translation, Special Issue on Embedded MT, 2003.
8. Probst, Katharina and L. Levin. Challenges in Automated Elicitation of a Controlled Bilingual Corpus, 9th International Conference on Theoretical and Methodological Issues in Machine Translation (TMI-02), 2002.
9. Sherematyeva, Svetlana and S. Nirenburg. Towards a Unversal Tool for NLP Resource Acquisition, Second International Conference on Language Resources and Evaluation (LREC-00), 2000.

# Investigation of Intelligibility Judgments

Florence Reeder

George Mason University
The MITRE Corporation
freeder@mitre.org

**Abstract.** This paper describes an intelligibility snap-judgment test. In this exercise, participants are shown a series of human translations and machine translations and are asked to determine whether the author was human or machine. The experiment shows that snap judgments on intelligibility are made successfully and that system rankings on snap judgments are consistent with more detailed intelligibility measures. In addition to demonstrating a quick intelligibility judgment, representing on a few minutes time of each participant, it details the types of errors which led to the snap judgments.

## 1   Introduction

Intelligibility is often measured through judgment on a one to five scale where five indicates that the translation is as coherent and intelligible as if it were authored in the target language. Varied definitions of intelligibility exist (e.g., [1], [11], [13]). The definition provided through the ISLE work [6] reflects historical definitions and are used here. Intelligibility is the "extent to which a sentence reads naturally." Natural reading can be the degree of conformance to the target language. In the case of this experiment, the target language is English and it can be said to measure the degree of Englishness.

In language teaching, Meara and Babi [7] tested assessors' abilities to make a distinction between Spanish native speakers (L1) and language learners (L2) for written essays. The experiment's main premise was that professional language examiners tend to make snap judgments on student exams. They showed assessors essays one word at a time, asking them to identify the author as L1 or L2. They counted the number of words before an attribution was made as well as success rates for the assessors. This is an intelligibility or coherence test since the essay topics were open-ended.

For eighteen assessors and 180 texts, assessors could accurately attribute L1 texts 83.9% and L2 texts 87.2% of the time. Additionally, they found that assessors could make the L1/L2 distinction in less than 100 words. It took longer to successfully attribute the author's language when the essay was written by a native speaker (53.9 words) than by a language learner (26.7 words). This means that the more intelligible an essay was, the harder it was to recognize. They ascribe this to the notion that L1 writing "can only be identified negatively by the absence of errors, or the absence of awkward writing" [7]. While they did not select features that evaluators used, they hypothesized a "tolerance threshold" for low quality writing. Once the threshold had

R.E. Frederking and K.B. Taylor (Eds.): AMTA 2004, LNAI 3265, pp. 227–235, 2004.
© Springer-Verlag Berlin Heidelberg 2004

been reached through either a major error or several missteps, the assessor could confidently attribute the text. The results are intuitive in that one would expect the presence of errors to be a strong determiner of intelligibility. On the other hand, it represents a measurement of the intuition, and the number of words needed is surprising small given the size of the average exam (over 400 words). The question arises, "Can the test be adapted for human translation (HT) and machine translation (MT) output?"

## 2    Experimental Setup

The data selected had been used in previous MT evaluations [13], representing previously scored data. The DARPA-94 corpus consists of three language pairs, French-English, Spanish-English and Japanese-English, containing one hundred documents per language pair taken from news texts. The texts are roughly 400 words apiece. For each source language document, two reference translations accompany the MT outputs. DARPA-94 is well-suited here because it has human intelligibility judgments. In the selected Spanish-English collection, five MT systems participated. The first fifty available translations for each system were chosen as well as one of two reference translations.[1] Headlines were removed as they represent atypical language usage. The extracts were taken from the start of each article. Sentence boundaries were preserved, therefore, each text was between 98 and 140 words long. Each text fragment was placed on a separate page along with an identifier and a scoring area.

Fifty participants were recruited where 98% were native English speakers and 2% had native English fluency. Participants were divided between those at least familiar with Spanish at 56%, and those with no Spanish at 44%. Subjects were heavily weighted towards computer competency, with 84% as computing professionals and none having no competence. MT knowledge was also spread between those with some familiarity at 38%; those with some NLP or language capability at 40%; and those with no familiarity, 22%.

Each subject was given a set of six extracts which were a mix of MT and HT. No article was duplicated within a test set. Text order was mixed within a test set so that the system and HT orders varied. Participants were given test sheets with a blank piece of paper for overlay. They were instructed use the overlay to read the article line-by-line and were told to circle the word at which they decided as soon as they could differentiate between HT and MT. Half of the subjects were given no information about the human's expertise level, while the other half were told that the HT was done by a professional translator. To facilitate snap judgment, subjects were given up to three minutes per text, although few came close to the limit.

---

[1] For one of the systems, nearly twenty documents were missing at the time of the experiment. These twenty were at the end of the selected sample and were augmented from the next group of 20.

# 3   Distinguishing Between HT and MT

Subjects were able to correctly attribute the translations 87.7% of the time. This determination is slightly above that reported for the L1/L2 distinction which averaged 85.6% [7]. For MT systems, the recognition rate was 87.6% which is comparable to the L2 attribution of 87.2% [7]. Surprisingly, at 88%, the successful attribution of HT was higher than the native speaker attribution rate of 83.9% [7]. Therefore, HT can be differentiated from MT in less than one hundred words.

In looking at the details of the scores, three of the fifty test subjects correctly identified only 50% of the texts. Another three subjects missed two of the texts with 88% being able to differentiate with less than one misattribution. Of this 88%, the group was evenly split between one error and no errors. Post-test interviews showed that one judge assumed pathological cases, such as a non-native English speaker translating Spanish to English, and another had little computer experience and considered computers more capable than humans.

# 4   Correctness as a Predictor of Intelligibility

The assumption is that given the high rate of computer savvy personnel in testing, a system producing less intelligible output or lower fluency scores would be more accurately attributed as having been computer generated. Measurement is through looking at the attribution accuracy (percent correct) versus the intelligibility (fluency) score (Table 1). Systems with higher intelligibility scores are less accurately differentiated from HT. As the fluency increases for systems, the percentage of correctly attributed texts decreases. While this can be seen (Figure 1), analysis shows a Pearson correlation of $R = -0.89$ (significant at 0.05). The negative correlation reflects the fact that as fluency increases differentiation from HT decreases. The Spearman correlation of -1 (significant at 0.01) is even stronger.

Given that the attributions were done on only part of the texts, we also looked at the fluency scores assigned for those parts of the texts that were part of the test. The original DARPA-94 scores were aggregates of individual sentence scores. Subjects were shown a text one sentence at a time and asked to score that sentence on a 1-5 scale where a score of five represents the greatest fluency. For a given text, scores were then averaged and divided by five resulting in a score which fell between zero and one. To look at partial text fluency, we took the scores for individual sentences used in the test, averaged them and divided by five. These are shown (third column of Table 1). When looking at the score correlations to partial text fluency, the result is close with a Pearson correlation of $R = -0.85$ (significant at 0.07). Partial fluency scores correlate with overall fluency scores at $R = 0.995$.

While the percentage correct does correlate with fluency for MT systems, like with other metrics such as BLEU [8]`, introducing HT causes the correlation to degrade. When HT is added in, scores do not follow the trend of lower intelligibility conforming to higher judgment accuracy with a correlation of -0.45 (significant at 0.32). This is because the HT examples have significantly higher fluency scores than MT, yet are able to be distinguished from MT.

**Table 1.** System Accuracy Scores, Fluency (FLU), Partial Text Fluency (FLUPAR)

| SYS | % CORRECT | FLU | FLUPAR |
|---|---|---|---|
| PANGLOSS | 0.96 | 0.21 | 0.35 |
| LINGSTAT | 0.94 | 0.31 | 0.43 |
| GLOBALINK | 0.92 | 0.43 | 0.54 |
| SYSTRAN | 0.86 | 0.46 | 0.54 |
| PAHO | 0.70 | 0.58 | 0.63 |
| EXPERT | 0.88 | 0.90 | 0.89 |
| AVG | 0.87 | 0.48 | 0.56 |

**Fig. 1.** Correct Attribution Rate Versus Fluency

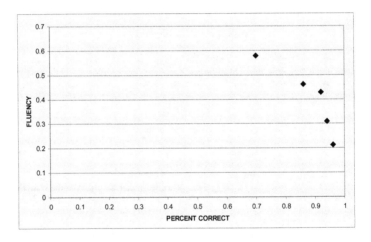

## 5    Words Needed as a Predictor of Intelligibility

The number of words needed to differentiate MT from HT increases for more intelligible systems. Texts with higher fluency scores are reasonably expected to contain fewer errors, meaning that it will take a more words to distinguish a text as MT. Results (Table 2, Figure 2) show that the number of words for decision does increase as fluency increases. The word count increases because more intelligible systems tend to have fewer errors per word. While the correlations are not as strong for the systems only case at $R^2 = 0.84$ (significant at 0.08), when the HT scores are include, the correlation improves to 0.95 (significant at 0.004). This confirms the idea that the presence of errors contributes significantly to the distinction. Looking at partial fluency and percentage of words as opposed to number of words improves the scores to some extent ($R^2 = 0.87$ for systems only).

**Table 2.** Number of Words for Decision Point

| SYSTEM | # WORDS | FLUENCY |
|---|---|---|
| Pangloss | 17.6 | 0.21 |
| Globalink | 25.9 | 0.43 |
| Systran | 31.7 | 0.46 |
| Lingstat | 33.8 | 0.31 |
| Paho | 37.6 | 0.58 |
| Human | 62.2 | 0.90 |
| AVG | 34.8 | 0.48 |

**Fig. 2.** Number of words versus intelligibility (human included)

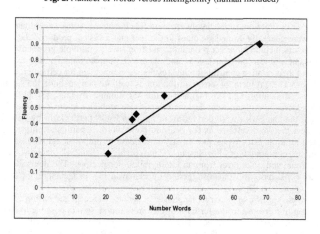

## 6   Error Types as Predictors of Intelligibility

Having established that the snap judgment test correlates well with intelligibility, it remains to determine if there are error types which play a large part in the decision process (Table 3). For this stage of the effort, only correctly attributed MT output is analyzed. This decision is due to the fact that MT, rather than HT, is of interest. Only correct attributions were included because these would provide useful information for training a system to correctly attribute MT as well.

**Table 3.** Error Types According to Number, Percentage of Total

| ERROR TYPE | DESCRIPTION | NUM | PER |
|---|---|---|---|
| PREPS | Incorrect, extra or missing preposition | 437 | 21.31 |
| ORDER | Word ordering | 351 | 17.11 |
| CAP-ERROR | Capitalization error | 206 | 10.04 |
| NE-ERROR | Named entity error | 189 | 9.22 |
| ARTICLE | Incorrect, extra or missing article | 153 | 7.46 |
| VERB-FORM | Verb form, particularly tense | 146 | 7.12 |
| PRONOUNS | Incorrect, extra or missing pronoun | 144 | 7.02 |
| NTW | Not translated word | 121 | 5.90 |
| NE-ARTICLE | Article before the named entity | 108 | 5.27 |
| SEMANTICS | Major semantic errors | 92 | 4.49 |
| AGREEMENT | Agreement in number and gender | 61 | 2.97 |
| PUNCT | Punctuation | 23 | 1.12 |
| NEGATION | Negation, particularly verbs | 11 | 0.54 |
| CONJ-COO | Conjunction and coordination | 9 | 0.44 |
| TOTAL | | 2051 | |

Some error types are immediately apparent.Not translated words, other than proper nouns, were generally immediate clues to the fact that a system produced the results. Other factors include incorrect pronoun translation such as multiple pronouns output, inconsistent preposition translation, and incorrect punctuation. To determine the errors and their relative contribution, the results were annotated for certain broad error categories. The problem of error attribution is well-known in both the language teaching community (e.g., [5], [4]) and in the MT community (e.g., [3], [12]). The categories used, therefore, were designed to mitigate problems in error attribution. In addition, the categories were derived from the data itself, particularly by looking at errors near the word selected as the decision point word. A particular phrase can be assigned multiple error types, particularly in the case of prepositional phrases versus noun-noun compounding. For instance "the night of Sunday" contains both a prepositional and order error from an intelligibility perspective. The items identified here are consistent with those suggested by Flanagan [3]. In fact, three of the five Class 1 errors identified by Flanagan (capitalization, spelling, article) are here. The other two are specific to the target languages in her study (accent and elision).

The top five errors account for 65% of the errors found, so it is possible to theorize that a system which could detect these could accurately measure intelligibility while being diagnostic as well. The top five error categories are prepositions; word ordering; capitalization errors; named entity errors and incorrect, extra or missing articles. If the named entity article category is included in articles in general, then articles are the third highest with 12.73% and the overall percentage of the top five is over 70%. Surprisingly, not translated words account for only six percent of the error categories, although these were repeatedly mentioned as a giveaway clue in the post-test interviews. Performing a linear regression analysis on the individual categories did not demonstrate a clear indicating factor for predicting intelligibility. We further analyzed the results into category types.

### 6.1 Surface Errors

Three types of errors fall into the surface errors category: capitalization errors; not-translated words; and punctuation errors. Not-translated words are an obvious indicator of machine ability. These could be accounted for explicitly. Not-translated words accounted for 9.9% of the selected words. That is, when a word was selected as the decision point, only in 9.9% of the cases was that word a not-translated one. On the other hand, only 17% of the not-translated words were selected ones, therefore, explicitly using these would is less indicative of decision factors than initially assumed. Capitalization accounts for over 10% of the errors, another readily measured feature, particularly for named entities and sentence beginnings.

### 6.2 Syntactic Errors

Syntactic errors form the majority of errors in this analysis. Two types of categories are those which have an edit distance component through the insertion, deletion and substitution of lexical items. In this type are incorrect, extra or missing prepositions; word ordering, including with incorrect noun-noun compounding and extra prepositions (i.e., **school of law** rather than **law school**); incorrect, extra or missing articles which do not include articles before named entities; incorrect, extra or missing pronouns, including indefinite pronouns and lists of pronouns (i.e., **he/she/it**) cases. The second type of errors is more related to agreement issues such as incorrect verb form, particularly tense; incorrect negation, particularly verbal; incorrect conjunction or coordination term used; and incorrect agreement in gender or number.

### 6.3 Semantic Errors

Only two error types are semantic: named entity errors and semantic errors. Named entity errors have been studied ([9], [10]) and a tool for measuring these exists. Major semantic errors will be difficult to diagnose and I limited these to ones primarily of spatial, temporal or event relationship. For instance, one system repeatedly listed a date as "east Tuesday" as opposed to "last Tuesday". Work in capturing and conveying semantic information is an active research area (e.g., [2]), so it is unlikely that an automated system could be designed to measure these at this time.

### 6.4 Post-test Interview Results

Post-test interviews have consistently shown that the deciders utilized error spotting techniques, although the types and sensitivities of the errors differed from subject to subject. Some errors were serious enough to make the choice obvious, while others had to occur more than once to push the decision above a threshold. One subject reported a tendency to want confirmation, saying that they could have guessed at the first line, but wanted to see the second just to be sure. Others reported wanting to be able to add a confidence measure to their judgments.

Test subjects used a variety of errors in vocabulary, grammar and style as indicators. The consensus was that a text that was not perfect was machine-generated. Lexical cues included "strange words", not-translated words, and extra words although misspellings were often forgiven. Other subjects recognized "convoluted constructs" such as too many prepositional phrases in a row, phrases starting with incorrect prepositions or verbal phrases in the infinitive form. Cumbersome sentence constructions that "didn't flow smoothly" involved choppy phrases strung together, long sentences, word ordering and literal translations, with one participant describing the grammar as "pathetic".

Those participants who did not immediately attribute weak translations to MT generally made either no assumptions of translation quality or attributed poor human translation to some of the cases. One described assuming the translator to be a non-native English speaker. Others supposed that since English is hard to learn and that even human translators can make mistakes.

## 7   Conclusions and Future Work

This work demonstrates that raters can make accurate intelligibility judgments with very little data. The impact of this is that it is conceivable to build an automated evaluation for intelligibility which relies on very little text, as opposed to those metrics which rely on corpora of test data. In addition, there are specific error types which contribute to the judgment which would enable diagnostic evaluation tools to be constructed. While it is not news to the MT community that certain types of errors contribute to judgments of poor intelligibility, it is unusual to have both the number and types quantified. Having said this, work still needs to be done in several dimensions. The first is to look at a system-by-system breakdown at the percentages and plot this against intelligibility scores to determine the weight that each type of error brings to the intelligibility score. Secondarily, a closer look at the error occurring at the word selected may indicate definitive features for decision making. Finally, this work proves out ideas of measuring "Englishness" of English-target MT. On the other hand, it argues not for measuring the positive amount of English conformance, but the negative degree of non-conformance to English standards. This indicates that it may be possible to build an error detection and correction post MT-module to improve MT output.

**Acknowledgement.** The views expressed in this paper are those of the author and do not reflect the policy of the MITRE Corporation. Many thanks to the anonymous reviewers for their astute and helpful comments.

# References

[1]     ALPAC. 1966. Language and machines: Computers in Translation and Linguistics. *A Report by the Automatic Language Processing Advisory Committee.* Division of Behavioral Sciences, National Academy of Sciences, National Research Council, Washington, D.C.

[2]     Farwell, D., Helmreich, S., Dorr, B., Habash, N., Reeder, F., Miller, K., Levin, L., Mitamura, T., Hovy, E., Rambow, O., Siddharthan, A. 2004. Interlingual Annotation of Multilingual Text Corpora. In Proceedings of Workshop on Frontiers in Corpus Annotation. NAACL/HLT 2004.

[3]     Flanagan, M. 1994. Error Classification for MT Evaluation. In Technology Partnerships for Crossing the Language Barrier:  Proceedings of the First Conference of the Association for Machine Translation in the Americas, Columbia, MD.

[4]     Heift, G. 1998. Designed Intelligence: A Language Teacher Model. Unpublished Ph.D. thesis. Simon Fraser University.

[5]     Holland, V.M. 1994. Lessons Learned in Designing Intelligent CALL: Managing Communication across Disciplines. *Computer Assisted Language Learning*, 7(3), 227-256.

[6]     Hovy E., King M. & Popescu-Belis A. 2002. Principles of Context-Based Machine Translation Evaluation. *Machine Translation*, 17(1), p.43-75

[7]     Meara, P. & Babi, A. 1999. Just a few words:  how assessors evaluate minimal texts. Vocabulary Acquisition Research Gp. Virtual Lib. www.swan.ac.uk/cals/vlibrary/ab99a.html

[8]     Papenini, K., Roukos, S., Ward, T. & Zhu, W-J. 2002. Bleu: a Method for Automatic Evaluation of Machine Translation. *Proceedings of ACL-2002*, Philadelphia, PA.

[9]     Papenini, K., Roukos, S., Ward, T., Henderson, J., & Reeder, F. 2002. Corpus-based comprehensive and diagnostic MT evaluation: Initial Arabic, Chinese, French, and Spanish results. In *Proceedings of Human Language Technology 2002*, San Diego, CA.

[10]    Reeder, F., Miller, K., Doyon, J., White, J. 2001. "The Naming of Things and the Confusion of Tongues: An MT Metric", *MT-Summit Workshop on MT Evaluation*, September.

[11]    Van Slype, G. 1979. *Critical Methods for Evaluating the Quality of Machine Translation.* Prepared for the European Commission Directorate General Scientific and Technical Information and Information Management. Report BR-19142. Bureau Marcel van Dijk.

[12]    White, J. 2000. Toward an Automated, Task-Based MT Evaluation Strategy. In Maegaard, B., ed., Proceedings of the Workshop on Machine Translation Evaluation at LREC-2000. Athens, Greece.

[13]    White, J., et al. 1992-1994. *ARPA Workshops on Machine Translation.* Series of 4 workshops on comparative evaluation. PRC Inc. McLean, VA.

# Interlingual Annotation for MT Development

Florence Reeder[2], Bonnie Dorr[3], David Farwell[4], Nizar Habash[3],
Stephen Helmreich[4], Eduard Hovy[5], Lori Levin[1], Teruko Mitamura[1], Keith Miller[2],
Owen Rambow[6], and Advaith Siddharthan[6]

[1] Carnegie Mellon University {teruko,lsl}@cs.cmu.edu,
[2] Mitre Corporation {keith,freeder}@mitre.org,
[3] University of Maryland {bonnie,nizar}@umiacs.umd.edu,
[4] New Mexico State University {david,shelmrei}@crl.nmsu.edu,
[5] University of Southern California, hovy@isi.edu,
[6] Columbia University {rambow, as372}@cs.columbia.edu

**Abstract.** MT systems that use only superficial representations, including the current generation of statistical MT systems, have been successful and useful. However, they will experience a plateau in quality, much like other "silver bullet" approaches to MT. We pursue work on the development of interlingual representations for use in symbolic or hybrid MT systems. In this paper, we describe the creation of an interlingua and the development of a corpus of semantically annotated text, to be validated in six languages and evaluated in several ways. We have established a distributed, well-functioning research methodology, designed a preliminary interlingua notation, created annotation manuals and tools, developed a test collection in six languages with associated English translations, annotated some 150 translations, and designed and applied various annotation metrics. We describe the data sets being annotated and the interlingual (IL) representation language which uses two ontologies and a systematic theta-role list. We present the annotation tools built and outline the annotation process. Following this, we describe our evaluation methodology and conclude with a summary of issues that have arisen.

## 1 Introduction

An interlingua (IL) is a semantic representation which mediates between source and target languages in interlingua-based machine translation (MT). If a system supports multi-language translation, the design of the IL becomes more complex, due to the number of languages represented. Even though the aim of an IL is to capture language-independent semantic expressions, it is difficult to design an IL that covers all known languages, and there is no universally acceptable IL representation currently in existence. In practice, researchers have designed IL representations for particular sets of languages, in order to cover the necessary set of semantic expressions for MT [15].

The "Interlingual Annotation of Multilingual Corpora" (IAMTC)[1] project focuses on the creation of a semantic representation system along with a multilingual corpus

---

[1] http://aitc.aitcnet.org/nsf/iamtc/

R.E. Frederking and K.B. Taylor (Eds.): AMTA 2004, LNAI 3265, pp. 236–245, 2004.
© Springer-Verlag Berlin Heidelberg 2004

for validating the IL. The establishment of a multilingual, semantically annotated corpus, with an associated interlingual representation, is potentially very important for MT research and development. The ambitious project (started September 2003) reported here involves six languages (Arabic, French, Hindi, Japanese, Korean and Spanish), 125 source news articles in each language and a total source corpus of about one million words. Each source article has been translated into English by three different professional translators, and the six bilingual corpora have been semantically annotated. Since the aims and basic structure of the project are discussed elsewhere [5], we describe the three stages of IL representation being developed and the annotation process. The evaluation methodology is examined along with a proposed MT-based evaluation.

## 2    Translation Divergences

A somewhat unique aspect of this project is its focus on multiple English translations of the same text. By comparing the annotations of the source text and its translations, any differences indicate one of three general problems: potential inadequacies in the interlingua, misunderstandings by the annotators, or mistranslations. By analyzing such differences, we can sharpen the IL definition, improve the instructions to annotators, and/or identify the kinds of translational differences that occur (and decide what to do about them).

Consider the first two paragraphs of K1E1 and K1E2 (two English translations of Korean text K1):

> *K1E1: Starting on January 1 of next year, SK Telecom subscribers can switch to less expensive LG Telecom or KTF. ... The Subscribers cannot switch again to another provider for the first 3 months, but they can cancel the switch in 14 days if they are not satisfied with services like voice quality.*
>
> *K1E2: Starting January 1st of next year, customers of SK Telecom can change their service company to LG Telecom or KTF ... Once a service company swap has been made, customers are not allowed to change companies again within the first three months, although they can cancel the change anytime within 14 days if problems such as poor call quality are experienced.*

First, if the interlingua term repository contains different terms for *subscriber* and *customer*, then the single Korean source term will have given rise to different interpretations. Here, we face a choice: we can ask annotators to explicitly search for near-synonyms and include them all, or we can compress the term repository to remove these near-synonyms. Second, K1E1 contains *less expensive*, which K1E2 omits altogether. This could be either one translator's oversight or another's incorporation of world knowledge into the translation. Third, is *voice quality* the same as *call quality*? Certainly *voice* is not the same as *call*. What should the interlingua representation be here—should it focus merely on the poor *quality*, skirting the modifiers altogether? Before we could address these more intriguing cases, we faced the necessity of building an IL representation which was increasingly abstract while maintaining a level of feasibility from an annotation perspective. This led to the approach described in the next section.

## 3   The Interlingual Representation

The interlingual representation comprises three levels and incorporates knowledge sources such as the Omega ontology and theta grids [16]. The three levels of representation are referred to as *IL0, IL1* and *IL2*. We have performed the annotation process incrementally, with each level incorporating additional semantic features and removing syntactic ones. Having designed and evaluated through *IL1*, we are now looking at *IL2* issues which will be documented in the future. *IL2* is designed to be the interlingual level that abstracts away from most syntactic idiosyncrasies of the source language.

*IL0* is a deep syntactic dependency representation including part-of-speech tags for words and a parse tree that makes explicit the syntactic predicate-argument structure of verbs. The parse tree contains labels referring to deep-syntactic function, normalized for voice alternations. Function words' contribution is represented as features or semantically void punctuation. While this representation is syntactic, disambiguation decisions, such as relative clause and PP attachment, have been made, and the presentation abstracts as much as possible from surface-syntactic phenomena. *IL0* (Figure 1) is constructed by hand-correcting the output of a dependency parser, showing annotators how textual units relate syntactically when making semantic judgments

*IL1* is an intermediate semantic representation associating semantic concepts with lexical units like nouns, adjectives, adverbs and verbs. It replaces *IL0* syntactic relations, like *subject* and *object*, with thematic roles, like *agent, theme* and *goal*. Thus, *IL1* neutralizes different alternations for argument realization. In progressing from *IL0* to *IL1*, annotators select semantic terms to represent the nouns, verbs, adjectives, and adverbs present in each sentence (the output is shown in Figure 2). These terms are represented in the 110,000-node Omega ontology [16], which has been built semi-automatically from sources including WordNet [6], Mikrokosmos [14], Upper Model [1] and SENSUS [12].

Each verb in Omega is assigned one or more grids specifying the theta roles of arguments associated with that verb. Theta roles are abstractions of deep semantic relations that generalize over verb classes. The theta grids used in our project were extracted from the Lexical Conceptual Structure Verb Database (LVD) [4]. The WordNet senses assigned to each entry in the LVD link the theta grids to the verbs in the Omega ontology. In addition to the theta roles, the theta grids specify syntactic realization information, such as Subject, Object or Prepositional Phrase, and the Obligatory/Optional nature of the argument. The set of theta roles used, although based on research in LCS-based MT [3, 8], has been simplified for this project.

*IL1* is not an interlingua; it does not normalize over all linguistic realizations of the same semantics. In particular, it does not address how the meanings of individual lexical units combine to form the meaning of a phrase or clause. It also does not address idioms, metaphors and other non-literal uses of language. Further, *IL1* does not assign semantic features to prepositions; these continue to be encoded as syntactic features of their objects, which may be annotated with thematic roles such as *location* or *time*.

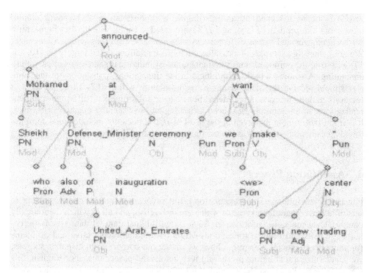

**Fig. 1.** Example of IL0 for "Sheikh Mohamed, who is also the Defense Minister of the United Arab Emirates, announced at the inauguration ceremony that 'we want to make Dubai a new trading center.'"

---

*The study led them to ask the Czech government to recapitalize CSA at this level.*

```
[30, lead, V, lead, Root, LEAD<GET, GUIDE]
      [20, study, N, study, AGENT, SURVEY<WORK, REPORT]
      [40, them, N, they, THEME, ---, ---]
      [60, ask, V, ask, PROPOSITION, ---, ---]
            [90, government, N, government, GOAL,
                  AUTHORITIES, GOVERNMENTAL-ORGANIZATION]
               [80, Czech, Adj, Czech, MOD,
                     CZECH~CZECHOSLOVAKIA, ---]
            [110, recapitalize, V, recapitalize, PROP,
                  CAPITALIZE<SUPPLY, INVEST]
               [120, csa, N, csa, THEME, AIRLINE<LINE, --
                     -]
            [160, at, P, value_at, GOAL, ---, ---]
               [150, level, N, level, ---, DEGREE,
                     MEASURE]
                  [140, this, Det, this, ---, ---, ---
                        ]
```

**Fig. 2.** Sample IL1 Representation

*IL2* is being designed as an interlingua, a representation of meaning that is reasonably independent of language. *IL2* is intended to capture similarities in meaning across languages and across different lexical/syntactic realizations within a language. We are gathering examples of extended paraphrase relations based largely on [10, 13, 17] and from the corpus of multiple translations of individual source texts that we are annotating. Assuming a basic faithfulness in the translations, translations of the same text should receive the same semantic representation within *IL2*. These paraphrase relations include morphological derivation; clause subordination; different argument realizations; noun-noun phrases; head switching and overlapping meaning. However, it is important to note that even at the level of *IL2*, it does not include some complex linguistics phenomena, such as discourse analysis and pragmatics.

## 4   Annotation Process

For any given subcorpus, the annotation effort involves assignment of IL content to sets of at least 3 parallel texts, 2 of which are in English, and all of which theoretically communicate the same information. Such a multilingual parallel data set of source-language texts and English translations offers both unique perspective and problems for annotating texts for meaning. Since we gather our corpora from disparate sources, we standardize a text before presenting it to automated procedures. For English, this means sentence boundary detection, but for other languages, it involves segmentation, chunking of text, and other operations. The text is then parsed with Connexor [18], and the output is viewed and corrected in TrED [9]. The revised deep dependency structure produced by this process is the *IL0* representation for that sentence. To create *IL1* from *IL0*, annotators use Tiamat, a tool developed specifically for this project. This tool enables viewing the *IL0* tree with easy reference to current IL representation, ontology, and theta grids.

The annotators are instructed to annotate all nouns, verbs, adjectives, and adverbs. This involves choosing all relevant concepts from Omega – both concepts from Wordnet SYNSETs and those from Mikrokosmos. In addition, annotators are instructed to provide a semantic case role for each dependent of a verb. LCS verbs are identified with Wordnet classes and the LCS case frames are supplied where possible. The annotator, however, is often required to determine the set of roles or alter them to suit the text. In both cases, the revised or new set of case roles are noted and sent to a reviewer for evaluation and possible permanent inclusion.

Three manuals comprise markup instructions: a users' guide for Tiamat, including procedural instructions, a definitional guide to semantic roles, and a manual for creating a dependency structure (IL0). Together these manuals allow the annotator to understand (1) the intention behind aspects of the dependency structure; (2) how to use Tiamat to mark up texts; and (3) how to determine appropriate semantic roles and ontological concepts. In choosing a set of appropriate ontological concepts, annotators are encouraged to look at the name of the concept and its definition, the name and definition of the parent node, example sentences, lexical synonyms attached to the same node, and sub- and super-classes of the node.

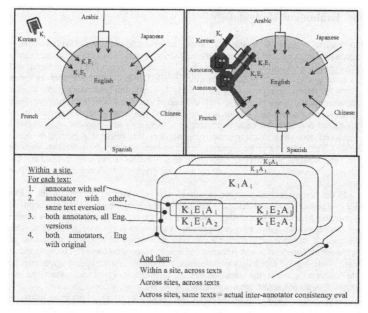

**Fig. 3.** Annotation Procedure

We have designed a round-robin annotation schedule in which each site's two annotators annotate both translated texts from their own site, one annotator annotates the source language text from his or her own site, and the other annotates a translated text from some other site (see Figure 3). In this way, we can compare across text source and its translations, across the two translations alone, across a site's annotators, across different sites' annotators, and across all the annotators.

In our first production run, lasting 3 weeks, annotators annotated 144 texts (6 source texts x 2 translations x 2 annotators x 6 sites). It takes approximately 5 hours to annotate a text of 350 words. Annotators are not allowed to communicate with one another until after the annotation is complete at all sites, following which they discuss problems in a countrywide telephone meeting. To test for the effects of coding two texts that are semantically close (since they are both translations of the same source document), the order in which the texts were annotated differed from site to site. Half of the sites marked one translation first, and the other half of the sites marked the second translation first. Another variant tested was to interleave the two translations, so that two similar sentences were coded consecutively.

## 5   Evaluation Methodology

In order to evaluate the annotators' output, an evaluation tool was also developed to compare the output and to generate the evaluation measures. The reports generated by the evaluation tool allow the researchers to look at both gross-level phenomena, such as inter-annotator agreement, and at more detailed points of interest, such as lexical items on which agreement was particularly low, possibly indicating gaps or other inconsistencies in the ontology. Two evaluation strategies have been applied: inter-annotator agreement and annotator reconciliation. For inter-annotator agreement, the annotated decisions for each word and each theta role are recorded. Agreement is measured according to the number of annotators that selected a particular role or sense. For annotator reconciliation, each annotator reviews the selections made by the other annotators and votes (privately) as to whether or not it is acceptable. The annotators discuss results, followed by a second private vote. Since the reconciliation process is on-going, we will not report these results.

In the first evaluation path, we measured inter-annotator agreement. While Kappa [2] is a standard measure for inter-annotator agreement, measuring it for this project presented difficulties. Calculating agreement and expected agreement when a number of annotators can assign zero or more senses per word is not straight-forward. Also, because of multiple annotators, we calculate an average of pair-wise agreement per word for all annotator pairs. Because multiple categories (senses) can be assigned for each word, we are faced with two decisions: a) do we count explicit agreement, i.e. the annotators select the same sense; or b) implicit agreement, when the two annotators do not select the same sense? Also, we must account for cases when no concept is provided in Omega. Later we can explore the option of applying weighting to Kappa using Omega's hierarchical structure to compute similarity amongst options. Two approaches are described.

For a specific word and pair of annotators who have made one or more selections of semantic tags, agreement is measured as the ratio of the number of agreeing selections to the number of all selections. Agreement is measured based on positive selections only, i.e., when the two annotators select the same semantic tag as opposed. For a word $W$, with a set of $n$ possible semantic tags $S_i$, the function $N(S_i)$ is defined as the sum of the selections made by the two annotators $A_1$ and $A_2$. Pair-wise agreement for a specific word is defined as:

$$\text{Agreement}_{word} = \frac{\sum_i^n N(S_i) \cdot (N(S_i) - 1)}{\sum_i^n N(S_i)}$$

Pair-wise agreement is measured as the average of agreement over all the words in a document. The overall inter-annotator agreement is measured as the average of pair-wise inter-annotator agreement of every pair of annotators. To calculate Kappa, we estimate chance agreement by a random 100-fold simulation where the number of concepts selected and concepts selected are randomly assigned, restricted by the number of concepts per word in Omega. If Omega has no concepts associated with the word, the chance agreement is computed as the inverse of the size of all of Omega

(1/110,000). Then chance agreement is calculated exactly as the overall agreement is calculated.

An alternative for calculating agreement is the implicit agreement case which looks at each sense on which a decision can be made as a different test case. Agreement for a word is calculated for each annotator pair and word agreement is the average of the pair-wise agreement. Calculating kappa then involves constructing a 3 by 3 matrix S where S[0,0] is the number of times both annotators did not pick a sense; S[1,1] is the number of times both annotators picked a sense. S[0,1] and S[1,0] contain mismatched selections. Proportion of agreement is S[0,0]+S[1,1] divided by the number of senses. Each row and column of S is then summed, so that S[0,2] is the number of times $A_1$ did not select a sense and S[1,2] is the number of $A_1$ selected a sense. In this case, kappa is calculated as:

$$\text{Kappa} = \frac{2 * ((S[0,0]*S[1,1]) - (S[0,1] * S[1,0]))}{(S[0,2]*S[2,1] + S[2,0]*S[1,2])}$$

When using this calculation method, it is possible to have a zero denominator when both annotators pick all of or none of the senses. These cases are counted separately and are removed from the calculation. No weighting is used at this time.

# 6   Results

The dataset has six pairs of English translations (250 words apiece) from each of the source languages. The ten annotators were asked to annotate nouns, verbs, adjectives and adverbs only with Omega concepts. The annotators selected one or more concepts from both WordNet and Mikrokosmos-derived nodes. Annotated verb arguments were assigned thematic roles. An important issue in the data set is the problem of incomplete annotations which may stem from: (1) lack of annotator awareness of missing annotations; (2) inability to finish annotations because of an intense schedule; and (3) ontology omissions for words for which annotators selected DummyConcept or no annotation at all. For 1,268 annotated words, 368 (29%) have no Omega WordNet entry and 575 (45%) do not have Omega Mikrokosmos entries.

To address incomplete annotations, we calculate agreement in two different ways that exclude annotations (1) by annotator and (2) by word. In the first calculation, we exclude all annotations by an annotator if annotations where incomplete by more than a certain threshold. Table 1 shows the average number of included annotators over all documents (A#), the Average Pair-wise Agreement (APA) and Kappa for the theta roles, the Mikrokosmos portion of Omega and the WordNet portion of Omega. The table is broken down by different thresholds for exclusion.

Again, since annotators did not annotate some texts or failed to choose an Omega entry, two types of agreement are reported. The first is agreement based on counting cases where all senses are marked with zero as perfect agreement with a kappa of 1; the second excludes zero cases entirely (Table 2). In eliminating zero pairs the agreement does not change significantly.

**Table 1.** Scores for explicit sense marking

|              | 5% | | | 10% | | |
|--------------|------|-------|-------|------|-------|-------|
|              | **A#** | **APA** | **Kappa** | **A#** | **APA** | **Kappa** |
| **MikroKosmos** | 3.50 | 0.745 | 0.743 | 4.42 | 0.731 | 0.730 |
| **WordNet**     | 6.08 | 0.660 | 0.657 | 7.00 | 0.654 | 0.650 |
| **Theta Roles** | 5.75 | 0.538 | 0.509 | 6.58 | 0.549 | 0.521 |
|              | | **50%** | | | **100%** | |
| **Mikrokosmos** | 6.33 | 0.611 | 0.609 | 9.42 | 0.455 | 0.454 |
| **WordNet**     | 8.33 | 0.598 | 0.594 | 9.42 | 0.517 | 0.513 |
| **Theta Roles** | 8.00 | 0.485 | 0.452 | 9.42 | 0.392 | 0.354 |

**Table 2.** Implicit agreement numbers

|              |            | All cases | | Exclude zero-pairs | |
|--------------|------------|-----------|-----------|-----------|-----------|
|              | **Zero-Pairs** | **Agree** | **Kappa** | **Agree** | **Kappa** |
| **Theta Roles** | 78.58  | 0.945 | 0.418 | 0.943 | 0.392 |
| **WordNet**     | 112.16 | 0.886 | 0.564 | 0.879 | 0.534 |
| **Mikrokosmos** | 258.5  | 0.811 | 0.522 | 0.784 | 0.433 |

## 7  Future Work and Conclusions

Since one goal is to generate an IL representation that is useful for MT, we plan to measure the ability to generate accurate surface texts from the IL representation as annotated. This work will involve obtaining EXERGE [7] and Halogen [11] and writing a converter between the IL format and those expected by generation tools. We can then compare the generated sentences with source texts through a variety of standard MT metrics. This will serve to determine if the elements of the representation language are sufficiently well-defined and if they serve as a basis for inferring interpretations from semantic representations or (target) semantic representations from interpretations. This approach is limited to English generation for the first pass as these tools are more readily available.

By providing an essential, and heretofore non-existent, data set for training and evaluating natural language processing systems, the resultant annotated multilingual corpus of translations is expected to lead to significant research and development opportunities for machine translation and a host of other natural language processing technologies, including question answering (e.g., via paraphrase and entailment relations) and information extraction. Because of the unique annotation processes in which each stage (IL0, IL1, IL2) provides a different level of linguistic and semantic information, a different type of natural language processing can take advantage of the information provided at the different stages. For example, IL1 may be useful for information extraction in question answering, whereas IL2 might be the level that is of most benefit to machine translation. These topics exemplify the research investigations that we can conduct in the future, based on the results of the annotation.

**Acknowledgement.** This work has been supported by NSF ITR Grant IIS-0326553.

# References

[1]     Bateman, J.A., Kasper, R.T., Moore, J.D., & Whitney, R.A. 1989. A General Organization of Knowledge for Natural Language Processing: The Penman Upper Model. Unpublished research report, USC/Information Sciences Institute, Marina del Rey, CA.

[2]     Carletta, J. C. 1996. Assessing agreement on classification tasks: the kappa statistic. Computational Linguistics, 22(2), 249-254

[3]     Dorr, B. 1993. Machine Translation: A View from the Lexicon, MIT Press, Cambridge, MA.

[4]     Dorr, B. 2001. LCS Verb Database, Online Software Database of Lexical Conceptual Structures and Documentation, University of Maryland. http://www.umiacs.umd.edu/~bonnie/LCS_Database_Documentation.html

[5]     Farwell, D., Helmreich, S., Dorr, B., Habash, N., Reeder, F., Miller, K., Levin, L., Mitamura, T., Hovy, E., Rambow, O., Siddharthan, A. 2004. Interlingual Annotation of Multilingual Text Corpora. In Proceedings of Workshop on Frontiers in Corpus Annotation. NAACL/HLT 2004.

[6]     Fellbaum, C. (ed.). 1998. *WordNet: An On-line Lexical Database and Some of its Applications.* MIT Press, Cambridge, MA.

[7]     Habash, N.    2003. Matador: A Large Scale Spanish-English GHMT System. In Proceedings of the MT Summit, New Orleans, LA.

[8]     Habash, N., B. Dorr, & D. Traum, 2002. "Efficient Language Independent Generation from Lexical Conceptual Structures," Machine Translation, 17:4.

[9]     Haji , J; Vidová-Hladká, B; Pajas, P. 2001. The Prague Dependency Treebank: Annotation Structure and Support. In Proceeding of the IRCS Workshop on Linguistic Databases, University of Pennsylvania, Philadelphia, USA, pp. 105-114.

[10]    Hirst, G.. 2003. Paraphrasing paraphrased. Invited talk at Second International Workshop on Paraphrasing, 41st Annual Meeting of the ACL, Sapporo, Japan.

[11]    Knight, K. and Langkilde, I. 2000. Preserving Ambiguities in Generation via Automata Intersection. American Association for Artificial Intelligence conference (AAAI'00).

[12]    Knight, K., & Luk, S.K. 1994. Building a Large-Scale Knowledge Base for Machine Translation. Proceedings of AAAI. Seattle, WA.

[13]    Kozlowski, R., McCoy, K., Vijay-Shanker, K. 2003. Generation of Single-Sentence Paraphrases from Predicate/argument Structure using Lexico-grammatical Resources. Second International Workshop on Paraphrasing, 41st ACL, Sapporo, Japan.

[14]    Mahesh, K., & Nirenberg, S. 1995. A Situated Ontology for Practical NLP. Proc. of Workshop on Basic Ontological Issues in Knowledge Sharing at IJCAI-95. Montreal, Canada.

[15]    Mitamura, T., E. Nyberg, J. Carbonell. 1991. An Efficient  Interlingua Translation System for Multilingual Document Production. Proc. of 3$^{rd}$ MT Summit. Washington, DC.

[16]    Philpot, A., M. Fleischman, E.H. Hovy. 2003. Semi-Automatic Construction of a General Purpose Ontology. Proc. of the International Lisp Conference. New York, NY. Invited.

[17]    Rinaldi, F., Dowdall, J., Kaljurand, K., Hess, M., Molla, D. 2003. Exploiting Paraphrases in a Question Answering System. 2$^{nd}$ International Workshop on Paraphrasing, 41st ACL.

[18]    Tapanainen, P. & T Jarvinen. 1997. A non-projective dependency parser. In the 5$^{th}$ Conference on Applied Natural Language Processing, Washington, DC.

# Machine Translation of Online Product Support Articles Using a Data-Driven MT System

Stephen D. Richardson

Natural Language Processing Group
Microsoft Research
One Microsoft Way
Redmond, Washington 98052
USA
steveri@microsoft.com

**Abstract.** At AMTA 2002, we reported on a pilot project to machine translate Microsoft's Product Support Knowledge Base into Spanish. The successful pilot has since resulted in the permanent deployment of both Spanish and Japanese versions of the knowledge base, as well as ongoing pilot projects for French and German. The translated articles in each case have been produced by MSR-MT, Microsoft Research's data-driven MT system, which has been trained on well over a million bilingual sentence pairs for each target language from previously translated materials contained in translation memories and glossaries. This paper describes our experience in deploying this system and the (positive) customer response to the availability of machine translated articles, as well as other uses of MSR-MT either planned or underway at Microsoft.

## 1 Introduction

The NLP group at Microsoft Research has created and begun internal deployment throughout Microsoft of MSR-MT [1], a data-driven machine translation (DDMT) system that has been trained on over a million translated sentences taken from product documentation and support materials in English and each of four languages: French, German, Japanese, and Spanish. MSR-MT has been used to translate Microsoft's Product Support Services (PSS) knowledge base into each of these languages. A multitude of additional opportunities to use MSR-MT exists at Microsoft, including in product localization and in many other groups like PSS, where translation of large amounts of material has not yet been considered because of cost and time constraints. Microsoft stands to save or otherwise realize the value of tens of millions of dollars in translation services annually using MSR-MT.

With an annual translation budget of hundreds of millions of dollars, Microsoft is still unable to translate massive amounts of documentation and other materials. The public PSS knowledge base, for example, contains over 140K articles and 80M words of text. Because of translation costs, generally only a few thousand articles have been

R.E. Frederking and K.B. Taylor (Eds.): AMTA 2004, LNAI 3265, pp. 246–251, 2004.

translated into each of the major European and Asian languages annually, providing only a sampling of online support to a growing international customer base. Meanwhile, hundreds more articles are added and/or updated on a weekly basis. Increasing costly phone support has been the only solution in the past to this chronic problem for PSS. Groups responsible for the content available on the Microsoft Developer Network (MSDN) and Microsoft's Technet are facing similar challenges. There are yet other groups at Microsoft whose budgets have not yet begun to allow them to think about translating their materials generally, especially those customized for and targeted to specific international customers.

Using translation memory (TM) tools such as TRADOS, the Microsoft localization community has been able to realize substantial savings in translating product documentation, which is often highly repetitive, "recycling" anywhere from 20% to 80% of translated sentences. But with a company-wide average recycling rate of around 40%, there is still a greater portion of text that must be translated from scratch, thus incurring costs averaging from 20 to 50 cents per word, depending on the language. Text volumes, together with the translation budget, continue to increase.

## 2 Translation of Microsoft's Product Support Knowledge Base

Facing escalating translation and phone support costs, PSS approached an MT vendor a few years ago about the possibility of using their commercial system. The vendor proposed a pilot to show how their system could be (manually) customized to produce better quality machine translations. For English to Spanish, $50K was requested to cover the pilot customization period of a few months, with the understanding that this would lead to a full-fledged customization and ongoing maintenance agreement. The initial and projected costs were a formidable barrier to acceptance by PSS of this customized MT system.

PSS then turned to the Microsoft Research's NLP group for help. An agreement was reached through which PSS supported the finishing touches on MSR-MT for an English-to-Spanish pilot.

After a period of further development, MSR-MT was trained overnight on a few hundred thousand sentences culled from Microsoft product documentation and support articles, together with their corresponding translations (produced by human localizers using the TRADOS translation memory tool). As reported at AMTA 2002 [2], the system was deployed and over 125,000 articles in the knowledge base (KB) were automatically translated into Spanish, indexed, and posted to a pilot web-site. A few months later, customer satisfaction with the articles, as measured by surveying a small sample of the approximately 60,000 visits to the web site, averaged 86% -- 12 points higher than for the English KB!

It appears that the Spanish users were so happy to have all the articles in their own language that they were willing to overlook the fact that their quality was less than that of human translations. Nevertheless, the "usefulness" rate (i.e., the percentage of customers feeling that an article helped solve their problem) for the machine translated articles was about 50%, compared to 51% for human translated Spanish articles and just under 54% for English articles. PSS management was excited to see that the potential of MSR-MT to lower support line call volume could be nearly the same as for human-translated articles.

Based on the results of the pilot experiment, PSS decided on a permanent deployment of MSR-MT for Spanish. In April 2003, articles translated by MSR-MT, interspersed with (many fewer) human translated ones, went live for Spanish-speaking countries at http://support.microsoft.com. One may access the Spanish articles by visiting the web site, clicking on "International Support," and choosing "Spain" as the country. Spanish queries may then be entered for the KB and pointers to both human and machine translated articles will be listed, the later being indicated by the presence of an icon next to the title containing two small gears.

For the five month period from September 2003 through January 2004, the permanent deployment of the Spanish KB achieved a 79% customer satisfaction rate (compared to 86% during the pilot and 73% for the original US English KB) and solid 55% usefulness rate (compared to 50% during the pilot and 57% for the US English). While the satisfaction rate has levelled off a bit as users have apparently become accustomed to the availability of KB articles in their language, it is still higher than the original English. Thus more continues to be better in spite of imperfect translations, with 20 times more articles in Spanish than before MT output was available.

We attribute the rise in the usefulness rate in part to the fact that the coverage and accuracy of MSR-MT were significantly enhanced after the pilot and before the permanent deployment by increasing the set of bilingual sentence pairs used to train the system from 350K to 1.6M. This was achieved by gathering data from additional translation memories for many more products and newer versions of products. We deemed this especially important after the pilot as we observed a number of sparse data deficiencies due to the vast variety of products discussed in the KB articles. The result was a 10% jump in BLEU score (from .4406+/-.0162 to .4819+/-.0177) on a test set of PSS article sentences for which we had human translations.

**Table 1.** Comparison of customer survey results for the Japanese and Spanish pilots and for the permanent Spanish and US English deployments

|  | Japanese Pilot (2 mos) | Spanish Pilot (4 mos) | Spanish Permanent (5 mos) | US English Permanent (5 mos) |
|---|---|---|---|---|
| % of customers who are satisfied with KB | 71% | 86% | 79% | 73% |
| % of customers who were helped to solve their issues using KB | 56% | 50% | 55% | 57% |
| % of customers who thought information is easy to understand | 72% | N/A | 69% | 87% |
| Number of surveys per month | 120 | 95 | 229 | 49K |
| Number of page hits per month | 8K | 15K | 175K | 39M |

With the success of the Spanish KB, our next (and more ambitious) target was a Japanese version. After training MSR-MT with over 1.2M sentence pairs, the Japanese pilot KB (with 140K+ articles) was deployed during the last two months of 2003. For a language that is admittedly tougher to translate and a user community that has a reputation for being hard to please, the overall satisfaction rate for the modest pilot was a surprising 71% and the usefulness rate was 56%—both very comparable to the original US English rates. Table 1 compares the customer survey results for the Japanese and Spanish pilots together with the permanent deployment survey results for Spanish and US English. The success of this pilot led to a permanent deployment of the Japanese KB in March 2004, containing both human and machine translated articles in like fashion to the Spanish KB. With careful scrutiny of and feedback on the Japanese KB by internal Microsoft users as well as external users, an updated version of the KB was posted online in June 2004 and is enjoying a very positive reception (to be reported when this paper is presented). A screen shot from one of the articles in the Japanese KB is displayed in Figure 1.

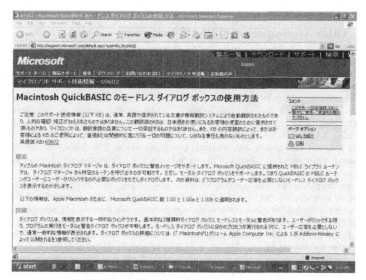

**Fig. 1.** Japanese KB article machine translated by MSR-MT

In the first quarter of 2004, pilots were begun of both French and German versions of the KB, translated by MSR-MT. It is anticipated that permanent deployments for these languages will be made available later this year. Work is also ongoing to create versions of MSR-MT capable of translating from English into Italian, Chinese, and Korean, as well as into other languages important to Microsoft's international business.

MSR-MT has provided customized MT output based on previously translated technical texts, thus enabling a cost-effective solution for the translation of Microsoft's PSS knowledge base into multiple languages. Traditional methods, using human translators and translation memory technology, would require an investment of approximately $15M-$20M per language to accomplish the same task, and would be hard pressed to keep up with the constant flow of updates and additions. Traditional commercial MT systems, such as those employed to translate the 5,000 documents in Autodesk's support data base [3] and the 8,000 documents in Cisco's data base [4] require costly and lengthy manual customization, although efforts are underway to apply automation to portions of this process. To our knowledge, the application of MSR-MT to the task of translating the PSS knowledge base is the first time that a data-driven MT system as been employed to translate a production-level support data base of this size and product scope. The data driven MT paradigm holds great promise of cost effective MT for a variety of similar applications at Microsoft as well as at numerous other multinational companies.

## 3   Other Applications of MSR-MT Underway

To address the need to reduce increasing localization costs where polished translations are required, we have integrated MSR-MT into the TRADOS translator's workbench. In the absence of an exact recycled alternative, we provide a machine-translated suggestion in the translation memory (TM) that the human translator can choose and edit if desired. This results in a measurable increase in translation throughput. In a recent experiment conducted in a tightly controlled usability lab setting, 3 translators translated 16 different documents with and without MT output in the TM, and were shown with statistical significance to be 35% faster with the MT output than without it. Details of this experiment will be reported separately in the future.

In the process of experimenting with MT post-editing, we have confirmed what others have already observed: that consideration of human factors is crucial, and that training is required to maximize post-editing efficiency. A number of MT post-editing pilots are in progress or planned for this year, involving the four languages currently supplied by MSR-MT. In facilitating localization, as in the publication of raw MT for certain applications, Microsoft stands to realize savings of millions of dollars.

Another area for potential cost savings using MSR-MT is in dealing with the product feedback recorded by a group within PSS that analyzes customer concerns, new feature requests, and customer task scenarios as they are reported during customer support phone calls. Previously, only feedback coming from English-speaking customers was analyzed and channelled back to the product groups, as there were no means nor translation budget to handle the growing volume of cases (now about 50% of all cases worldwide) from non-English-speaking users. Efforts are underway to make use of MSR-MT, which is currently trained to translate both to and from English and the four languages mentioned above, to enable the translation of customer cases into English, and the subsequent analysis of this data for the improvement of Microsoft's products.

Finally, we have provided limited availability of MSR-MT as a web service on Microsoft's internal corporate network to users of Word 2003 (which includes just about everyone) through the translation function located in the Task Pane. By default this function provides access to $3^{rd}$ party MT providers via the Internet. Currently, the same version of MSR-MT, trained to translate Microsoft technical texts (such as PSS articles) to and from English and the four languages previously mentioned (and also including a Chinese to English pair), is available either on a server or as a download-able service to run on the client's machine. Deployment of MSR-MT in this context enables a variety of other uses, and provides a means for groups to explore other applications of MT in their own areas of responsibility.

# References

1. Richardson, S., Dolan, W., Menezes, A., Pinkham, J.: Achieving commercial-quality translation with example-based methods. In: Proceedings of MT Summit VIII, Santiago de Compostela, Spain (2001) 293-298
2. Dolan, W., Pinkham, J., Richardson, S.: MSR-MT: The Microsoft Research machine translation system. In: Machine Translation: From Research to Real Users: Proceedings of the AMTA 2002 Conference. Tiburon, California, USA (2002) 237-239
3. Flanagan, M. and McClure, S. IDC Bulletin #25019, June (2001)
4. Shore, R. Cisco Systems and SYSTRAN: an ongoing partnership in MT. Unpublished user presentation at AMTA 2002 Conference, Tiburon, California, USA (2002)

# Maintenance Issues for Machine Translation Systems

Nestor Rychtyckyj

Manufacturing Engineering Systems
Ford Motor Company
nrychtyc@ford.com

**Abstract.** At AMTA-2002 we presented a deployed application of Machine Translation (MT) at Ford Motor Company in the domain of vehicle assembly process planning. This application uses an MT system developed by SYSTRAN to translate Ford's manufacturing process build instructions from English to Spanish, German, Dutch and Portuguese. Our MT system has already translated over 2 million instructions into these target languages and is an integral part of our manufacturing process planning to support Ford's assembly plants in Europe, Mexico and South America. A major component of the MT system development was the creation of a set of technical glossaries for the correct translation of automotive and Ford-specific terminology. Due to the dynamic nature of the automobile industry we need to keep these technical glossaries current as our terminology frequently changes due to the introduction of new manufacturing technologies, vehicles and vehicle features. In addition, our end-users need to be able to test and modify translations and see these results deployed in a timely manner. In this paper we will discuss the tools and business process that we have developed in conjunction with SYSTRAN in order to maintain and customize our MT system and improve its performance in the face of an ever-changing business environment.

## 1 Introduction

We have been utilizing a Machine Translation system at Ford Motor Company since 1998 within Vehicle Operations for the translation of our process assembly build instructions from English to German, Spanish, Portuguese and Dutch. This system was developed in conjunction with SYSTRAN Software Inc. and is an integral part of our worldwide process planning system for manufacturing assembly. The input to our system is a set of process build instructions that are written using a controlled language known as Standard Language. The process sheets are read by an artificial intelligence (AI) system that parses the instructions and creates detailed work tasks for each step of the assembly process. These work tasks are then released to the assembly plants where specific workers are allocated for each task. In order to support the assembly of vehicles at plants where the workers do not speak English, we utilize MT technology to translate these instructions into the native language of these workers. Standard Language is a restricted subset of English and contains a limited vocabulary

R.E. Frederking and K.B. Taylor (Eds.): AMTA 2004, LNAI 3265, pp. 252–261, 2004.
© Springer-Verlag Berlin Heidelberg 2004

of about 5000 words that also include acronyms, abbreviations, proper nouns and other Ford-specific terminology. In addition, Standard Language allows the process sheet writers to embed comments within Standard Language sentences. These comments are ignored by the AI system during its processing, but have to be translated by the MT system. Standard Language also utilizes some structures that are grammatically incorrect and create problems during the MT process. Therefore, the development of a translation system for these requirements entailed considerable customization to the SYSTRAN translation engines as well as a lot of effort in building the technical glossaries to enable correct translation of Ford-specific manufacturing terminology. We described the process of building this system in a previous paper [1]; our focus of this paper is to discuss the process and methodology of MT system maintenance.

Section 2 will provide an overview of the existing manufacturing process at Ford and describe how MT is part of that process. In Section 3 we will discuss Standard Language in more detail and illustrate some of the issues that need to be addressed during the translation process. The next section will discuss the process of MT maintenance and show what needs to be done to keep our technical glossaries and translation software up to date. We will also describe some of the new tools that have been developed by SYSTRAN in order to facilitate this process. Our paper concludes with a discussion of future work and our view of the role that MT will continue to play in Ford's manufacturing processes.

## 2   Machine Translation for Vehicle Assembly

The machine translation system utilized at Ford is integrated into the Global Study Process Allocation System (GSPAS). The goal of GSPAS is to incorporate a standardized methodology and a set of common business practices for the design and assembly of vehicles to be used by all assembly plants throughout the world. GSPAS allows for the integration of parts, tools, process descriptions and all other information required to build a motor vehicle into one system and provides the engineering and manufacturing communities a common platform and toolset for manufacturing process planning. GSPAS utilizes Standard Language as a requirement for writing process build instructions and we have deployed an MT solution for the translation of these process build instructions.

The translation process at Ford for our manufacturing build instructions is fully automated and does not require manual intervention. All of the process build instructions are stored within an Oracle database; they are written in English and validated by the AI system. AI validation consists of parsing the Standard Language sentence, analyzing it and matching the description to the appropriate work description in the knowledge base and creating an output set of work instructions, their associated MODAPTS codes and time required to perform each operation. MODAPTS codes (Modular Arrangement  of Predetermined Time Standards) are used to calculate the time required to perform these actions. MODAPTS is an industrial measurement system around the world [2]. A more complete description of the GSPAS AI system can be found in [3].

After a process sheet is validated and the AI system generates the appropriate MODAPTS codes and times, a process engineer will release the process sheet to the appropriate assembly plants. A vehicle that is built at multiple plants needs to have these process sheets sent to each of these assembly plants. The information about each local plant is stored in the database and those plants that require translation are picked out by the system. The system then selects the process sheets that require translation and starts the daily translation process for each language. Currently we translate the process build instructions for 24 different vehicles into the appropriate language. English-Spanish is the most commonly used language pair as it supports our assembly plants in Spain, Mexico and South America.

The machine translation system was implemented into GSPAS through the development of an interface into the Oracle database. Our translation programs extract the data from an Oracle database, utilize the SYSTRAN system to complete the actual translation, and then write the data back out to the Oracle database.

Our user community is located globally. The translated text is displayed on the user's PC or workstation using a graphical user interface through the GSPAS system. It runs on Hewlett Packard workstations under the HP UNIX operating system. The Ford multi-targeted customized dictionary that contains Ford technical terminology was developed in conjunction with SYSTRAN and Ford based on input from engineers and linguists familiar with Ford's terminology.

One of the most difficult issues in deploying any translation is the need to get consistent and accurate evaluation of the quality of your translations (both manual and machine). We are using the J2450 metric developed by the Society of Automotive Engineers (SAE) as a guide for our translation evaluators [4]. The J2450 metric was developed by an SAE committee consisting of representatives from the automobile industry and the translation community as a standard measurement that can be applied to grade the translation quality of automotive service information. This metric provides guidelines for evaluators to follow and describes a set of error categories, weight of the errors found and calculates a score for a given document. The metric does not attempt to grade style, but focuses primarily on the understandability of the translated text. The utilization of the SAE J2450 metric has given us a consistent and tangible method to evaluate translation quality and identify which areas require the most improvement.

We have also spent substantial effort in analyzing the source text in order to identify which terms are used most often in Standard Language so that we can concentrate our resources on those most common terms. This was accomplished by using the parser from our AI system to store parsed sentences into the database. Periodically, we run an analysis of our parsed sentences and create a table where our terminology is listed in use of frequency. This table is then compared to the technical glossary to ensure that the most-commonly used terms are being translated correctly. The frequency analysis also allows us to calculate the number of terms that need to be translated correctly to meet a certain translation accuracy threshold.

A machine translation system, such as SYSTRAN's, translates sentence by sentence. A single term by itself cannot be translated accurately because it may correspond to different parts of speech depending on the context. Therefore, it is necessary to build sample test cases for each word or phrase that we will need to test for translation accuracy. This test case utilizes that term in its correct usage within the sentence. A file containing these translated sentences (known as a test corpus) is used as a baseline for regression testing of the translation dictionaries. After the dictionary is updated, the test corpus of sentences is retranslated and compared against the baseline. Any discrepancies are examined and a correction is made to either the baseline (if the new translation is correct) or the dictionary (if the new translation is incorrect).

The translation quality is evaluated both by SYSTRAN linguists and the users of the system. We have had difficulty in measuring our progress as opinions of translation quality vary significantly between translation evaluators. We have also allowed the users to manually override the translated text with their preferred translation. These manual translations are not modified by the system, but have to be redone each time that the process sheet is revised.

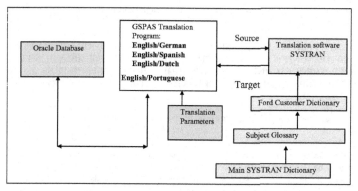

**Fig. 1.** Machine Translation in GSPAS

## 3 Standard Language

Standard Language is a controlled language that provides for the expression of imperative English assembly instructions at any level of detail. All of the terms in Standard Language with their pertinent attributes are stored in the GSPAS knowledge base in the form of a semantic network-based taxonomy as shown in Figure 2. Certain word categories in the language possess specific semantics as defined by the engineering community. Verbs in the language are associated with specific assembly instructions and are modified by significant adverbs where appropriate. For example, the phrases *inspect*, *visually inspect* and *manually verify* all have different interpreta-

tions  Information on tools and parts that are associated with each process sheet is
used to provide extra detail and context.

The Standard Language sentence is written in the imperative form and must contain a verb phrase and a noun phrase that is used as the object of the verb. Any additional terms that increase the level of detail, such as adverbs, adjuncts and prepositional phrases are optional and may be included at the process writer's discretion.
The primary driver of any sentence is the verb that describes the action that must be
performed for this instruction The number of Standard Language verbs is limited and
each verb is defined to describe a single particular action. For example, the verbs
*position* and *seat* have different meanings and cannot be used interchangeably. The
object of the verb phrase is usually a noun phrase that describes a particular part of
the vehicle, tool or fastener. Standard Language allows the usage of modifiers that
provide additional detail for those objects. The process sheet writer may use prepositional phrases to add more detail to any sentence. Certain prepositions have specific
meaning in Standard Language and will be interpreted in a predetermined manner
when encountered in a sentence. For example, the preposition *using* will always signify that a tool description will follow. Figure 2 shows how the Standard Language
sentence "Feed 2 150 mm wire assemblies through hole in liftgate panel" is parsed
into its constituent cases.

(S (VP (VERB FEED)) (NP (SIMPLE-NP (QUANTIFIER 2) (DIM (QUANTIFIER
150) (DIM-UNIT-1 MM)) (ADJECTIVE WIRE) (NOUN ASSEMBLY))) (S-PP (S-
PREP THROUGH) (NP (SIMPLE-NP (NOUN HOLE) (N-PP (N-PREP in) (NP
(SIMPLE-NP (ADJECTIVE LIFTGATE) (ADJECTIVE OUTER) (NOUN
PANEL)))))))

**Fig. 2.** Example of parsed Standard Language sentence

As mentioned previously, Standard Language process sheets are checked by the AI
system for correctness. Any errors are flagged by the system and returned to the engineer to be fixed before the process sheet can be released to the assembly plant. The
process engineers are also trained in the proper way to write sheets in Standard Language. Other utilities, such as an on-line help facility and written documentation are
provided to assist the process engineer in the writing of correct process sheets in
Standard Language. The vehicle assembly process is very dynamic; as new vehicles
and assembly plants are added to the system, it requires that Standard Language also
evolve. Changes to Standard Language are requested and then approved by the Industrial Engineering organization; these changes are then added into the system by
updating the DLMS knowledge base. Figure 3 shows the graphical user interface that
is used to maintain the DLMS knowledge base.

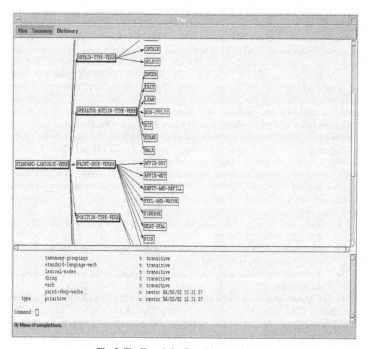

**Fig. 3.** The Knowledge Base Manager (KBM)

The greatest improvements to machine translation quality can be made by limiting the expressiveness and grammar of the source text by imposing restrictions on that text. This restricted language improves the quality of translation by limiting both the syntax and vocabulary of the text that will be translated. These restrictions must be enforced through the use of a checker that will accept or reject text based on its compliance with those rules.

## 4  System Maintenance

As previously discussed, we have spent considerable time and effort to create a set of customized technical glossaries that are used during the translation process. These glossaries were developed in conjunction with SYSTRAN and with subject matter experts from Ford Motor Company. However, since Standard Language and the Ford terminology is always evolving, it soon became obvious that we needed to develop a process to modify and add terminology to our technical glossaries in a timely manner.

The initial release of our MT system was designed so that all updates to the technical glossaries required SYSTRAN to create and compile a new set of dictionaries that would include the new changes. SYSTRAN would need to test these dictionaries through their internal quality control program and then deliver the updates to Ford. We would also need to test the updates against our internal benchmarks and deploy them into production if the result of the testing was acceptable. The entire process would be delayed if any problems were discovered during testing. This approach was too cumbersome and time-consuming and was not viable for the long term.

Our first attempt to build a process for on-line dictionary management led to the development of an Excel spreadsheet based system by SYSTRAN. This approach allowed us to modify the translation of an existing term or phrase and add new terminology to the spreadsheet. At any point we could recompile the entire spreadsheet and create a new set of translation dictionaries. These dictionaries would then be tested against our benchmarks and deployed if all of the translations were correct. However, there were still significant shortcomings to this approach:

- There was no way to test any individual term for accuracy without recompiling the entire dictionary.
- Each recompilation of the dictionary required that all of the sample translations be tested again for accuracy.
- There was no way to monitor or control the changes that were being made to the spreadsheet.

SYSTRAN developed a web-based system known as the SYSTRAN Review Manager (SRM) that addressed all of these shortcomings. The SRM was deployed on a Ford internal server that allowed us to control and monitor the access to the application. Our user community was trained to use this tool and it gave them the following benefits:

- Automation of the testing process: a user can make a change to the technical glossaries and immediately run a translation that will test to see how the change impacts the translation quality.
- The SRM allows users to create and modify different versions of user-defined dictionaries without impacting changes that are being made by a different user.
- Test corpuses can be loaded and analyzed directly within the SRM.
- The web-based architecture of the SRM allows our users to access the system without any additional software or hardware requirements.
- The SRM provides very quick turn-around time for the process of modifying and deploying an updated translation glossary.

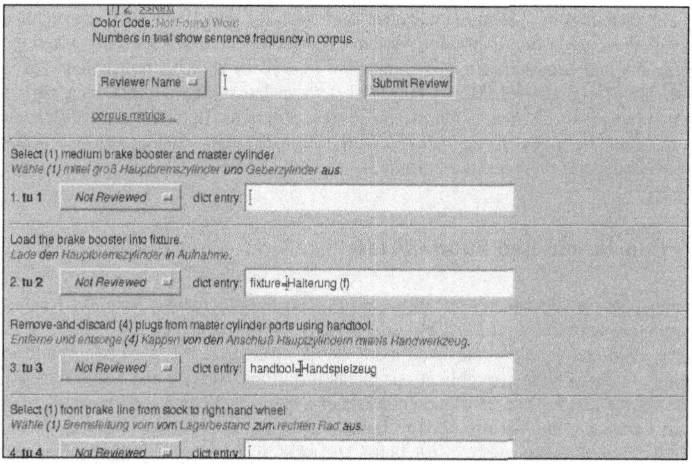

**Fig. 4.** SYSTRAN Review Manager

Another important facet in dictionary maintenance deals with the analysis and customization of the source text. We have previously described some of the techniques we have been using to clean up the source text to improve translation quality. In this section we will discuss additional capabilities we have added into the system to improve the translation of the free-form text. A Standard Language element may contain embedded free-form text that is ignored by the AI system; however this text must be translated and sent to the assembly plants. This free-form text usually consists of additional information that may be useful to the operator on the assembly line. Below is an example of Standard Language with embedded free-form text comments.

Figure 5: PLACE TWO MOULDINGS INSIDE HEATER {TAPE SIDE UP}

The text inside the curly brackets {TAPE SIDE UP} is not really part of the sentence; it actually describes the position of the "mouldings". Therefore, a translation system that processes this sentence as one entity would not generate an accurate translation. We need to be able to tell the system that the clause inside the curly brackets should be treated independently of the rest of the sentence. This problem is solved by embedding tags into the source text before it gets translated. These tags function identify comments and provide the translation program with information about how these comments should be translated. Short comments are processed differently from long comments within Standard Language regarding translation parameters (dictionaries and segmentation).

Another facet of system maintenance deals with the underlying software architecture that supports our translation system. Translation in GSPAS involves a set of programs that communicate with a database as well as with the translation engines and technical glossaries. Most changes to the translation engine processing also require changes to the translation pre-processing programs. In addition, modifications to the database model or upgrades to the operating system require extensive testing and validation of the translation results.

## 5  Conclusions and Future Work

In this paper we discussed some of the issues related to the maintenance of a machine translation application at Ford Motor Company. This application has been in place since 1998 and we have translated more than 2 million records describing build instructions for vehicle assembly at our plants in Europe, Mexico and South America. The source text for our translation consists of a controlled language, known as Standard Language, but we also need to translate free-form text comments that are embedded within the assembly instructions. The most difficult issue in the development of this system was the construction of technical glossaries that describe the manufacturing and engineering terminology in use at Ford. Our application uses a customized version of the SYSTRAN Software translation system coupled with a set of Ford-specific dictionaries that are used during the translation process. The automotive industry is very dynamic and we need to be able to keep our technical glossaries current and to develop a process for updating our system in a timely fashion.

The solution to our maintenance issues was the development and deployment of the SYSTRAN Review Manager. This web-based tool allows our users the capability to test and update the technical glossaries as needed. This has reduced our turnaround time for deploying changes to the dictionaries from 2 months to less than 48 hours. The SYSTRAN Review Manager runs on an internal Ford server and is available for use by our internal customers.

System maintenance is an on-going issue. We still require additional capabilities to improve our translation accuracy and to expand our system to other type of source data, including part and tool descriptions. We have already introduced XML tagging into our free-form comment translation and are working with SYSTRAN to enhance that capability and improve translation accuracy. Our current AI system in GSPAS already parses Standard Language into its components and we would like to pass that information over to the translation system to improve the sentence understanding that should lead to higher accuracy.

Our experience with Machine Translation technology at Ford has been positive; we have shown that customization of a translation system can lead to very good results. It is also essential to put a process in place that allows for the timely testing and upgrades to the technical glossaries. We are confident that further enhancements to the technology, such as tagging of terminology, will lead to better results in the future and improve the use and acceptance of machine translation in the corporate world.

# References

1.  Rychtyckyj, N., (2002), "An Assessment of Machine Translation for Vehicle Assembly Process Planning at Ford Motor Company", Machine Translation: From Research to Real Users, 5th Conference of the Association for Machine Translation in the Americas, AMTA 2002 Tiburon, CA, USA, October 2002 Proceedings, pp. 207-215, Springer-Verlag.
2.  International MODAPTS Association (IMA) (2000), "MODAPTS: Modular Arrangement of Predetermined Time Standards -- The Language of Work"
3.  Rychtyckyj, N.: "DLMS: Ten Years of AI for Vehicle Assembly Process Planning," AAAI-99/IAAI-99 Proceedings, Orlando, FL, AAAI Press (1999) 821-828
4.  Society of Automotive Engineers: J2450 Quality Metric for Language Translation, www.sae.org (2002)

# Improving Domain-Specific Word Alignment with a General Bilingual Corpus

Hua Wu and Haifeng Wang

Toshiba (China) Research and Development Center
5/F., Tower W2, Oriental Plaza, No.1, East Chang An Ave., Dong Cheng District
Beijing, 100738, China
{wuhua, wanghaifeng}@rdc.toshiba.com.cn

**Abstract.** In conventional word alignment methods, some employ statistical models or statistical measures, which need large-scale bilingual sentence-aligned training corpora. Others employ dictionaries to guide alignment selection. However, these methods achieve unsatisfactory alignment results when performing word alignment on a small-scale domain-specific bilingual corpus without terminological lexicons. This paper proposes an approach to improve word alignment in a specific domain, in which only a small-scale domain-specific corpus is available, by adapting the word alignment information in the general domain to the specific domain. This approach first trains two statistical word alignment models with the large-scale corpus in the general domain and the small-scale corpus in the specific domain respectively, and then improves the domain-specific word alignment with these two models. Experimental results show a significant improvement in terms of both alignment precision and recall, achieving a relative error rate reduction of 21.96% as compared with state-of-the-art technologies.

## 1 Introduction

Bilingual word alignment is first introduced as an intermediate result in statistical machine translation (SMT) [3]. Besides being used in SMT, it is also used in translation lexicon building [8], transfer rule learning [9], example-based machine translation [13], translation memory systems [12], etc.

In previous alignment methods, some researchers modeled the alignments as hidden parameters in a statistical translation model [3], [10] or directly modeled them given the sentence pairs [4]. Some researchers use similarity and association measures to build alignment links [1], [11], [14]. In addition, Wu [15] used a stochastic inversion transduction grammar to simultaneously parse the sentence pairs to get the word or phrase alignments. However, All of these methods require a large-scale bilingual corpus for training. When the large-scale bilingual corpus is not available, some researchers use existing dictionaries to improve word alignment [6]. However, few works address the problem of domain-specific word alignment when neither the large-scale domain-specific bilingual corpus nor the domain-specific translation dictionary is available.

In this paper, we address the problem of word alignment in a specific domain, in which only a small-scale corpus is available. In the domain-specific corpus, there are

R.E. Frederking and K.B. Taylor (Eds.): AMTA 2004, LNAI 3265, pp. 262–271, 2004.

two kinds of words. Some are general words, which are also frequently used in the general domain. Others are domain-specific words, which only occur in the specific domain. In general, it is not quite hard to obtain a large-scale general bilingual corpus while the available domain-specific bilingual corpus is usually quite small. Thus, we use the bilingual corpus in the general domain to improve word alignments for general words and the bilingual corpus in the specific domain for domain-specific words. In other words, we will adapt the word alignment information in the general domain to the specific domain.

Although the adaptation technology is widely used for other tasks such as language modeling, few literatures, to the best of our knowledge, directly address word alignment adaptation. The work most closely related to ours is the statistical translation adaptation described in [7]. Langlais used terminological lexicons to improve the performance of a statistical translation engine, which is trained on a general bilingual corpus and used to translate a manual for military snipers. The experimental results showed that this adaptation method could reduce word error rate on the translation task.

In this paper, we perform word alignment adaptation from the general domain to a specific domain (in this study, a user manual for a medical system) with four steps. (1) We train a word alignment model using a bilingual corpus in the general domain; (2) We train another word alignment model using a small-scale bilingual corpus in the specific domain; (3) We build two translation dictionaries according to the alignment results in (1) and (2) respectively; (4) For each sentence pair in the specific domain, we use the two models to get different word alignment results and improve the results according to the translation dictionaries. Experimental results show that our approach improves domain-specific word alignment in terms of both precision and recall, achieving a 21.96% relative error rate reduction.

The remainder of the paper is organized as follows. Section 2 introduces the statistical word alignment method and analyzes the problems existing in this method for the domain-specific task. Section 3 describes our word alignment adaptation algorithm. Section 4 describes the evaluation results. The last section concludes our approach and presents the future work.

## 2 Statistical Word Alignment

In this section, we apply the IBM statistical word alignment models to our domain-specific corpus and analyze the alignment results. The tool used for statistical word alignment is GIZA++ [10]. With this tool, we compare the word alignment results of three methods. These methods use different corpora to train IBM word alignment model 4. The method "G+S" directly combines the bilingual sentence pairs in the general domain and in the specific domain as training data. The method "G" only uses the bilingual sentence pairs in the general domain as training data. The method "S" only uses the bilingual sentence pairs in the specific domain as training data.

### 2.1 Training and Testing Data

We have a sentence aligned English-Chinese bilingual corpus in the general domain, which includes 320,000 bilingual sentence pairs, and a sentence aligned English-

Chinese bilingual corpus in the specific domain (a user manual for a medical system), which includes 546 bilingual sentence pairs. From this domain-specific corpus, we randomly select 180 pairs as testing data. The remained 366 pairs are used as domain-specific training data. [1]

The Chinese sentences in both the training set and the testing set are automatically segmented into words. Thus, there are two kinds of errors for word alignment: one is the word segmentation error and the other is the alignment error. In Chinese, if a word is incorrectly segmented, the alignment result is also incorrect. For example, for the Chinese sentence "诊断床面的警告标签" (Warning label for the couch-top), our system segments it into "诊断/床/面的/警告/标签". The sequence "床面的" is incorrectly segmented into "床/面的(couch/taxi)", which should be "床面/的(couch-top/of)". Thus, the segmentation errors in Chinese may change the word meaning, which in turn cause alignment errors.

In order to exclude the effect of the segmentation errors on our alignment results, we correct the segmentation errors in our testing set. The alignments in the testing set are manually annotated, which includes 1,478 alignment links.

## 2.2  Overall Performance

There are several different evaluation methods for word alignment [2]. In our evaluation, we use evaluation metrics similar to those in [10]. However, we do not classify alignment links into sure links and possible links. We consider each alignment $(s, t)$ as a sure link, where both $s$ and $t$ can be words or multi-word units.

If we use $S_G$ to represent the alignments identified by the proposed methods and $S_C$ to denote the reference alignments, the methods to calculate the precision, recall, and f-measure are shown in Equation (1), (2) and (3). According to the definition of the alignment error rate (AER) in [10], AER can be calculated with Equation (4). Thus, the higher the f-measure is, the lower the alignment error rate is.

$$precision = \frac{|S_G \cap S_C|}{|S_G|} \tag{1}$$

$$recall = \frac{|S_G \cap S_C|}{|S_C|} \tag{2}$$

$$fmeasure = \frac{2*|S_G \cap S_C|}{|S_G| + |S_C|} \tag{3}$$

$$AER = 1 - \frac{2*|S_G \cap S_C|}{|S_G| + |S_C|} = 1 - fmeasure \tag{4}$$

With the above metrics, we evaluate the three methods on the testing set with Chinese as the source language and English as the target language. The results are

---

[1] Generally, a user manual only includes several hundred sentences.

shown in Table 1. It can be seen that although the method "G+S" achieves the best results among others, it performs just a little better than the method "G". This indicates that adding the small-scale domain-specific training sentence pairs into the general corpus doesn't greatly improve the alignment performance.

**Table 1.** Statistical Word Alignment Results

| Method | Precision | Recall | AER |
|--------|-----------|--------|--------|
| G+S | 0.7140 | 0.6942 | 0.2961 |
| G | 0.7136 | 0.6847 | 0.3014 |
| S | 0.4486 | 0.4066 | 0.5735 |

## 2.3 Result Analysis

We use $A$, $B$ and $C$ to represent the set of correct alignment links extracted by the method "G+S", the method "G" and the method "S", respectively. From the experiments, we get $|A|=1026$, $|B|=1012$ and $|C|=601$ and get two intersection sets $|D|=|A \cap C|=524$ and $|E|=|B \cap C|=516$. Thus, about 14% alignment links of $C$ are not covered by $B$. That is to say, although the size of the domain-specific corpus is very small, it can produce word alignment links that are not covered by the general corpus. These alignment links usually include domain-specific words. Moreover, about 13% alignment links of $C$ are not covered by $A$. This indicates that, by combining the two corpora, the method "G+S" still cannot detect the domain-specific alignment links. At the same time, about 49% of alignment links in both $A$ and $B$ are not covered by the set $C$.

For example, in the sentence pair in Figure 1, there is a domain-specific word "multislice". For this word, both the method "G+S" and "G" produce a wrong alignment link (multislice, 扫描) while the method "S" produces a correct word alignment link (multislice, 多扫描层). However, the general word alignment link (refer to, 参见) is detected by both the method "G+S" and the method "G" but not detected by the method "S".

**Fig. 1.** Alignment Example

Based on the above analysis, it can be seen that it is not effective to directly combine the bilingual corpus in the general domain and in the specific domain as training data. However, the correct alignment links extracted by the method "G" and those extracted by the method "S" are complementary to each other. Thus, we can develop a method to improve the domain-specific word alignment based on the results of both the method "G" and the method "S".

Another kind of errors is about the multi-word alignment links[2]. The IBM statistical word alignment model only allows one-to-one or more-to-one alignment links. However, the domain-specific terms are usually aligned to more than one Chinese word. Thus, the multi-word unit in the corpus cannot be correctly aligned using this statistical model. For this case, we will use translation dictionaries as guides to modify some alignment links and get multi-word alignments.

## 3  Word Alignment Adaptation

According to the result analysis in Section 2.3, we take two measures to improve the word alignment results. One is to combine the word alignment results of both the method "G" and the method "S". The other is to use translation dictionaries.

### 3.1  Bi-directional Word Alignment

In statistical translation models [3], only one-to-one and more-to-one word alignment links can be found. Thus, some multi-word units cannot be correctly aligned. In order to deal with this problem, we perform translation in two directions (English to Chinese, and Chinese to English) as described in [10]. The GIZA++ toolkit is used to perform statistical word alignment.

For the general domain, we use $SG_1$ and $SG_2$ to represent the alignment sets obtained with English as the source language and Chinese as the target language or vice versa. For alignment links in both sets, we use $i$ for English words and $j$ for Chinese words.

$$SG_1 = \{(A_j, j) \mid A_j = \{a_j\}, a_j \geq 0\} \tag{5}$$

$$SG_2 = \{(i, A_i) \mid A_i = \{a_i\}, \ a_i \geq 0\} \tag{6}$$

Where, $a_x (x = i, j)$ represents the index position of the source word aligned to the target word in position $x$. For example, if a Chinese word in position $j$ is connected to an English word in position $i$, then $a_j = i$. If a Chinese word in position $j$ is connected to English words in positions $i_1$ and $i_2$, then $A_j = \{i_1, i_2\}$.

Based on the two alignment sets, we obtain their intersection set, union set[3] and subtraction set.

Intersection: $SG = SG_1 \cap SG_2$

Union: $PG = SG_1 \cup SG_2$

Subtraction: $MG = PG - 2 * SG$

---

[2] Multi-word alignment links means one or more source words aligned to more than one target word or vice versa.

[3] In this paper, the union operation does not remove the replicated elements. For example, if set one includes two elements $\{1, 2\}$ and set two includes two elements $\{1, 3\}$, then the union of these two sets becomes $\{1, 1, 2, 3\}$.

Thus, the subtraction set contains two different alignment links for each English word.

For the specific domain, we use $SF_1$ and $SF_2$ to represent the word alignment sets in the two directions. The symbols $SF$, $PF$ and $MF$ represents the intersection set, union set and the subtraction set, respectively.

### 3.2 Translation Dictionary Acquisition

When we train the statistical word alignment model with the large-scale bilingual corpus in the general domain, we can get two word alignment results for the training data. By taking the intersection of the two word alignment results, we build a new alignment set. The alignment links in this intersection set are extended by iteratively adding word alignment links into it as described in [10].

Based on the extended alignment links, we build an English to Chinese translation dictionary $D_1$ with translation probabilities. In order to filter some noise caused by the error alignment links, we only retain those translation pairs whose translation probabilities are above a threshold $\delta_1$ or co-occurring frequencies are above a threshold $\delta_2$.

When we train the IBM statistical word alignment model with the small-scale bilingual corpus in the specific domain, we build another translation dictionary $D_2$ with the same method as for the dictionary $D_1$. But we adopt a different filtering strategy for the translation dictionary $D_2$. We use log-likelihood ratio to estimate the association strength of each translation pair because Dunning [5] proved that log-likelihood ratio performed very well on small-scale data. Thus, we get the translation dictionary $D_2$ by keeping those entries whose log-likelihood ratio scores are greater than a threshold $\delta_3$.

The corpus used to build $D_1$ is the 320,000 sentence pairs in the general domain. The corpus used to build $D_2$ is the 366 sentence pairs on the manual for a medical system. By setting thresholds $\delta_1 = 0.1, \delta_2 = 5$ and $\delta_3 = 50$, we get two translation dictionaries, the statistics information of which is showed in Table 2.[4]

**Table 2.** Translation Dictionary Statistics

|                              | $D_1$   | $D_2$ |
| ---------------------------- | ------- | ----- |
| Unique English Words         | 57,380  | 728   |
| Multi-Words                  | 18,870  | 28    |
| Average Chinese Translations | 2.1     | 1.1   |

In the translation dictionary $D_1$, the multi-words accounts for 32.89% of the total words. In the translation dictionary $D_2$, the number of multi-words is small because the training data are very limited.

---

[4] The thresholds are obtained to ensure the best compromise of alignment precision and recall on the testing set.

### 3.3 Word Alignment Improvement

With the statistical word alignment models and the translation dictionaries trained on the corpora in the general domain and the specific domain, we describe the algorithm to improve the domain-specific word alignment in this section.

Based on the bi-directional word alignment, we define $SI$ as $SI = SG \cap SF$ and $UG$ as $UG = PG \cup PF - 4 * SI$. The word alignment links in the set $SI$ are very reliable. Thus, we directly accept them as correct links and add them into the final alignment set $WA$. In the set $UG$, there are two to four different alignment links for each word. We first examine the dictionary $D_1$ and then $D_2$ to see whether there is at least one alignment link of this word included in these two dictionaries. If it is successful, we add the link with the largest probability or the largest log-likelihood ratio score to the final set $WA$. Otherwise, we use two heuristic rules to select alignment links. The detailed algorithm is described in Figure 2.

| |
|---|
| **Input:** Alignment sets $SI$ and $UG$ |
| (1)  For alignment links in $SI$, we directly add them into $WA$.<br>(2)  For each English word $i$, we first find its alignment links in $UG$, and then do the following:<br>  a) If there are alignment links found in the translation dictionary $D_1$, we add the link with the largest probability to $WA$.<br>  b) Otherwise, if there are alignment links found in the translation dictionary $D_2$, we add the link with the largest log-likelihood ratio score to $WA$.<br>  c) If both a) and b) fail, but three links select the same target words for the English word $i$, we add this link to $WA$.<br>  d) Otherwise, if there are two different kinds of links for this word: one target is a single word, and the other target is a multi-word unit and the words in the multi-word unit have no link in $WA$, add this multi-word alignment link to $WA$. |
| **Output:** Updated alignment set $WA$ |

**Fig. 2.** Word Alignment Adaptation Algorithm

Figure 3 lists four examples for word alignment adaptation. In example (1), the phrase "based on" has two different alignment links: one is (based on, 基于) and the other is (based, 基于). And in the translation dictionary $D_1$, the phrase "based on" can be translated into "基于". Thus, the link (based on, 基于) is finally selected according to rule a) in Figure 2. In the same way, the link (contrast, 造影) in example (2) is selected with the translation dictionary $D_2$. The link (reconstructed, 再现) in Example (3) is obtained because there are three alignment links selecting it. For the English word "x-ray" in Example (4), we have two different links in $UG$. One is (x-ray, X) and the other is (x-ray, X射线). And the single Chinese words "射" and "线" have no alignment links in the set $WA$. According to the rule d), we select the link (x-ray, X射线).

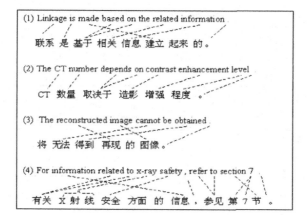

**Fig. 3.** Alignment Adaptation Example

## 4    Evaluation

In this section, we compare our methods with three other methods. The first method "Gen+Spec" directly combines the corpus in the general domain and in the specific domain as training data. The second method "Gen" only uses the corpus in the general domain as training data. The third method "Spec" only uses the domain-specific corpus as training data. With these training data, the three methods can get their own translation dictionaries. However, each of them can only get one translation dictionary. Thus, only one of the two steps a) and b) in Figure 2 can be applied to these methods. All of these three methods first get bi-directional statistical word alignment using the GIZA++ tool, and then use the trained translation dictionary to improve the statistical word alignment results. The difference between these three methods and our method is that, for each source word, our method provides four candidate alignment links while the other three methods only provides two candidate alignment links. Thus, the steps c) and d) in Figure 2 cannot be applied to these three methods.

The training data and the testing data are the same as described in Section 2.1. With the evaluation metrics described in section 2.2, we get the alignment results shown in Table 3. From the results, it can be seen that our approach performs the best among others. Our method achieves a 21.96% relative error rate reduction as compared with the method "Gen+Spec". In addition, by comparing the results in Table 3 and those in Table 1 in Section 2.2, we can see that the precision of word alignment links is improved by using the translation dictionaries. Thus, introducing translation dictionary results in alignment precision improving while combining the alignment results of "Gen" and "Spec" results in alignment recall improving.

**Table 3.** Word Alignment Adaptation Results

| Method | Precision | Recall | AER |
|--------|-----------|--------|--------|
| Ours | 0.8363 | 0.7673 | 0.1997 |
| Gen+Spec | 0.8276 | 0.6758 | 0.2559 |
| Gen | 0.8668 | 0.6428 | 0.2618 |
| Spec | 0.8178 | 0.4769 | 0.3974 |

**Table 4.** Multi-Word Alignment Results

| Method | Precision | Recall | AER |
|--------|-----------|--------|--------|
| Ours | 0.5665 | 0.4083 | 0.5254 |
| Gen+Spec | 0.4339 | 0.096 | 0.8430 |
| Gen | 0.5882 | 0.083 | 0.8541 |
| Spec | 0.5854 | 0.100 | 0.8292 |

In the testing set, there are 240 multi-word alignment links. Most of the links consist of domain-specific words. Table 4 shows the results for multi-word alignment. Our method achieves much higher recall than the other three methods and achieves comparable precision. This indicates that combining the alignment results created by the "Gen" method and the "Spec" method increases the possibility of obtaining multi-word alignment links. From the table, it can be also seen that the "Spec" method performs better than both the "Gen" method and the "Gen+Spec" method on the multi-word alignment. This indicates that the "Spec" method can catch domain-specific alignment links even when trained on the small-scale corpus. It also indicates that by adding the domain-specific data into the general training data, the method "Gen+Spec" cannot catch the domain-specific alignment links.

## 5    Conclusion and Future Work

This paper proposes an approach to improve domain-specific word alignment through alignment adaptation. Our contribution is that, given a large-scale general bilingual corpus and a small-scale domain-specific corpus, our approach improves the domain-specific word alignment results in terms of both precision and recall. In addition, with the training data, two translation dictionaries are built to select or modify the word alignment links and to further improve the alignment results. Experimental results indicate that our approach achieves a precision of 83.63% and a recall of 76.73% for word alignment on the manual of a medical system, resulting in a relative error rate reduction of 21.96%. This indicates that our method significantly outperforms the method only combining the general bilingual corpus and the domain-specific bilingual corpus as training data.

Our future work includes two aspects. First, we will seek other adaptation methods to further improve the domain-specific word alignment results. Second, we will also use the alignment results to build terminological lexicons and to improve translation quality and efficiency in machine translation systems.

# References

1.  Ahrenberg, L., Merkel, M., Andersson, M.: A Simple Hybrid Aligner for Generating Lexical Correspondences in Parallel Tests. In Proc. of the 36th Annual Meeting of the Association for Computational Linguistics and the 17th Int. Conf. on Computational Linguistics (ACL/COLING-1998) 29-35
2.  Ahrenberg, L., Merkel, M., Hein, A.S., Tiedemann, J.: Evaluation of Word Alignment Systems. In Proc. of the Second Int. Conf. on Linguistic Resources and Evaluation (LREC-2000) 1255-1261
3.  Brown, P.F., Della Pietra, S., Della Pietra, V., Mercer, R.: The Mathematics of Statistical Machine Translation: Parameter estimation. Computational Linguistics (1993), Vol. 19, No. 2, 263-311
4.  Cherry, C., Lin, D.K.: A Probability Model to Improve Word Alignment. In Proc. of the 41st Annual Meeting of the Association for Computational Linguistics (ACL-2003) 88-95
5.  Dunning, T.: Accurate Methods for the Statistics of Surprise and Coincidence. Computational Linguistics (1993), Vol. 19, No. 1, 61-74
6.  Ker, S.J., Chang, J.S.: A Class-based Approach to Word Alignment. Computational Linguistics (1997), Vol. 23, No. 2, 313-343
7.  Langlais, P.: Improving a General-Purpose Statistical Translation Engine by Terminological Lexicons. In Proc. of the 2nd Int. Workshop on Computational Terminology (COMPUTERM-2002) 1-7
8.  Melamed, D.: Automatic Construction of Clean Broad-Coverage Translation Lexicons. In Proc. of the 2nd Conf. of the Association for Machine Translation in the Americas (AMTA-1996) 125-134
9.  Menezes, A., Richardson, S.D.: A Best-First Alignment Algorithm for Automatic Extraction of Transfer Mappings from Bilingual Corpora. In Proc. of the ACL 2001 Workshop on Data-Driven Methods in Machine Translation (2001) 39-46
10. Och, F.J., Ney, H.: Improved Statistical Alignment Models. In Proc. of the 38th Annual Meeting of the Association for Computational Linguistics (ACL-2000) 440-447
11. Smadja, F., McKeown, K.R., Hatzivassiloglou, V.: Translating Collocations for Bilingual Lexicons: a Statistical Approach. Computational Linguistics (1996), Vol. 22, No. 1, 1-38
12. Simard, M., Langlais, P.: Sub-sentential Exploitation of Translation Memories. In Proc. of MT Summit VIII (2001) 335-339
13. Somers, H.: Review Article: Example-Based Machine Translation. Machine Translation (1999), Vol. 14, No. 2, 113-157
14. Tufis, D., Barbu, A.M.: Lexical Token Alignment: Experiments, Results and Application. In Proc. of the Third Int. Conf. on Language Resources and Evaluation (LREC-2002) 458-465
15. Wu, D.K.: Stochastic Inversion Transduction Grammars and Bilingual Parsing of Parallel Corpora. Computational Linguistics (1997), Vol. 23, No. 3, 377-403

# A Super-Function Based Japanese-Chinese Machine Translation System for Business Users

Xin Zhao[1], Fuji Ren[1], and Stefan Voß[2]

[1] Faculty of Engineering, University of Tokushima
Tokushima, Japan 770-8506, {zhao, ren}@is.tokushima-u.ac.jp
[2] Institute of Information Systems, University of Hamburg
20146 Hamburg, Germany, stefan.voss@uni-hamburg.de

**Abstract.** In this paper, a Japanese-Chinese Machine Translation (MT) system using the so-called Super-Function (SF) approach is presented. A SF is a functional relation mapping sentences from one language to another. The core of the system uses the SF approach to translate without going through syntactic and semantic analysis as many MT systems usually do. Our work focuses on business users for whom MT often is a great help if they need an immediate idea of the content of texts like e-mail messages, reports, web pages, or business letters. In this paper, we aim at performing MT between Japanese and Chinese to translate business letters by the SF based technique.

## 1  Introduction

Machine translation describes computer-based translation between human languages and is one of the oldest large-scale applications of computer science. In today's increasingly networked world, the need for systems to translate documents to and from a variety of languages is expanding. While useful MT technology is currently available, it is not yet capable of providing both high-quality and wide-domain performance simultaneously. Techniques such as Statistical MT and Example-Based MT (EBMT) add new capabilities and possibilities to the older tried-and-true methods and theories of MT.

Over the past decades a considerable growth of the number and diversity of experiments in various MT paradigms (Rule-Based MT, Knowledge-Based MT, and EBMT) has been observed [10,5]. For instance, a Glossary-Based MT (GBMT) engine provides an automatic translation for various language pairs by using a bilingual phrasal dictionary (glossary) for phrase-by-phrase translations. A GBMT system is quite simple and quick to be developed. Moreover, the user keeps full control of all language resources used by the system.

In this paper we apply a recent MT paradigm called Super-Function Based Machine Translation (SFBMT) to improve the GBMT. SFBMT uses a specific function in the translation engine to enhance the translation quality and to reduce the glossary quantity. In the system the SF itself is used to translate without syntactic and semantic analysis as many MT systems usually do.

R.E. Frederking and K.B. Taylor (Eds.): AMTA 2004, LNAI 3265, pp. 272–281, 2004.

While the benefits derived from MT can be categorized into many classes, one important class of real users consists of business users. For them, MT can provide benefits in a number of ways. If one likes to understand the general meaning of some document such as e-mail or a business letter, MT can be used to scan through those texts and return the requested information in a short amount of time. It can also help users to screen many large documents in order to identify documents that warrant more accurate translation.

With the increasing business between Japan and China, Japanese-Chinese business letters become more and more important. Here, we apply our approach for respective business users. Section 2 discusses the SFBMT approach and relates it to other engines. Sections 3 and 4 describe the user requirements and provide some experimental results. Finally, some conclusions are given.

## 2    Super-Function

A Super-Function is a function that shows some defined relations between a source (original) language sentence and a target language sentence [9,15]. In the sequel we discuss the SF concept and briefly put it into perspective with respect to other approaches from the literature.

### 2.1    SF Definition

A SF can be represented using a formal description:

$$SF\_O(O\_STRing, O\_VARiable) \rightarrow SF\_T(T\_STRing, T\_VARiable)$$

$O$: Original language    $STRing$: Natural language character string
$T$: Target language     $VARiable$: Word, phrase, sentence, paragraph, etc.

A SF can also be rewritten as $f(X_1, X_2, ...., X_n)$. Here, the SF $f$ consists of $n$ variables $X_i$ $(i = 1, ..., n)$. To understand the concept, we provide an example:[1]
SF1:
$< J > X_1$ HAOMOTOSHITE $X_2$ TO $X_3$ NIHANBAISARETEORIMASU.
$< C > X_1$ ZHUYAO XIAOWANG $X_2$ HE $X_3$.
**English:**    The product is mainly sold to Germany and the U.S.
**Japanese:**    SEIHIN HAOMOTOSHITE DOITSU TO BEIKOKU NIHAN-BAISARETEORIMASU.
**Chinese:**    CHANPIN ZHUYAO XIAOWANG DEGUO HE MEIGUO.

We assume that a sentence consists of some constant and some variable parts. By replacing the variable parts one can get a multitude of different sentences. Based on this prerequisite, we can use a SF to describe the detailed relation of those constant and variable parts between a source and a target language

---

[1] For ease of readability we do not use original Japanese and Chinese character sets but use some phonetic spelling instead. SFs in Japanese/Chinese are indicated by $< J >/< C >$, respectively.

**Fig. 1.** Example of DG

**Table 1.** Example of a Node Table    **Table 2.** Example of an Edge Table

| No | Language-J | Language-C |
|----|-----------|-----------|
| 1 | $\phi$ | $\phi$ |
| 2 | haomotoshite | zhuyaoxiaowang |
| 3 | to | he |
| 4 | nihanbaisareteorimasu. | . |

| No | Location | | Kind |
|----|---|---|------|
| | -J | -C | |
| 1 | 1 | 1 | noun |
| 2 | 2 | 2 | proper noun |
| 3 | 3 | 3 | proper noun |

sentence pair. That is, a SF consists of the constant parts which are extracted from the source and the target language sentence pair and the corresponding positions of the variable parts.

## 2.2  SF Architecture

A SF may be represented, e.g., by means of a Directed Graph (DG). In a DG strings are represented by nodes and variables are represented by edges (see Fig. 1 for the above example SF1). The purpose of introducing the DG is to use a finite state technique in matching between a SF and a sentence.

Another architecture of a SF is a Transformation TaBle (TTB). It consists of a Node TaBle (NTB) and an Edge TaBle (ETB). For SF1 the construction of NTB and ETB is described using Tables 1 and 2. Language-J in NTB is a string of Japanese, Language-C is a string of Chinese; Location-J and -C in ETB indicate the location relationship between Japanese and Chinese. Kind in ETB indicates the kind of variable or condition. At present, we use a TTB to represent a SF. However, it is easy to transform a DG into a TTB and vice versa.

## 2.3  Robust SF

At the beginning, we construct some Robust SF (RSF). Constructing RSFs aims at enhancing the robustness of MT. The following is an example:

RSF1:

$< J > X_1$ {NP} NI TSUITE $X_2$ {NP} GA/HA ARU*.

$< C >$ DUIYU $X_1$ {NP} FAXIANYOU $X_2$ {NP}.

The symbol { } indicates the attribute of a variable. Because the SFBMT does not perform a syntactic analysis, attributes can be found easily, such as NP→ noun, pronoun, ..., SF. Using attributes in an RSF increases the chance of finding a corresponding SF from the SF base. If only nouns are considered as variables, they can be omitted. Compared with RSF, a SF is much more specific. Especially, when a sentence consists only of variable parts an attribute should be added to get a correct translation. The symbol * represents all inflected forms and / indicates a possible choice. That is, in RSF1 the node GA/HA ARU* can be matched by (1) GA ARU, (2) GA ARI, (3) GA ARIMASU, (4) HA ARU, (5) HA ARI, and (6) HA ARIMASU.

### 2.4  Process of SFBMT

The SFBMT uses a bilingual dictionary and the SF concept to produce a translation of a source text. An input sentence is first analyzed morphologically and then matched with the source sentence and a SF. SFBMT produces a sentence-by-sentence translation of the source text, falling back on a phrase-by-phrase and a word-by-word translation when no SF matches the input sentence. Here, we just consider the case of sentence-by-sentence translation. The process of SFBMT consists of the three major parts:

**Morphological Analysis:** General morphological analysis was developed as a method for structuring and investigating the total set of relationships contained in multi-dimensional, non-quantifiable, problem complexes [16]. Japanese text poses challenges for automatic analysis due to the language's complex constructions. Text must be accurately segmented by common application functions like parsing, indexing, categorizing, or searching. Morphological analysis is often a prerequisite to performing operations on text of any language.

**Super-Function Matching:** A SF is represented by a NTB and an ETB. Matching a SF is simply matching each node of the NTB and confirming the kind of each edge in the ETB.

**Morphological Translation:** After obtaining the SF by the SF matching, the target language variable parts are rearranged, according to the location relationship in the ETB, into the string parts to get the translated sentence. Usually, it is suggested that an unknown word is treated as a noun to match a SF, and a translation is generated using the string of the unknown source language word. However, for Japanese as a specific language, we define some rules to decide if an unknown word is a verb or a noun.

### 2.5  Related Research

SFBMT has its roots in different concepts including GBMT. Here, we give a brief overview of some related work.

**Pattern-Based MT (PBMT):** The basic idea of PBMT is to translate from a source language into a target language using Translation Patterns (TP). A TP is defined as a pair of Context Free Grammar (CFG) rules, and zero or more syntactic head and link constraints for certain symbols [11,13]. The difficult problems with PBMT are how to translate light-verb phrases and how to find the pair of CFG rules. The SF of SFBMT is like the TP of PBMT in structure.

However, because the nodes of a SF have no semantic attributes, SFBMT has not the mentioned problems of the PBMT.

**Glossary-Based MT:** A GBMT engine uses a bilingual glossary and a bilingual dictionary to produce a translation of phrases in a source text. A GBMT system (see, e.g., [3,14]) produces phrase-by-phrase translation, falling back on a word-by-word translation when no phrase from the glossary matches the input. Thus, the size of the glossary and the flexibility of the pattern language are crucial for good translations. However, the GBMT system lacks of translation accuracy and readability. In SFBMT, by introducing the SF variables, the glossary quantities will be reduced, and by the SF the translation quality will be improved, such as word order and conventional expressions.

**Example-Based MT:** EBMT is essentially translation by analogy. A basic premise in EBMT is that, if a previously translated sentence occurs again, the same translation is likely to be correct. In many cases an EBMT does not provide a translation by itself, but suggests similar sentences in the target language thus helping to ensure the consistency of style and terminology. Over the years, so-called light or shallow versions of EBMT have been proposed [8,12,1,2]. In the translation process, such a system can look up all matching phrases in the source language and performs a word-level alignment on the entries containing matches to determine a translation. Portions of the input for which there are no matches in the corpus do not generate a translation but can be translated by using a bilingual dictionary and a phrasal glossary.

Shallow EBMT performs no deep linguistic analysis, but compares surface strings (possibly with some morphological analysis), in this respect it is very similar to SFBMT. However, a shallow EBMT engine may be unable to properly deal with translations that do not involve one-to-one correspondences between source and target words. In SFBMT, by extracting the constant parts (SF) out of a sentence and matching them with the SF base for translation, these problems may be overcome.

## 3    SF-Based Japanese-Chinese MT for Business Users

The 21st century may be called the century of Asia. Almost all Asian countries including China and Japan raised the position in the international community and became centers noteworthy within the world. Especially the interdependence relation between Japan and China had pursued considerable developments generally in each area of politics, economy, diplomacy and the culture, etc. The demand for Japanese-Chinese MT systems has increased rapidly to promote the trade between Japan and China. Here, we aim at performing the MT between Japanese and Chinese to translate business letters by the SF based technique. That is, we consider the needs and requirements of business users as a starting point for the development of a Japanese-Chinese MT system.

The business letter is a document typically sent externally to those outside a company but is also sent internally within a company. There are six most common types of business letters (referring, e.g., to inquiries, orders, or adjust-

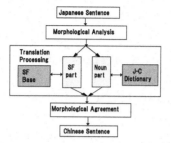

**Fig. 2.** Outline of the Translation

ments), and for each common type of business letters, the basic format and the outline are very similar. Based on the special functionalities and properties of business letters, in our system we only look at nouns as variables for translation. The outline of the translation is as follows (see also Fig. 2).

The translation system consists of five major parts:

1. The inputted Japanese sentence is written in a file.
2. Morphological Analysis: The Japanese sentence is morphologically analyzed by ChaSen (a free Japanese morphological analyzer). ChaSen analyzes the specified file in the morpheme and outputs the result.
3. Translation Processing: First of all, the nouns are extracted from the file which resulted after the morphological analysis. Then the words between nouns are tied together to build a node of a SF. The nouns are written into a noun file, and the parts of the SF are written to a node file which is matched with the SF base to search for the corresponding Chinese SF part. By using the bilingual dictionary the nouns are then translated into Chinese.
4. Morphological Agreement: Based on the order of nouns in an ETB a rearrangement of the nouns within the Chinese node parts takes place.
5. A translation sentence is outputted to a browser.

## 4   Experiment and Evaluation

In this section, we describe some experiments for evaluating the system. The **Translation Corpus** for our experiments consists of 391 letters with about 4,100 sentences of Japanese and Chinese extracted from two books [7,4]. We have a Japanese-English **Bilingual Dictionary** JEB-V015 (general vocabulary is 230,000 words). In order to perform the test experiment based on the dictionary, we generated a simulated Japanese-Chinese bilingual dictionary. For **Building the SF Base** we have manually extracted about 2700 SFs from the above corpus. The SFBMT has been implemented in Perl. Furthermore, a simple user interface has been realized in Javascript and HTML. All experiments have been run on a Celeron(R) with 2.20GHz 256MB RAM under WindowsXP.

### 4.1   Example

In the practical experiment, we unite the NTB and the ETB to express the SF. We use the above example SF1 to explain the detailed translation process.

**Japanese:**   SEIHIN HAOMOTOSHITE DOITSU TO BEIKOKU NIHAN-BAISARETEORIMASU.

$\Longrightarrow$(Perform morphological analysis)
SEIHIN|HA|OMOTOSHITE|DOITSU|TO|BEIKOKU|NI|HANBAI|SA|RE|TE| ORI|MASU.

$\Longrightarrow$(Extract the nouns)
$X_1$|HA|OMOTOSHITE|$X_2$|TO|$X_3$|NI|HANBAI|SA|RE|TE|ORI|MASU.

$\Longrightarrow$(Tie words between nouns together and construct a Japanese SF part from them)   $X_1$|HAOMOTOSHITE|$X_2$|TO|$X_3$|NIHANBAISARETEORIMASU.

$\Longrightarrow$(Match the Japanese SF part with the SF base and output the corresponding Chinese SF part)   $X_1$|ZHUYAOXIAOWANG|$X_2$|HE|$X_3$|.

$\Longrightarrow$(Rearrange the SF part and translated nouns, if necessary)
$X_1$|ZHUYAOXIAOWANG|$X_2$|HE|$X_3$|.

$\Longrightarrow$(Output the Chinese sentence)
**Chinese:**   CHANPIN ZHUYAOXIAOWANG DEGUO HE MEIGUO.

Firstly, we do the morphological analysis for the inputted sentence, extract the nouns into the noun file and translate them using the dictionary. Then we tie the words between nouns together and regard them as a SF to match it with the SF base, output the corresponding Chinese SF part, and adjust the order of nouns to rearrange the SF part and nouns.

When extracting a SF from the corpus, according to various problems, we may need to perform different ways of processing, e.g., in case that the nouns in the Japanese and the Chinese sentence are not corresponding. For example:

**English:**   We trust that the price could be accepted by you.
**Japanese:**   JYOUKI NEDAN HA OUKENEGAERUNI CHIGAINAITO SIN-JITEORIMASU.
**Chinese:**   XIANGXIN SHANGSHU JIAGE NENGBEI GUIFANG SUOJIE-SHOU.

In this example, there are only two nouns (underlined) in the Japanese sentence, but the corresponding Chinese sentence could not be expressed correctly and fluently by using only two nouns. In this case, we should add the needed noun [GUIFANG] into the part of the Chinese SF for getting the correct translation. That is, when the nouns in the Japanese and the Chinese sentence do not match exactly, we add the corresponding nouns into the SF part.

Japanese letters often use classical grammar patterns. There are many set expressions and honorific expressions used in formal letters, especially for business letters. A typical business letter in Japanese also abounds in many ritualistic elements and polite circumlocution. With respect to these expressions or preliminary greetings and a complimentary closing part, we have defined a number of SFs for translation. Some examples are as follows.

SF2:

**Table 3.** Result of the Evaluation Experiment

| Sentence | Success | SF is in agreement |
|----------|---------|--------------------|
| 250 | 183 | 204 |
|  | (73%) | (81%) |

$< J > X_1$ HA $X_2$ NO $X_3$ WOITADAKIARIGATOUGOZAIMASU.
$< C > X_1$ DUOMENG $X_2$ $X_3$, JINZHI XIECHEN.
SF3:
$< J > X_1$ $X_2$ NO $X_3$ WO TAMAWARI ATSUKUONREIMOUSHIAGEMASU.
$< C > X_1$ CHENGMENG GUIGONGSI $X_2$ $X_3$, ZAICISHENBIAOXIEYI.

Sometimes, depending on the categories of business letters (Business-to-Business Letters (B2B), i.e. other businesses, internal business, and Business-to-Consumer Letters (B2C), i.e. consumers, general public), the same sentence can have a different translation, such as:

**Japanese:** MASUMASU GOSEIEI NOKOTOTO OYOROKOBI MOUSHI-AGEMASU.
**Chinese1:** (In B2C letters)  XINWEN XIANSHENG SHIYEFADA, SHENTI-JIANKANG, KEXIKEHE.
**English1:** I am happy to hear that you are well and prosperous.
**Chinese2:** (In B2B letters)  XINWEN GUIGONGSI SHIYERIYICHANG-SHENG, SHENBIAOZHUHE.
**English2:** I am happy to hear about the prosperity of your company.

In such a case, when defining the SF we provide some reference options so that the users can choose the correct translation based on that.

### 4.2   Evaluation Experiment

After having collected the 391 business letters from [4,7] we have chosen a sample of 250 sentences from a different source [6] for evaluation purposes. When a translated sentence is identical with the estimated sentence we consider it as a success. Due to the existence of synonyms the translation of nouns is not included as an evaluation criterion. The result of the experiment is shown in Table 3.

In the 250 evaluating sentences, 183 (73%) sentences have been translated successfully and 204 (81%) sentences have a SF that is available in the SF base. There are 21 (8%) sentences which have a SF from the SF base but have different translation sentences compared to the evaluating sentences. The reason is, that even if we can get the same Japanese SF part and the kind of nouns with the SF base, the Chinese SF part can be different, such as:

**English:** The import goods of our company are seasonal goods.
**Japanese:** TOUSYA YUNYUU NO SYOUHIN HA KISETSUSYOUHIN DE-ARU.
**Chinese:** WOSHE JINKOUDE SHANGPIN JIJIEXING SHI HENQIANGDE.
**Translation Chinese:** WOSHE JINKOUDE SHANGPIN SHI JIJIESHANG-PIN.

By the SF of this example we can get the corresponding Chinese SF part from the SF base. However, as it is different from the original Chinese evaluation sentence, we obtain a different translation.

The following is a successful example (with noun parts underlined):

**English:**  The matter pointed out in your letter was chiefly investigated.

**Japanese:**  OMOTOSHITE <u>KISIN</u> SHITEKINO <u>JIKOU</u> NITSUITE <u>CYOUSA</u> WOOKONATTA.

**Chinese:**  ZHUYAOJIU <u>GUIHAN</u> SUOZHICHUDE <u>XIANGMU</u> JINXINGLE <u>DIAOCHA</u>.

Because of the difference between the Japanese Hiragana and Kanji characters we do not always obtain the correct translation as we have expected. For solving this problem we can output the pronunciation from the result of the morphological analysis and use it to get the correct translation.

Analyzing sentences which could not find the corresponding SF in the SF base reveals another problem: the difference of the ending of a word. Due to the difference between [∼?] and [∼.] or [∼DA.] and [∼DESU.] in the following example we could not get the corresponding SF in the SF base. RSFs can help us to deal with such problems.

**Japanese:**  SARAISYUU ATARI GOTSUGOU HAIKAGADESYOUKA ?
SF ⇒ $X_1$ ATARI $X_2$ HAIKAGADESYOUKA.

**Japanese:**  ANOSYOUHIN HAHONTOUNO KOUKYUHINDA.
SF ⇒ ANO $X_1$ HAHONTOUNO $X_2$ DESU.

## 5   Conclusions and Future Work

In this paper we have considered a Super-Function approach and described the architecture of a Japanese-Chinese MT system based on its basic principle. The result of the experiment and our experience show that using the SF in the translation system to translate without syntactic and semantic analysis as many MT system usually do, will enhance the translation quality and reduce the glossary quantity. At present, the scale of the SF may still be increased, the current translation accuracy can be improved in some cases and we need to enhance the performance of the system to gain better user acceptance. We consider improving the translation accuracy by making corrections to the dictionary, extending the scale of the SF and improving the translation of non-standard sentences.

Future work concerns the following aspects: 1) We should develop an algorithm for automatically acquiring high quality SFs from parallel corpora. 2) Translation speed can be increased by using an advanced finite state technique for high speed matching between the SF and a sentence. 3) With the increase of the number of SFs, the translation quality will increase, too. Increasing the number of RSFs would be very helpful. Furthermore, it will be of interest to extend the experimentation for the current system, but also to extend the research to other language pairs. Based on business users' needs applying our MT functionality for conducting inter-company oriented supply chain contracts is challenging. To summarize, we have made substantial progress with our MT application and plan to continue using this technology.

## References

1. R.D. Brown. Adding linguistic knowledge to a lexical example-based translation system. In *Proceedings of the 8th International Conference on Theoretical and Methodological Issues in Machine Translation*, pages 22–32. Chester, 1999.
2. R.D. Brown. Automated generalization of translation examples. In *Proceedings of the 18th International Conference on Computational Linguistics (COLING-2000)*, pages 125–131. Saarbrücken, 2000.
3. R. Frederking, D. Grannes, P. Cousseau, and S. Nirenburg. An MAT tool and its effectiveness. In *Proceedings of the DARPA Human Language Technology Workshop*, Princeton, NJ, 1993.
4. K. Fujimoto, L. Zhang, and H. ShiYun. *Chinese-Japanese Business Letters Encyclopedia*. TOHU Shoten, 1995.
5. J. Hutchins. Machine translation today and tomorrow. In G. Willée, B. Schröder, and H.-C. Schmitz, editors, *Computerlinguistik: Was geht, was kommt?*, pages 159–162, Sankt Augustin, 2002. Gardez.
6. http://www.jusnet.co.jp/business/bunrei.html. June 2004 (date of last check).
7. K. Maruyama, M. Doi, Y. Iguchi, K. Kuwabara, M. Onuma, T. Yasui, and R. Yokosuka. *Writing Business Letters In Japanese*. Original Japanese edition published by The Japan Times, Ltd., 2003.
8. S. Nirenburg, S. Beale, and C. Domashnev. A full-text experiment in example-based machine translation. In *Proceedings of the International Conference on New Methods in Language Processing*, pages 78–87. Manchester, 1994.
9. F. Ren. Super-function based machine translation. *Communications of COLIPS*, 9(1):83–100, 1999.
10. S. Sato. MBT2: A method for combining fragments of examples in example-based translation. *Artificial Intelligence*, 75:31–49, 1995.
11. K. Takeda. Pattern-based context-free grammars for machine translation. In *Proceedings of the 34th Annual Meeting of the Association for Computational Linguistics*, pages 144–151, 1996.
12. T. Veale and A. Way. Gaijin: A bootstrapping, template-driven approach to example-based MT. In *Proceedings of the NeMNLP '97 New Methods in Natural Language Processing*. Sofia, 1997.
13. H. Watanabe. A method for extracting translation patterns from translation examples. In *Proceedings TMI-93*, pages 292–301, 1993.
14. R. Zajac and M. Vanni. Glossary-based MT engines in a multilingual analyst's workstation architecture. *Machine Translation*, 12:131–151, 1997.
15. X. Zhao, F. Ren, S. Kuroiwa, and M. Sasayama. Japanese-Chinese machine translation system using SFBMT. In *Proceedings of the Second International Conference on Information*, pages 16–21, Beijing, 2002. Tsinghua University.
16. F. Zwicky. *Discovery, Invention, Research – Through the Morphological Approach*. Macmillan, Toronto, 1969.

# Author Index